Climate Adaptation for Architects

Architecture must adapt to protect people from the threat of climate change. About half of the world's population lives in contexts that are highly vulnerable to climate change as hazards continue to intensify, with global disasters projected to reach 560 events per year by 2030, or 1.5 events every day.

The accelerating frequency and intensity of disasters underscores the urgency to prepare for severe events to protect people, communities, and essential systems but also to protect the environment which provides shelter, livelihoods, cultural heritage, and public functions. This book provides a comprehensive reference of climate adaptation design tactics and a toolkit for adaptation to shocks and stresses, outlining the process for architects and designers to:

- Understand the risks posed by climate change to the built environment.
- Reduce the risks to people and the built environment from natural hazards.
- Reduce human vulnerability to shocks and stresses by strengthening resilience and adaptive capacity.
- Design the built environment to adapt to changes over its lifetime.
- Design buildings and cities to reduce dependence on fossil fuels.
- Preserve biodiversity and support natural resources.

Climate Adaptation for Architects presents 45 adaptation tactics responding to the most consequential effects of climate change: heat, water, wind, and resource scarcity. Each chapter includes images, a definition, background information, key design considerations, potential impacts, and resources for further information. This is a valuable resource for every architect, landscape architect, urban planner, developer, and policymaker.

Allison H. Anderson, FAIA, is the founding principal of unabridged Architecture, a firm recognized for incorporating sustainability, climate change adaptation, and resilience across a wide variety of project scales. Allison was the first LEED-Accredited Professional in Mississippi, focused on sustainability. After Hurricane Katrina devastated her community, unabridged Architecture began exploring resilience and climate adaptation. Her research is included in the Oxford Research Encyclopedia of Natural Hazard Science, the AIA Resilient Project Process Guide, AIA Climate Action Playbook, and the AIA Framework for Design Excellence. Allison has taught architecture at the University of Texas, Tulane University, and Louisiana State University. She is a Fellow of the American Institute of Architects.

'Resilience for architects is a matter of understanding how climate hazards threaten to damage and destroy a building and making hundreds of well-informed design decisions. Allison Anderson's book, *Climate Adaptation for Architects*, is written with the obvious insight of a practicing architect who has made those hundred of decisions many times and lives up to the responsibility to make buildings that will stand the tests of increasing risks'.

David Perkes, AIA, Professor,
Mississippi State University

'The rising number of climate-related disasters worldwide make investing in adaptation increasingly critical. This is an essential resource for designers working at multiple scales to ensure that planning, infrastructure, and buildings are prepared for disasters'.

Amy Chester, Director, Rebuild by Design

'Resilient design is essential if we choose to protect people and property from a warmer, more chaotic climate. Luckily, the path forward is clear thanks to *Climate Adaptation for Architects: A Design Toolkit*. With design strategies that cover the full breadth of challenges we face, every architect now has the tools necessary to design for the future we know is coming'.

Corey Squire, author of *People, Planet, Design: A Practical Guide To Realizing Architecture's Potential*

'*Climate Adaptation for Architects provides* essential knowledge to drive the crucial need to integrate resilience and adaptation into the built environment. The book is a comprehensive guide to adaptive design solutions at all scales – from materials to community scale, from theory to application. The clear organization by risk category, with great illustrations, makes the book easily accessible as a go-to guide. It should be an indispensable resource for all architects, from students to seasoned professionals'.

Mary Ann Lazarus, FAIA LEED Fellow,
Architect and Consultant, Cameron MacAllister Group, Adjunct Faculty,
Washington University in St. Louis

Climate Adaptation for Architects

A Design Toolkit

Allison H. Anderson

Routledge
Taylor & Francis Group
LONDON AND NEW YORK

Designed cover image: Allison H. Anderson.

First published 2026
by Routledge
4 Park Square, Milton Park, Abingdon, Oxon OX14 4RN

and by Routledge
605 Third Avenue, New York, NY 10158

Routledge is an imprint of the Taylor & Francis Group, an informa business

British Library Cataloguing-in-Publication Data
A catalogue record for this book is available from the British Library

Library of Congress Cataloging-in-Publication Data
Names: Anderson, Allison (Architect), author.
Title: Climate adaptation for architects: a compendium of strategies for resilience / Allison Anderson.
Description: Abingdon, Oxon; New York, NY: Routledge, 2025. |
Includes bibliographical references and index. |
Identifiers: LCCN 2025004639 | ISBN 9781032702919 (hardback) |
ISBN 9781032702865 (paperback) | ISBN 9781032702964 (ebook)
Subjects: LCSH: Architecture and climate.
Classification: LCC NA2541 .A53 2025 | DDC 720.1/03–dc23/eng/20250519
LC record available at https://lccn.loc.gov/2025004639

ISBN: 978-1-032-70291-9 (hbk)
ISBN: 978-1-032-70286-5 (pbk)
ISBN: 978-1-032-70296-4 (ebk)

DOI: 10.4324/9781032702964

Typeset in AZO
by codeMantra

MIX
Paper | Supporting responsible forestry
FSC® C013056

Printed and bound in Great Britain by
TJ Books, Padstow, Cornwall

Contents

INTRODUCTION

The dangers associated with climate change were creeping into conversations early in the 2000s but the effects were expected to be decades away. There remained in me a suspicion that, perhaps, a house at 15 feet above sea level and one block from the Gulf of Mexico, might not be the safest place when sea levels rose. My husband, also an architect, and I purchased a lot on higher ground – a whopping 20 feet above sea level – and built a house to demonstrate our commitment to sustainability: thick walls and extra insulation, polished concrete slab to avoid redundant finishes, pervious paving to manage stormwater, and a grass roof just to prove it could be done. We moved into the house in July 2005. Five weeks later, Hurricane Katrina roared ashore with a 28-foot storm surge.

When we returned after evacuating for the storm, uncertain of what we would find, the house was still standing. The visible waterline on the walls was as high as I could reach. Storm surge had found the weakest point and created its own flood vents, battering through windows and walls on opposite sides of the house, retreating quickly but leaving behind a toxic swamp of mud and debris. Our house had acted as a bulwark to protect two neighbouring houses from sliding off their foundations. It also protected a brother and sister who swam out of the second floor of their house on the beach and took shelter beneath the grass roof because 'it was the only thing that wasn't moving'. The architects' house had survived and a lot of people wanted to know why. Instead of becoming a showcase for sustainability it became an example of resilience.

A single storm cannot be attributed to climate change but impacts seemed to accelerate from that point forward: clusters of storms accompanied by higher storm surges, ravenous wildfires that aren't extinguished for months, and climbing temperatures, each year hotter than the last record-breaking year.

Throughout the years of hurricane recovery and rebuilding, I began to examine how the built environment fails, adapts, and thrives in adversity. Our studio designed buildings to survive the worst-case scenarios and buildings that are sacrificial. We explored global examples to learn how people respond to climate hazards and reduce impacts. We investigated building materials and assemblies to find solutions for our hot, humid climate. I read thousands of papers and books and evaluated wildly speculative solutions for a world with more heat, water, and wind and fewer resources to go around. I canvassed other fields – military history, medicine, mathematics – to assimilate their recommendations on preparing for uncertainty.

The planet is entering into an era of precarity. The structures and systems we expected to last for generations have proven fragile and the communities in which we build are becoming increasingly vulnerable. We are entering a future unrecognisable to our parents, bearing a past unfamiliar to our children.

Climate-sensitive hazards can be categorised into four threats: heat, water, wind, and scarcity.

- **Heat** is the deadliest weather-related killer across the globe, responsible for nearly half a million premature deaths a year and becoming progressively more dangerous, with record-breaking highs and extended heat waves now commonplace.
- **Water** is insidious, ubiquitous, unstoppable. Without adaptation, by the end of this century up to 4.6% of the global population will flood annually from 25–123 cm of global mean sea-level rise[1] and even more of the population subject to fluvial (river), and pluvial (rainfall) flooding.
- **Wind** intensity is increasing with climate change, with storms characterised by

DOI: 10.4324/9781032702964-1

stronger gusts and more frequent lightning strikes propelling wildfires.
- **Scarcity** is beginning to affect the things we eat, drink, and use every day, impacting human security, causing resource conflicts, and prompting large-scale climate migration.

It is presumptuous to claim that architecture can solve the climate crisis. However, the resource-reliant construction sector has played a critical role in contributing to climate change, with buildings responsible for over 40% of greenhouse gas emissions, giving architecture and construction a key role in climate mitigation. Our role in climate adaptation is even more clearly defined by two questions: How can architecture and communities better prepare for climate change? And how can the built environment better prepare for disasters?

Resilient buildings, sites, and communities won't spare us from the disruption ahead. Adaptation won't halt the speed or scale of climate change but it can act as a shock absorber against the impacts to the built environment and the people it serves. The power of architecture to translate cultural values into physical form will remain testamentary for many years if they are resistant to the impacts of climate change; if they are not, the financial and environmental repercussions will haunt communities for a similar period of time.

A NOTE ON THE STRUCTURE

Each chapter of this book includes a **Definition** of the adaptation measure, the **Background** in which the measure was developed and tested, and the context in which it might be successful. **Key Design Considerations** outlines questions, recommendations, implementation steps, and metrics for success. At the end of each chapter are notes describing the **Impact** or long-term changes resulting from implementing these strategies across four systems:

- **Social** focuses on the well-being of people and communities, defining the effect of the adaptation measure on equity and justice, quality of life, displacement, and losses.
- **Environmental** describes the effect on the natural environment and ecosystem services, as well as the compromises that may limit the resources available to the future.
- **Economic** accounts for the costs and benefits of implementing the measure, including construction costs, economic growth, resource efficiency, and economic stability.
- **Spatial** outlines the ways that measures may modify patterns in the built environment, intensify or reduce density, reform access to nature, abandon hazardous zones, and establish new settlements.

Resources suggest further reading on the topic or referenced texts.

Architecture is the ultimate act of optimism, and architects and planners are visionaries of the future. This book offers precedents, solutions, and guidance to create a safe, just, and prepared built environment to rewrite the climate future, if only we have the courage to respond. We must go to work now to change the trajectory of global heating and adapt the built environment to protect people at risk and future generations.

NOTE

1 Hinkel, J. et al. 2014. Coastal Flood Damage and Adaptation Costs under 21st Century Sea-Level Rise. *PNAS*, February 2014, 111, 3292–3297. https://doi.org/10.1073/pnas.1222469111.

PART I

Heat

Of all the climate hazards, responding to hotter temperatures outside seems like the easiest - simply turn on the air conditioning. However, the mechanical systems to heat and cool buildings, sized for the predicted loads when they were installed perhaps decades ago, can't keep up. A substantial proportion of the world's existing buildings is not energy efficient or may not have AC at all, and if those buildings install AC, their greenhouse gas emissions would contribute even more to climate change. Chronic exposure to extreme heat places a strain on systems and causing individual mechanical systems to fail, aggregating demand to overwhelm the ailing electrical grid, and inducing outages.

Increased heat is changing the typical meteorological year, partially due to the widespread use of air conditioning. Before WWII there were very few residential AC units but by the 1980s houses and cars were rarely built without them. Heating, ventilation, and air conditioning - HVAC - uses the highest percentage of power in a building and produces 7% of the global greenhouse gas emissions. Outdoor temperatures are climbing, and by 2080 the number of extreme heat days will be 100–250 times the present number,[1] leading to an ever-increasing demand for air conditioning.

The rising demand isn't equitably fulfilled. Air conditioning works for those who can afford it, dividing the world into cool, productive retreats or exposure to sweltering, barbaric heat. Places that never needed AC before, such as the large urban agglomerations of London and Moscow, are racing to install units that will make summer temperatures bearable. Places with a long history of hot weather now face dangerously high temperatures and no nighttime relief. Parts of the globe are becoming unsurvivable.

Architecture has a significant role in mitigating and adapting to climate change. At the Community scale, **Heat Response Networks** prepare communities for temporary periods of extreme heat with cooling centres, mobile services, and water distribution to save lives. Implementing a **Policy of Shade** promotes heat island relief through trees, canopies, and mutual shading, especially in areas of historic disinvestment. **Urban Cooling with Water** introduces water in combination with air movement and shade to cool neighbourhoods. **Cool Corridors** recognise the value of extending fingers of green through the city, connecting and giving comfort for pedestrians, cyclists, transit riders, and others.

The Site scale contributes to heat relief through the design of **Reflective + Absorptive Sites** that reduce local heat islands. Site planning also prepares for associated impacts of **Wildfire Protection** and poor **Air Quality**.

At the Building scale, **Passive Design + Passive Survivability** explores how energy-efficient buildings remain cool even during power outages to preserve the lives of occupants. **Solar Control** presents a variety of solutions to prevent direct heat gain. **Cool Envelopes** suggest methods for controlling heat transfer between outside and inside. **Building Electrification** prepares for a shift away from fossil fuels to a clean electrical grid. **Uninterruptible Power** describes the win–win strategy of renewable energy systems to fulfil daily needs and provide reliable backup power in an emergency.

The building sector has made incomprehensible contributions to greenhouse gas emissions but now has the opportunity to mitigate emissions and adapt to a hotter world.

NOTE

1 Coffel, E. et al. 2018. Temperature and Humidity Based Projections of a Rapid Rise in Global Heat Stress Exposure during the 21st Century. *Environmental Research Letters* 13, no. 1. https://doi.org/10.1088/1748-9326/aaa00e

HEAT RESPONSE NETWORKS

1

ADAPTATION **HEAT** SCALE **COMMUNITY**

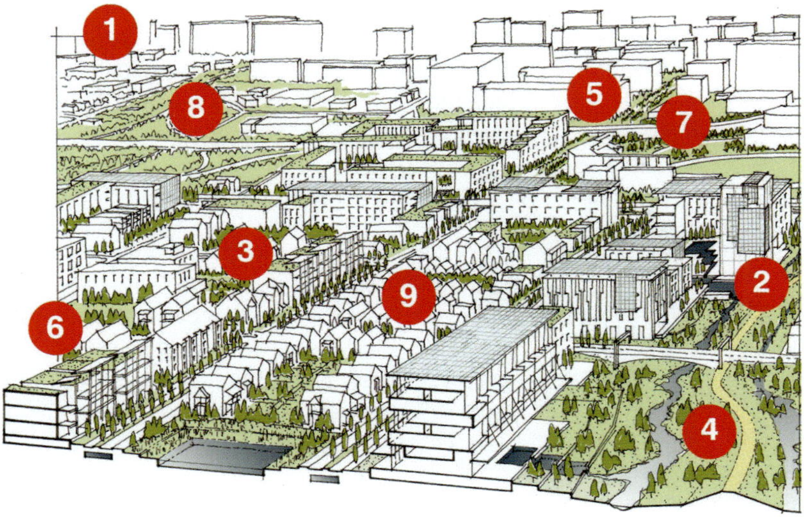

Figure 1.1: Extreme heat is the deadliest climate-related disaster. A heat-sensor network forms an essential part of a city's data collection and emergency response system.

1. An Emergency Operations Centre monitors the network and issues automated calls, texts, and emails when a heat warning is triggered, providing the location of cooling centres, and sharing emergency numbers. Messages warn residents to minimise energy use to avoid brownouts and guide people to local assistance.
2. Fixed, mobile, and satellite-based sensors placed across the city collect micro-climate data to identify areas for mobilisation.
3. Local cooling centres are opened at schools, churches, community centres, libraries, and museums to give people a retreat from the heat, with extended hours to cover the hottest parts of the day.
4. Drinking water distribution points are set up throughout the city and public water fountains dispense cool, potable water. Shower stations are set up for humans and pets.
5. On-demand transportation takes elderly and handicapped residents to cooling centres. Additional health care response is mobilised to check on vulnerable people.
6. Occupational safety protocols for outside workers recommend crews take more frequent breaks, drink plenty of water, and adjust working hours to avoid the hottest part of the day.
7. Sporting event dates or times are rescheduled to take advantage of cooler weather. Athletes are warned to pace themselves, wear lightweight and light-coloured clothing, ensure adequate hydration, and limit outdoor activity during the hottest part of the day.
8. Outdoor cooling centres offer shade, drinking water, seating, and misters.
9. Areas with a green equity gap are prioritised to relieve localised heat islands.

A heat response network is a bio-meteorological system which monitors human thermal comfort. Sensors measure air temperature, sunlight intensity, and humidity in real time, and assess the presence of shade and wind as mitigating factors for heat. The resulting thermal index indicates the relative heat stress which can guide communities about when and where to mobilise additional resources to support at-risk residents. Community response activities are triggered at a predetermined heat-health threshold where heat poses a threat to people's health, based on the temperature at which there was previously a surge in deaths due to extreme heat or an increase in hospital admissions.

DOI: 10.4324/9781032702964-3

BACKGROUND

Climate change is driving temperatures higher for longer periods in summer months, affecting cities and people that are unprepared for extreme heat. There is wide spatio-temporal variability of temperature in cities, depending not only on the time of day and season but on the context: the amount of paving, building orientation, the presence of shade, and local weather patterns. Buildings, sidewalks, and roadways retain heat and trap airflow, causing temperatures to rise in daylight and remain high throughout the night.

The impacts of climate change are distributed unevenly among the population. People with the highest risk of death or serious illness from heat are older adults, very young children, people with mental health issues and chronic diseases, unhoused, outdoor workers, and non-native speakers. Poverty has grave impacts at both weather extremes, affecting people unable to heat their homes in winter or cool them in summer, or forcing households to economise on energy consumption to a point that negatively impacts the inhabitants' health and wellbeing. A legacy of poorly insulated older homes, inefficient appliances, and the high cost of energy also results in a high proportion of household expenditures on energy, resulting in energy poverty.

Cities can employ heat sensor networks to identify the potential for heat stress, especially in heat islands that overlap with areas of high concentrations of vulnerable people, to learn where excessive heat places people at greater risk. Heat response networks are an effort to protect public health against excessive heat. When extreme heat in Barcelona reaches 33.4°C (92°F) for three consecutive

Figure 1.2: Barcelona Climate Shelters include schools, museums, libraries, and parks. They open to the public from 15 June to 15 September each year, for the hours that the buildings are open. Park spaces are improved with cooling fountains, gardens and green walls, solar shading, and shade trees. Barcelona City Council.

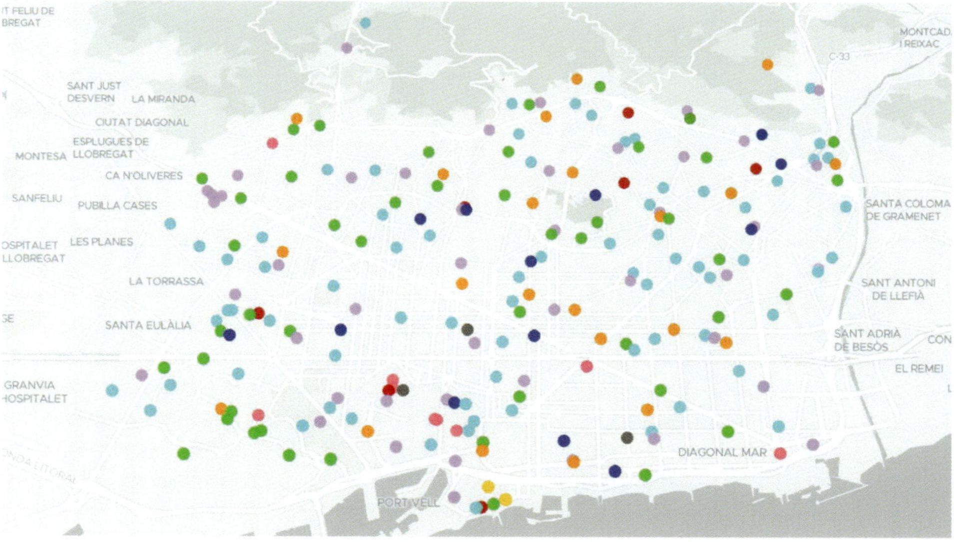

Figure 1.3: Barcelona Climate Shelters are spread throughout the city, with physical and digital wayfinding. Barcelona City Council. A map is available at: https://www.barcelona.cat/barcelona-pel-clima/ca/accions-concretes/xarxa-de-refugis-climatics.

days, the plan is activated with operations to move elderly and vulnerable people into air-conditioned climate shelters, distribute water in public spaces, and provide emergency medical services. The city ensures water and energy utilities to homes are maintained, preventing shutoff for nonpayment of bills. The city is also investing in renovating existing buildings as shelters, expanding solar energy generation, and creating cooling gardens co-located with schools. The shaded gardens improve thermal comfort on the playground, with seating, drinking water, pervious surfaces, and drought-resistant vegetation.

Unprecedented heat in Paris foreshadows a hotter future. The one day of extreme heat per year that the city endures at present is projected to grow to 10–25 heat wave days per year by the end of the century. The 2017 heat wave illustrated the contribution of paved schoolyards to a hotter microclimate. In a city with only 5.8 m^2 of greenspace per inhabitant, the two issues coalesced in a single solution: transform asphalt playgrounds into urban cooling centres. Schools are located within 200 m of most Parisian homes, so the conversion affects every *arondissement* and every resident. The OASIS (Openness, Adaptation, Sensitisation, Innovation, and Social Ties) programme uses permeable paving, overhead shade structures, fountains, rainwater recovery, drought-resistant plants, and pedagogical gardens to teach children about nature and gardening. Schools open the climate-adapted spaces to elderly residents during heat waves and to the public outside of school hours. Paris plans to develop 300 garden play yards and shaded walking routes, with a mobile app to guide people to cooler public spaces.

Improvements such as these require public investment and a demonstration that the benefits from such a programme will outweigh the costs. A cost-benefit analysis of a Hot Weather Health Watch/Warning System studied Philadelphia, PA, during the period from 1995 to 1998.[1] Excessive heat

Figure 1.4: Paris schoolyards are transformed into outdoor cooling centres with permeable paving, overhead shade structures, fountains, rainwater recovery, and drought-resistant plants.

OASIS Schoolyard, Urban Innovative Actions Initiative, EU.

Figure 1.5: A network of outdoor drinking fountains across the city are a critical component of a heat-response network with locations marked on physical and digital maps.

warnings were issued when the daytime heat index was expected to exceed 40.5°C (105°F) for more than 3 hours per day on two consecutive days, or whenever the daytime heat index was expected to exceed 46°C (114°F) for any length of time. Preventative actions included warning residents of the heat wave, providing a heat-line service connecting people to resources, and not shutting off essential services (electricity and water) due to missed payments. The actions had direct costs to the city, including additional wages for Emergency Medical Service crews but the study estimated the costs to the city did not exceed $10,000 per day of the heatwave. The most consequential benefit of the programme was saving an average of two lives for each day of the heat wave.

KEY DESIGN CONSIDERATIONS

Utilise a sufficient number of heat sensors to forecast real-time and future conditions to capture microclimate variations within the city. Include fixed sensors, mobile systems to measure trends, and satellite data.[2] Place some sensors at the height of a human, between 0.7 m to 2.5 m, to collect data at the sidewalk level.

Map and analyse socially vulnerable populations and overlay heat islands. The United States is developing the National Integrated Heat Health Information System (www.heat.gov) to compare temperatures of disadvantaged and non-disadvantaged census tracts.

Improve emergency preparedness by ensuring people know where to go. Efficient heat response networks include comprehensive emergency communications, heat safety tips, advice on keeping temperatures under control inside the home, information about how to reach emergency transportation and medical services, and the location of cooling centres. Create awareness through networks of trusted people: community and church leaders, teachers, and local service providers. Provide physical and digital signage to guide people to cooling centres, along with the hours of operation and services available.

Disperse cooling centres across the city, ideally within a ten-minute walk of every residence. Libraries, museums, community centres, and churches may have space that can operate independently from their normal functions to manage an influx of temporary users or extend operating hours beyond normal staffing. Note that schools may be in session during many of the hottest months and operate during the hottest part of the day and therefore may be unable to accommodate people in unsupervised groups due to security concerns.

Cooling centres must provide shade, seating, fans or air conditioning, and restrooms. They should have storage for emergency supplies: first aid, drinking water, extra seating, and other necessities. They may also offer charging points, Wi-Fi networks, and access to other resources.

Create outdoor cooling centres with 24-hour access to fans, shade, misters, and drinking water. Provide direct access from the street. Enhance parks and gardens with features for people to rest with air movement and access to drinking water. Plant trees to provide a cool canopy of shade. Transform asphalt-covered surfaces into absorptive ground surfaces.

Create a network of shaded routes throughout the city. Replant corridors, expand green infrastructure, and improve access to parks and urban gardens. (Chapter 5: Cool Corridors.)

Correct the 'park equity gap' in low-income neighbourhoods and areas with higher populations of people of colour, which typically have higher temperatures relative to adjacent neighbourhoods in the same city and fewer open spaces to find relief.

Transform outdoor spaces to tackle heat by including outdoor drinking water fountains, pools, and rainwater recovery. Plant shade trees and drought-resistant vegetation. Remove areas of impervious surface and replace with native groundcover.

Construct trellises or vegetated walls to intercept direct sun and shield from reflected heat, as well as awnings, pergolas, and solar shades.

IMPACT

Social: Heat monitoring and early response systems can save lives in a heat wave. Tailor responses to prioritise hotter neighbourhoods with greater exposure to heat stress, areas with fewer resources to cope with extreme heat.[3]

Environmental: Measuring and mapping heat islands prioritises the areas most in need of cooling strategies. The success of nature-based solutions to manage heat promotes awareness of the benefits conferred by nature and catalyses further sustainable development.

Economic: Heat has negative impacts on the economy, disrupting productivity, industrial production, construction activities, and the electrical grid. Although heat response networks have direct costs to the city, these costs are negligible when measured against the lives saved during heatwaves.[4]

Spatial: Data from heat sensors can map localised anomalies where cities can focus to transform heat islands into cool, green oases.

NOTES

1 Ebi, K.L., T.J. Teisberg, L.S. Kalkstein, L. Robinson, and R.F. Weiher. 2004. Heat Watch/Warning Systems Save Lives Estimated Costs and Benefits for Philadelphia 1995–98. *Bulletin of the American Meteorological Society*, 1 August, 1067–1074. https://doi.org/10.1175/BAMS-85-8-1067.

2 Yang, J. and E. Bou-Zeid. 2019. Designing Sensor Networks to Resolve Spatio-Temporal Urban Temperature Variations: Fixed, Mobile or Hybrid? *Environmental Research Letters* 14, 074022. https://doi.org/10.1088/1748-9326/ab25f8.

3 Harlan, S.L., A.J. Brazel, L. Prashad, W.L. Stefanov, and L. Larsen. 2006. Neighborhood Microclimates and Vulnerability to Heat Stress. *Social Science & Medicine* 63, no. 11, 2847–2863. https://doi.org/10.1016/j.socscimed.2006.07.030.

4 Ebi et al. (2004).

RESOURCES

- The International Federation of Red Cross and Red Crescent Societies (IFRC): *City Heatwave Guide for Red Cross Red Crescent Branches*. Accessed at: https://www.ifrc.org/sites/default/files/2019_RCCC-Heatwave-Guide-for-RCRC-Branches-1.pdf
- Sitzoglou, M. 2023. OASIS Takes Off! – Final Journal. Urban Innovative Actions, Lille, France. Accessed at: https://www.uia-initiative.eu/en/pdf/3058

2 A POLICY OF SHADE

ADAPTATION **HEAT** SCALE **COMMUNITY**

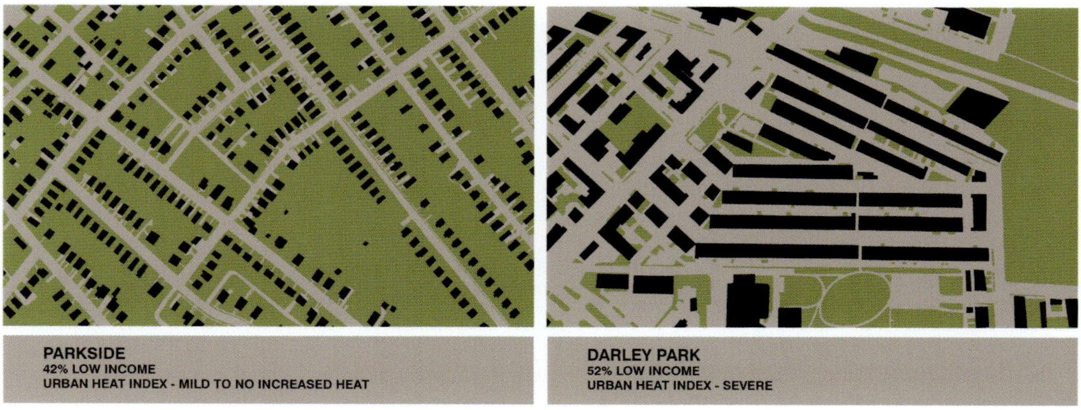

Characteristics of the built environment have a significant impact on concentrating and trapping heat in urban areas, with street and building surface temperatures from 18°F to 27°F hotter (in daylight) and from 9°F to 18°F warmer (at night) than rural areas.[1] Instituting a policy of shade can encourage improvements in the built environment to reflect rather than absorb heat. A shaded street with an overhanging tree canopy filters light, offering shelter from the discomfort of oppressive heat and glare. In a hot climate, shade is a measure of health and a statement of community values which prioritises wellbeing and seeks to distribute it equitably.

Figure 2.1: The amount of greenspace has a profound effect on heat profiles in two Baltimore neighbourhoods. Parkside (left) has 42% low-income residents and a mild- to no-increases in the heat profile due to large areas of greenspace. Darley Park has 52% low-income residents and severe increases to heat, making temperatures up to 8°F hotter. The two communities are less than 2.5 miles apart.

DOI: 10.4324/9781032702964-4

BACKGROUND

Sunshine is a welcome boon to human health, elevating moods, reducing stress, and activating the immune system but too much sunlight can lead to heat stress, skin cancer, and eye damage. As temperatures rise, communities must increase shading in the public realm to manage heat. Implementing a policy of shade enlivens public spaces and incorporates shade at the street level, using building overhangs and massing, trees and vegetation along streets and in the interstitial spaces between buildings, and adding shade structures in exposed areas where trees are not appropriate.

Shade has a crucial role in the prevention of skin cancer, incidences of which have increased dramatically in the last decades. The Earth's orbit is closer to the sun in the southern hemisphere during its summer than in the northern hemisphere; this difference, plus lower pollution levels and clearer air, results in 15% higher solar UV intensity during the southern hemisphere summer. The Shade Working Group in New South Wales, Australia developed a coordinated and strategic shade policy agenda in response to public health concerns about skin cancer.[2] Local strategic planning focused on a wide range of actions to enhance shade, expand the urban tree canopy, construct shade canopies, and mitigate climate change.

The provision of shade has long been a tenet of good planning in hot climates. The Law of the Indes, issued by King Phillip of Spain in 1573, guided the planning and establishment of new towns in the Americas and Asia. Law 115 reads, 'Around the plaza as well as along the four principal streets which begin there, there shall be arcades, for these are of considerable convenience to the merchants who generally gather there'.[3] The standard encouraged cities to provide shade in places where people gather at peak times to protect pedestrians and tradespeople.

Figure 2.2: Tree canopies block solar radiation from reaching the ground and heating up materials such as asphalt. Trees also cool the environment via the process of transpiration, which consumes heat energy that would otherwise raise air temperatures.

Shade has a legacy of inequity in the United States, where streets in many low-income neighbourhoods were built with higher densities and narrow rights-of-way, leaving little space for trees, medians, and sidewalks. The urban heat intensity (UHI) is typically lower in census tracts with high median income and a higher population of white people, with higher UHI in communities of colour and low-income neighbourhoods.[4] Studies correlate historically redlined areas (the discriminatory and systematic denial of services to residents of certain areas, based on their race or ethnicity) with consistent patterns of higher temperatures, varying by as much as 7°C from wealthier neighbourhoods.[5] The social distribution of shade is a public good and issues of equity should be considered in decisions about where to expand urban shade canopies.

KEY DESIGN ISSUES

Institute community policies to increase shade. Conduct a shade audit at sites where shade is important, such as parks, paths, swimming pools, public spaces, playgrounds, schoolyards, beaches, and sports fields. Prioritise investments in shade based on the time of use (midday is the critical protection time), the length of use (full day taking precedence), and the level of use (the number of people at the site). Include the effects of reflected UV radiation and the types of ground cover present. Based on these factors, assess the need for improved shade at the site.

Shade acts as a physical barrier from direct and indirect sources of UV radiation. It can be built (overhangs and roofs) or natural (trees and vegetation) to cast shadows opposite the sun's position. Shade creates comfortable outdoor spaces, extending the period of use through the summer's heat.

Plant trees strategically to create a continuous canopy of shade where people are walking and standing, and allow the tree canopy to extend over streets, where traffic permits. Plant a diversity of vegetation to create a succession of experiences, of perfume, colour, texture, and foliage. Linear forests have benefits for stormwater management, improve air quality, and increase biodiversity.

Established trees provide broader shade canopies more quickly than newly-planted replacements. Maintain trees and vegetation buffers along streets, alleys, and between lots. Prevent construction site clearing and the unnecessary removal of trees. Prevent unnecessary trimming at power lines. Require tree protection throughout the construction phase and prevent materials storage or parking within the drip line.

Ensure that tree planters offer adequate space and soil for urban street trees. In narrow sidewalk zones, select trees that won't grow bushy and prevent movement along the sidewalk. Avoid planting in places where roots may damage foundations or underground utilities. When there is little room within the right-of-way for trees, plant and maintain vegetated screens, hedges, shade walls, and trellises.

Trees with dense foliage create more shade. If heat constitutes a year-round hazard, plant evergreen species; if winter sun is desirable, plant deciduous species.

Architectural shading devices for public spaces include arcades, awnings, galleries, and both temporary and permanent canopies. Overhanging planes are most efficient when the sun is at its highest point in the middle of the day, while vertical fins protect against early morning and late afternoon sun.

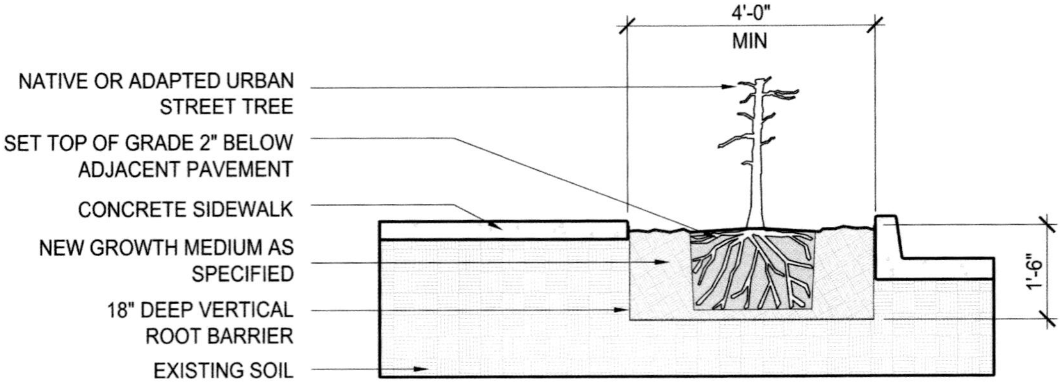

Figure 2.3: Street trees in the right-of-way should be planted to accommodate full maturity, even if the growth will take decades. The target soil requirements depend on the mature canopy size: a tree with a large canopy of 8 m diameter needs a soil volume of 30 m^3; a small tree with 5 m canopy diameter has a target soil volume of 5 m^3.

Figure 2.4: A catalogue of rooftop shade options: shade sail, tree planter, pergola, trellis, vertical screen, retractable fabric awning, and living wall.

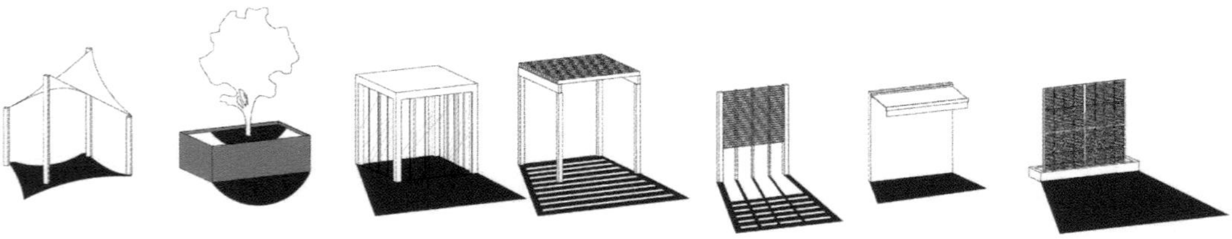

Arrange buildings to shade each other and exterior spaces in mutual shading patterns. Narrow 'shade canyons' create social and circulation spaces in the interstices between structures. Narrow courtyards can have shade coverings or open to the sky to allow cross-ventilation and flush out hot air. Place buildings close together in hot, arid climates to shade each other in the early morning and late afternoon when the sun is low in the sky.

Maximise shade on building rooftops and roadways, areas that would be otherwise fully exposed to absorb heat. At noon on a clear summer day, a flat (horizontal) surface receives about 1,000 watts of sunlight per square meter (U.S. latitudes). Adding buildings to a city footprint typically increases the urban temperature, but with as little as a 1% increase in shadows cast on the rooftops of adjacent can result in average temperature decreases of between 0.13% and 0.31%.[6] Recognise that the cooling effect of shading adjacent roofs must be balanced by its impact on solar power generation capacity.

Shade structures can be built in a wide variety of configurations, permanent or temporary. Consider demountable shade structures for places that need shade occasionally.

IMPACT

Social: Shade improves thermal comfort and mitigates the effects of global heating. Correcting the green deficit and improving shade throughout urban zones can reduce energy burdens on low-income households. Shade inspires more people to get outside in hot seasons, with physical and mental health benefits.

Environmental: Trees decrease urban temperatures due to shading, reflection, and evapotranspiration. The effects can be significant: reducing temperatures by 6°C (12°F) when planting areas equal about 20% of the city area, and about 10°C (20°F) when planted areas equal 50% of the city.[8] The expanded tree canopy reduces stress on ecosystems, improves stormwater management, and increases biodiversity.

Economic: Planting trees along street corridors has direct benefits for street maintenance; 20% shading over a street extends the service life of the pavement by 11%, realising a 60% saving in resurfacing costs over 30 years. Shade canopies also cool private properties and reduce energy demand, especially in neighbourhoods with narrow setbacks from the street. Tree-lined parking improves commercial sales in adjacent retail outlets and well-maintained green spaces increase property values.

Spatial: Shaded streets clearly define the boundary of the vehicular zone, calming traffic speeds and promoting pedestrian safety. Tree cover and greenery contribute to the community streetscape, character, identity, and standard of living.

Adjustable shades - retractable, sliding, and roll-up - are modified over the course of a day or a season in response to the sun orientation. Lightweight tension membranes can be removed for cleaning or during high winds.

Air temperatures are 4–8°F cooler in shaded parking lots than in unrelieved asphalt lots. Shade trees in parking lots reduce surface asphalt temperatures by 20°C (36°F) and vehicle interior temperatures by 26°C (47°F). Cooler parking lot temperatures also reduce ozone concentrations and hydrocarbon emissions from parked cars due to fuel evaporation.[7] A reasonable target goal is to achieve 50% shading of all hardscape within 10 years of planting.

Require a percentage of parking areas to have solar photovoltaic canopies that produce electricity and shield cars and pavement from direct sun. France requires parking lots with 80 or more spaces to be covered with solar shades; and in parking lots with over 400 spaces, 50% must be covered with solar by 2025.

NOTES

1 U.S. Environmental Protection Agency. 2008. Urban Heat Island Basics. In *Reducing Urban Heat Islands: Compendium of Strategies* (pp. 1–22). https://www.epa.gov/heat-islands/heat-island-compendium
2 Shade Policy Framework, Cancer Council of Victoria, Australia. Accessed August 8, 2023 at: https://www.sunsmart.com.au/downloads/shade/shade-policy-framework.pdf
3 Law 116 continues, "but for purposes of defense in areas where there are horses, it would be better if they are wide." English translation by Axel Mundigo and Dora Crouch. 1977. The City Planning Ordinances of the Laws of the Indies Revisited, Part I. *Town Planning Review* 48, no. 3, 247–268. Accessed at: https://www.liverpooluniversitypress.co.uk/doi/10.3828/tpr.48.3.g58m031x54655ll5
4 T. Chakraborty, A. Hsu, D. Manya, and G. Sheriff. 2020. A Spatially Explicit Surface Urban Heat Island Database for the United States: Characterization, Uncertainties, and Possible Applications. *ISPRS Journal of Photogrammetry and Remote Sensing* 168, 74–88. https://doi.org/10.1016/j.isprsjprs.2020.07.021.
5 J.S. Hoffman, V. Shandas, and N. Pendleton. 2020. The Effects of Historical Housing Policies on Resident Exposure to Intra-Urban Heat: A Study of 108 US Urban Areas. *Climate* 8, no. 1, 12. https://doi.org/10.3390/cli8010012.
6 Y. Park, J.-M. Guldmann, and D. Liu. 2021. Impacts of Tree and Building Shades on the Urban Heat Island: Combining Remote Sensing, 3D Digital City and Spatial Regression Approaches. *Computers, Environment, and Urban Systems* 88, July 2021, 101655. https://doi.org/10.1016/j.compenvurbsys.2021.101655.
7 K.I. Scott, Simpson, J.R., and McPherson, E.G. 1999. Effects of Tree Cover on Parking Lot Microclimate and Vehicle Emissions. *Journal of Arboriculture* 25, no. 3, 129–142.
8 L.O. Myrup. 1969. A Numerical Model of the Urban Heat Island. *Journal of Applied Meteorology* 8, 908–918.

RESOURCES

- King, E.L., S. Thompson, and N. Groskops. 2022. Integrating Shade into the Healthy Built Environment Agenda: The Approach Taken in NSW, Australia. *Public Health Research & Practice* 32, no. 1, e3212206. https://doi.org/10.17061/phrp3212206
- Park, Y., J.-M. Guldmann, and D. Liu. 2021. Impacts of Tree and Building Shades on the Urban Heat Island: Combining Remote Sensing, 3D Digital City and Spatial Regression Approaches. *Computers, Environment, and Urban Systems* 88, July 2021, 101655. https://doi.org/10.1016/j.compenvurbsys.2021.101655

URBAN COOLING WITH WATER

3

ADAPTATION **HEAT** SCALE **COMMUNITY**

For millennia, people have used water to reduce temperatures in the urban environment through reflecting pools, splashing fountains, deep tanks, and slender water courses. Water decreases air temperature through evaporative cooling and heat absorption but water alone isn't sufficient to remedy the heat island effect. Water in combination with shade and air movement is an effective way to amplify cooling in the urban environment, relieving heat and creating cool refuges.

Figure 3.1: Ponds located in open squares or parks have a cooling effect on surrounding areas, especially if shaded by trees on the east and west sides. Urban water features can reduce temperatures up to 8°C.

DOI: 10.4324/9781032702964-5

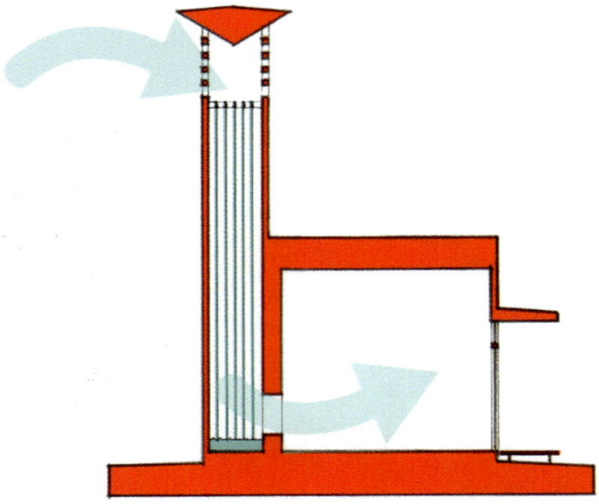

Figure 3.2: The first evaporative wind towers were built approximately 1,200 years ago in the arid regions of Iran and are still used in the Middle East. Air enters at tall wind towers and is drawn past conduits filled with water and over pools at the bottom, introducing cooler and more humid air to adjacent interior spaces.

BACKGROUND

Water shapes the experience of a place. Cities like Rome make the presence of water tangible and immediate with urban fountains that splash, leap, trickle, and ultimately fall to rest. Water satisfies the human need for delight, quenching physical and spiritual thirst. Water features enhance the visual and acoustic beauty of public space; they serve as landmarks, meeting places, respites, and interactive play areas. Water movement mixes water and air together, an alchemy that turns liquid into vapour and evaporates heat from the urban environment with a greater effect on temperature than a still pool.

Ancient civilisations employed water to cool buildings and settlements exposed to heat, using indigenous practices that are still in use today.

- Ancient Egyptians filled a porous earthenware jar with water and placed it in a window so that air could blow over and around it. The hot, dry air quickly absorbed condensation from the jar and created an effective evaporative cooling mechanism.
- Wind towers collect outside air and draw it into the building, directing airflow over vertical water conduits in the tower and pools of water at the base to activate the natural evaporative system. They are useful at the civic scale to direct airflow into small open spaces surrounded by buildings.
- Tropical areas use swimming pools as a natural thermal cooling device. Locating a shaded pool between the prevailing winds and a sleeping room boosts evaporative cooling before the air is circulated through interior spaces.[1]
- *Uchimizu* is the Japanese practice of splashing rainwater or greywater onto the ground or roadways to cool the surrounding air. A campaign to honour this traditional Japanese practice was conducted in 2003 in Tokyo, with a reported decrease in temperature of 1°C.
- India uses *tatties*, frames filled with dried grasses that are kept wet with catch basins, set into openings. A mechanical version of this – a *thermantidote* – introduces a fan to blow air through the tatties. W.G. Osborne described these in *The Court & Camp of* Runjeet Sing (1840).[2]

> *The thermometer at 112 all day in our tents, notwithstanding tatties, phermanticlotes (sic), and every possible invention that was likely to lessen the stifling heat.... All sorts of experiments to keep themselves cool are tried by the different unhappy individuals in camp; I think mine the most successful. Dig a large hole in the ground, in the centre of your tent, and then place your table over it to form a sort of inner roof, and prevent the sun from shining down upon you. Make your bheestie [water carrier] water the floor of the hut, and then hang a wet sheet over the hole like a hammock,*

Figure 3.3: Introducing water in the urban landscape can affect city temperatures, with the most significant reductions derived from combining several techniques - shading, water vapourisation, and natural ventilation - around water bodies.

> *pegged to the ground on the edge of the pit to prevent its touching the bottom; take off all your clothes, and get into it, and by having a skin of water thrown over you every ten minutes, you may perhaps get the temperature down to 100, which would be a perfect heaven to what we are now enduring.*

Technology has developed new ways of delivering water to the urban environment. Misters are highly water-efficient, using a small amount of water (as little as 1–2 gallons per hour) to create a fine mist and cover a large surface area. Street-level misters enhance pedestrian comfort by targeting the upper body, which has more human sweat glands and skin temperature receptors, than the lower body.[3] The optimal locations for mist systems are places where people are exposed to heat for long periods such as transit stops, outdoor dining areas, or queues. People prefer indirect misting at the periphery, rather than the wetness that can come from direct exposure to the mist nozzles.[4] Mist cooling is best suited to environments where airflow can increase the evaporation rate, particularly in hot, dry climates, but they also work in humid environments as nebulisation uses a small amount of water to minimise increased humidity.

Inviting people to engage with water connects humans to nature, the water cycle, and water across the globe. Does the water invite contact, from the rolling of trousers and paddling to complete immersion? Or would splashing in them disrupt the dignity and serenity of the pool? The architecture of water and its myriad forms can invite or deter interaction without barriers to enjoyment.

KEY DESIGN CONSIDERATIONS

Lakes, rivers, and wetlands regulate urban ambient temperatures by 1–2°C, a result of water's thermal heat retention and evaporative cooling. Large water bodies like big water reservoirs and rivers can reduce heat by 3.3°C, intermediate size water bodies like inland lakes by 2.1°C, and ponds by 1.6°C, consistent with the amount of open space that is adjacent.[5]

In high-traffic pedestrian areas, wetting the sidewalk in morning and afternoon reduces temperatures in places where there may not be room for trees or shade.[6] To get good results, weather conditions should be above 20°C (68°F) and sunny. The spray must run continuously for several hours at a time to have an effect; expected temperature drop may be 0.79°C at 1.5 m above grade and 0.57°C at 4 m above grade. If city-wide wetting is deployed, up to 2°C of relief may be obtained.

Spraying fountains improve the thermal environment through cooling and humidifying through interaction (heat, mass, and

Figure 3.4: A wind tower in Masdar City, UAE, directs airflow through the structure to cool a central courtyard at the Masdar Institute Campus. Masdar Official.

momentum transfer) between the sprayed droplets and air, creating droplets with trajectory, diameter, and temperature. The cooling effects of a fountain can be felt on the leeward side of the spray, with temperature reductions from 1 to 4°C depending on wind speed and distance from the spray.

A blue roof is essentially a roof-mounted pond, a non-vegetated storage system designed to allow the structure to retain stormwater. It is installed over a sealed roof membrane and typically utilises check dams or trays with porous, light-coloured stone to capture and temporarily detain stormwater before it is released. Stormwater detained by blue roofs evaporates, especially during warm, sunny weather, with the remainder directed to roof drains. Blue roofs may be used on buildings with a relatively flat roof pitch and adequate load capacity to handle the excess weight of the system and the water. Surface temperatures at blue roofs are 5°C cooler than gravel roofs.[7]

Evaporative wind towers are passive systems that require no energy to assist with thermal comfort. Wind towers direct outside air into a building, often channelling it over pools of water at the base of the tower or past vertical conduits mounted on the tower walls. Air passing these conduits is evaporatively cooled and its density is increased; the cooler air is heavier than the ambient air, resulting in a downward circulation into the living space.

Figure 3.5: Shaded canals, such as this one in Amsterdam, can have an urban cooling effect of 6°C. Allison Anderson.

European cities primarily built canals for trade but recognise a cooling effect near the canals. Canals also act as ventilation channels, lowering the air temperature as wind blows over the water. Provide stairs for water access and water misters in sunlit areas to further improve thermal comfort and interest. Unshaded canals may have reductions between 0.3°C and 1.6°C within a 100 m of the canal during the hottest hours of the day.[8] When the water is shaded by trees, the temperature may be 6°C lower than adjacent areas of the city.

Ponds located in open squares or parks have a cooling effect, especially if shaded by trees on the east and west sides. Bridges or walkways enhance the sensation of coolness as people cross the pond. Shade from trees planted beside – or within – water bodies significantly enhances the cooling effect, and variations in tree canopy height or offset rows of trees create more turbulent airflow.[9] The potential temperature reduction can reach 8°C.[10]

IMPACT

Social: Water enhances social spaces and encourages people to linger, observe, and interact with urban water features. The cooling effect of water counteracts high temperatures and encourages extended use of public spaces.

Environmental: Reduced temperature in urban areas lowers the demand for energy, mitigating greenhouse gas emissions. The reduction in heat also reduces the formation of ground-level ozone and creates more favourable conditions for a variety of plant and animal species.

Economic: Water attracts people to engage in commercial and recreational activities, with a direct correlation between the time spent in commercial corridors and a rise in economic activity.

Spatial Integration: Water has an unparalleled aesthetic appeal. Watching water move, hearing its sounds, and feeling the tactile qualities of water enlivens the urban environment. Water contributes to a more varied and pleasurable spatial dynamic by defining cooler corridors, squares, and resting points.

Overhead misters enhance the urban environment by creating pockets of cool, refreshing air with a fine spray of water. The largest reductions occur where there is a combination of mist and shade. The average reduction can be as much as 8°C, which makes mist cooling an asset in managing local heat islands.

Placing misting systems at multiple levels can have an even greater effect on urban temperatures. One study placed misters at the rooftop, outdoor terrace, and exterior air conditioning unit of an apartment in a building in Osaka, Japan. The mist systems reduced energy consumption for cooling inside the apartment by over 80% and reduced exterior temperatures by 0.9°C.[11]

NOTES

1 Hoque, S. and N. Iqbal. 2015. Building to Net Zero in the Developing World. *Buildings* 5, no. 1, 56–68. https://doi.org/10.3390/buildings5010056.

2 Osborne, W.G. 1840. *The Court and Camp of Runjeet Sing*. London: Henry Colburn, Publisher. Accessed at: https://gurmatveechar.com/books/English_Books/The.Court.and.Camp.of.Maharaja.Ranjit.Singh.Ji.by.W.G.Osbourne.(GurmatVeechar.com).pdf

3 Desert, A., E. Naboni, and D. Garcia. 2020. The Spatial Comfort and Thermal Delight of Outdoor Misting Installations in Hot and Humid Extreme Environments. *Energy & Buildings* 224, 110202. https://doi.org/10.1016/j.enbuild.2020.110202.

4 Desert et al. (2020).

5 Jacobs, C., L. Klok, M. Bruse, J. Cortesão, S. Lenzholzer, and J. Kluck. 2020. Are Urban Water Bodies Really Cooling? *Urban Climate* 32, 100607. https://doi.org/10.1016/j.uclim.2020.100607.
6 Hendel, M., P. Gutierrez, M. Colombert, Y. Diab, and L. Royon. 2016. Measuring the Effects of Urban Heat Island Mitigation Techniques in the Field: Application to the Case of Pavement-Watering in Paris. *Urban Climate* 16, 43–58.
7 Föllmi, D., L. Corpel, A. Solcerova, and J. Kluck. 2023. Influence of Blue-Green Roofs on Surface and Indoor Temperatures over a Building Scale. *Nature-Based Solutions* 4, 100076. https://doi.org/10.1016/j.nbsj.2023.100076.
8 Climatelier. 2018. REALCOOL. Amsterdam Institute for Advanced Metropolitan Solutions. Accessed at: http://climatelier.net/projects/research/realcool-really-cooling-water-bodies-in-cities/
9 Climatelier (2018).
10 Climatelier (2018).
11 Narumi, D., K. Shigematsu, and Y. Shimoda. 2012. Effect of the Evaporative Cooling Techniques by Spraying Mist Water on Reducing Urban Heat Flux and Saving Energy in Apartment House. *Journal of Heat Island Institute International* 7, 175–181. Accessed at: http://heatisland2009.lbl.gov/docs/221000-narumi-doc.pdf.

RESOURCES

- Climatelier REAL COOL - Really Cooling Water Bodies in Cities. Accessed at: https://climatelier.net/projects/research/realcool-really-cooling-water-bodies-in-cities/
- Water-Smart Cities: Livesley, S., V. Marchionni, P.K. Cheung, E. Daly, and D.E. Pataki. 2020. Water Smart Cities Increase Irrigation to Provide Cool Refuge in a Climate Crisis. *Earth's Future* 9, no. 1. https://doi.org/10.1029/2020EF001806

COOL CORRIDORS

4

ADAPTATION **HEAT** SCALE **COMMUNITY**

Cool corridors are designed to provide relief from high temperatures in the urban landscape. They are characterised by shade and other features to serve pedestrians and bicyclists: vegetation, drinking water, and stormwater improvements. Cool corridors should interconnect throughout the city to form a network of shaded routes through the city leading to commercial areas, schools, public services, parks, libraries, and other destinations.

Figure 4.1: Cool corridors have features to serve everyone on the community, regardless of age or ability: pedestrians, bicyclists, motorists, and transit riders. Cool corridors are also complete streets with multiple mobility options including expanded pedestrian zones, separated bicycle lanes, dedicated transit zones, carefully designed roadways and intersections, and trees and vegetation for shade.

DOI: 10.4324/9781032702964-6

BACKGROUND

Heat can be deadly, especially for people who work, move, or spend a significant portion of the day outside. People without access to automobiles experience high exposure to outdoor heat, a population which often includes the elderly, children, and other vulnerable populations. Cool corridors address the dual issues of excess heat and poor air quality, the two most dangerous environmental factors affecting populations in urban areas; over 4.6 million people die from heat-related issues each year and around 4 million people die each year from exposure to fine particulate outdoor air pollution.[1] High levels of air pollutants and extreme heat coincide due to the role of photochemistry in ground-level ozone formation.[2] Transforming streets into cool corridors is a solution for reducing urban temperatures where people circulate through greenways, linear parks, and green oases throughout the city.

Planting street trees to shade paths across the city is the most effective solution to reduce temperature and improve air quality. The city of Medellín, Colombia, has planted 800,000 trees and 2.5 million plants along 30 *corredores verdes* since 2016, connecting 18 main roads, 12 streams, and 124 parks. The objectives of this programme, to reduce temperatures and improve air quality, have resulted in localised temperature reductions up to 8°C and a cooling effect of 2°C across the city. Air quality improvements also show promise; Medellín's annual particulate matter (PM2.5) levels are three times the WHO guidelines for safe limits but the medians and verges are helping to offset the growth in emissions from private vehicles. The tree planting programme has led to a 34.6% increase in cycling in the city.

Figure 4.2: A map of the *corredores verdes* in Medellín, Colombia. Cooling the central, high-traffic corridors improves heat islands and air quality for the many other users of the street: pedestrians, cyclists, and transit riders.

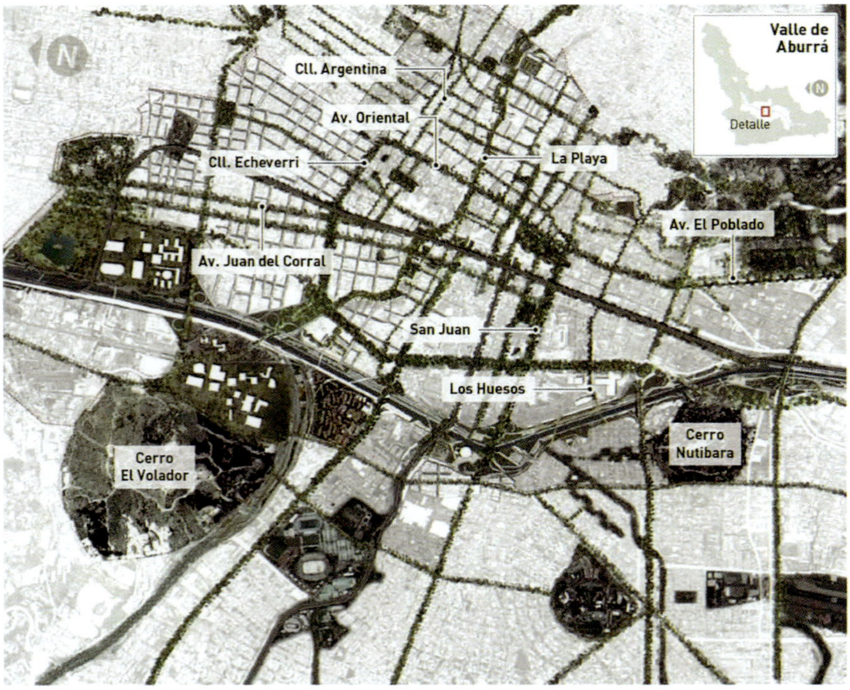

Complete streets are designed to enable safe, convenient, and comfortable travel for users of all ages, abilities, and mobility type, including walking, cycling, riding public transport, driving automobiles, and delivering goods. Dedicating space for trees within an existing right-of-way isn't always easy but narrower vehicle lanes can leave more space for sidewalks, separated bike lanes, and landscape. A U.S. investigation on speed, travel lane width, and safety found that narrowing travel lanes of roadways with speeds up to 35 mph to 3 m (9 feet) is associated with significantly lower numbers of traffic crashes, improving both vehicle and pedestrian safety. Slightly larger lanes (3.4 m) accommodate oversized trucks in streets above 35 mph that serve as transit or freight corridors.[3]

Streets that are oriented to funnel winds or conduct cool air from high elevations into valleys also serve as cool corridors. The city of Stuttgart, Germany, hired a meteorology

Figure 4.3: The design of Stuttgart's ventilation channels has been guided by a map of its urban climate that was first drawn up by the climatology office in 1998. Maps showing wind patterns, flows of cool air, air pollution concentrations, and urban hot spots provide a blueprint for dealing with heat in this densely populated valley basin. Source: Stuttgart Office of Climatology.

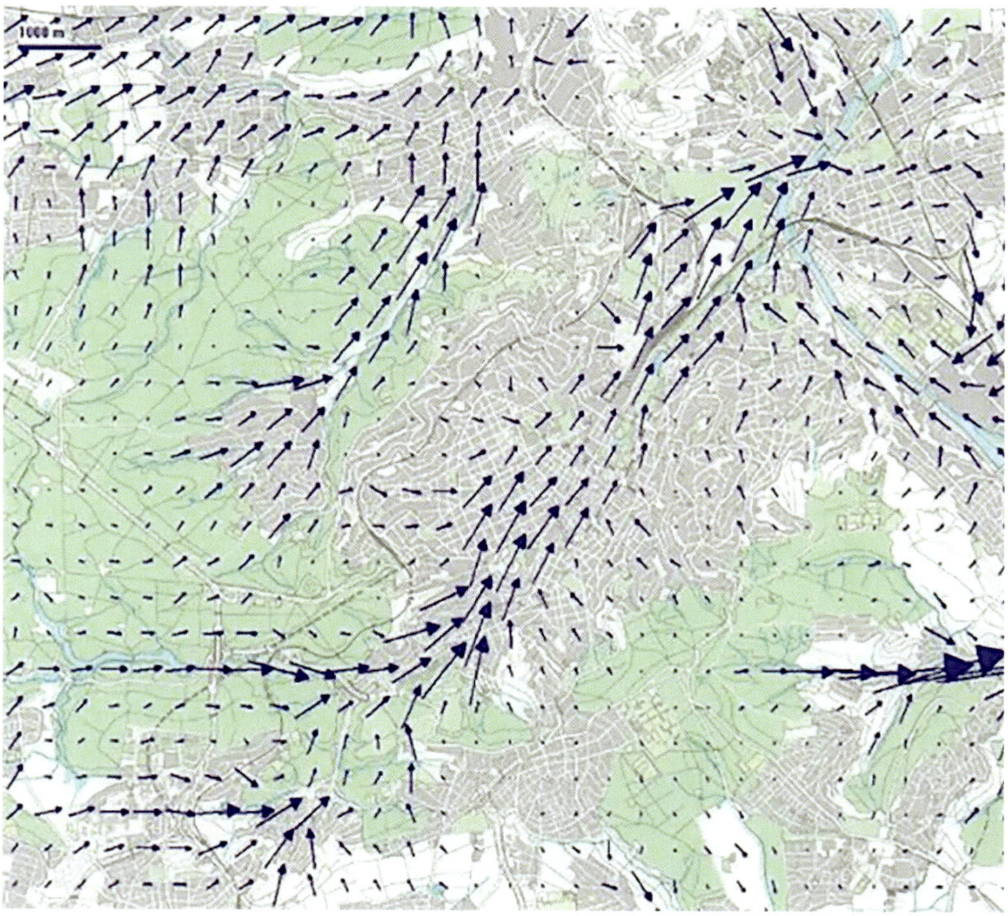

graduate in 1938 to study climate conditions and their relationship to urban development when demands for access to light, ventilation, and exposure to sunlight to counteract tuberculosis and other diseases established environmental hygiene as a priority in the early twentieth century. The city climatologist recognised the potential ventilation effect of topographic conditions to channel air from the mountain slopes into the valley, cooling and disseminating pollutants such as sulphur dioxide and carbon monoxide generated by industrial plants in the city. The city's current land use plan protects ventilation corridors from development in order to maintain cooling airflows, encourages the creation of new greenspace, and prevents uses that could add potential emissions.[4]

The cooling benefits of a densely-planted corridor extend beyond the immediate edge of the street. As air moves along a corridor with shade trees, plantings, and bioswales, cooler air flows into intersecting streets, creating pockets of relief from the heat in neighbouring areas. Distributing green corridors throughout the city allows more neighbourhoods to gain advantages from cooler temperatures.

KEY DESIGN CONSIDERATIONS

Cities can prioritise where to invest in cool corridors by considering: streets where people would walk or bike if more shade existed there; streets adjacent to schools where children and caregivers gather; streets that people would use to walk or bike to a destination where parking is scarce; streets that could benefit from more shade for retail and restaurant customers; and areas with a concentration of people over the age of 65, who are more vulnerable to the adverse effects of air pollution and extreme heat but are more likely to use public transport.[5]

Complete corridors include transit improvements. Provide shaded seating at transit stops. Create a system with frequent and reliable service to decrease exposure time. Include alert systems and online schedules to help riders avoid extended wait times.

A sidewalk serves multiple functions and a 1.5 m (5 foot) wide path (a standard dimension in many cities) is often insufficient. U.S. National Association of City Transportation Officials (NACTO) identifies four sidewalk

Figure 4.4: Sidewalk zones include: (1) the Frontage Zone functions as an extension of the building; (2) the Pedestrian Through Zone is the accessible pathway parallel to the street; (3) the Street Furniture Zone accommodates lighting, benches, kiosks, landscape, and bike parking; and (4) the Enhancement Zone may include stormwater management, curb extensions, or bike lanes. NACTO: https://nacto.org/publication/urban-street-design-guide/street-design-elements/sidewalks/

zones: (1) the frontage zone, which serves as an extension of the building; (2) the pedestrian zone, which allows pedestrian circulation; (3) the street frontage zone, which includes street furniture and amenities such as lighting, benches, utility poles; and (4) the enhancement or buffer zone, with parklets, stormwater management, bike racks, bike lanes, and parking. These zones increase street activity with corollary economic benefits.

Pathways to schools are important routes for children and caregivers on their daily commutes. Communities that encourage children to walk or bike to school will become safer places for everyone to walk and bike. Paths leading to schools and playgrounds should be shaded and continuous, with marked, signalised, or guarded crosswalks.

Green corridors that serve as essential connections in the urban environment should remain safe and accessible at all hours. Dark-sky compliant lighting with good visibility and security encourage nighttime use.

Protected bike lanes are essential to prevent collisions between bicycles, cars, and pedestrians. Protected bike lanes have physical separation from moving motor vehicle traffic: posts, bollards, curbs, planters, or parked cars. They are exclusively designated for people on bicycles and run parallel to the roadway. Streets with protected bike lanes have 90% fewer injuries per mile than those with no bike infrastructure.[6] People are also much more likely to use protected bike lanes. Because they shorten crossing distances, New York City found that protected bike lanes also reduced injury rates for pedestrians, in some cases up to 65% fewer incidents.[7]

Dedicated transit lanes may install alternative surface treatments between the rails, including permeable gravel, grass, or wildflower mixes. Medians separating transit lanes from roadways can include space for a tree canopy, transit stops, lighting, benches, and planters.

Figure 4.5: Recognising the ecosystem value of trees and nature promotes investment in nature-based infrastructure. Residents of Waveland, Mississippi created 'price tags' to highlight the ecosystem benefits from urban street trees that were under threat by road widening projects, resulting in these trees being preserved. Allison Anderson.

Consider narrowing vehicle travel lanes. Streets that are good candidates for lane width reduction are 35 mph or below and have low traffic volume, limited on-street parking, very little street curvature, and fewer lanes.

Trees are part of the infrastructure of a city with values derived from the ecosystem services they provide. Street trees planted in the public right-of-way are a key part of the green infrastructure for stormwater management, cooling, and beautification. Cities can ensure that initial investments in green corridors remain effective with dedicated maintenance and replacement schedules.

Planting the right tree in the right place is essential. Tree species must be selected using a variety of spatial and physical characteristics: climate, species, size, tree spacing, sight lines, growth profiles, available planting space, soils, irrigation, pest control, seasonal changes, maintenance regimes, and other factors.

The Air Pollution Tolerance Index (APTI)[8] is used to assess how tolerant plant species are of air pollution and identify plant species that can assist with pollution removal. It is determined by four biochemical limits of a tree species: ascorbic acid, total chlorophyll content, pH of the leaf extract, and relative water content. The Index classifies trees as tolerant or sensitive to pollutants, helping communities select appropriate species.

Planting a mix of species provides food and habitat for different species of birds and can increase resilience to disease. Avoid over-specialisation by using a variety of tree species, and consider using native evergreen and coniferous trees to maintain year-round benefits. Ensure that non-native species do not have the potential to become invasive.

Consider both overhead and underground utilities before planting. Underground pipes can be damaged during planting and trees planted near underground lines may be damaged if the lines need to be dug up for repairs. Overhead lines may be damaged by tree limbs during high wind events and overzealous tree pruning by a municipality can harm or disfigure trees near power lines.

IMPACT

Social: Cool corridors improve quality of life for the entire community when the sidewalk becomes a space for social interaction, comfortable movement, convenient access to meet daily needs, and safe conditions at all times of day. Planting trees and vegetation provides aesthetic value, shade, and thermal comfort, among other benefits.

Environmental: Beyond regulating temperature and improving air quality, planted corridors also lower greenhouse gas emissions by reducing energy use in adjacent structures that benefit from the corridor shading. The vegetation creates habitat for birds, insects, and other animals, and sequesters carbon dioxide.

Economic: Shaded streets improve property values in both residential and commercial districts. Streets with active transportation infrastructure increase pedestrian counts and bike ridership, with economic benefits to retail and restaurant uses along the street.

Spatial: Cool corridors integrate nature into the city fabric and the places where people live, work, and travel. Distributed across the city, a network of green corridors provides immediate access to the natural world.

NOTES

1 Sources for Heat-Related Excess Deaths: The Lancet. Accessed at: https://www.thelancet.com/journals/lanplh/article/PIIS2542-5196(21)00081-4/fulltext
Air pollution deaths: UNEP website, accessed at: https://www.unep.org/interactives/air-pollution-note/

2 Fever, S.K., J.D.W. Kahl, A.E. Kalkbrenner, R.M. Cerón Bretón, and J.G. Cerón Bretón. 2022 Mar 11. A New Combined Air Quality and Heat Index in Relation to Mortality in Monterrey, Mexico. *International Journal of Environmental Research and Public Health* 19, no. 6, 3299. https://doi.org/10.3390/ijerph19063299.

3 Johns Hopkins Bloomberg School of Public Health. 2023. Narrow Lanes Save Lives: A Way to Make Our Communities Safer and Healthier. Accessed at: https://narrowlanes.americanhealth.jhu.edu/

4 Climate Adapt Website. 2024. Stuttgart: Combating the Heat Island Effect and Poor Air Quality with Ventilation Corridors and Green-Blue Infrastructure. Accessed 4 February 2024 at: https://climate-adapt.eea.europa.eu/en/metadata/case-studies/stuttgart-combating-the-heat-island-effect-and-poor-air-quality-with-green-ventilation-corridors

5 City of Phoenix. 2024. Cool Corridors Program. Accessed 4 February 2024 at: https://www.phoenix.gov/streets/coolcorridors

6 Teschke, K., M.A. Harris, C.C. Reynolds, M. Winters, S. Babul, M. Chipman, M.D. Cusimano, J.R. Brubacher, G. Hunte, S.M. Friedman, M. Monro, H. Shen, L. Vernich, and P.A. Cripton. 2012 Dec. Route Infrastructure and the Risk of Injuries to Bicyclists: A Case-Crossover Study. *American Journal of Public Health* 102, no. 12, 2336–2343. https://doi.org/10.2105/AJPH.2012.300762.

7 New York City Department of Transportation (NYCDOT). 2014. *Protected Bicycle Lanes in NYC*. Accessed 4 February 2024 at: https://www.nyc.gov/html/dot/downloads/pdf/2014-11-bicycle-path-data-analysis.pdf.

8 Molnár, E.V. et al. 2020. Air Pollution Induced Vegetation Stress – The Air Pollution Tolerance Index as a Quick Tool for City Health Evaluation. *Ecological Indicators* 113, 106234. https://doi.org/10.1016/j.ecolind.2020.106234.

RESOURCES

- Complete Streets: Urban Street Design Guide. National Association of City Transportation Officials. 2013. Accessed at: https://nacto.org/publication/urban-street-design-guide/
- Narrow Traffic Lanes: Narrow Lanes Save Lives: A Way to Make Our Communities Safer and Healthier. 2023. Johns Hopkins Bloomberg School of Public Health. Accessed at: https://narrowlanes.american health.jhu.edu/

REFLECTIVE + ABSORPTIVE SITES

5

ADAPTATION **HEAT** SCALE **SITE**

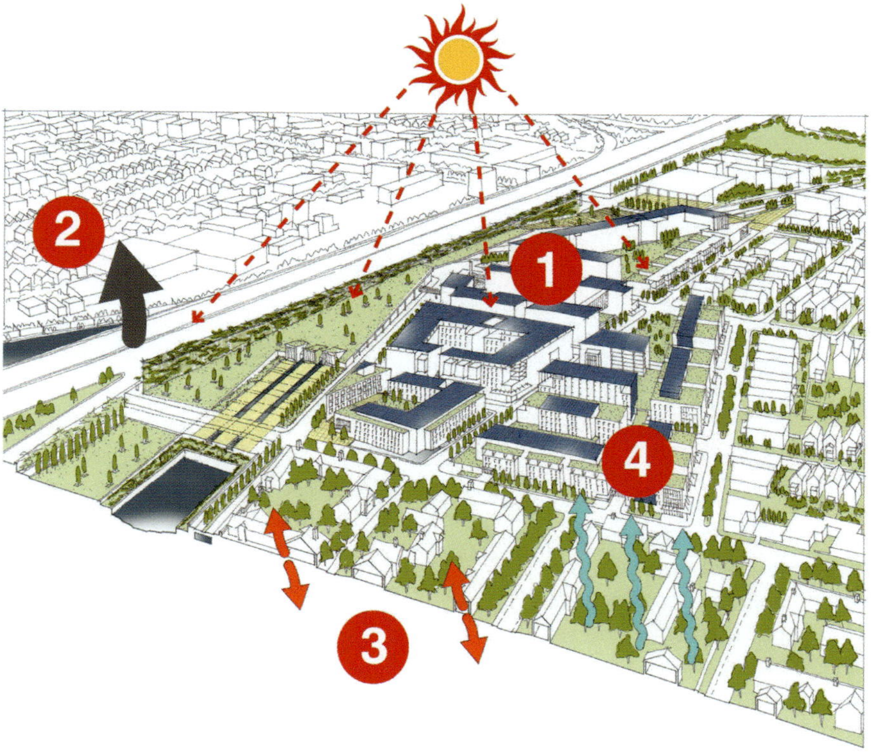

Urban areas are subject to higher temperatures than rural communities due to the higher density of buildings and pavements, and to the solar energy absorbed by asphalt and concrete. Among the many options proposed to cool heat islands, incorporating more permeable ground surfaces may have the greatest impact because it stimulates the evaporative cooling effect, allowing water to evaporate from the pavement pores and extracting heat from the air through the change from a liquid to a gas. Increasing the solar reflectance (SR) of materials also helps by reducing heat storage and re-radiation.

Figure 5.1: The urban environment raises air temperature through: (1) radiation, (2) convection, and (3) conduction. Reflective and absorptive surfaces provide countermeasures like (4) evaporation to improve microclimates at sites.

DOI: 10.4324/9781032702964-7

BACKGROUND

The surface of a city is covered with roads and pavements, concrete, and asphalt, engulfing up to 45% of the land,[1] with much of the remaining area covered by buildings. Global predictions estimate that urban land expansion will increase by 2050, raising the average summer air temperature between 0.5°C and 3°C.[2] These stark projections make it increasingly important to manage heat islands and reduce daytime and nighttime temperatures. Absorptive sites, which allow water to infiltrate the ground and evaporate when temperatures rise, are a critical tool to catalyse urban cooling and conduct heat away from the zone where people live and move.

The physics of heat exchange occurs through **radiation**, **convection**, **conduction**, and **evaporation**.

Radiation is the transmission of heat energy (in the form of particles or waves) through materials or space. In the built environment, the sun heats the ground plane and building surfaces in its direct path but solar radiation is tempered by shade from clouds, trees, or overhead planes such as canopies or awnings. When solar radiation hits a pavement surface, part of it is reflected and part of it is stored and re-radiated. Natural materials - trees, plants, and soil - store less heat and reflect heat better than urban materials.

Convection transfers heat between the pavement surface and the air as warm air rises at a rate depending on flow conditions, fluid properties, and the roughness of the surface. Asphalt and concrete absorb and store heat, but permeable versions of these pavements have a larger surface area due to air voids and rougher surfaces, promoting airflow through the pavement to reduce heat energy storage.

Conduction occurs through direct contact between the layers of the pavement with the ground and air. Heat is transferred from hotter materials to colder materials through microscale interactions from the pavement into the ground. Higher density materials have more efficient conduction because less air exists inside that material to provide insulation. Using thermally conductive materials to transfer heat into the subgrade can effectively reduce heat accumulation and reduce pavement temperatures. These include graphite fibres, steel fibres, vertical steel rods, or quartzite aggregates that may be added to asphalt to improve the thermal conductivity of the pavement. The results range from a 1°C to 3°C reduction of peak surface temperature using steel fibres to almost 3.73°C using quartzite aggregate.[3]

Evaporation occurs as water evaporates and absorbs latent heat from the surroundings. Evaporative pavements hold water within their structure, with more air voids than conventional pavement. Vegetation also reduces air temperature by releasing water to the air and dissipating ambient heat; plants are more effective at evaporative cooling than pavements because of their greater surface area.

Approximately 90% of paved roads across the globe use hot mix asphalt, characterised by dark surfaces which absorb 80–95% of sunlight. Solar radiation is stored in the blacktop, which can be 19.5°C (35°F) hotter than a vegetated surface. The Solar Reflectance Index (SRI) measures a material's response to solar radiation using SR, which measures the fraction of solar energy that is reflected, and Thermal Emittance, which is the relative ability of the surface to radiate heat. The SRI is a value between 0 and 1, where 0 is standard black and 1 is standard white; the lower the SRI, the hotter a material is likely to become in sunlight. The varying physical properties describe why light colours with high reflectivity feel cooler in hot temperatures. SRI value changes over the life of a material as dirt is deposited on the surface, surfaces weather or abrade, or UV radiation affects the colour. The typical SRI values for standard pavements (with no cleaning) are:

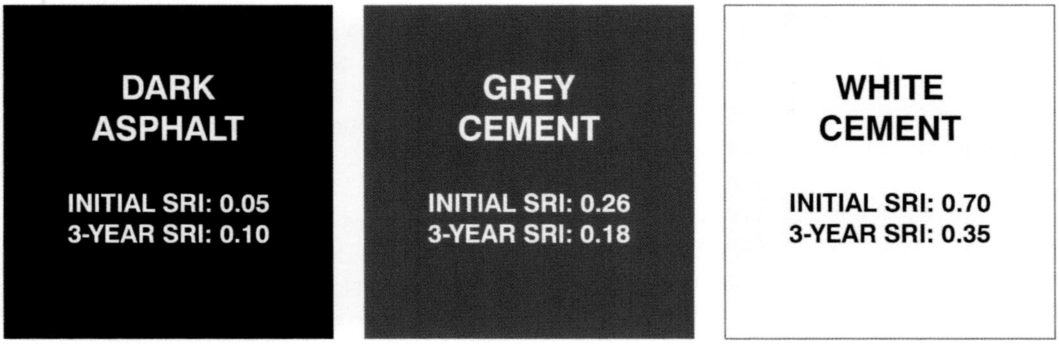

Figure 5.2: Solar Reflectance Index (SRI) of common hardscape materials. A lower number indicates the material will be hotter when exposed to sunlight. The recommended SRI at initial installation is 0.33; of the three options, only white cement concrete meets the standard for cool pavement.

Figure 5.3: Two types of pervious paving. At left: porous geogrid cells planted with grass can result in temperatures 2.61°C lower than asphalt due to evaporation and high solar reflectivity. At right, interlocking concrete pavers can have 6.6°C lower surface temperature than cast grey concrete.

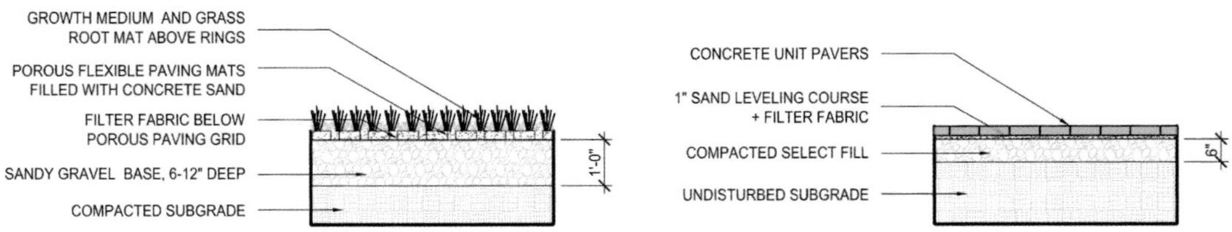

KEY DESIGN CONSIDERATIONS

Minimise the extent of paved surfaces. Reduce road lane widths, the number of parking spaces, and the length of paved driveways. Where hard surfaces are required for accessibility, select permeable paving where appropriate.

The components of a permeable paving system include: the pavement surface; subsurface base and storage reservoir; and edge restraints. Additional components may include an underdrain system and geotextile fabric to reduce weed growth.

Geo-grid options include infill with glass or gravel, which are also infiltrative but have varying thermal properties. Geo-grids planted with grass activate the process of transpiration, as roots move moisture from deep within the soil to the surface, subsequently evaporating and cooling the pavement. However, the sustainability of the vegetation is dependent on local moisture, the amount of traffic, and other variables.

Pervious concrete incorporates large pore spaces to facilitate evaporation and reduce heat storage. However, pores can become clogged by debris, requiring vacuum sweeping to maintain permeability.

Interlocking concrete pavers are set on a porous subbase and interstitial spaces are filled with rocks, gravel, sand, or soil. These surfaces can support excess loading conditions such as heavy vehicles, fire trucks, and even commercial airliners in apron and cargo loading areas.

Avoid the use of artificial turf, which can cause contact burns and skin injuries for humans and pets.

Urban geometry and scale influences heat retention and potential cooling measures. Large plazas, squares, and open-sided areas allow airflow to mitigate heat buildup, while semi-enclosed 'sun traps' reflect radiation and create heat spots. Large projects use Computational Fluid Dynamics to model the effect of size, orientation, various pavement materials, and potential shading options to determine optimal solutions to relieve heat.

Pavements are complex systems with many variables. Conditions that affect pavement temperatures include: dirt and wear upon a surface due to daily foot and vehicle traffic; impediments to convection such as parked cars; and shading caused by people, cars, vegetation, and neighbouring structures.

Figure 5.4: Surface temperatures of six types of ground covers, from left: artificial turf, gravel, pervious asphalt, asphalt, pervious concrete, and grey cement concrete. Artificial turf can be up to 16°C (60°F) hotter than natural turf, potentially causing skin injuries to athletes as well as contributing to the heat island effect.

Figure 5.5: Infiltrative zones are comprised of pervious paving or landscaped areas allowing infiltration to bioretention cells. The cells detain water to reduce surface flooding, supply water to tree roots and accelerate evaporative cooling. Mississippi State University, Gulf Coast Community Design Studio.

Provide shade over hardscapes using trees and plants to shade pavements. Use existing plant material or plant new vegetation that will provide shade over paved areas on the site within ten years of planting, however, do not compromise tree health by placing pavements within the drip line of existing trees. Ensure there is adequate stormwater storage to supply water to tree roots and accelerate evaporative cooling.

Pavements can be shaded with vegetated structures such as trellises, screens, living walls, and green screens. Shade can also be enhanced with architectural structures: canopies, pergolas, awnings, galleries, arcades, and other horizontal planes.

Select pavement materials with a high SRI. The SRI should be 0.33 at initial installation and the three-year aged SRI at least 0.28.

The choice of material has tremendous implications for embodied carbon in addition to their heat storage capacity. Asphalt cement is extracted via distillation and cooling during the petroleum refining process. The materials are shipped to a production plant to be combined with aggregates which have been heated and dried to a temperature between 150 and 170°C. The embodied energy use for hot mix asphalt production is 0.0238 kg/CO_2e per kilogram; one cubic metre of asphalt weighs 2,200–2,700 kg.

To make Portland cement concrete, materials are heated to high temperatures (1,500°C) in a kiln to obtain clinker. After the clinker is cooled, small amounts of gypsum are added to obtain Portland cement. The cement is shipped to local concrete plants and mixed with cement, aggregate, water, and admixtures. The embodied energy use for Portland cement concrete is 0.1055 kg/CO_2e per kilogram[4]; one cubic metre of concrete weighs 2,000–2,600 kg.

IMPACT

Social: Reducing the heat island effect provides localised comfort through lower air temperatures, reduces peak energy demands, and results in fewer heat-related risks.

Environmental: Enhancing the tree canopy in cities can improve biodiversity if a variety of native and adapted species are planted. Cool pavements and absorptive sites improve air quality by decreasing temperatures and slowing the chemical reactions that create smog. Permeable paving improves water quality through stormwater filtration and increases storage capacity in the soil and groundwater aquifer.

Economic: If pavement reflectance throughout a city were increased from 10 to 35%, air temperature could potentially be reduced by 0.6°C (1°F), which would result in lower energy demand and associated cost savings.

Spatial: Creating tree cover and shading over pavements has a significant impact on the urban form, appearance, and thermal comfort. Reflective pavements enhance visibility at night, possibly reducing street lighting requirements. Permeable pavements reduce surface stormwater, improving pedestrian and vehicular safety.

NOTES

1 Golden, J.S. and K.E. Kaloush. 2006. Mesoscale and Microscale Evaluation of Surface Pavement Impacts on the Urban Heat Island Effects. *International Journal of Pavement Engineering* 7, no. 1, 37–52, https://doi.org/10.1080/10298430500505325.

2 Vujovic, S., B. Haddad, H. Karaky, N. Sebaibi, and M. Boutouil. 2021. Urban Heat Island: Causes, Consequences, and Mitigation Measures with Emphasis on Reflective and Permeable Pavements. *CivilEng* 2, no. 2, 459–484. https://doi.org/10.3390/civileng2020026.

3 Pan, F., J. Pei, G. Zhang, Y. Wen, J. Zhang, and R. Li. 2022. Building the Cooling Roads with High Thermal Conductivity Pavements to Relieve Urban Heat Island Effect. *Construction and Building Materials* 346, 128276. https://doi.org/10.1016/j.conbuildmat.2022.128276.

4 White, P., J.S. Golden, K.P. Biligiri, and K. Kaloush. 2010. Modeling Climate Change Impacts of Pavement Production and Construction. *Resources, Conservation and Recycling* 54, no. 11, 776–782. https://doi.org/10.1016/j.resconrec.2009.12.007.

RESOURCE

- U.S. Environmental Protection Agency. 2012. Cool Pavements. In: *Reducing Urban Heat Islands: Compendium of Strategies*. Draft. Accessed at: https://www.epa.gov/heat-islands/heat-island-compendium.

WILDFIRE PROTECTION

6

ADAPTATION **HEAT** SCALE **SITE**

Wildfires are increasing in frequency and intensity across the globe. Fires are growing in extent, currently consuming an average 865 million acres of land each year due to hotter weather and increasing fuel loads. Wildfires are growing in severity due to human incursions into the wildland-urban interface (WUI) and the expansion of infrastructure with potential ignition sources: electrical powerlines, roadways, rails, and pipelines. Design strategies protect the built environment from wildfire by retreating from the WUI, reducing biomass, protecting ignition sources, hardening the building envelope against embers, and providing auxiliary water features.

Figure 6.1: Wildfire protection considers three zones around a building: 0-5 feet = Immediate Zone; 5-30 feet = Intermediate Zone; and 30-200 feet = Reduced Fuel Zone.

DOI: 10.4324/9781032702964-8

BACKGROUND

Climate change is supercharging wildfires across the planet, with a projected global increase in wildfire of 29% by 2100. Increased heat boosts the amount of biomass developed throughout longer growing seasons and heightens the combustibility of biomass due to low moisture levels. Hotter temperatures unleash more intense storms and multiply lightning strikes that can ignite a wildfire. Climate change is causing greater variability in precipitation amounts which can propel explosive growth in spring or excessive dryness in autumn. In a cooler world, fire typically followed a diurnal pattern, losing energy in direct relation to the sun's absence; a hotter world increases night-time temperatures and the intensity at which wildfires can burn at night. The hotter climate also increases the range of insect infestations and arboreal disease which can result in tree mortality, adding fuel to the fire.[1]

As humanity continues to encroach on wild lands and expand the WUI, the chance of wildfire increases. Construction in the WUI places combustible materials and buildings directly adjacent to habitats that contain massive amounts of fuel. Impervious surfaces such as roadways and rooftops interrupt the replenishment of groundwater resources that can extinguish fires. New construction materials often contain petrochemicals, which accelerate fire at lower temperatures and release toxic chemicals into the environment when burned. Landscaping introduces ornamental, often invasive plant species that rapidly spread wildfire. Closer contact raises the risk of accidental and intentional acts of ignition from powerlines, roadways, and railroad tracks. The new residents at the periphery fear fire, preferring to suppress fire management and prolong the fire return interval, which creates higher fuel loads and results in more intense fires. Humans have become accidental arsonists.[2]

The WUI covers less than 5% of global land surface but is home to nearly half of the world's population, with high concentrations in Europe and North America. More than one-third of American homes and over half of Canadian homes are located in the WUI.[3] The most fire-prone U.S. states are expecting population increases between 15% and 40% by 2050, with a corresponding demand for housing. Driven by drier winters, more variable rainfall, longer and hotter summers, and intensified winds, wildfire occurrences are expected to rise in many parts of the globe.

The conflict between human activities and fire isn't diminishing, so solutions must be devised at three scales to address wildfire protection:

- The macroscale is primarily associated with forestry and emergency strategies, including forest management, fuel reduction, emergency management, and infrastructure for suppression. These decisions are not typically the domain of architects and are therefore not addressed here.
- The mesoscale corresponds to preventive measures to keep settlements safe: clustering houses, clearing firebreaks, creating fire refuges, locating power lines underground, and augmenting water supply points.
- The microscale is engaged at individual sites and buildings in the 'home ignition zone', to reduce exposure, harden the building envelope against ignition, and provide exterior sprinklers and on-site water storage.[4]

KEY DESIGN CONSIDERATIONS

MESOSCALE

Evaluate the fire risk. Depending on the site location, check: North American Seasonal Fire Assessment and Outlook (NOAA) at https://toolkit.climate.gov/tool/north-american-seasonal-fire-assessment-and-outlook; England and Wales Fire Severity Index at https://www.metoffice.

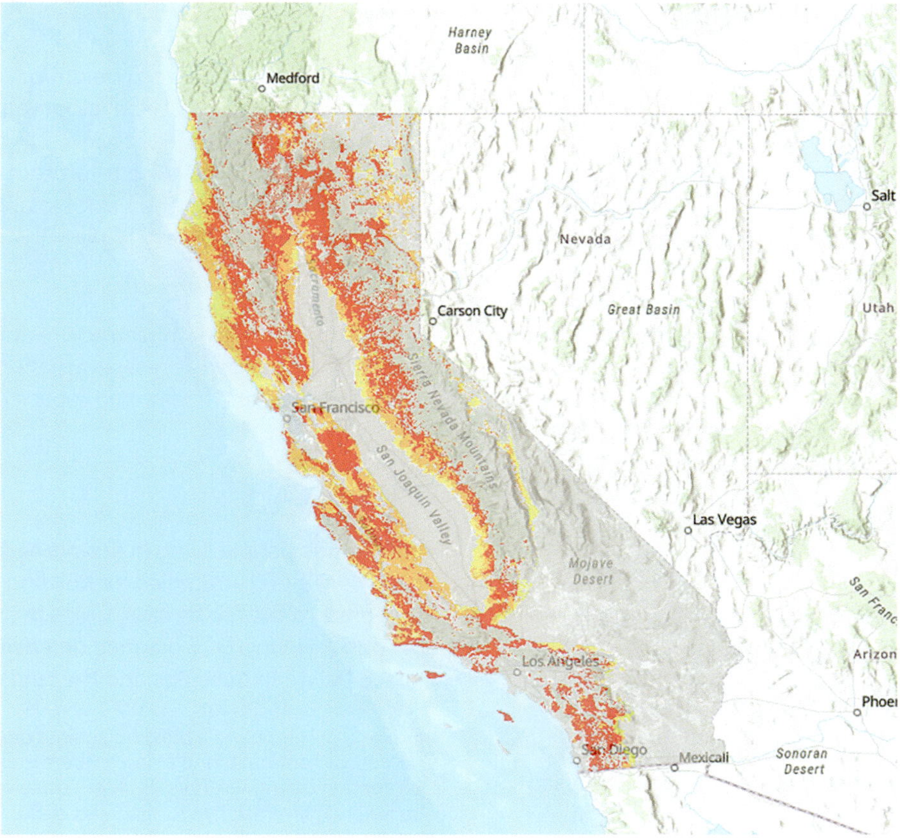

Figure 6.2: California maintains a map of Fire Hazard Severity Zones (classified as moderate, high, and very high) based on fuel loading, slope, fire weather, areas where winds have been identified as a major cause of wildfire spread, and other relevant factors.

gov.uk/public/weather/fire-severity-index/#?tab=map&fcTime=1708884000&zoom=5&lon=-4.00&lat=55.74; the European Commission's Copernicus Emergency Management Service at https://effis.jrc.ec.europa.eu/apps/effis_current_situation/; or local information sources.

Understand fire behaviour. The fire triangle is made up of three points: available fuel, weather conditions (fire sustains itself more easily in high temperatures and wind acts as a flamethrower), and topography (wildfires burn up steep slopes faster and more intensely than along flat ground).

There are several measures that determine imminent fire risk. The Fine Fuel Moisture Code measures the dryness of needles, leaves, and forest litter in a range from 0 to 101. The Duff moisture code rates the average moisture content of loosely compacted organic matter on the forest floor. The Drought Code represents the dryness of deeper soils, trees, and logs. The Buildup Index measures the total fuel available for combustion and the density of flammable biomass, ranging from 0 to an unlimited number. Explore the range of measures for a site to recognize patterns.

High fire risk zones are related to distance, topography, and orientation. Sun-facing slopes receive direct heat gain and become hotter than slopes facing other directions, making them more susceptible to fire. Flames race upslope because they are closer to the fuel dehydrating, preheating, and ignition, the flames creating an updraft that increases the speed. Distance from fuel sources also plays a role: areas within 50 m (150 feet) of wildland are at highest risk, properties within 2.4 km (1.5 miles) are in the ember zone, with lower risks beyond this distance.

Lot size and placement of structures determine the structure-to-structure exposure. Separation distances have significant impact on fire propagation in the WUI. Low-density developments with separation between structures less than 15 m (50 feet) have lower potential losses from structure-to-structure ignition, with an inherently low potential for urban conflagration. Moderate density developments with structures separated by 7.5 to 15 m (25 to 50 feet) can be hardened against fire exposure from neighboring structures. High-density developments with structures separated less than 7.5 m (25 feet) require each building to protect against structural ignition, as the risk of losing the entire community is very high.[5]

Identify the protective infrastructure available around the site: road access, evacuation routes, water supplies, and firefighting capacity.

MICROSCALE

Indigenous people living in fire-prone locations have developed strategies for building in response to the fire threats. China in the second millennia BCE planned defensible space between buildings and the landscape,

Figure 6.3: Hardening a building against direct flames, radiant heat, and flying embers improves protection during wildfires. Building-scale strategies include: (1) fire-resistive roofing and cladding; (2) enclosed soffits; (3) improved windows and doors; (4) vestibule entrances; and (5) fire-resistive plants and mulch. An air quality dashboard warns building users about current fire risks.

placed water sources strategically to douse fires, developed fire-resistant wall assemblies, and used steep roofs and covered eaves to prevent embers from entering the building.[6]

Reduced Fuel Zone, 10–60 m (30–200 feet): maintain an extended firebreak where possible as embers can fly 2.4 km (1.5 miles). Maintain landscaping to decrease the severity of a possible fire by removing dead plant material, lower tree branches, and other ladder fuels. Create an ember-resistant zone around outbuildings, firewood, and propane tanks.

Intermediate Zone, 1.5–9 m (5–30 feet): reduce ignition pathways leading to the structure. Maintain vegetation to maximum 10 cm (4-inch) height and keep it watered. Clear a 2 m (6 feet) wide by 2.5 m (8 feet) high safety zone within 5 m of the structure. Maintain areas around fences, as this is an area where embers can collect. Remove dead vegetation, including piles from pruning and firewood. Locate firewood and large propane tanks at least 9 m from any structures. Trim upper branches of trees to ensure at least 3 m of space between the canopies of neighbouring trees and work with neighbours to address trees near the property line that affect both properties. Ask the power company to remove branches that are near power lines. Choose low growing, fire-resistant plants[7] and minimise layered plantings that provide ladder fuels. Keep low-growing bushes and shrubs in small groupings of no more than three shrubs to establish a discontinuous path of vegetation. Remove hedges and bushes that create a pathway for fire. Place accessory structures at least 3 m away from the dwelling.[8]

Immediate Zone, 0–1.5 m (0–5 feet): reduce fire exposure near the structure. Remove all vegetation, groundcover, wood mulch, pine straw, rubber mulch, and other combustibles. Trim branches that overhang the roof to create a 1.5 m clear zone. Install an edge of hardscape such as gravel, pavers, river rocks, steppingstones, or concrete; this will also reduce the potential for termite infestation. Ensure there is a minimum of 15 cm (6 inches) vertical separation of noncombustible siding material at the base of each structure. Replace combustible fencing in this zone with noncombustible alternatives such as chain link. Do not park or store any vehicles, boats, RVs, or ATVs within 5 feet of the structure; store these items in a closed garage or park them at least 30 feet away. Move extra vehicles, gas canisters, and other petrochemical products to a safe location during periods of high fire threat.[9]

Provide driveways and turnarounds for fire apparatus to access three sides of the property.

Harden the building against embers which can originate from adjacent parcels or farther afield.[10] The roof is the most vulnerable area of the home because of its large surface area; replace combustible roofs with a Class A roof. Embers can ignite vegetative debris that has accumulated on the roof surface or in gutters; remove vegetative debris regularly and install a noncombustible and corrosion-resistant metal drip edge to provide protection for the sheathing and fascia.

Close gaps at eaves where embers could land or pass through into the attic. Screen vents with fine mesh and fill gaps with caulk. Enclose the under-eave area with noncombustible material to create a protected soffit.

Cover the chimney and stovepipe outlets with noncombustible screens. Use a metal screen material with openings no smaller than 3/8-inch (10 mm) and no larger than 1⁄2-inch (13 mm) to minimise embers leaving the chimney. Close the fireplace flue during fire season when the chimney is not in use. Install metal step flashing at roof-to-siding intersections to reduce vulnerability to embers.

Avoid storing combustible items (plywood, cardboard boxes, newspapers, and magazines) near attic and crawlspace vents. Use a minimum 3 mm (1/8-inch) noncombustible corrosion resistant metal mesh screen or flame- and ember-resistant vents.

Exterior walls are especially vulnerable to direct exposure from flames or prolonged exposure to radiant heat from burning vegetation or a neighbouring structure. High fire exposures (flames from large sources such as a burning residence) are very difficult to address by hardening the structure, because both the roof and wall assembly need to be hardened not only to withstand exposure but also to withstand it for the entire exposure duration.

Use noncombustible siding (stucco, aluminium, or fibre cement), especially when neighbouring buildings are within 9 m. In areas that are particularly vulnerable, such as at roof-to-wall transitions, replace siding with a noncombustible product. New construction should have a one-hour fire-rated wall assembly at exterior walls.

Direct exposure and radiant heat can ignite combustible siding such as wood and vinyl. Although the initial surface flammability of vinyl siding is lower than that of oak or redwood, fires grow more quickly when travelling through petrochemical products, and vinyl siding products deform and melt when exposed to heat from nearby fires, exposing underlying sheathing. Burning vinyl can release toxic components, such as chlorine gas and dioxin, into the environment. Avoid siding products that develop toxic smoke when burned.

Create an ember-resistant zone under the footprint and around all decks to reduce the likelihood of under-deck flame exposure. If a deck overhangs a slope, create and maintain an effective defensible space downslope of the deck to reduce the chance of flames reaching the underside of the deck. Apply metal flashing on top of and a few inches down the side of the support joists. Steel supports also reduce the vulnerability of the deck from both flames and embers. At wood decks, increase the size of the gap between deck boards to 1/4 inch so that vegetative debris can fall through rather than accumulate on the deck. If a deck is made of combustible decking materials, replace the board closest to the home with a noncombustible material. In new deck construction, consider using noncombustible or higher density decking products. Routinely clear debris from under the deck and move combustible deck furniture (especially those with woven components that can trap embers) inside or relocate away from the house when fire threatens.

When replacing windows, choose multi-pane options containing tempered glass. If neighbours or outbuildings are within 9 m, consider deployable noncombustible shutters to provide additional protection. Install insect screens in all operable windows, which increase ember resistance and also decreases radiant heat exposure. Close all windows when a wildfire threatens.

Seal garage doors to minimise the entry of embers into the garage. Add a battery back-up to the garage door motor so that the garage can be opened or closed if the power is out. Close garage doors when a wildfire threatens.

Provide an auxiliary water supply, especially at sites which are difficult to access or may be far from alternative water sources. The Australian architect Glenn Murcutt is known for incorporating bushfire-resistant features into his designs. The Simpson-Lee house is built with non-flammable materials and has a reflecting pool that supplies water to the roof-mounted sprinkler system in case of fire.

Automated wildfire sprinkler systems track the development and progress of wildfires and automatically trigger water sprinklers and biodegradable firefighting foam. When fire advances within a certain radius of the building, the system is activated. Water and foam are released from sprinklers within the intermediate zone; at the immediate zone, sprinklers at the roof and eaves wet the exterior with overlapping radii to provide coverage in high winds. If the primary water supply is interrupted or experiences a drop in pressure, the system switches to a secondary water source, such as a swimming pool or water tank.

Figure 6.4: The Simpson Lee House by Architect Glenn Murcutt uses bushfire-resistant construction and features a reflecting pool that can be used as an auxiliary source of water in case of fire. Lawrence Speck.

IMPACT

Social: Each year, global wildfires displace millions of people and damage properties, crops, and livelihoods. In addition to physical losses, the trauma inflicted by fires affects the human ability to adapt.

Environmental: Settlements and buildings that reduce the spread of wildfires also minimise their contribution of greenhouse gases to the atmosphere. The more wildfires burn, the more forests potentially turn from carbon sinks into carbon emitters. Preventing buildings at the WUI from burning also reduces their contribution to the formation of toxic gases, which can spread for hundreds or thousands of miles.

Economic: There are direct losses from wildfire including properties, crops, and timber, and the cost of services to fight fires. There are also indirect economic impacts from wildfires: loss of ecological services, interruptions to tourism, health effects, displacement costs, and productivity losses. Research suggests that the total cost of a wildfire is typically 10–50 times its suppression costs. Preparing buildings and settlements to avoid these losses has a tremendous payback: fire hazard mitigation saves $4 for every $1 spent.[11]

Spatial Integration: The type of large lot development with defensible space needed for wildfire protection can engender settlement patterns of low-density sprawl in WUI areas. However, buildings in close proximity within wildfire zones can cause wildfires to spread more quickly through direct ignition. One solution is to cluster buildings constructed with ignition-resistant materials and maintain the recommended setbacks from wildlands.

NOTES

1 Sterry, M. 2022. Design for Wildfire: Architecture as Catalyst for Virtuous Not Vicious Wildfire Activity. *The Routledge Companion to Ecological Design Thinking* 1, 424–436.

2 Sterry (2022).

3 Mowery, M. and D. Punchard. 2021. Land Use Planning Approaches in the Wildland-Urban Interface. Community Wildfire Planning Center. Accessed at: https://www.communitywildfire.org/wp-content/uploads/2021/02/CWPC_Land-Use-WUI-Report_Final_2021.pdf.

4 Moritz, M. and V. Butsic. 2020. *Building to Coexist with Fire: Community Risk Reduction Measures for New Development in California*. University of California Agriculture and Natural Resources Pub 8680. https://doi.org/10.3733/ucanr.8680.

5 Maranghides, A. et al. 2022. NIST Technical Note 2205: WUI Structure/Parcel/Community Fire Hazard Mitigation Methodology. Accessed at: https://nvlpubs.nist.gov/nistpubs/TechnicalNotes/NIST.TN.2205.pdf.

6 Sterry (2022).

7 List of the Most Fire-Resistant Plants. Western Fire Chiefs Association. Accessed at: https://wfca.com/wildfire-articles/fire-resistant-plants/.

8 IBHS. https://ibhs1.wpenginepowered.com/wp-content/uploads/Wildfire-Ready-Home-Prep-Upgrades.pdf.

9 Insurance Institute for Business & Home Safety. Prepare and Protect Your Home from Wildfire. Accessed at: https://ibhs1.wpenginepowered.com/wp-content/uploads/Wildfire-Ready-Home-Prep-Upgrades.pdf.

10 Building recommendations are drawn from the recommendations in the Wildfire Home Retrofit Guide published by University of Nevada, Reno: https://www.readyforwildfire.org/wp-content/uploads/Wildfire_Home_Retrfit_Guide-1.26.21.pdf.

11 National Institute of Building Sciences. 2019. Natural Hazard Mitigation Saves: 2019 Report. https://www.nibs.org/projects/natural-hazard-mitigation-saves-2019-report.

RESOURCES

- International Wildland-Urban Interface Code. 2021. International Code Council, Washington DC. Accessed at: https://codes.iccsafe.org/content/IWUIC2021P2
- Wildfire Home Retrofit Guide. University of Nevada, Reno. Accessed at: https://www.readyforwildfire.org/wp-content/uploads/Wildfire_Home_Retrfit_Guide-1.26.21.pdf

AIR QUALITY

7

ADAPTATION **HEAT** SCALE **SITE**

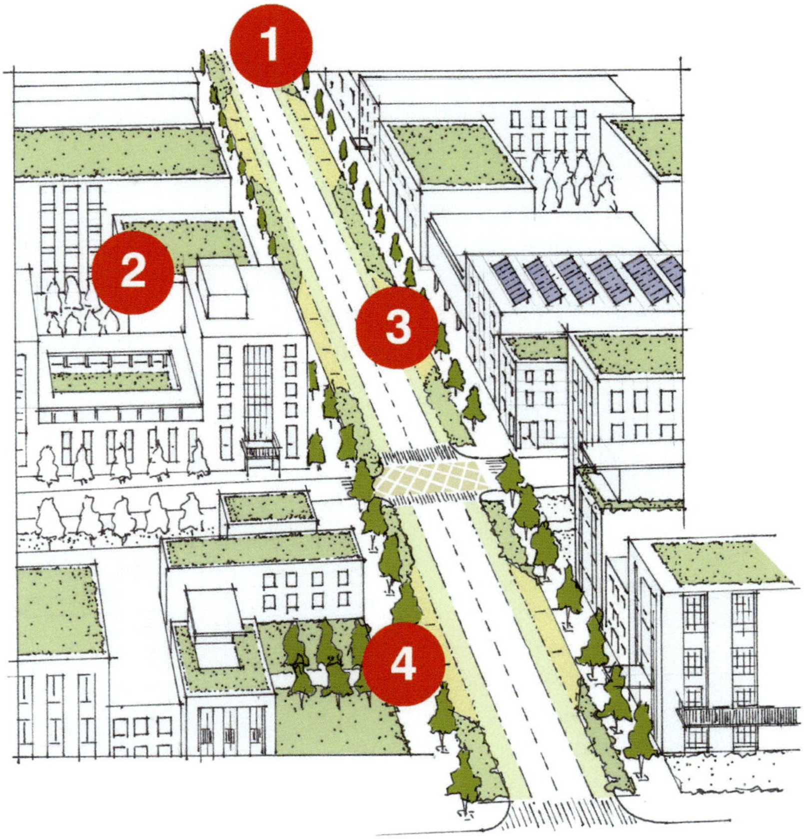

A warming climate impacts air quality with significant effects on human health, especially respiratory and cardiovascular systems. Poor air quality also affects ecosystems and plant growth and limits the effectiveness of solar renewable energy. Improving air quality begins outdoors by reducing the emissions which contribute to ground-level ozone production, aeroallergens, and particulate matter (PM). At the building edge, designers can reduce the infiltration of polluted outdoor air into indoor spaces through effective air barriers, controlled entryway systems, and filtering outside air. Inside the building, eliminating fossil fuel-burning equipment, reducing moisture, and using low-volatile organic compound (VOC) products help manage indoor air quality.

Figure 7.1: Reducing outdoor pollution targets three sources: ozone, aeroallergens, and particulate matter. (1) Reduce the use of fossil-fuel vehicles. (2) Improve building energy efficiency. (3) Separate vehicle lanes from people with distance and vegetation. (4) Select hypoallergenic plants.

DOI: 10.4324/9781032702964-9

BACKGROUND

Poor outdoor air quality is the result of three factors: ozone, aeroallergens, and PM. Current levels of ground-level ozone are responsible for thousands of premature deaths each year, tens of thousands of hospital visits, and millions of cases of acute respiratory symptoms. High pollen concentrations and longer pollen seasons are increasing allergic sensitisation and asthma episodes, affecting productivity at work and school. Breathing in particulate matter smaller than 2.5 microns in diameter ($PM_{2.5}$) is associated with serious chronic and acute health effects, including lung cancer, chronic obstructive pulmonary disease, cardiovascular disease, and asthma. Air quality across the globe is getting worse and the World Health Organisation reports that 99% of the global population regularly breathe air that does not meet minimum health standards.

The changing climate is modifying the global weather patterns, which influence the formation and prevalence of outdoor air pollutants such as ground-level ozone (O_3). Ozone is not a direct emission but is the result of chemical reactions between nitrogen oxides (NO_x) and VOCs. It forms when pollutants emitted by cars, power plants, industrial facilities, chemical solvents, and other sources react chemically in the presence of sunlight. Higher temperatures increase the rate of ozone formation and extend ozone life in the atmosphere. Ozone is most likely to reach unhealthy levels on hot, sunny days in urban environments, and when a local air mass stagnates over a period of several days. Although emission sources that form ozone are expected to decrease in the next few decades, meteorological conditions will become more favourable to forming ozone, a paradox known as the 'climate penalty'.

Rising levels of carbon dioxide (CO_2) promote plant growth, including species that release aeroallergens. Aeroallergens are substances present in the air that stimulate an allergic response in sensitised individuals. Rising levels of CO_2 also affect the allergenicity (a measure of how much particular allergens affect people) and expand the spatial distribution and seasonal length of pollen. Aeroallergens include tree, grass, and weed pollen, as well as indoor and outdoor moulds. Common ragweed (*Ambrosia artemisiifolia*) is one of the most common sources of allergens and an invasive annual weed that invades heavily disturbed habitats to replace native plant communities. Heavy rainfall is associated with spikes in aeroallergen concentrations, creating further concerns from climate change. Changes in length of the growing season of certain allergenic pollens may increase airborne ragweed pollen by over 25 days in some areas, as well as species of oak, pine, and others. Birch pollen is projected to produce peak values up to 2.3 times higher than in the baseline year 2000 with start dates of the pollen season advancing by two to four weeks. Landscape architects can manage aeroallergens through the careful selection of plants and specification of diverse plant communities.

The principal constituents of airborne PM include sulphate, nitrate, ammonium, organic carbon, elemental carbon, sea salt, and dust. While emissions of sulphur dioxide (SO_2), NO_x, and black carbon are projected to decline substantially in some countries over the next few decades due to regulatory controls, wildfires are projected to grow in number and severity, offsetting these improvements. Wildfire smoke contains ozone precursors and fine particulate matter ($PM_{2.5}$ < 2.5-μm diameter), and the smoke from large wildfires can travel hundreds or thousands of miles with impacts far from the source. Dust is another contributor to PM; the severity and extent of drought has been projected to increase as a result of climate change, accompanied by soil erosion into airborne particles.

Most exposure to high levels of ozone occurs outdoors but indoor exposures, while lower, occur for much longer time periods. Indoor

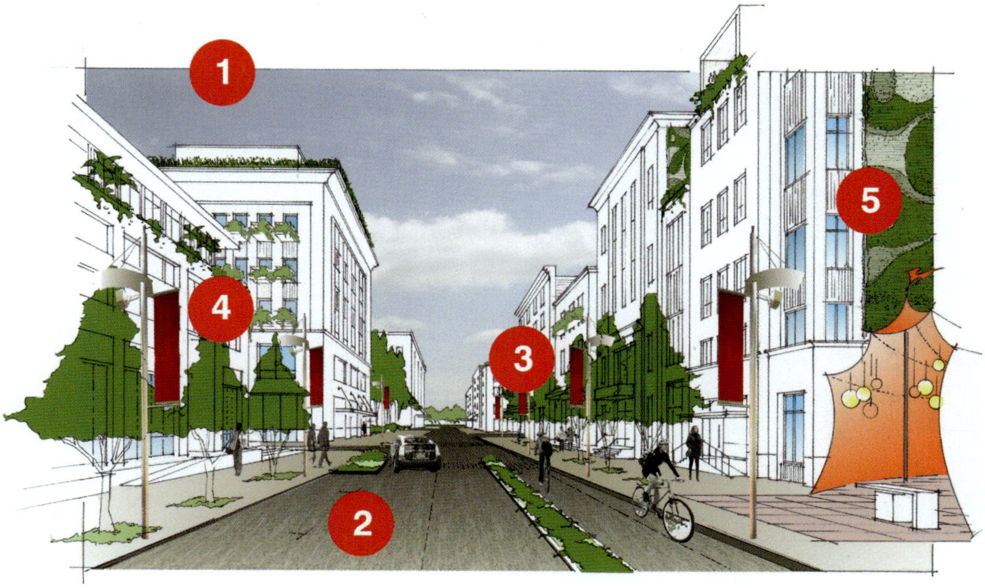

Figure 7.2: Design streets that increase pollutant dispersal: (1) mixed height buildings encourage air mixing; (2) low speed roadways with no parking or idling, and limited braking and acceleration. Intercept pollutants with: (3) street trees; (4) balcony planters; and (5) living walls.

ozone concentrations are usually about 10%–50% of outdoor concentrations; however, since people spend most of their time indoors, their exposure to ozone is mostly from indoor air. About 45%–75% of a person's overall exposure to ozone occurs indoors.[1]

KEY DESIGN CONSIDERATIONS

Critical measures for adaptation are comprised of reducing outdoor air pollution, managing aeroallergens, and improving indoor air quality.

REDUCING OUTDOOR AIR POLLUTION

Ozone pollution is increasing due to rising quantities of pollutants such as NO_x and VOCs interacting with heat and sunlight. Reducing the compounds that contribute to ozone – such as emissions from industrial facilities and electrical utilities that burn fossil fuels, vehicle exhaust, gasoline vapours, and chemical solvents – helps limit the formation of ground-level ozone. Decarbonising the electrical grid mitigates ozone production.

Reduce the use of fossil fuel-burning vehicles. Start-up, idling, and miles travelled produce NO_x and other pollutants. Support cleaner methods for urban mobility – electric transit, bicycles, and walking. Incentivise the use of electric vehicles. Provide charging stations for electric vehicles powered by renewable energy.

Reduce exposure to vehicle exhaust by separating vehicle travel lanes from pedestrian and bike paths. Use trees and vegetation, distance, and other barriers to intercept pollutants.

Figure 7.3: Trees capture significant quantities of atmospheric particles from the atmosphere to improve local air quality. Conifers may be the best choice for pollution-control plantings due to their bushy structure and high surface area, with the advantage of retaining their foliage during the winter. Allison Anderson.

Conserve electricity use in buildings, especially in places which still depend on fossil fuels (coal and natural gas) as the primary source of electricity.

Adopt and enforce ordinances to prevent windblown dust and open burning of waste. Establish composting centres for yard waste instead of burning.

Plants are more effective at capturing particulate pollution than they are at taking up gaseous pollutants such as ozone. Trees provide a surface area for particulates to land, so select species with rough or hairy leaves, dense leaves and twigs, large stomatic pores, and a tolerance for urban sites. A UK-based study found that Corsican pine (*Pinus nigra*) collected more of the coarse particle (PM_{10}) and fine particle ($PM_{2.5}$) material than other trees tested: whitebeam (*Sorbus aria*), cypress (*Cupressocyparis leylandii*), field maple (*Acer campestre*), or poplar (*Populus deltoides*).[2]

Create buffers around industrial facilities, refineries, and other concentrated sources of PM using distance and dense vegetation. Advocate for more efficient environmental controls and design buildings in fenceline communities with improved ventilation and advanced air filtration equipment to offset some of the most critical impacts.

MANAGING AEROALLERGENS

Ragweed and other significant allergenic plants grow more quickly, produce more pollen per plant, and have greater allergenicity under increased atmospheric carbon. Global warming and a longer growing season are facilitating the migration of invasive plant species, allowing allergenic species to expand across new geographic ranges. Control invasive plants that produce common allergens, such as ragweed, with approved herbicides.

Studies indicate that increasing native plant species richness, in addition to herbicides, provides an eco-friendly method of control. The greater the native species richness in each habitat, which includes both the number of species and the number of individuals in each plot, the higher the control rate of ragweed by preventing seed yield and dispersal.[3] Replant areas disturbed by human activities - roadside verges, wastelands, railway embankments, construction sites, and the edges of fields - with a rich mix of native plants to prevent invasive growth.

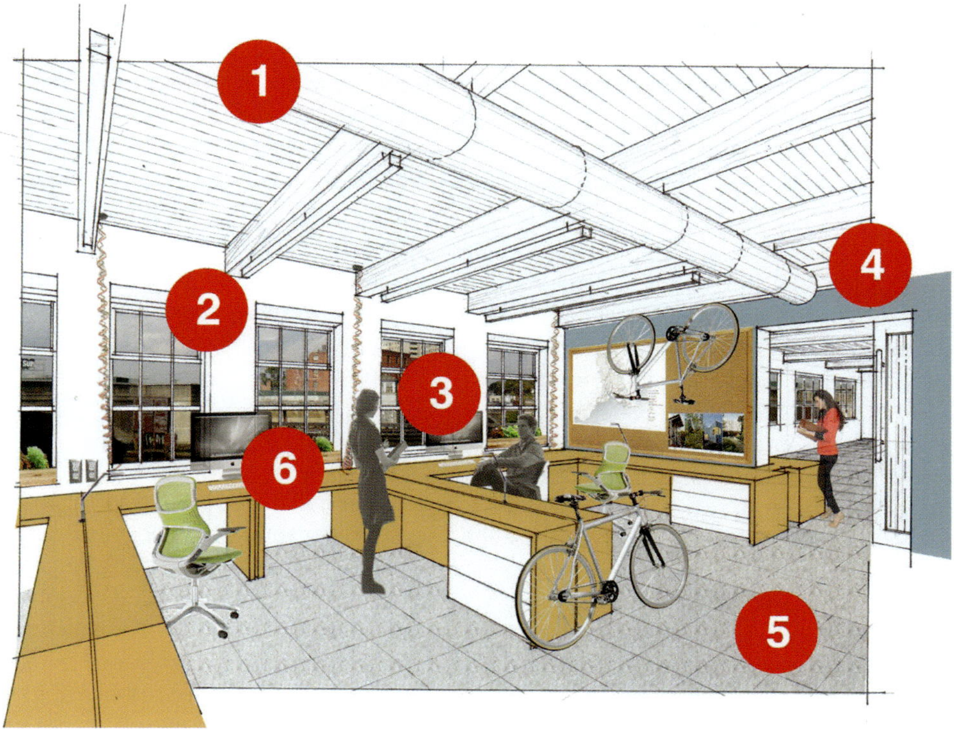

Figure 7.4: Improve indoor air quality by: (1) decarbonising the building; (2) monitoring outdoor air quality; (3) providing a continuous air barrier; (4) using high-efficiency particulate (HEPA) filters; (5) specifying low-VOC finishes and furnishings; and (6) supplying sufficient air exchange to maintain CO_2 levels below 600 ppm.

Consider species' pollen production habits prior to plant selection. Plants with high pollen counts are often deciduous, wind-pollinating, and prolific. Trees that produce high levels of pollen likely to trigger allergies include many common landscape species, such as birch, elm, cedar, oak, olive, pine, and poplar.

Establish hypoallergenic green spaces. Low-allergen species rely on birds or insects for pollination, rather than wind-borne distribution. Low-allergen species include fruit trees such as apple, pear, plum, and pomegranate, as well as magnolia, red maple, English yew, and holly.

IMPROVING INDOOR AIR QUALITY

Monitor indoor and outdoor air concentrations of ozone and PM. Check reputable sources for information on local conditions: UK AIR (https://uk-air.defra.gov.uk/), Air Now in the United States (https://www.airnow.gov/), and the European Air Quality Index (https://www.eea.europa.eu/themes/air/air-quality-index).

Consider ozone levels, PM, and allergens to determine appropriate building operations. If outdoor air quality is compromised by any of these three issues, natural ventilation is not recommended and additional air filtration is advised.

Communicate the current air quality condition on a building dashboard or bulletin for building tenants. Monitor pollen concentrations and take action during high pollen seasons to prevent outdoor air from contaminating interior spaces. Monitor indoor air with CO_2 sensors in the breathing zone and CO monitors. These are often required in residential units, hotel rooms, and continuous care facilities but even if not required, monitors provide baseline information about indoor air quality.

Prevent exterior contamination at air intakes. Locate air intakes away from high-traffic roadways, loading docks and parking areas, and roof-mounted exhausts. Elevate and secure air intakes at facilities that may be targets for chemical, biological, and radiation attacks. Ensure the concentration of outdoor air contaminants measured at outdoor air intakes are below acceptable thresholds. The allowable annual average is defined by the NAAQS (or local equivalent), available at: https://www.epa.gov/criteria-air-pollutants/naaqs-table.

The required volume of outdoor air intake is determined by the type of space, occupancy, and mechanical system. Minimum ventilation rates are published in ASHRAE Standard 170-2008, Section 7 or local equivalents. It is helpful to understand the relationship between CO_2 and indoor air quality in relation to productive learning and working environments.

- 420 ppm is a normal range for CO_2 levels in outside air.
- Below 1,000 ppm represents a normal range for indoor CO_2 levels.
- At 1,000–1,400 ppm, impacts include the decline of cognitive abilities by 15%, accompanied by drowsiness and fatigue.
- Above 1,400 ppm, occupants may experience the decline of cognitive abilities by 50%, with headaches and an inability to focus.

It is recommended to keep indoor air quality close to 400 ppm and below 800 ppm. If this threshold is exceeded, add ventilation to the space.

The most critical step towards reducing PM indoors is to decarbonise the building. Cooking with gas stoves creates nitrogen dioxide, carbon monoxide, formaldehyde, and airborne particles ($PM_{2.5}$) that range hoods do not effectively remove. Gas fireplaces, water heaters, furnaces, and other equipment also contribute contaminants to indoor air. Replace natural gas, woodburning, and other carbon-based fuel appliances with all-electric equipment. Smoking inside buildings should be prohibited.

Most of the air and particulate pollution enters a building at the doors. Design an entryway system to capture dirt and particulates in the vestibule or entrance. This requires a minimum 3 m (10 feet) grate of slotted grilles that allow for cleaning underneath, or textured mats that can be easily cleaned or replaced. Vestibules with pressurised air improve indoor air quality at high-volume entrances and in hospitals.

Air also enters a building through openings and cracks, bypassing filters and bringing outdoor air pollutants inside. Weatherise, caulk, insulate, and create a continuous air barrier to prevent the migration of outdoor air, contaminants, and vapour into interior spaces. Test the barrier's efficacy using a blower door test and thermal imaging.

Climate change may drive more heavy precipitation events and other severe weather that allows water or moisture entry. Outdoor humidity is the largest contributor to indoor dampness, creating the conditions for condensation and mould growth. Vestibules reduce the migration of warmer and more humid air from outside to inside. Desiccants remove moisture from inside air.

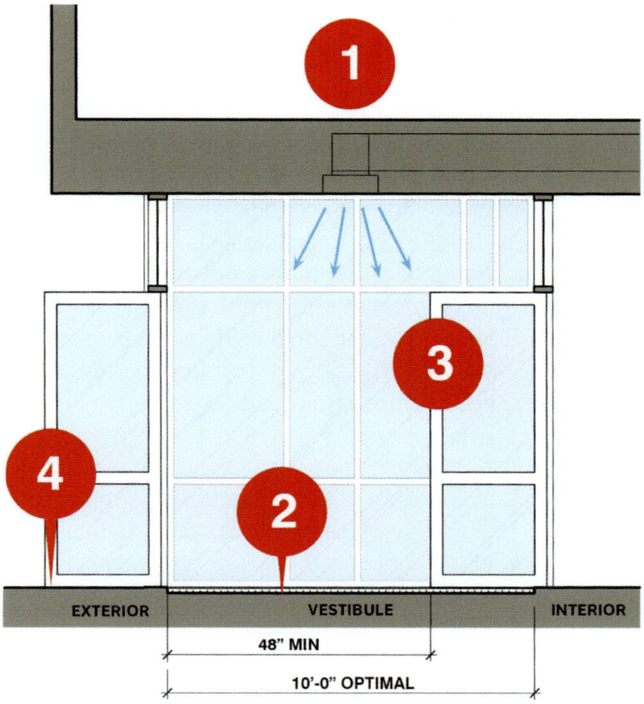

Figure 7.5: A building vestibule reduces air infiltration at areas with high pedestrian traffic, creating an air lock that captures airborne dirt and particulate pollution to prevent it from entering the building and recirculating through ventilation systems. A conditioned vestibule has: (1) air supply but no return to create positive pressure and assist with the air lock; (2) recessed flooring grilles with alternating slats of aluminium and carpet to remove dirt, liquids, snow, and debris from shoes; (3) non-porous finishes; and (4) exterior finishes to reduce moisture.

Power outages due to more frequent extreme weather events can lead to lack of dehumidification, filtration, and air circulation, leading to mould growth, increased levels of carbon monoxide, and increased levels of contaminants. Uninterruptible power provides continuous ventilation to prevent mould growth within the building.

Indoor air can contain a mix of chemical and biological contaminants including carbon monoxide (CO), carbon dioxide (CO_2), fine particles ($PM_{2.5}$), nitrogen dioxide (NO_2), formaldehyde, radon, mould, and pollen. VOCs are emitted by paints and lacquers, paint strippers, cleaning supplies, pesticides, building materials, furnishings, office equipment, correction fluids, copy paper, glues, adhesives, permanent markers, and photographic solutions. VOCs are emitted not just from coatings but also from the containers themselves, spread in the process of application, and are released as the material dries. Source control of VOCs is critical for indoor air quality; establish a maximum project VOC budget and specify low- or non-emitting finishes and furniture. Comply with jurisdictional VOC content requirements such as the European Decopaint Directive[4] or the California Air Resources Board VOC Limits.[5]

The Living Building Challenge (LBC) Red List[6] represents the 'worst in class' materials, chemicals, and elements prevalent in the building products industry that are known to pose serious risks to human health. Projects pursuing LBC certification must avoid the Red List chemical classes in 90% of the new materials but other projects may use the Red List to improve indoor air quality.

Create a clean room when outdoor air quality reaches critical levels. Identify a room that can be isolated from outside air to create a clean room if wildfire smoke or high levels of contaminants are present in outside air. Create a tight seal at windows and exterior doors, and minimise the number of entries and exits through a single interior door. Discard clothes and shoes that have been worn outdoors prior to entering the clean room.

If outdoor air exceeds recommended concentrations of contaminants, set central-ducted air conditioning and heating systems to 'on' to ensure air is being filtered constantly, rather than 'auto', which runs the system intermittently. If the system brings fresh air in, close the outside air intake so that it operates in recirculation mode to prevent outdoor smoke from getting inside.

Commercially available filters with a minimum MERV 13 rating can remove bacteria, wildfire smoke, and respiratory droplets. High-efficiency particulate air filters at MERV 17 or higher can theoretically remove 99.97% of dust, pollen, mould, bacteria, and airborne particles with a size of 0.3 microns (μm); particles that are larger or smaller are trapped with even higher efficiency. An ultra-low particulate air filter can theoretically remove 99.999% of dust, pollen, mould, bacteria, and airborne particles with a minimum particle penetration size of 0.12 μm. During periods of critical pollution exposure, change filters frequently to trap PM, at least every 2–4 weeks, or any time the filter appears saturated with particulates.

Mechanical carbon filters are appropriate for clearing gaseous VOCs from the air but they do not have an appreciable effect on removing particles. Ozone and electronic air cleaners using ionisers or UV light can emit ozone and other free-radical species as a by-product and are less effective than other filtering technologies at dealing with particulates.

IMPACT

Social: Poor air quality is often an environmental justice issue, as those with greater resources can choose to put greater distance between their home and sources of pollutants such as high-traffic roadways, industrial plants, and city agglomerations. Access to high-performance indoor ventilation systems and air filtration may also depend on capital.

Environmental: Reducing air pollutants at the source mitigates climate change and reduces impacts to weather patterns, rising sea levels, and disruptions to ecosystems. Emissions of sulphur dioxide (SO_2) and nitrogen oxides (NOx) can lead to the formation of acid rain, which damages soil, water bodies, and vegetation, impacting ecosystems and aquatic life. Fine PM settles on land and water surfaces, negatively impacting soil quality, water quality, and aquatic ecosystems.

Economic: Air pollution affects crop yields and quality with impacts to food production. Chronic exposure to air pollution can lead to decreased productivity among workers, absenteeism, or decreased work capacity, especially for outdoor workers. Pollution levels can also lead to decreases in real estate property values, and to identity, perception, and demand, affecting tourism.

Spatial Integration: Create buffers to concentrated sources of pollution and separate people from high-traffic roadways, industrial plants, and other places with poor air quality.

NOTES

1 Nazaroff, W.W. and C.J. Weschler. 2022 Jan. Indoor Ozone: Concentrations and Influencing Factors. *Indoor Air* 32, no. 1, e12942. https://doi.org/10.1111/ina.12942.

2 Beckett, K., P. Freer-Smith, and G. Taylor. 2000. Effective Tree Species for Local Air Quality Management. *Journal of Arboriculture* 26, 995–1003.

3 Wang, H. et al. 2022. Reduced Invasiveness of Common Ragweed (Ambrosia artemisiifolia) Using Low-Dose Herbicide Treatments for High-Efficiency and Eco-Friendly Control. *Frontiers in Plant Science Section Functional Plant Ecology* 13. https://doi.org/10.3389/fpls.2022.861806.

4 https://eur-lex.europa.eu/LexUriServ/LexUriServ.do?uri=OJ:L:2004:143:0087:0096:EN:PDF

5 https://ww2.arb.ca.gov/our-work/programs/coatings/architectural-coatings/voc-limits

6 https://living-future.org/red-list/#red-list-and-watch-list-casrn-guide

RESOURCES

- Hypoallergenic Tree Species: Allergy-Free Gardening: The Best and Worst Trees for Allergies. New York Sinus Center. Accessed at: https://www.nysinuscenter.com/2017/06/best-and-worst-trees-for-allergies/
- Living Building Challenge Red List. International Living Future Institute. Accessed at: https://living-future.org/red-list/

PASSIVE DESIGN, PASSIVE SURVIVABILITY

8

ADAPTATION **HEAT** SCALE **BUILDING**

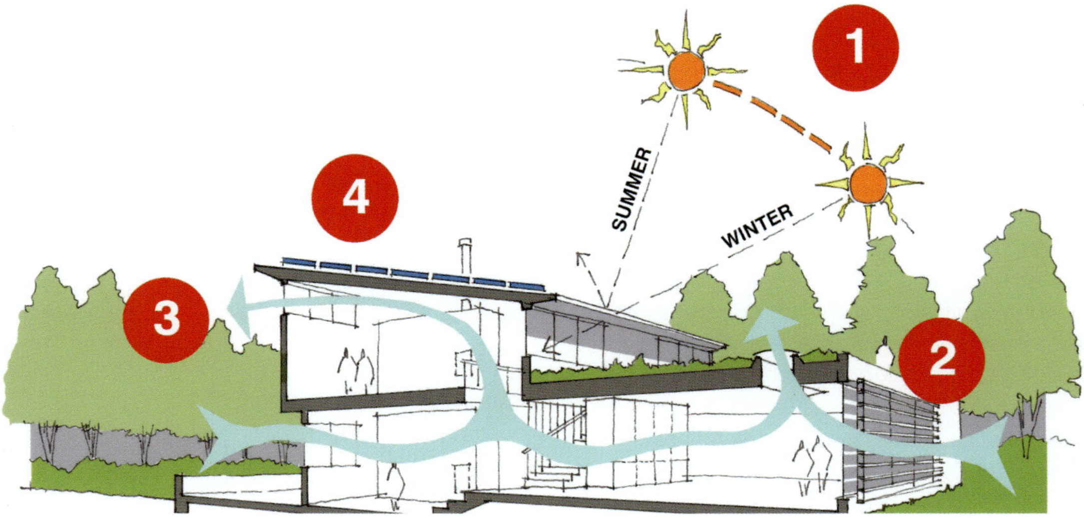

Passive design examines the specific site and climate to take advantage of seasonal solar patterns, diurnal temperature changes, air flow, and pressure differences to reduce the heat inside a building. Passive survivability is the building's capacity to maintain habitable conditions for occupants during an extended loss of power and water. Residential structures where people shelter in place after a disaster event or occupy during a power outage should be capable of sustaining life and provide some measure of comfort.

Figure 8.1: Passive survivability strategies include: (1) deflecting heat gain in summer and allowing solar penetration in winter; (2) high insulation values; (3) natural ventilation; and (4) renewable energy generation and storage.

DOI: 10.4324/9781032702964-10

BACKGROUND

Residential buildings can quickly reach unsafe temperatures during power outages, even in typical winter and summer conditions that are not considered extreme. Highly energy-efficient buildings maintain habitable conditions for longer periods, making this approach not only critical for achieving sustainable operations but as a resiliency measure. The key passive design principles include orientation and shading, a high-performance building envelope, daylighting, and natural ventilation.

Before determining building envelope performance targets, before selecting heating, ventilating and cooling systems, and before considering renewable energy, the building's orientation and form determine heat gain or loss.[1] Orientation affects how much solar heat gain is captured for useful heat in the winter and the amount of cooling load necessary to remove heat in the summer. The building's orientation also facilitates or impedes airflow for natural ventilation. Optimising building orientation and form requires designers analyse options early in the design process and allow the results to influence the fundamental design of the building.

Site and programme often dictate building orientation but where possible a building should be oriented with the long axis parallel to the equator. A narrow floor plate with a deep overhang facing the midday sun shields interior spaces from summer heat gain but permits winter heat and daylight to penetrate the building. East and west elevations are more efficiently shaded with vertical fins instead of unfeasibly deep overhangs. Orientation also determines a building's readiness to meet net-zero targets. Preparing for renewable energy generation with photovoltaics at the roof indicates the roof should slope down towards the equator. The optimal tilt for solar photovoltaic panels correlates to the latitude of the site in degrees: the optimal tilt for London at 51° latitude is 34° from vertical; the optimal tilt for Catania, Italy at 37° latitude is 27° from vertical.[2]

An extremely well-insulated building, such as a Passivhaus, protects against heat and cold and is likely to maintain habitable temperatures for many days, even in a power outage. Better thermal envelopes and more efficient HVAC systems are the core of passive design but geometry plays a surprising and important role. Energy transfer occurs wherever exterior surfaces meet the outdoor environment, making the surface area of a building a critical third variable. Buildings with a compact surface area perform better than complex or elongated forms to reduce energy transfer.

Architects can calculate the Area Ratio – the surface area of the building (walls, roof, and floor) divided by the floor area – to compare different building shapes for efficiency. The larger the area ratio, the more energy the building uses to heat and cool each unit of floor area. Complex footprints affect the area ratio and amount of heat transfer, with measurable losses in energy efficiency. Buildings designed with party walls, such as townhouses and terraced housing, create proportionately less surface area because of reductions in the exposed surface area, making them more thermally efficient.

Designers recognise a trade-off between: (1) a compact form that minimises heat transfer and (2) a rectangular footprint that invites daylighting, cool-season solar gain, and natural ventilation. A large building with a square floor plate may be highly efficient in minimising heat transfer but much of the floor area will be too far from the perimeter to take advantage of daylighting, views, and operable windows. Overall, larger buildings use more energy per square foot, often due to inefficient shape.[3]

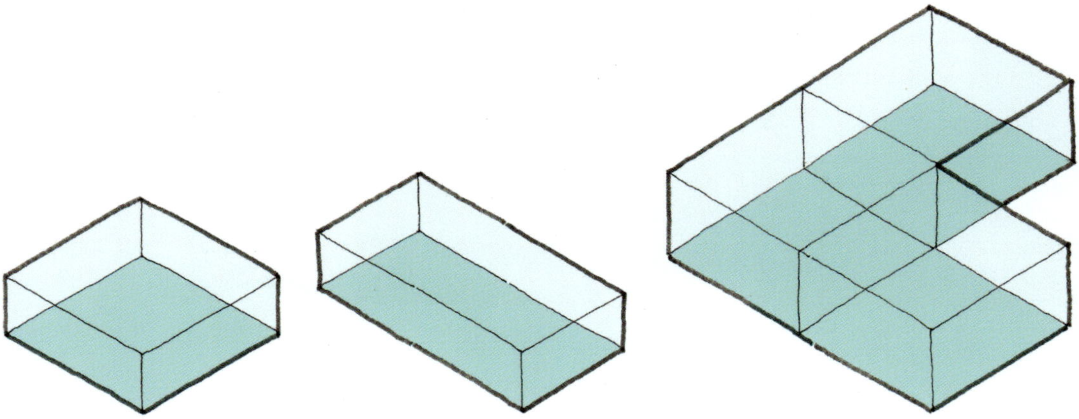

Figure 8.2: The Area Ratio equals the surface area of the building (walls, roof, and floor) divided by the floor area. The ratio compares different building shapes for efficiency, with larger area ratios requiring more energy to heat and cool each unit of floor area.

The area ratio of a square is always 1.64, a rectangle 1.68. A complex building shape calculates the area ratio by multiplying the surface area by the floor area; these three squares joined together to form an L-shaped building have a ratio of 2.33.

Architects use sectional and three-dimensional analysis to study solar radiation penetration for shading and daylighting. This analysis reveals opportunities to shield sections of the building from the most intense heat gain, provide daylighting using windows and clerestories, design light shelves to direct light deep into the floor plate, and integrate skylights and light wells to deliver daylighting to lower floors of large buildings. Daylighting allows safe movement and some activities to take place in the absence of artificial lighting.

Orientation to prevailing winds enhances natural ventilation strategies. A wind rose shows the typical distribution of wind speed, direction, and frequency, which impacts a building's ability to provide natural ventilation. The building form and openings can be rotated to defend the interior from harsh winds or invite airflow for ventilation. When wind blows towards a building facade, positive air pressure is directed towards operable windows on the windward side while a natural vacuum effect draws air out of windows on the leeward side, propelling cross ventilation. Note that the IPCC forecasts a worldwide slowing of average wind speeds by up to 10% by 2100, which may reduce the effectiveness of natural ventilation.[4]

Buildings can manipulate form to exploit the Venturi effect, where wind speed increases as air funnels from a wide opening through a narrow constriction. A dogtrot is an example from the southern U.S. vernacular, with enclosed areas split into two volumes, one on either side of a deep porch opening from front to back. Breezes accelerate in the gap between the buildings, making it the coolest place to rest, the reason for its idiomatic name.

Passive survivability is a building's ability to maintain life-support conditions in the event of an extended loss of power, heating fuel, or water. Severe weather of all kinds is increasing - violent storms, brownouts from heat waves, and flooding - with the potential to interrupt services to buildings for an extended period and leave occupants at risk. Passive survivability uses passive

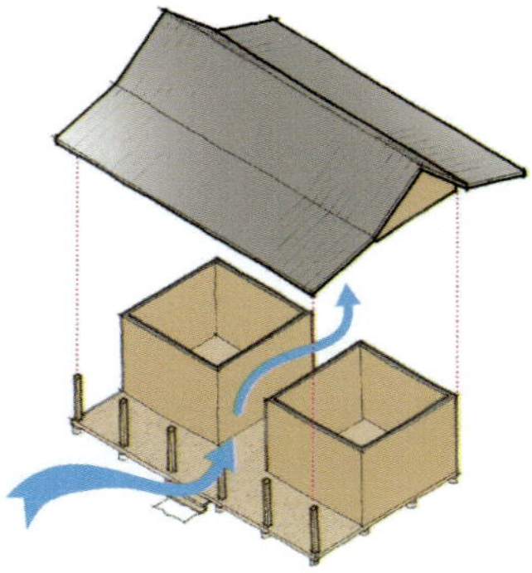

Figure 8.3: A vernacular solution for keeping spaces cool is the dogtrot, a common building type in the southern United States. A dogtrot places enclosed volumes on either side of a covered open space and uses the Venturi effect to accelerate and funnel airflow through the opening. Photo of the Shaw Homestead Restoration is courtesy of the Mississippi Gulf Coast National Heritage Area.

design principles to avoid cooling loads, amplify natural ventilation, enable passive solar gain in winter, and provide daylighting. These measures prepare for extreme weather conditions and create a habitable zone in extended power outages.

The thermal habitability zone is wider than the standard psychrometric comfort zone (see Sidebar). The Habitability Zone defines the conditions that will generally keep people safe, if not comfortable. An average low temperature of 12°C (54°F) standard effective temperature (SET) and an average low temperature of 30°C (86°F) SET will keep a person with average stature and physical condition safe. Differences in age, health, and physiology may require adjusting the parameters to fit specific needs, although residential buildings should not exceed extremes beyond 32°C (90°F) or drop below 10°C (50°F).

KEY DESIGN CONSIDERATIONS

PASSIVE DESIGN

Analyse temperature projections at the project site. Extreme heat is considered to be a period of high heat and humidity with temperatures above 32°C for at least two to three days. In extreme heat, the body works harder to maintain a normal temperature, which can lead to death in vulnerable people. Consider how many degree days over 32°C (90°F) are expected now? How many in 2075?

Simulate solar irradiation at the site by developing a sun angle diagram or computer model to identify summer and winter patterns. Model adjacent building and landscape features that might provide shading now and in the future.

Develop design options for distributing volumetric mass on the site. Where possible, orient the building so that the long axis faces the equator and the east and west facades are shorter than the north and south. Provide deep overhangs on the façade facing the equator. Develop massing and shading options to protect the building from early morning or late afternoon summer sun.

Develop options for fenestration patterns and shading options. Model these to determine their effect on heat gain, access to daylighting, and natural ventilation.

Prepare the building for solar energy by providing a large, contiguous, sun-facing area for solar panels. These areas should avoid shading from overhanging trees, roof projections, or adjacent structures.

Calculate the Area Ratio to compare different building shapes for efficiency. The formula used to determine the Area Ratio is: Surface Area of the building (walls, roof, and floor) divided by Floor Area. The smaller the Area Ratio, the more efficient it is, due to a lower potential for heat transfer through the building envelope.

Heat Transfer through a wall depends on the amount of surface area, the thermal conductivity of the envelope, and the temperature difference on its surfaces. The heat transmission equation that calculates conductive heat loss or gain from a building is:

$$Q = (A/R) \times (T_{indoor} - T_{outdoor})$$

Q = heat transmission
A = exterior surface area of the building walls, floor, and roof
R = thermal resistance of the envelope (R-value)
T_{indoor} = indoor air temperature
$T_{outdoor}$ = outdoor air temperature

Manipulate the building massing by right-sizing the programme, developing a compact form, or minimising the surface area by attaching to adjoining buildings. These design choices reduce surface area, thereby reducing the potential for heat transfer.

Building fewer large buildings is typically less costly and more efficient than building a greater number of smaller buildings. For a given total floor area and width, shorter buildings are generally more economical while mid-rise buildings have better environmental performance.[5]

Develop options for the building massing to optimise heat reduction through mutual shading: stepped floor plate, rotated volumes, cantilevers, subtraction, and additive forms. In addition to the impact on design, examine the potential energy profiles of each option.

There are often conflicts between the ideal building form and the street grid or lot size. If a narrow lot or existing features constrain the ideal building placement, use other passive design strategies to provide shading and limit heat gain.

Identify prevailing wind speed, direction, and frequency to find the optimal orientation for natural ventilation strategies. Model massing options to funnel airflow towards areas of the building where air circulation is desirable.

Interior separations restrict the potential for natural ventilation when compared to open interiors with less compartmentalisation. Align openings from one side of the structure to the other to encourage cross ventilation. A good example is the American shotgun house, so named because a shotgun shell fired at the front door will continue straight through the back door.

High ceilings encourage heat stratification because warm air is lighter than cold air, creating a temperature gradient between the floor and the ceiling. High ceilings keep warm air away from the zone people occupy. High outlets, openings or exhausts, can exhaust warmer air. Note that ceiling fans will destratify the air in a room, although if rotating counterclockwise (the direction recommended in summer) it will provide a downdraft that makes the air feel cooler.

Buoyancy-driven ventilation uses the stack effect to promote airflow throughout the building. Inlets are located near the base of the structure and a tower or atrium has high outlets to propel the stack effect.

Study building massing that generates turbulence along the façade as a cooling strategy. Uneven heights, serrated edges, overlapping forms, and serpentine curves increase friction. This approach can allow designers to exploit localised air movement to increase airflow and reduce heat.

PASSIVE SURVIVABILITY

Maintain habitable temperatures inside the building without the use of power. Insulate, weatherise, and make other improvements to the building envelope and shading to perform well during power interruptions. Recommendations for the minimum insulation and air sealing of the building envelope include:

- Wall R-values of R-25
- Roof R-values of R-50
- Window assembly R-values of R-4.3
- Air tightness of less than 1.5 ACH at 50 Pa[6]

Ensure operable windows are provided in residential buildings to permit natural ventilation and cooling without power. Many windows have stops that limit the opening to 11.5 cm (4.5 inches); address child safety concerns with alternate measures.

Choose reliable backup power and prioritise loads to remain powered. Fossil fuel-free systems such as cogeneration and solar power can be more reliable than diesel generators that are operated only in an emergency. Cogeneration and solar systems must be designed to operate on island mode in power outages. Solar power may be insufficient to supply all power over the course of a 24-hour period so prioritise the circuits that feed the refrigerator and microwave, fans, radios, phone chargers, and minimal lighting. In a larger building, emergency lighting, fire alarm system, and one elevator should remain powered. To operate around the clock, the system will require battery storage, which has a significant impact on the cost of the system.

In cold climates, add hookups for temporary generators and boilers to serve multi-family, healthcare, and senior housing facilities. Extended service disruptions impact vulnerable residents with greater consequences.

Supply drinking water without power by providing alternative potable water access in multi-family residential units. This can be a fixture in a common area that is supplied through pressure in the public water main.

Enhance building water reserves with potable water tanks mounted high on the building to feed fixtures with gravity pressure.

Ensure toilets and sinks work without power. At least one lavatory and water closet sensor control device must be able to function for two weeks without electrical power. Manual flushing and faucet control devices remain operational in the absence of electricity.

HUMAN THERMAL COMFORT

Humans are comfortable within a narrow range of temperatures. Thermal comfort is determined by multiple variables, including air temperature, radiant temperature, air movement and speed, humidity, clothing, work rate, age, size, weight, and fitness level. The psychrometric chart shows relationships between air temperature and relative humidity with data points representing site conditions at a specific location, times, and dates. The area identified as the 'comfort zone' is overlaid, showing the range of temperature and humidity levels at which occupants are satisfied with the thermal conditions. The thermal comfort zone is highly variable depending on climate, project type, programme, and the anticipated level of clothing worn by the occupants.

After plotting the air conditions and overlaying the comfort zone, it is possible to see how passive design strategies can extend the comfort zone:

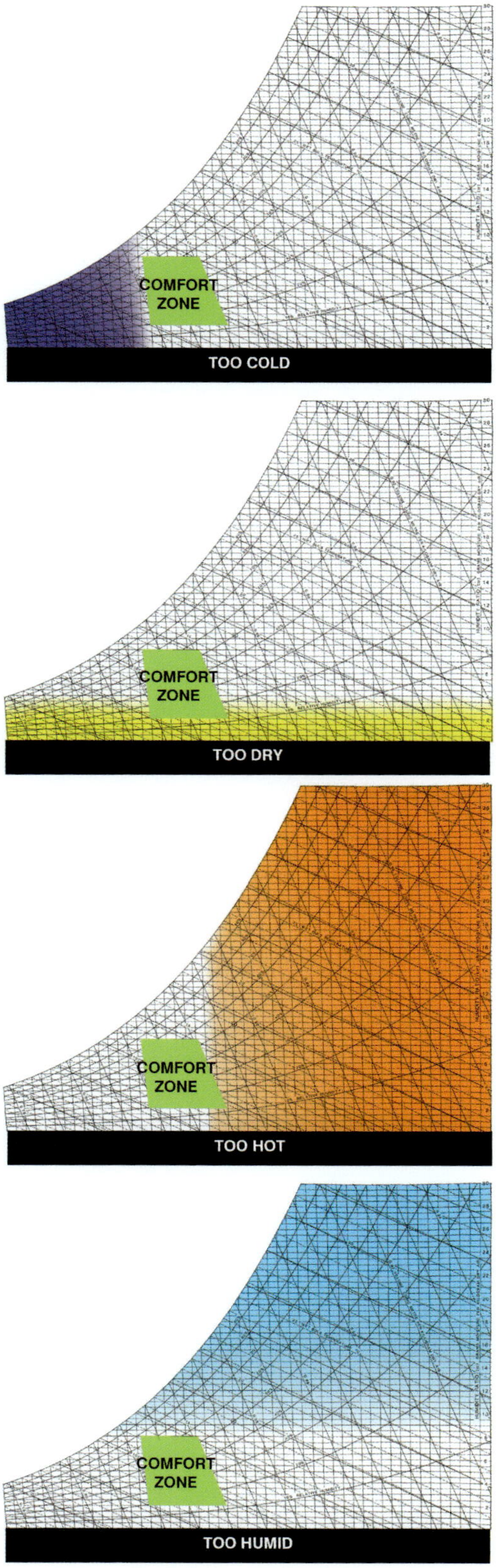

Figure 8.4: A psychrometric chart displays the dry bulb temperature (air temperature, shown along the horizontal axis at the bottom); dew point temperature (temperature of condensation, shown in horizontal lines); wet bulb temperature (temperature of evaporation, shown in diagonal lines extending downward from the saturation curve); relative humidity (the percentage of water vapour in the air compared to how much the air can hold, represented in curves through the chart); and other variables. The Comfort Zone (in green) represents the range where occupants are satisfied with surrounding thermal conditions, neither too cold or hot, too dry or humid.

- When data points fall to the right of the comfort zone, it is necessary to reduce the air temperature, increasing air flow with natural ventilation. If this is not sufficient, mechanical cooling must be added.
- When data points fall to the left of the comfort zone, an increase in air temperature is necessary, incorporating solar heat gain or with high thermal mass materials. If this is not adequate, then mechanical heating must be added.
- When relative humidity is too low, it can be increased with evaporative cooling.
- When relative humidity is too high, it can be decreased with the use of desiccants.

IMPACT

Social: Passive design improves the liveability of a building year-round and tempers increasing heat from climate change. Passive survivability saves lives in a disaster or extended interruption of services.

Environmental: Making building forms more compact and reducing surface area also minimises resource use and embodied carbon in construction; creating highly energy-efficient buildings reduces operational carbon. Both actions mitigate future climate change.

Economic: Buildings that achieve Passive Survivability standards will be more energy-efficient, with corresponding reductions in energy demand and operational cost.

Spatial Integration: Classic passive design strategies inform vernacular buildings: in hot, humid locations, deep overhangs and porches on the south façade, large windows on the north, and smaller windows on the east and west. These and other proven techniques shape the urban context in which new structures will be placed. New buildings may use advanced modelling to solve unique problems and deliver passive survivability.

NOTES

1 Depecker, P. et al. 2001. Design of buildings shape and energetic consumption. *Building and Environment* 36(5), 627–635. Accessed at: https://www.sciencedirect.com/science/article/pii/S0360132300000445

2 Jacobson, M.Z. and V. Jadhav. 2018. Optimal Solar Tilt Angles: World Estimates of PV Optimal Tilt Angles and Ratios of Sunlight Incident upon Tilted and Tracked PV Panels Relative to Horizontal Panels. *Solar Energy* 169, 55–66. Accessed at: https://www.sciencedirect.com/science/article/pii/S0038092X1830375X?via%3Dihub

3 Squire, C. 2023. *People, Planet, Design: A Practical Guide to Realizing Architecture's Potential*. Island Press, Washington DC, p. 155.

4 IPCC WGI Interactive Atlas, Surface wind change % – Near Term (2021–2040). Accessed at: https://interactive-atlas.ipcc.ch/regional-information#eyJ0eXBlIjoiQVRMQVMiLCJjb21tb25zIjp7ImxhdCI6MTE1NDQyMiwibG5nIjo4MzYxNjgsInpvb20iOjMsInByb2oiOiJFUFNHOjU0MDMwIiwibW9kZSI6ImNvbXBsZXRlX2F0bGFzIn0sInByaW1hcnkiOnsic2NlbmFyaW8iOiJzc3AxMjYiLCJwZXJpb2QiOiJuZWFyIiwic2Vhc29uIjoieWVhciIsImRhdGFzZXQiOiJDTUlQNiIsInZhcmlhYmxlIjoic2ZjV2luZCIsInZhbHVlVHlwZSI6IlJFTEFUSVZFX0FOT01BTFkiLCJoYXRjaGluZyI6IkRJU0FCTEVEIiwicmVnaW9uU2V0IjoiY29udGluZW50IiwiYmFzZWxpbmUiOiJXTU8yIiwicmVnaW9uc1NlbGVjdGVkIjpbXX0sInBsb3QiOnsiYWN0aXZlVGFiIjoicGx1bWUiLCJtYXNrIjoibm9uZSIsInNjYXR0ZXJZTWFnIjpudWxsLCJzY2F0dGVyWVZhciI6bnVsbCwic2hvd2luZyI6ZmFsc2V9fQ==

5 Mosey, G. and B. Deal. 2021. Optimizing Multi-Family Building Massing for Affordability and Envelope Performance: An Investigation of the Trade-Offs Implicit in Low Rise Residential Buildings. *Buildings* 11, no. 3, 99. https://doi.org/10.3390/buildings11030099

6 Urban Green. 2013. NYC Building Resiliency Task Force: Report to Mayor Michael Bloomberg and Speaker Christine C. Quinn. Accessed at: https://www.urbangreencouncil.org/building-resiliency-task-force/

RESOURCES

- Passive Building Principles: PassivHaus Institute. Accessed at: https://www.phius.org/passive-building/what-passive-building/passive-building-principles
- Passive Survivability: Alex Wilson. 2021. Passive Survivability: Understanding and Quantifying the Thermal Habitability of Buildings during Power Outages. In *Climate Adaptation and Resilience Across Scales*. Oxford: Routledge. Accessed at: https://www.taylorfrancis.com/chapters/oa-edit/10.4324/9781003030720-9/passive-survivability-alex-wilsonArea Ratios: F.D.K. Ching and I.M. Shapiro. 2021. *Green Building Illustrated*, Second Edition. New York: Wiley.

9 SOLAR CONTROL

ADAPTATION **HEAT** SCALE **BUILDING**

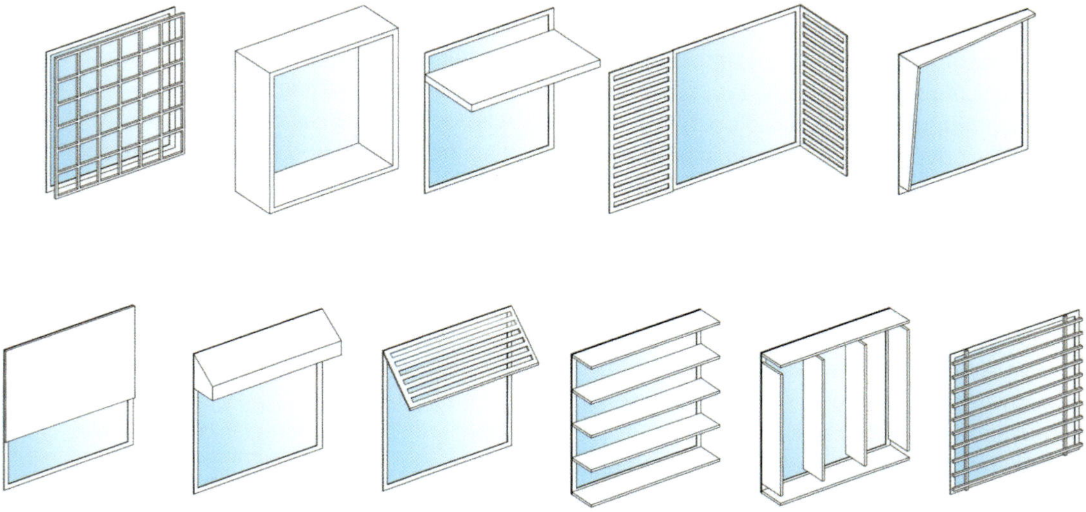

Sunlight grazes the planes of a building, providing welcome heat and light and also undesirable heat gain and glare. Shading devices reduce solar heat gain and other negative effects of sunlight by controlling direct sun penetration. Shading devices installed at the exterior façade block solar radiation before it passes through glazing, an approach that can reduce solar heat gain by 80% and cooling loads by 30% or more.[1] Solar shading regulates performance and offers limitless possibilities for architectural responses to orientation.

Figure 9.1: A catalogue of exterior shading devices: trellis/screen, recessed window, fixed horizontal light shelf, movable shutters, fixed shades, operable shades, awnings, Bahama shutter, horizontal louvers, vertical louvers, and ceramic pipe screens.

DOI: 10.4324/9781032702964-11

BACKGROUND

Building façades become animated with shading. There are horizontal projections and vertical ribs; picture-frame boxes; egg-crate screens; repositionable louvers and jalousies; slanted and shaped fins; perforated, slatted, sliding, and folding shutters; Bermuda shutters with fixed props; sail-shaped extrusions; opaque or transparent curtains; intricate wooden screens; brise-soleils; taut fabric shades; awnings; and recessed openings. Before the advent of artificial climate control, building occupants depended on exterior shading and less-effective interior curtains to protect spaces from heat and glare.

Shading devices are so intrinsic to architecture and culture that they define elements of vernacular design. Asked about the single most important measure of building performance, the architect Todd Walker said, 'Does the building have a south-facing porch?'[2] In the hot, humid climate of Memphis, Tennessee, an extended roof along the south side of a building is a ubiquitous feature found in nearly every building in the American south, regardless of architectural style.

Shading at the exterior delivers better performance than other options such as coated glazing or interior window coverings. If glazing is not shaded, it can become a source of radiant heat at interior spaces by transmitting solar radiation and emitting long-wave radiation. A lack of shading can cause problems with glare from extreme contrasts in luminance, which can cause discomfort and make visual tasks more difficult. External shading reduces transmittance and helps filter or block glare,

Figure 9.2: A south-facing porch is the most common vernacular heat control strategy in the American south. Principal Todd Walker, FAIA of archimania ranks it the single most critical measure of building performance. Archimania Office, Memphis, TN.

Figure 9.3: Indian jaali screens influenced the design of Le Corbusier's brise-soleil at the Punjab and Haryana High Court, Chandigarh. A jaali compresses airflow through a carved screen, causing air to move faster and penetrate farther into interior spaces.

which is characteristic of early morning and later afternoon sunlight penetrating through glazing.

Le Corbusier coined the term *brise-soleil* in the 1930s to describe a baffle to moderate light, a modern decoration grounded in utility and therefore acceptable. The shading innovation was described in a letter from Clive Entwistle, British architect and translator of Le Corbusier, as 'a splendid element, the key to infinite combinations ... magnificent clothes, adaptable to all climates'.[3] Corbusier manipulated his 'sun-breaker' screens to great effect.

> *A scheme can therefore be devised, based on precise data: (a) the course of the sun on every day of the year; (b) problems of the latitude of the place under consideration: for instance, the sun must never touch a pane of glass during the summer period, between the two equinoxes, but in winter the sun may be perfectly bearable.*[4]

Corbusier and others learned from ancient masters. The *jaali* is a screen of perforated stone or latticed wood carved in ornamental patterns which are derived from calligraphy, geometric shapes, and natural motifs of trees and vines. Small openings in the screen compress airflow in conformance with the Venturi effect, causing air to move faster through the spaces of the screen. This cools the air and allows it to penetrate farther into adjacent spaces. In India's humid zones, where the *jaali* screen was refined, craftsmen developed screens with an optimal ratio of 80–90% open to solid to dispel early morning and late afternoon sun.[5]

KEY DESIGN CONSIDERATIONS

Orient buildings with the long axis parallel to the equator. The south side (in the northern hemisphere or north side in the southern hemisphere) faces the sun for much of the day, making a horizontal overhang the most efficient shading device. A sun-facing overhang casts shadows from high solar angles during the hottest part of the year and invites low sun in the winter. A horizontal overhang also creates deep porches and sheltered spaces for activities.

The east and west sides of a building are the most difficult areas to shade due to the low angle of the sun in the morning and evening

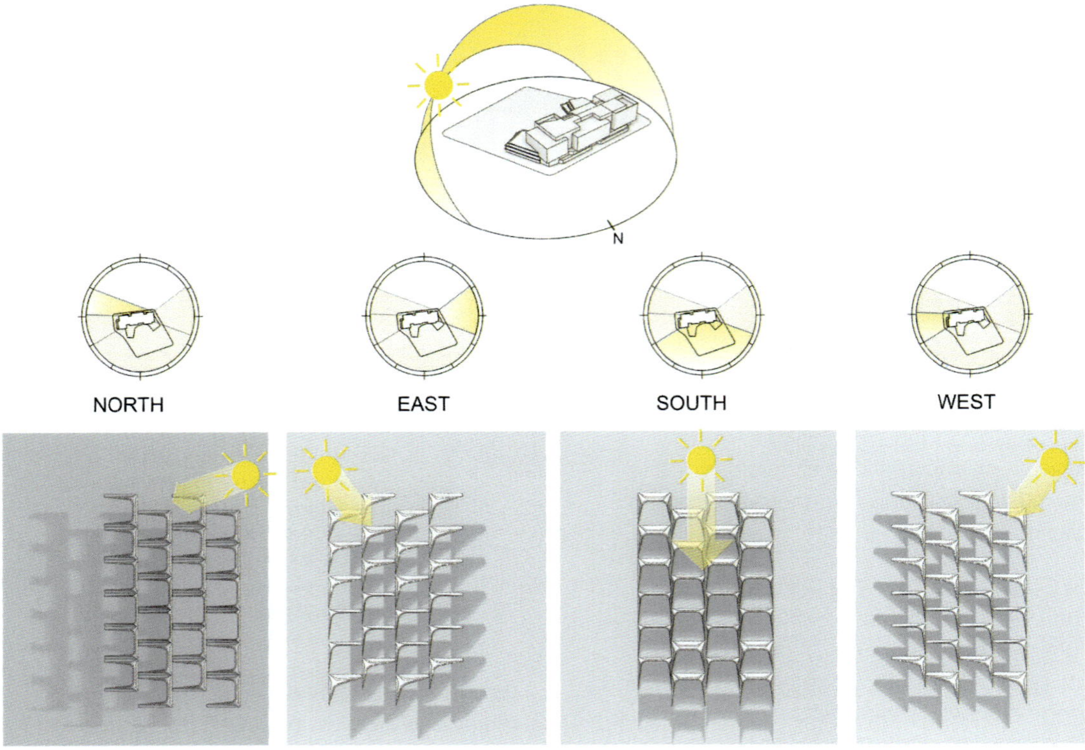

hours. Shading devices on east and west sides employ vertical fins or L-shaped extrusions to reduce direct solar gain.

The north side (in the northern hemisphere or south side in the southern hemisphere) faces away from the sun most of the time and may only have direct solar radiation in early morning and late evening hours in midsummer. Northern light is more diffuse and typically requires less control for glare, which is the reason that north-facing skylights are beloved by artists and loft-dwellers.

Identify site features that may affect solar heat gain, such as neighbouring buildings or trees that block direct sunlight, or bodies of water that reflect sunlight at lower angles. Include these elements, as well as trees at full maturity, in site analyses and energy models.

Figure 9.4: Solar shades were modelled to determine the most efficient method to deflect direct solar heat gain and maximise natural light exposure for occupants while reducing glare with the perforated leading edge of the shades. From left: at this latitude and orientation, a minor amount of solar gain is received from the northwest façade, requiring additional shading. East-facing perforated shades block early morning sunlight with an L-shaped fin. Horizontal extensions block solar radiation from high-altitude sunlight on the south side. West-facing perforated shades block late afternoon sunlight with an L-shaped fin. Harvard University Science and Engineering Complex, Allston, Massachusetts. Architect: Behnisch Architekten.

Energy modelling in the early design phase helps designers visualise the implications of different shading options and their capacity to cast shadows, protect openings from solar heat gain, and provide daylighting. Establish solar shading and cooling performance targets in the early design phase. Test a variety of options and modify design strategies using different shading devices, configurations, dimensions, and materials until performance targets are met. Architects can expect exterior shading devices to reduce cooling loads by about 30%.[6]

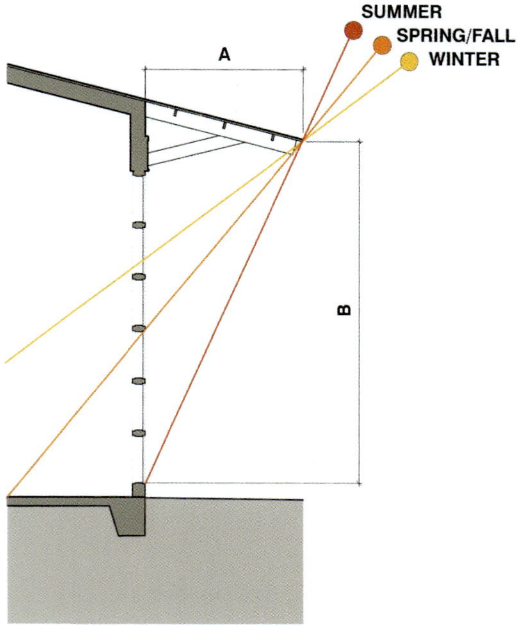

Figure 9.5: The optimal overhang to prevent heat gain in summer and invite welcome heat in winter depends on the building's latitude, orientation, and function, requiring energy modelling. A general rule of thumb for initial design is: overhang distance (A) should equal 1/4 the height of the opening (B) in latitudes 28°–32°; A should be 1/3 of B in latitudes 36°–40°; and A should be 1/2 of B in northern latitudes 44°–56°, where there is less sun and (typically) less heat gain.

Louvers are orthogonal, repetitive, parallel units including fixed or dynamic fins, blades, slats, laths, or tubes designed to limit light penetration or airflow. Louvers allow airflow through, which reduces the need for additional bracing against wind uplift. A general rule of thumb for using louvers to shade windows is a ratio of projection depth to height equal to 0.5. This means louvers spaced 30 cm (1 foot) apart would need to be 15 cm (6 inches) deep; louvers 25 mm (1 inch) apart would be 12.5 mm (1/2 inch) deep.[7] Louvers can be made of glass, wood, metal, or ceramic; many of these materials have high embodied carbon so compare the life cycle costs before selecting a system.

Scrims made of perforated metal, mesh, or semi-opaque tensile fabric, block visible light transmittance based on the ratio of solid to open space. A dark-coloured solar screen can block 80% of UV radiation but only 40% of the views offering a reasonable trade-off.

Intercept solar radiation at high levels of the building to reflect heat upwards and reduce the overall heat island effect. Low-level shading devices can keep pavements from absorbing heat, contributing to a cooler micro-climate and improving the pedestrian environment.

Automated solar tracking can be highly efficient but manual control over window shading is always welcome so that occupants can adjust the light to respond to seasonal changes and serve a variety of functions, from a discussion group to a video presentation.

Design shade devices to have multiple benefits. Horizontal planes built of solid materials also extend protection from rain. A light shelf has dual functions: shading a lower window and reflecting light deep into the building through an upper window. Some shading devices can collect and channel rainwater to on-site storage, while others integrate solar panels to generate renewable energy.

In high-wind environments, secure exterior shading so it does not become detached or contribute unexpected uplift forces that may damage the building.

Architectural shading devices can be combined with trees and vegetated screens to shade walls and openings at low levels, reducing heat gain either year-round (evergreen trees and screens) or in summer (deciduous trees). Consider planting a variety of species with different vining patterns to grow foliage at different heights: for example, in coastal Mississippi, landscape architect Ed Blake planted a palette of three species - bougainvillea, crossvine (*Bignonia capreolata*), and jasmine (*Trachelospermum jasminoides)* - to cover a vertical greenscreen over 7.5 m (24 feet) high.

IMPACT

Social: Solar shading improves indoor thermal comfort by reducing heat gain and UV exposure. Shading enhances comfort and productivity in the workplace by reducing distractions caused by glare. These improvements lead to more pleasant living and working environments and contribute to well-being. Efficient shading improves passive survivability conditions for occupants during a power outage and reduces health impacts from prolonged heat exposure.

Environmental: Shading devices reduce direct heat gain on walls and windows, reducing cooling loads and mitigating operational energy demand and the corresponding greenhouse gas emissions. Shading at pedestrian areas reduces temperatures at the ground level, improving the microclimate of the site. Shade screens and overhangs can reduce bird mortality.

Economic: Reduced demand for cooling offers operational energy cost benefits, as well as lower initial equipment costs, which may offset the cost of shading solutions.

Spatial: A city crafted with infinite combinations of shading creates human scale in tall structures, orients people to cardinal directions, and creates shaded precincts at the ground and in the air.

NOTES

1 Shahdan, M.S., S.S. Ahmad and M.A. Hussin. 2018. External Shading Devices for Energy Efficient Building. *IOP Conference Series: Earth and Environmental Science* 117, 012034. https://doi.org/10.1088/1755-1315/117/1/012034
2 Walker, T. 2023. Remarks at AIA National Conference Session TH205. *The Framework for Design Excellence*, June 6, 2023.
3 Le Corbusier, Oeuvre Complete. Vol. IV, p. 113.
4 Le Corbusier. 1960. My Work, p. 111.
5 Sherif, A., A. El-Zafarany, and R. Arafa. 2012. External Perforated Window Solar Screens: The Effect of Screen Depth and Perforation Ratio on Energy Performance in Extreme Desert Environments. *Energy and Buildings* 52, 1–10. https://doi.org/10.1016/j.enbuild.2012.05.025
6 Shahdan, M.S., S.S. Ahmad and M.A. Hussin. 2018. External Shading Devices for Energy Efficient Building. *IOP Conference Series: Earth and Environmental Science* 117, 012034. https://doi.org/10.1088/1755-1315/117/1/012034
7 Squire, C. 2023. *People, Planet, Design*, Island Press: Washington DC, p. 181.

RESOURCE

- Olgyay, A. and V. Olgyay. 1957. *Solar Control & Shading Devices*. Princeton, NJ: Princeton University Press.

COOL ENVELOPES 10

ADAPTATION **HEAT** SCALE **BUILDING**

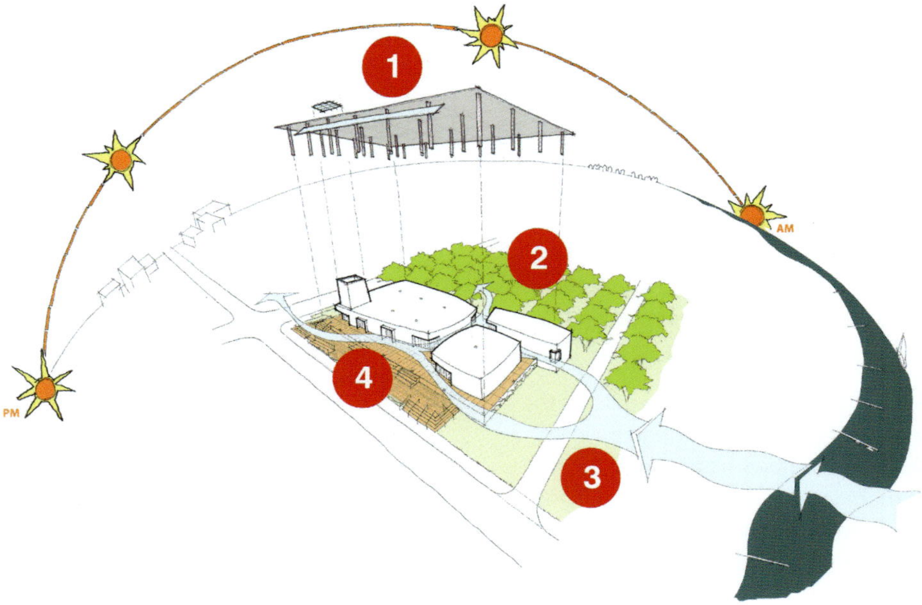

A cool envelope is a high-performance building envelope specifically designed to protect against increasing temperatures and more frequent heat waves. The envelope is a multi-layered assembly separating interior from exterior and distinguishing conditioned from unconditioned space. It is comprised of all the planes of the building: roof, walls, openings, floor, and foundation. The sum of materials in each plane determines its overall thermal resistance to heat gain or loss, which has a significant role in determining the thermal comfort of occupants and the amount of energy necessary for heating and cooling. A high-performance envelope reduces energy consumption for heating and cooling, improves thermal comfort for occupants, uses materials efficiently, introduces daylight and natural ventilation, and creates a durable barrier to the climate. Poor envelope performance exacerbates climate change by demanding more energy resources and increases risks to passive survivability in an extended grid interruption.

Figure 10.1: Waveland Business Centre has a double roof, the upper (1) with high albedo to reflect heat and shelter circulation spaces and building pods. The roof of each pod is insulated and the distance between the two roofs reduces heat transfer. (3) Pods are rounded to encourage airflow and (4) have super-insulated rainscreen and glazing.

DOI: 10.4324/9781032702964-12

BACKGROUND

Climate change is increasing the temperature differential between outside heat and conditioned indoor spaces; by the end of this century it will most likely be 2–3°C hotter outside than the pre-industrial average. The building envelope is an environmental separator to keep harsh outside conditions from affecting indoor spaces and tempering the conditions inside for occupant comfort. The envelope is responsible for controlling rain, air, vapour, and heat, listed in order of importance.[1] A cool envelope with continuous insulation and air barrier not only reflects and insulates against heat but it also protects the materials in the assembly itself, ensuring a long service life.

The science of thermodynamics regulates the movement of air and water through building envelope. Moisture flows from warm to cold and from more to less. Air moves from higher pressure to lower pressure. In hot climates, interior conditioned space is colder, and often drier, than the outside, so vapour is driven towards the inside of the enclosure unless the envelope resists these flows. As the temperature outside mounts, increased heat also raises humidity levels, as warmer air can hold greater amounts of moisture. Without adequate air and vapour barriers, infiltration can raise humidity levels in the wall assembly and continue through leaky joints to affect interior spaces.

There are six components of a cool envelope: structural frame, insulation, control layers, thermal mass, cladding and roofing materials, and openings.

Structural Frames: Thermal bridging is the heat exchange through thermal conductivity at elements that bridge the insulation of a wall or roof enclosure, when the outside temperature is significantly warmer or colder than the interior space. Wood, steel, and concrete structural framing conducts heat readily due to their lower thermal resistance, or R-value. Typical R-values for framing members: wood 2 × 4 equals R-4.38; steel stud is R-1.34; and concrete block R-1.89. If the frame is not thermally broken with non-conductive material inserted between inside and outside contact points, it can result in heat flow from high exterior temperatures towards cooler temperatures inside, reducing energy efficiency and potentially causing moisture problems. Thermal bridging usually results from framing members penetrating through building insulation layers. Buildings designed with thermal breaks can achieve up to 30% energy savings when compared to standard designs.

Insulation: The thermal boundary is a continuous insulation layer wrapped around a building, routed along the outer envelope (walls and roof) and possibly also at the ceiling and interior walls. The thermal boundary should be complete, with no gaps in the insulated shell of a building. Opaque building components must be well insulated with different recommendations for each climate zone. Use local climate projections for temperatures at the end of the century, and design for these temperatures rather than current conditions.

As the baseline for high-performance walls, the Energy Star program recommends walls R-10; roofs R-30 to R-60; and underfloor R-10 to R-20.[2] The current International Energy Conservation Code calls for minimum walls R-13 to R-30; underfloor R-13 to R-38; and roofs R-38 to R-60.[3] Passivhaus recommends insulation levels for walls R-40 to R-60; roofs R-60 to R-90; and slabs/underfloor R-30 to R-50.[4]

Control layers: A cool envelope includes barriers that protect the building from water, air, condensation, and energy loss. A building enclosure should dry outwards from the control layers and inwards from the control layers. There are four types of control layers: water control, air control, vapour control, and thermal control. In some buildings, the control layers are separate and at other times two or more are combined into a single weather barrier that stops rainwater, air, and vapour from infiltrating.

- Water Control: 'A sheet, spray or trowel-applied membrane or material layer that controls the passage of liquid water even after long or continuous exposure to moisture'.[6] The water control layer is designed to resist the penetration of rainwater into the building enclosure. Water control layers are installed on the warm side of the wall, so from the outside face of a wall, they are located either on top of the exterior sheathing, or behind exterior insulation. Provide ventilation space between the cladding and the water control layer to disconnect the vapour drive.
- Air Control: 'The air control layer system is the primary air enclosure boundary that separates indoor (conditioned) air and outdoor (unconditioned) air'. The air control layer stops outside air from infiltrating the building and depositing moisture within the building enclosure; prevents air leakage into the building; and avoids air leakage from the building, leading to a loss of energy efficiency. An airtight enclosure is necessary to establish conditioned space with particulate filtration, appropriate air changes, and temperature and humidity control. Air control layer systems are materials with a measurable resistance to airflow, including gypsum board, sealant, and insulation.
- Vapour Control: 'The component that is designed and installed in an assembly to control the movement of water by vapour diffusion'. The vapour control layer is commonly used in residential and small commercial construction; however, the selected materials often have a permeance that is either too low or too high. The International Building Code recognises the following classes:

  Class I: Vapour retarder materials with permeance of 0.1 perm or less. (This is the only material considered vapour impermeable.)
  Class II: Vapour retarder materials with permeance of 1.0 perm or less and greater than 0.1 perm.
  Class III: Vapour retarder materials with permeance of 10 perms or less and greater than 1.0 perm.
  Vapour retarder materials with permeance with greater than 10 perms are considered to be vapour permeable.

- Thermal Control: 'The components that are designed and installed in an assembly to control the transfer of heat'. These commonly include insulation products (see Sidebar) and also include confined gaps filled with air or other gases as found in windows, doors, ETFE, and inflated structures. Air is a good insulator because as a mostly empty space and its molecular configuration resists heat transfer.

	Energy Star	IECC	PassivHaus
Walls	R-10	R-13 R-30	R-40 R-60
Roofs	R-30 R-60	R-38 R-60	R-60 R-90
Underfloor	R-10 R-20	R-13 R-38	R-30 R-50

Figure 10.2: A comparison of Energy Star, International Energy Conservation Code, and PassivHaus recommendations for insulation at the building envelope.

Figure 10.3: A catalogue of insulation types and their embodied carbon per R-value. All GWP values are from the Embodied Carbon in Construction Calculator (EC3) Tool: https://www.buildingtransparency.org/ and are based on uncertainty adjusted GWP per 1 m^2.

SIDEBAR: INSULATION MATERIALS

Selecting an insulation material requires architects to consider several criteria: thermal resistance, thickness, chemical content, and embodied carbon. Inorganic insulation materials (fibreglass and mineral wool) have environmental impacts from a production process that demands high temperatures. Organic insulation materials - graphite polystyrene (GPS), polyisocyanurate thermal insulation (polyiso), expanded polystyrene foam (EPS), and extruded polystyrene foam (XPS) - are flammable and can emit toxic gases when heated to temperatures around 80°C. XPS uses polystyrene particles mixed with hydrofluorocarbon agents that allow the mixture to expand under pressure when cooling. It is neither a low-carbon nor low-toxicity material and it cannot be recycled, making it a poor material choice. Better choices for continuous insulation with lower global warming potential include:[5]

- Dense-pack blown cellulose has the lowest environmental impact among common insulation materials. It is a plant-based material made from recycled paper with R-3.2 to R-4 per 25 mm (1 inch) of thickness. It is treated with borate compounds to resist mould, fire, and pests. It is installed with a blower between studs.
- GPS incorporates air trapped within a polymer matrix containing graphite. The graphite reflects radiant heat energy like a mirror, increasing the material's resistance to the flow of heat, increasing in R-value as the temperature outside changes. The material contains styrene, which is a known carcinogen. Boards can be damaged by exposure to sunlight.
- Rockwool is a rigid stone wool insulation board that is made from natural volcanic rock. The rock is crushed and fed into a furnace where steel slag is added and the mixture is heated. The molten rock is poured onto a spinning machinwe where centrifugal force pulls the material through thousands of tiny holes, forming long strands of rock fibres. These are cured with hot air and shaped into boards or batts.
- EPS is made by evaporating pentane into polystyrene particles, which produces white, rigid closed-cell foam. The material has low thermal conductivity and a significant heat storage coefficient. EPS is extremely tough to degrade, ensuring long life but making recycling problematic.
- Polyisocyanurate is a rigid, closed cell, continuous foam board insulation. The 'closed' cells prevent air and moisture from entering between the cells or inside the foam. Rigid polyiso insulation board is sandwiched between face materials.

Thermal mass: Thermal mass provides inertia against temperature fluctuations. A material with high heat storage capacity prevents thermal energy from reaching the inner surface. Thermal mass is typically used in hot, arid climates where a thickened envelope retards heat transfer from the exterior to the interior during the day; it can also be used in cold, humid climates to prevent the loss of heat from the interior.

Optimal use of thermal mass can reduce a building's energy use, environmental footprint, and peak-energy loads, as well as increase occupant thermal comfort. Thermal mass

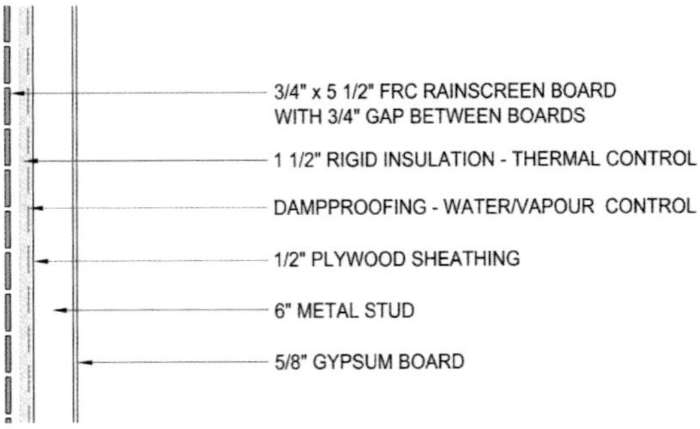

Figure 10.4: The wall section includes layers from outside to inside: cladding, control layers, structure, and interior finish. The 'perfect' wall.

can also be used as a thermal flywheel, an integrated strategy to provide passive heating or cooling in places with large diurnal temperatures swings (cooler at night and warmer in the day). As outside temperatures fluctuate throughout the day, thermal mass within the insulated enclosure absorbs heat energy when the surroundings are warmer than the mass, and releases it when the surroundings are cooler, thus regulating temperature fluctuations. Thermal mass also absorbs, stores, and releases heat from internal loads such as lights and computers. It is useful to note that in commercial buildings, placing thermal mass at the interior has greater impact because commercial buildings develop high internal loads as a result of lights, equipment and people - and people aren't usually present at night, when the stored heat is released.

CLADDING AND ROOFING MATERIALS

There are three key properties of every cladding and roofing material: reflectivity, thermal conductivity, and water-resistance. A cool roof is designed to reflect more sunlight than a conventional roof, absorbing less solar energy. Choose roofing materials with a high solar reflectance index (SRI). Less solar energy hits the walls than the roof and buildings have greater diurnal and annual variation in the amount of sunlight that hits exterior walls. This is the reason walls generally have less insulation than roofs, and why cool roofs are more effective than cool walls.

Most roofing materials have high thermal conductance, so insulation is used to counteract heat transfer. Some examples are listed below - higher numbers indicate greater thermal conductance.

- Thermoplastic Membrane (TPO): 0.025 W/mk
- Asphalt shingles: 0.5 W/mk
- Slate: 1.3–3.8 W/mk
- Steel sheets: 50 W/mk

The envelope must have water resistant properties to prevent water ingress into the structure. Water-shedding roofs use steeper slopes to direct water off the roof and are used in areas with heavy rains. Water-resistant roofs are made with materials that block water, such as rubber or metal, and can be used on flatter slopes. Many cladding materials are naturally impermeable, such as metal or glass; others, such as wood, are porous and need to be sealed to become water-resistant. Brick, stucco, and fibre-cement siding store water after rain exposure, acting as reservoirs that are charged during a rain event and discharge water afterwards in both inward and outward directions. These materials can be used as a rainscreen with a ventilated cavity behind to collect and direct water away from the inner control layers. The same principle applies to clay and concrete tile roofs.

Openings: Window performance is calculated based on the thermal resistance of the glazing, frame, and spacers, plus weatherstripping and hardware to ensure a tight seal. High-performance windows and doors commonly have insulated frames, insulating glass, low-E coatings, and tinted glazing. Performance testing includes:

- U-factor: The U-factor is a measure of how well the window assembly (not just the glass) resists heat flow. U-factor is the inverse of R-value indicating the insulation performance so the lower the number, the more thermally efficient the window. For example, a window with a U-factor of 0.18 has an R-value of about R-5.5. A target for a cool-temperate climate zone window is max 0.30 U-value (R-3.33); a skylight is max 0.25 U-value (R-4).[7] An energy-efficient door with no glass should have a U-factor of 0.17 or less; doors with about 50% glass must have 0.23 or less; and doors with more than 50% glass, 0.28 or less (southern zones) or 0.26 (northern zones).
- Solar Heat Gain Coefficient (SHGC). These values range from 0 to 1 and describe the amount of solar heat the window allows inside. A window with a low SHGC is more effective at keeping out solar radiation, while a window with a high SHGC doesn't block much heat. Common ranges are from 0.80 (allows 80% of solar heat to pass through) for uncoated clear glass to less than 0.20 (allows 20%) for highly-reflective coatings on tinted glass. A good target for a cooling-dominated climate is 0.30 (allowing 30%) or less, but values vary depending on the climate region of the project.
- Visible Transmittance. This represents the amount of the visible light spectrum that gets through the glass. The value ranges from 0 to 1 and the higher the value, the more light is allowed in for daylighting. Insulating windows range from 0.30 to 0.70 VT.
- Air Leakage. A rating of 0.30 or lower certifies that the window allows no more than 0.3 cubic feet per minute per square foot of window area in a 25-mph wind.
- Condensation Resistance. This measures how well a window resists forming condensation on the inside surface. A window that forms condensation is poorly insulated, allowing cold air to chill the glass. Measured from 1 to 100, the higher the number, the better the product resists condensation.

KEY DESIGN CONSIDERATIONS

GENERAL NOTES ON THE BUILDING ENVELOPE

Identify the climate zone and projections for future temperatures and rainfall. Review the minimum standards and consider higher performance targets if appropriate.

A cool envelope must control rain, air, and vapour, as well as heat. Higher temperatures are accompanied by greater capacity for air to hold moisture, so water control becomes even more critical as temperatures rise.

The International Building Code requires every climate zone (except ASHRAE zone 2B[8]) to have a continuous air barrier. Uncontrolled air movement through the building envelope can account for 50% of the heating load and a significant portion of the cooling load, equal to about 30% of the annual HVAC operating costs. An air-impermeable material has an air permeance equal to or less than 0.02 l/s-m^2 at 75 Pa pressure differential when tested according to ASTM E 2178 or E 283; anything with greater permeance is an air-permeable material. The best place for the air control layer is under the insulation layer so the air does not change temperature.

Blower door tests determine a building's airtightness and indicate areas that are poorly sealed, allowing air leakage. During the test, the analyst uses an infrared camera to pinpoint locations with thermal bridging, missing insulation, and air leakage. The analyst may also use a nontoxic smoke pencil to detect air leaks.

The most critical details ensure continuity of the control layers at every intersection, between the roof and wall, at plane changes, and at openings.

Design envelopes with the least amount of technology and systems necessary. This ensures that construction is straightforward and uses familiar materials and techniques, with fewer opportunities for error.

Investigate multi-layered systems for the building enclosure. Double walls, double roofs, and other redundancies can deliver better performance, especially if the window-to-wall ratio is higher than recommended.

ROOF

The roof of a building receives more direct sunlight than any other part of a building and roofing materials are often highly conductive, so thermal control is critical. Insulate beyond minimum code requirements.

Reflect sunlight to prevent the roof from absorbing heat. Use roofing materials with a high SRI equal to or greater than 78 for a low-slope roof (less than or equal to 2:12) and 29 for a steep-slope roof (greater than 2:12). The whitest white coating, which includes barium sulphate particles suspended in an acrylic base, can reflect 98.1% of sunlight, remaining cool to the touch even in the hottest part of the day. The paint can keep surfaces 19°F cooler than the ambient surroundings at night and cool surfaces 8°F below their surroundings under strong sunlight in midday. These products are on their way to market.[9]

Roofing materials should have high thermal emittance (TE), which refers to the efficiency with which a surface cools itself by emitting thermal infrared radiation. On a typical summer afternoon, a clean white roof that reflects 80% of sunlight will stay about 31°C (55°F) cooler than a grey roof that reflects only 20% of sunlight.[10]

The 'perfect roof' extolled by Joseph Lstiburek places the rainwater control under the insulation and ballast so that the essential water control layer is protected from UV radiation, heat, and water.

Most problems with water intrusion in the building enclosure occur where roofs meet walls. Maintain continuity between the water control layer at the roof with the water control layer at the walls, the air control layers, and the thermal control layers.

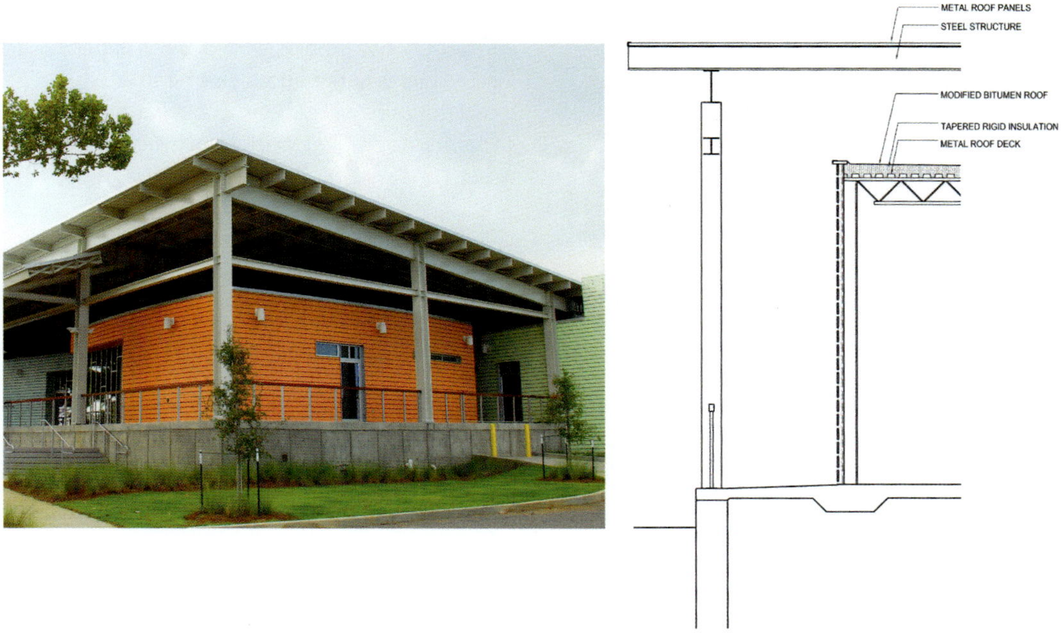

Figure 10.5: The double roof of Studio Waveland includes a superstructure of steel with metal roof panels to resist high winds and modified bitumen roofing over tapered insulation at building pods. This system places the rain control layer outside of the air, vapour, and thermal control layers protecting the structure.

A green roof is a type of cool roof. The earth and organic material acts as insulation, while also reducing direct heat gain on the roof membrane. Green roof temperatures can be 30–40°F lower than conventional roofs.[11]

Shading the roof is another way to keep it cool. Shade sails, trellises, and other roof features intercept sunlight and heat before it reaches the enclosure.

Roofs should be solar-ready, designed to accommodate solar panels in the future if not immediately. Photovoltaic arrays also shade the roof membrane, reducing direct heat gain. Design roof slopes to orient towards the prevailing sun direction, typically south- and west-facing in the northern hemisphere. Solar arrays on flat roofs can be adjusted to the optimal alignment, but sloped roofs have a fixed angle that can limit the potential for solar collection unless reverse-tilt racking is used to correct the solar panel to the optimal angle.

A double roof system consists of two separate roof layers. Double roofs shade the lower roof to keep the enclosure cool and provide a redundant skin to prevent water intrusion. The air space between the two roofs can be a few centimetres to a meter or more. A double roof system can reduce heat transfer by about 50%, and when the lower roof is insulated, it can reach an 85% reduction from a conventional roof.[12] However, double roofs in high wind zones may require additional structure to prevent wind uplift and the initial cost, embodied carbon, and maintenance costs will likely be higher than a single roof.

Blue roofs designed to detain and control roof drainage flow to increase on-site water storage and slow the release of stormwater runoff may also help to cool the structure below. A blue roof has both insulating and reflective effects, even at a depth of 150 mm (6 inches). The waterproofing membrane for a blue roof must be able to tolerate frequent ponding water events and longer durations; membranes with welded seams and monolithic membranes have a proven performance history. During hot summer days, the temperature of a blue roof is up to 12°C lower than a gravel roof, with up to 3°C higher minimum temperatures during cold winter nights.[13]

Existing roofs can be improved using cool roof coatings with high reflectance values to reduce air temperature and improve thermal comfort inside the structure, especially during the peak period of the day.

Radiant barriers do not have an R-value, so they don't add value on the inside of a roof or ceiling under the insulation because those locations are not on the high temperature side. If the attic has a minimum R-30 insulation, radiant barriers provide little benefit.

WALLS

The recommended wall insulation in ultra-low energy buildings is R-40 to R-60. Consider whether higher performance targets are appropriate and cost-effective.

Thermal bridging occurs with all types of structural framing: wood, steel, and concrete. Provide continuous insulation between the frame or bearing wall and the exterior. Where penetrations are necessary, use thermally-broken materials, frames, hardware, and insulating gaskets.

Avoid using vapour barriers where vapour retarders will suffice. Avoid using vapour retarders where vapour permeable membranes will suffice. Encourage drying mechanisms over wetting prevention.[14]

Define the level of permeance of the vapour control layer based on the climate zone and the construction type. The fundamental principle of vapour control is to keep water out and let it out if it gets in. Vapour barriers are intended to prevent assemblies from absorbing moisture but when they are incorrectly applied they may prevent assemblies from drying. Avoid installing vapour barriers (including vinyl wallcoverings) installed on the interior of air-conditioned enclosure, a practice linked to mouldy buildings. Avoid installing redundant vapour barriers to facilitate drying in at least one direction. These include foil-faced batts, radiant barriers, and vinyl wallcoverings.

Cool exterior walls are comprised of materials that reflect sunlight and cool themselves by releasing any heat that is absorbed. A high-albedo wall surface stays cooler and reduces the amount of heat conducted into the building. Raising the wall albedo of a building reduces its absorption of sunlight, which reduces cooling loads by 5% but increases heating loads by 13.95%.[15] The International Green Construction Code recommends a minimum SRI of 29 on east- and west-facing walls to reflect more morning and afternoon sunlight. Consider strategies such as screens or vegetation to mitigate localised problems. However, reflective walls can drive heat to surrounding buildings and spaces, creating pockets of higher heat.

The thermal conductivity of cladding materials varies widely, from virtually zero R-value for materials like sheet steel to high R-values for insulated panels. Granite conducts heat up to 3.9 W/mk, making granite cladding far more likely to conduct heat than hardwood cladding at 0.16 W/mk. In the middle of the materials spectrum are glass (0.8), brick (0.7), and structural concrete (1.4).[16] Note that material properties may change when exposed to rain; the thermal conductivity of wood can increase by 15% when wet. Use cladding materials that resist heat transfer with higher R-value materials or intercept heat with efficient insulation and ventilation cavities.

Porous materials such as brick, stucco, and fibre-reinforced concrete absorb water from rain events and discharge it afterwards in both inward and outward directions. Use these as a rainscreen with a ventilated cavity behind to direct water away from the interior of the wall assembly.

A double-skin or dynamic wall assembly can improve performance for facades with high amounts of glazing. They typically consist of an outer façade of laminated glass, an intermediate airspace that acts as a thermal buffer, and an inner façade with insulating glass units. The intermediate airspace can incorporate shading devices, walkways, vegetation, or maintenance platforms.

A rainscreen is essentially a shading device for the envelope behind. A rainscreen incorporates an outer cladding layer (the first line of defence against moisture) and an inner weather-resistant barrier (the second line of defence against moisture), separated by an air gap. The cladding prevents thermal bridging and moisture intrusion, while the insulating properties provided by the air gap improve thermal performance.

OPENINGS

A building's window-to-wall ratio (calculated by taking the Net Glazing Area and dividing it by the Gross Wall Area) should generally fall between 25% and 40% for the entire building, with the same proportion in each of the major spaces and HVAC zones. This is the sweet spot where daylight and views can be maintained but heat transfer is reasonable. A higher window-to-wall ratio reduces energy performance by increasing heat flow as many windows have R-values in the range of 2–5, rather than the 10–60 recommended at walls.

Advanced technologies offer promising options for high performance windows and doors, including: self-cleaning coatings (hydrophilic coatings using a transparent layer of titanium dioxide); dynamic or active windows that utilise materials that can adapt to external conditions; vacuum glazing to reduce heat transfer; photochromic glazing that can block sunlight in response to natural light incidence; thermochromic glazing that uses vanadium dioxide to change opacity; gasochromic glazing that uses tungsten oxide to regulate transparency; and photovoltaic glass to generate energy without compromising the visible transmittance.

SLAB, BASE, FOUNDATION

The optimal slab has a gravel sub-base layer that separates it from the earth and acts as a capillary break and a groundwater control layer. This stone layer should be drained and vented to the atmosphere. An unprotected slab provides a relatively porous avenue for moisture diffusion into the building envelope; a plastic/polyethylene vapour barrier should wrap the underside of the slab and grade beam to isolate the concrete from ground contact.

Insulate under the slab and vapour barrier only as required for the frost line in cold climates. In hot climates, direct contact with soil, which has a fairly consistent temperature, can help regulate temperatures inside by keeping the floor cool.

Provide thermal breaks at slab edges. Uncouple the flat plate of the slab from exposed stem walls around the edge with rigid insulation. This prevents heat gain or loss through the slab.

Raised floors with an encapsulated crawlspace should be designed like a mini-basement, with control layers including thermal insulation and a continuous, vapour- and air-barrier. Encapsulated crawlspaces require conditioning or dehumidification, which may be managed through a transfer grille or exhaust fans.

In hot, humid, and wet locations, passive design strategies include raising the building off the ground to prevent flooding; this also allows air to circulate completely around the structure for cooling. For raised floors with vented crawlspace, provide air, vapour, and thermal control layers under the floor to prevent moisture intrusion. Foil-faced rigid insulation R-20 or better, attached to the bottom of the joists, is recommended to manage vapour drive and provide a thermal barrier. Ensure the insulation is airtight by taping joints. For additional insulation, fiberglass insulation may be added between the joists with an airspace between the fiberglass and the subfloor.

IMPACT

Social: A cool envelope improves occupant comfort by keeping interior temperatures cooler during hot summer months. It improves passive survivability in the event of an extended grid interruption.

Environmental: Ultra-low energy buildings restrict energy use up to 120 kWh/m^2/yr (the PassivHaus standard) including heating, cooling, appliances, and household electricity. This reduces demand for fossil fuel electricity and mitigates greenhouse gas emissions and associated climate change.

Economic: A high performance envelope reduces the need for air-conditioning and cuts energy costs and associated greenhouse gas emissions. This improves grid stability and decreases peak energy demand by reducing air-conditioning needs during the hottest part of the year. Future energy costs are likely to be higher than current costs so energy efficiency offers an increasing return on investment.

Spatial: A cool envelope doesn't conform to any particular style but may have visible features that differentiate it from conventional structures: extended overhangs and shading, a window-to-wall ratio between 25 and 40, dynamic facades, double skins, and high-albedo finishes.

NOTES

1 Lstiburek, J. The Perfect Wall. Building Science. Com Corporation. Accessed at: https://buildingscience.com/documents/insights/bsi-001-the-perfect-wall
2 Recommended Home Insulation R-values. Accessed at: https://www.energystar.gov/saveathome/seal_insulate/identify_problems_you_want_fix/diy_checks_inspections/insulation_r_values
3 2021 International Energy Conservation Code. Accessed at: https://codes.iccsafe.org/content/IECC2021P2/chapter-4-re-residential-energy-efficiency
4 Lstiburek, J. "BSD-025" The Passive House (Passivhaus) Standard – A Comparison to other Cold Climate Low-Energy Houses. Accessed at: https://buildingscience.com/documents/insights/bsi-025-the-passivhaus-passive-house-standard#:~:text=Insulation%20levels%20of%20walls%20of,Window%20specifications%20are%20also%20demanding.
5 KPMB Lab. 2021. Embodied Carbon Values in Common Insulation Materials. Accessed at: https://www.kpmb.com/wp-content/uploads/2021/04/KPMB-LAB_Embodied-Carbon-in-Insulation.pdf
6 All definitions of control layers are from: Lstiburek, J. BSD-024: Vocabulary. Accessed at: https://buildingscience.com/sites/default/files/document/bsi-024_vocabulary_c.pdf
7 Table of Maximum Fenestration U-Factor Requirements for New Homes as Listed in the 2009–2021 IECC and IRC. Energy.gov. Accessed at: https://basc.pnnl.gov/images/table-maximum-fenestration-u-factor-requirements-new-homes-listed-2009-2021-iecc-and-irc
8 ICC. 2021. International Energy Conservation Code. C402.5.1 Air Barriers. Accessed at: https://codes.iccsafe.org/s/IECC2021P3/chapter-4-ce-commercial-energy-efficiency/IECC2021P3-CE-Ch04-SecC402.5.1
9 Wilson, M. 2020. The World's Whitest White Is Here – And It's Coming to a Roof Near You. Fast Company. Accessed at: https://www.fastcompany.com/90568342/the-worlds-whitest-white-is-here-and-its-coming-to-a-roof-near-you?_ga=2.206593243.979623333.1708372489-902524151.1708372489
10 Lawrence Berkeley Laboratory Heat Island Group. https://heatisland.lbl.gov/coolscience/cool-roofs
11 General Services Administration. 2011. The Benefits and Challenges of Green Roofs on Public and Commercial Buildings.
12 Omar, A.I., J. Virgone, E. Vergnault, D. David, and A.I. Idriss. 2017. Energy Saving Potential with a Double-Skin Roof Ventilated by Natural Convection in Djibouti. *Energy Procedia* 140, 361–373. https://doi.org/10.1016/j.egypro.2017.11.149.
13 Bono, S. and A. Bono. 2017. Design Considerations for Blue Roofs: Don't Get Inundated. *Building Enclosure*. Accessed at: https://www.buildingenclosureonline.com/articles/86698-design-considerations-for-blue-roofs
14 Lsiburek, J. BSD-106: Understanding Vapor Barriers. Accessed at: https://buildingscience.com/documents/digests/bsd-106-understanding-vapor-barriers
15 Zhang et al. 2018. Effect of Neighboring Cool Walls on HVAC Loads. Accessed at: https://www.energy.ca.gov/sites/default/files/2021-06/CEC-500-2019-040-APB.pdf
16 IES Virtual Environment System Material Database, Table 6: Thermal Conductivity, Specific Heat Capacity and Density. Accessed at: https://help.iesve.com/ve2021/table_6_thermal_conductivity__specific_heat_capacity_and_density.htm

RESOURCES

- Lstiburek, J.W. Insight Vocabulary. Accessed at: https://buildingscience.com/sites/default/files/document/bsi-024_vocabulary_c.pdf
- Passipedia: The Passive House Resource. Accessed at: https://passipedia.org/basics

BUILDING ELECTRIFICATION 11

ADAPTATION **HEAT** SCALE **BUILDING**

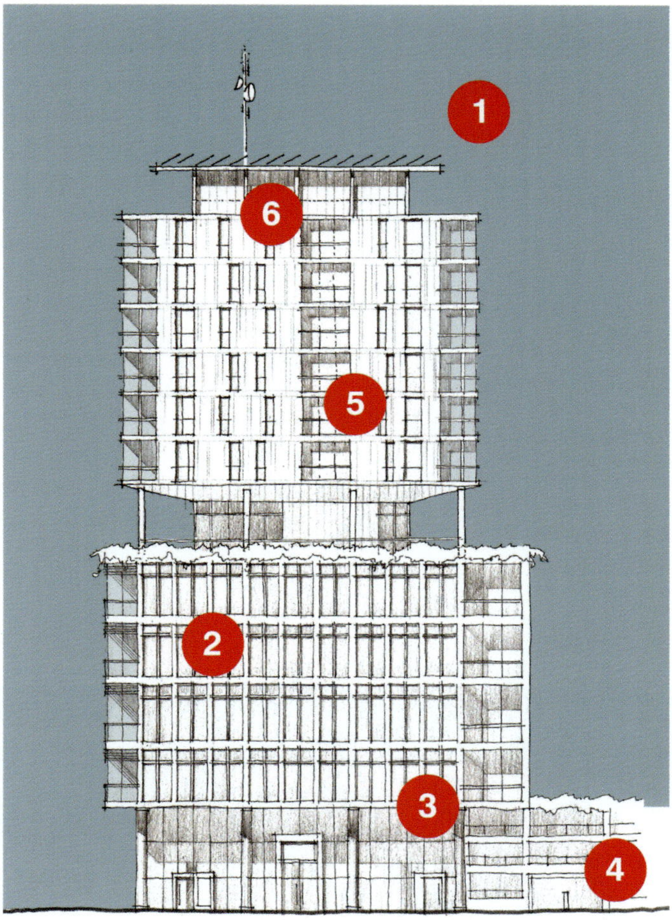

Building electrification supports a shift away from fossil fuels towards electricity generated from renewable sources: solar, wind, hydropower, and green hydrogen. Building electrification eliminates the indoor air pollution generated by gas furnaces, water heaters, and appliances; simultaneously, grid decarbonisation eliminates sources of greenhouse gas emissions and air pollutants from the extraction, refining, and burning of fossil fuels to make electricity. Electrification is the first step in preparing for a clean energy future, establishing the groundwork for uninterruptible power, and reducing inequity and long-term stressors.

Figure 11.1: 'Beneficial electrification' shifts demand away from fossil fuels in conjunction with deep energy efficiency retrofits and peak demand management. Different strategies are employed in commercial and office functions (lower section) and residential units (upper section).

DOI: 10.4324/9781032702964-13

BACKGROUND

Electrification has the potential to both mitigate climate change and improve adaptation. It eliminates the decentralised burning of fossil fuels for heat and cooking at individual properties, and reduces the demand for extracting, processing, and delivering gas, oil, or propane to buildings. Avoiding the worst effects of climate change requires the built environment to meet deep decarbonisation goals for energy use by eliminating carbon pollution in the construction and operation of buildings and infrastructure. Electrification is a crucial step towards reducing emissions and meeting climate goals. The next target is to decarbonise the electrical grid so that it runs on 100% renewable energy sources, a transformation that is underway; an IEA report shows that under existing policies and market conditions, global renewable power capacity is now expected to grow to 7,300 GW over the 2023–2028 period.[1] Improvements to the grid include expanding renewable generation capacity and creating greater flexibility to manage intermittent loads.

Electrification also forces a reckoning with the dangers to human health from exposure to carbon-based fuels. People today spend more time indoors than in past generations, breathing air with a concentration of pollutants 2–5 times higher than levels typically found outdoors. Many of the airborne contaminants come from carbon-based fuels

Figure 11.2: Land and Ocean Areas to support 100% renewable energy generation worldwide is shown in this graphic from the Land Art Generator. According to a report from the National Renewable Energy Laboratory, roughly 22,000 square miles of solar panel-filled land would be required to power the entire United States, including all 141 million households and businesses, based on 13–14% efficiency for solar modules.

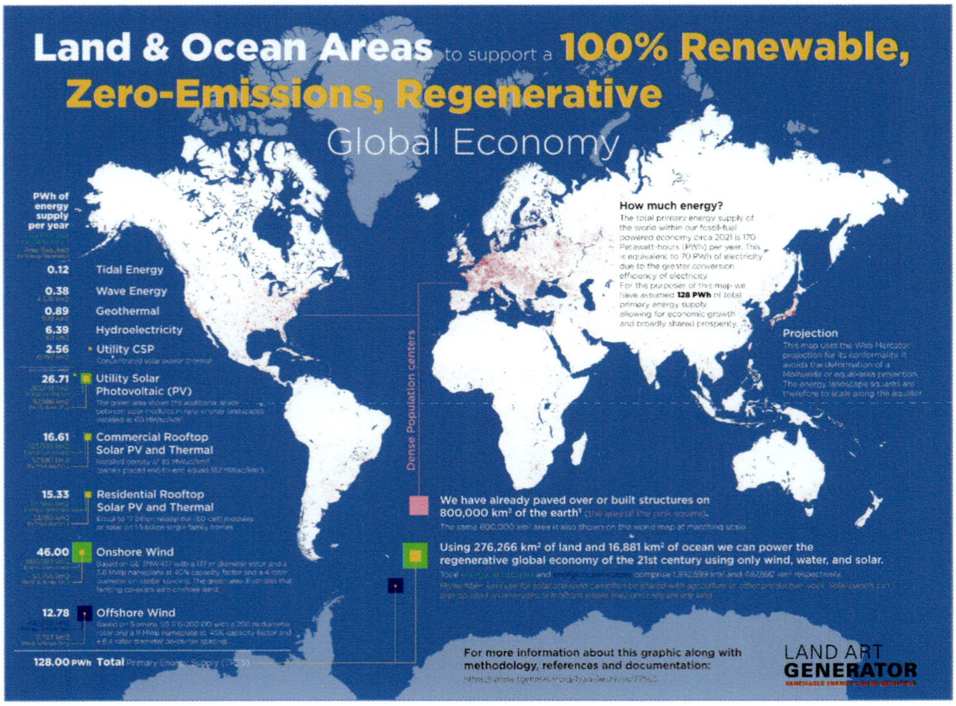

combusted within the building envelope: gases and particles from burning fuels such as wood, natural gas, kerosene, or charcoal, which generate carbon monoxide (CO), nitrogen dioxide (NO_2), polycyclic aromatic hydrocarbons (PAHs), formaldehyde, and particulate matter.

Decarbonising buildings prepares for grid energy interruptions by establishing an all-electric suite of equipment that can be powered by renewable energy sources in the event of an emergency. Solar power efficiency may be relatively high during heat waves, after hurricanes, or during periods of high demand that cause grid brownouts or interruptions. A few solar panels on a rooftop are sufficient to power essential receptacles: refrigerator, microwave, television, and fans. This can have profound lifesaving effects for vulnerable populations who may have difficulty in mobility or can ill afford to lose the contents of their freezer.

KEY DESIGN CONSIDERATIONS

PREPARING FOR A CLEAN ENERGY FUTURE

To achieve a fossil fuel-free electrical grid by 2035, rapid and sustained growth in solar and wind generation capacity is needed. Transformation of the electrical grid is underway in many parts of the world, with the rapid growth of renewable energy making up 70–80% of net new capacity in the United States and European Union. Asian and African countries are also making progress away from coal and liquefied natural gas (LNG) power plants. Additional transmission capacity, ranging from 1 to 3 times the existing capacity, is necessary to deliver energy from wind-laden regions to major load centres.

Improvements to the electrical grid are necessary to ensure grid harmonisation, which levels out demand peaks and valleys to create a more even distribution of demand and response. Gas and coal plants generate continuous power by burning fuel around the clock, but solar energy production fluctuates from day to night and wind energy shifts over the day and the season. This creates a mismatch between demand and supply. Grid-interactive buildings can anticipate or delay energy use to balance demands from utility providers. Demand-response can also save money for consumers and prevent brownouts during surges in demand.

The shortage of overnight and seasonal storage is a barrier to decarbonising the grid. Grid-scale batteries cushion the impact of peak supply from solar and wind installations, regulate frequency, and provide a reliable backup when renewable systems are offline. They also save money, by allowing power producers to store energy when it is readily available and supply the grid during times of peak demand.

Electric heating in harsh winter climates is finally cost-effective due to advances in heat pump efficiency in the last decade, making the worldwide transition to electric heating possible. Electric heat pumps can heat and cool spaces, resulting in lower initial costs as well as lower operating costs.

All-electric structures reduce initial construction cost by eliminating the need for gas piping, meters, and tap fees. Maintenance costs are also reduced throughout the building's service life. In existing buildings, the cost of shifting from gas to electrical appliances is repaid in less than 10 years.[2]

All-electric appliances are a key component in a slow-moving system change; every new gas appliance sold locks in higher emissions for

10–15 years, the life of the appliance. Every new structure that relies on fossil fuels to heat spaces or cook locks in higher emissions for 50 or more years.

Electric Vehicle (EV) charging during daylight hours is an optimal use of solar power. For this reason, place solar arrays at locations where there is a concentration of people in peak solar times: offices, schools, and shopping centres.

Figure 11.3: Arizona State University campus in Tempe, AZ uses photovoltaics to create a renewable energy canopy over public spaces to shield pedestrians from the sun and create lighted pathways at night. The university has on-site solar generation capacity of 23 MW with over 80,000 PV panels installed on the school's three campuses. Photo by Robert Ferry.

The World Health Organisation reports that illnesses attributable to household air pollution caused by the incomplete combustion of solid fuels and kerosene used for cooking causes 3.2 million people to die prematurely from to heart disease, stroke, cancer, and infections.

Fossil fuel generation plants produce high levels of outdoor air pollutants, affecting fenceline communities disproportionately inhabited by lower income residents. The shift to renewables will improve air quality in these areas, although many fear the loss of jobs.

Transitioning to all-electric appliances improves indoor air quality by reducing the pollutants generated by gas appliances and reducing concentrations of NOx, CO, and particulate matter. Gas appliances emit a range

of air pollutants, exacerbating respiratory conditions like asthma and allergies, illnesses that disproportionately affect low-income communities and communities of colour.

Weave renewable energy into already-built environments to cover rooftops, parking lots, highway corridors, public works sites, landfills, and other nontraditional spaces. Interlace solar arrays in parks as canopies, with grazing as agrivoltaics, and lakefronts. Design sufficient solar into each project to generate energy equivalent to that consumed within the structure.

RESPONDING TO DISASTER

When coupled with on-site renewable energy sources, all-electric appliances continue to operate during and after a disaster.
Solar panels enable daytime use for the essential circuits in a building, and batteries store energy for overnight use. Life-sustaining loads (medical equipment, emergency lighting, and communications) are typically about 10% of a facility's total load. Priority loads (refrigeration, fans) comprise another 15% of the total.

In a disaster event, power from the electrical grid may be restored more quickly than natural gas service. Although disasters can interrupt the electrical grid for hours or days, gas utilities may be disrupted for months or years if the supply piping requires repairs throughout the looped fuel system.

There are significant health hazards when backup power is generated using gas-powered generators, including the risk of electric shock, fire, and carbon monoxide poisoning. The U.S. Consumer Product Safety Commission estimates that about 85 people die in the United States each year from carbon monoxide poisoning from portable generators. African Americans are at higher risk from carbon monoxide poisoning from gas-fuelled generators in the United States, accounting for 23% of generator-related CO deaths, nearly double their share of the population.[3]

Greater reliance on renewables creates a decentralised grid, reducing the chance that an entire swathe of buildings will experience brownouts or interruptions at once. The redundancy of a renewable energy system improves community resilience by offering multiple options in a disaster.

Community microgrids (coordinated, local grids supported by renewables) decrease reliance on the overall grid. They span an entire substation grid area, potentially benefitting thousands of customers with indefinite backup power for lifesaving and priority loads. By serving customers in the immediate area, they also reduce transmission losses.

Grid interruptions exacerbate the equity gap. Low-income families have fewer resources if the power goes out. They may live in older, less well-insulated homes, with proportionately higher energy costs and a higher energy burden: 67% of low-income households pay more than 6% of their income on energy bills, a high energy burden; 60% pay more than 10% of their income for energy, a severe energy burden.[4]

Low-income families are susceptible to significant losses from extended power outages. They may lack the resources to adequately prepare for events that disrupt power, and the cascading effects of boil water notices and interruptions to heating or cooling. They have a greater risk of the loss of power causing spoilage and food shortages.[5]

IMPACT

Social: Building electrification results in cleaner air, subsequently improving human health and well-being. Addressing issues of equity related to electricity generation and environmental justice can improve conditions for historically underrepresented residents.

Environmental: Buildings that burn gas, propane, wood, and other fossil fuels for heating or cooking contribute significant emissions of CO_2e every year, equal to about 6% of global GHG emissions or 1.8 billion tonnes per year. Decarbonisation reduces GHG and improves air quality outdoors and indoors. Fossil fuel power plants require significant amounts of water for cooling, so decarbonisation also conserves water.

Economic: Replacing fossil fuel-powered systems and appliances in buildings reduces health and fire risk. Although decarbonising the power sector by 2035 would cost $330–740 billion in the United States alone, this would avoid 130,000 premature deaths with savings of $390–400 billion in avoided mortality costs. When avoided costs from increased severe weather are added, the United States could realise an overall net savings of $1.2 trillion.[6]

Spatial: Renewable energy increases the amount space devoted to energy generation; however, the effects on ecosystems, biodiversity, and human activity are lower than if the land were used for fossil fuel extraction. The worldwide land area needed for large-scale renewable energy (2020) is 1.261% of the world's land area; the current land area used for electricity extraction, refining, and generation is about 0.5%. Rising demand for energy by 2050 may require 3% of the world's land area, but employing the world's rooftops to produce solar power could contribute a considerable proportion of the space needed.[7]

NOTES

1 International Energy Agency. 2023. Renewables 2023. Accessed at: https://www.iea.org/reports/renewables-2023

2 Ye, Y. et al. 2023. A Perspective of Decarbonization Pathways in Future Buildings in the United States. *Buildings* 2023, no. 13, 1003. Accessed at: https://www.osti.gov/pages/servlets/purl/1974528

3 https://www.cpsc.gov/content/ Fatal-Incidents-Associated-with-Non-Fire-Carbon-Monoxide-Poisoning-from-Engine-Driven-Generators-and-Other-Engine-Driven-Tools-2011-2021

4 Driehobl, A. et al. 2020. How High Are Household Energy Burdens? American Council for an Energy-Efficient Economy. Accessed at: https://www.energy.gov/sites/default/files/2022-10/16.%20How%20high%20are%20household%20energy%20burdens_ds_0.pdf

5 Dugan, J. et al. 2023. Social Vulnerability to Long-Duration Power Outages. *International Journal of Disaster Risk Reduction* 85, February 2023, 103501. Accessed at: https://www.sciencedirect.com/science/article/pii/S2212420922007208

6 Denholm, P., P. Brown, W. Cole, et al. 2022. *Examining Supply-Side Options to Achieve 100% Clean Electricity by 2035*. Golden, CO: National Renewable Energy Laboratory. NREL/TP6A40-81644. Accessed at: https://www.nrel.gov/docs/fy22osti/81644.pdf

7 Nøland, J.K., J. Auxepaules, A. Rousset et al. 2022. Spatial Energy Density of Large-Scale Electricity Generation from Power Sources Worldwide. *Science Report* 12, 21280. https://doi.org/10.1038/s41598-022-25341-9

RESOURCE

- Rocky Mountain Institute, All Electric Homes: A Health Professional's Guide. Accessed at: https://rmi.org/all-electric-homes-a-health-professionals-guide/

UNINTERRUPTIBLE POWER

12

ADAPTATION **HEAT** SCALE **BUILDING**

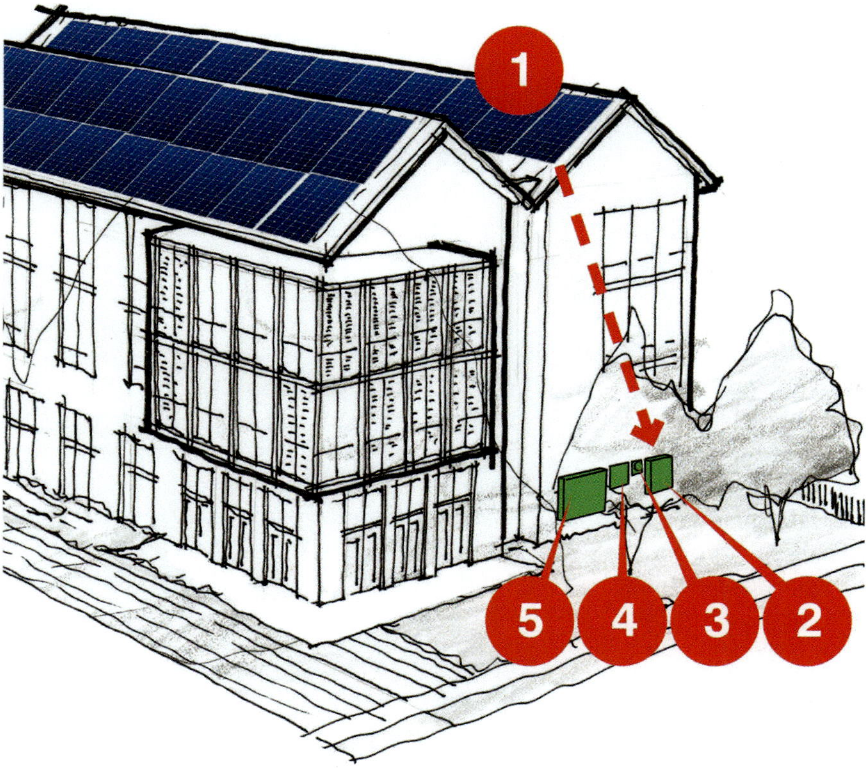

Grid electricity networks are experiencing pressure from intensifying climate change, aging transmission and distribution systems, and greater demands from population growth, higher cooling loads, and the rapid growth in data consumption. Disruptions to the grid interrupt the functioning of medical equipment, communications and security systems, heating and cooling systems, and refrigeration. Power outages will likely increase even in highly developed countries, driven by events such as heat waves, hurricanes, wildfires, and storms. Clean, uninterruptible power provides reliable generation to maintain essential operations with the associated benefit of mitigating climate change.

Figure 12.1: Elements of an uninterruptible solar renewable energy system include solar panels, racking and fastening systems, inverters, disconnect switch, electrical panel, battery storage, and an electric meter.

DOI: 10.4324/9781032702964-14

BACKGROUND

Rising global temperatures affect the entire electricity system. Electricity generation becomes less efficient at thermal power plants as the ambient air temperature increases; wind patterns change; and hydropower plants can be stranded by drought conditions. Transmission and distribution networks are affected by higher temperatures, which can melt and deflect above-ground power lines, while increasing wind speeds damage power poles and lines designed for lower windspeeds. Heat waves drive unprecedented demand, which may lead to rolling blackouts or grid failures. The risk of rolling urban blackouts lasting at least an hour and affecting at least 50,000 households increased by 151% between 2015 and 2021. These events cause discomfort for affected customers, with higher risks for people who rely on home medical equipment such as oxygen concentrators, infusion pumps, nebulisers, and electric wheelchairs. Traffic lights fail, fuel and water can't be pumped, and transit halts. The increasing number of electric vehicles remains immobile. The average global electricity customer experiences 5.7 outages per month.[1]

Short-term grid interruption is defined by the Lawrence Berkeley National Laboratory as lasting up to 16 hours. Food supplies are affected as refrigeration fails. Banks, shops, and restaurants close, offering no access to cash, essential goods, or alternate food supplies. The excess heat affects those with chronic illnesses such as cardiovascular disease, asthma, diabetes, and pulmonary disease, ensuring that hospitalisations will rise. Water supplies will likely be interrupted by the failure of pumps. Wastewater may be discharged without treatment, with corresponding impacts to water quality. Long-duration, widespread interruptions – so-called 'black sky' disruptions that last many weeks or months – will have catastrophic effects on local and national populations, economies, and the environment.

Decentralised renewable energy plays a role in mitigating and adapting to climate change. Solar power with battery storage reduces power disruptions by keeping the lights on and essential equipment running during severe weather. Two back-to-back Category 5 storms, Hurricanes Irma and Maria, struck Puerto Rico in 2017, knocking out 80% of the electrical grid. The death toll attributable to Hurricane Maria alone was estimated to be 4,645 people but about 10% of those deaths were due to an inability to access electricity needed for respiratory equipment. This was the second largest blackout in the world and the largest blackout in United States history.[2] The storm brought attention to the critical need for alternate power sources, and by the time Hurricane Fiona struck Puerto Rico in 2022, the island had installed over 42,000 rooftop solar arrays, many with battery backups. Although 1 million residents lost power, the businesses and residences with solar panels kept running.

Interruptions affect commercial entities by impeding services: offices must close facilities because of a lack of lighting, elevators, air conditioning, computing and communications; restaurants cannot safely store food, prepare food, or serve customers; and retail shops cannot maintain point-of-sale transactions, lighting, security, and thermal comfort. Industrial firms are unable to run machinery and other systems that manufacture components and goods. These costs are calculated as the 'value of lost load', and are added to the physical damage to the facility that results from power loss, such as goods and materials that cannot be reused or recovered, mould growth, vermin, vegetation growth, and other impacts.

A solar power system includes the following elements: solar panels, racking system, inverter, solar disconnect switch, electrical panel, battery storage, and an electric meter.

Figure 12.2: There are 42,000 solar power installations in Puerto Rico, transforming the energy landscape. The new generating capacity is eight times the number of solar arrays present at the end of 2016, before Hurricanes Irma and Maria hit the island. Photo by Karl Callwood.

- **Solar panels** use silicon, a semi-conductive element, to convert solar energy into direct current (DC) electricity. Efficiency ratings for solar panels measure the amount of power produced by the panel per m^2 and average efficiency falls between 18 and 24%.
- **Racking systems** have mounting hardware that align panels to face the sun, either through fixed or tracking mounts using roof-mounted clips, ballasts, or stand-alone racks. Most arrays can withstand 140 mph winds, or 2,400 Pascals, the unit in which panel wind resistance is measured. High-wind racking systems are engineered to meet 165 mph loading conditions for use in hurricane and high-wind zones.
- **Inverters** change DC electricity collected by the panels to the alternating current (AC) electricity used to power the building. String inverters collect all electricity in one place; microinverters attach to the underside of each panel and convert power individually. Microinverters offer 5–15% increase in production versus string inverters, which cap production of each panel by the lowest-producing panel in the string.
- A **Solar Disconnect Switch** separates the solar inverter from the electric grid in the event of a fire or to prevent electrocution of people working on the powerlines. It is required at all solar installations.

- The **Electric Panel** connects the inverter to a subpanel or panel to power the building. Subpanels are often used to isolate the critical loads of the building (life-sustaining and priority loads) from non-critical loads.
- **Battery storage** is a critical element for uninterruptible power. Renewable energy production in commercial facilities typically matches the peak demand hours and uses solar energy as it is produced. Residential electricity production peaks during the day but consumption peaks in the evening, so the battery charges during the day and discharges during evening hours, completing one full cycle per day or 7,300 cycles over a lifetime of 20 years.[3] In an uninterruptible system, batteries are fully charged prior to sending excess power to the grid. There are several battery types, including lithium ion (15–20 years life, high power density); lead acid (up to 20 years life); and nickel-cadmium batteries (20 years life, ability to handle a wide ambient temperature range of 20–40°C, but with difficulty in disposal and recycling at end of life).
- An **Electric Meter** is necessary for grid-connected solar installations. Net metering measures the flow of electricity demanded from the grid when panels are not producing, balanced against electricity supplied to the grid. Solar power contributes to offsetting energy costs each month.

Renewable power generation isn't without environmental impacts. There are consequences from extracting raw materials, manufacturing solar modules or turbines, and installation. Mining quartz sand for silicon cells or metal ore for thin-film cells and processing them into assemblies comprises 60–70% of the life cycle analysis in photovoltaic systems. In a traditional coal-fired plant, embodied energy makes up about 1% of the carbon emissions but operations and maintenance create 98% of the emissions, with decommissioning and disposal another 1%. The life-cycle analysis of photovoltaic energy totals 40 grams of CO_2 equivalent per kilowatt hour versus 1,000 grams of CO_2 equivalent per kilowatt hour for a coal plant.[4]

The U.S. Department of Defense is one of the largest consumers of energy in the world. Secretary of the Navy Ray Mabus made a powerful argument for renewable energy in 2010, saying,

> *Gasoline is the single thing we import most into Afghanistan.... For every 24 convoys, we lose a Marine, a soldier, a sailor or an airman: one in every 24 convoys. That is too high a price to pay for power.*[5]

Switching to on-site renewable power was the most effective way to reduce casualties, improve safety, and provide budget stability. The U.S. Navy established an ambitious goal in their 2022 climate adaptation report: to achieve 100% carbon pollution-free electricity by 2030, at least half of which is locally supplied clean energy to meet 24/7 demand.[6] The Navy anticipates deploying cyber-secure microgrids with long-duration battery storage to support critical missions and allow silent operation, improving survivability in conflict situations.

KEY DESIGN CONSIDERATIONS

Uninterruptible power maintains critical system functions during grid power disruption. In a disaster event, the priority loads for a home or office include: one elevator, telecommunications, phone chargers, medical systems, and refrigeration, emergency lighting, computers, and fans. Non-critical loads include: air conditioning, washing machine, dishwasher, water heater, iron, blender, general lighting, or other plug loads. To determine the size of the system needed, a standard rule of thumb is to calculate the total amount of power consumed by critical systems and multiply by 1.25, as electrical systems should not function at 100% load capacity. Consider how the system can be expanded in the future if additional equipment is installed or more loads are designated as critical.

Clean, uninterruptible power reduces the loss of food from spoilage. A refrigerator without power only keeps food safe for up to four hours, according to food safety guidelines from the U.S. Department of Agriculture. Socioeconomic status has a major impact on how critical safe food storage is to the family budget; lower income populations spend a higher proportion of their budget on food, and food loss from power failures has serious consequences.

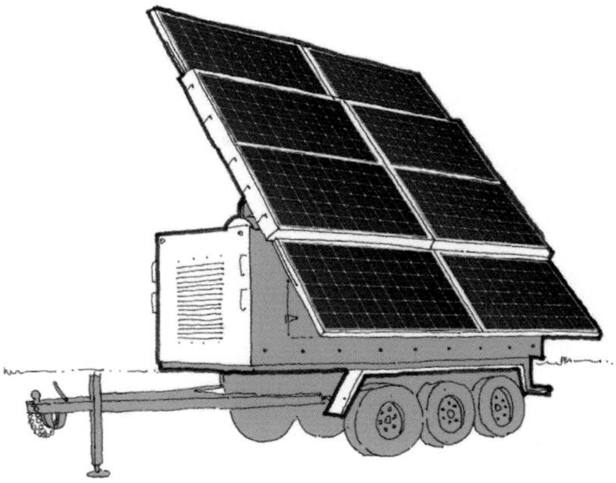

Figure 12.3: Mobile solar power units provide stand-alone photovoltaic power after a disaster. Units include multiple panels, an inverter, and batteries in an enclosed, ventilated trailer, along with external outlets and a transfer switch. Modules can be linked together to provide additional generation and storage capacity.

Global food losses from lack of cold storage are 20% of all production.[7] The availability of low-cost, clean, and uninterruptible power across the cold chain can reduce global food waste and improve profitability for farms, livestock operations, and the seafood industry.

Solar power provides a reliable and sustainable source of community power after natural disasters, when grid electricity may be compromised for days or weeks. Mobile modular solar arrays for emergency response can be transported to the disaster-affected area to provide reliable energy for essential infrastructure, powering emergency response, communication networks, water treatment, medical refrigeration, treatment centres, and community shelters. Mobile arrays can also recharge phones, radios, lights, and tools to assist in recovery efforts.

Understand the sustainability impact of renewable energy and battery hardware, including the embodied carbon footprint, hazardous substances, and disposal options. Regulations such as Restriction of Hazardous Substances (RoHS) and the European Union (EU) Registration, Evaluation, Authorisation, and Restriction of Chemicals (REACH), and Environmental Product Declarations improve transparency. Where possible, recycle batteries to ensure that toxic chemicals are safely extracted and disposed.

Solar power is silent and stealthy. Even at maximum generation capacity it remains noiseless and emissions-free in operation.

Cost-benefit analysis can determine the payback period for a clean, uninterruptible power system. Costs include the initial installation costs plus required maintenance and disposal. Benefits include avoided losses in damages and productivity, savings on energy bills, increased property values, potential incentives or tax credits, reduction

IMPACT

Social: Clean, uninterruptible power improves public health by providing a reliable power supply in severe weather, reducing the loss of critical food and medicines, and maintaining telecommunications services. They reduce energy costs for consumers over a payback period. Modular renewable systems provide access to energy in underserved areas and stabilise many social determinants of vulnerability (lack of health, education, and capacity for work productivity).[9]

Environmental: Substituting renewable energy with battery backup in place of diesel generators mitigates greenhouse gas emissions and improves the acoustic environment and air quality.

Economic: Direct and indirect economic losses stemming from the effects of extreme weather on the grid are consistently under-estimated.[10] The economic impact from production losses affects both suppliers and customers, whose upstream or downstream operations may be impeded. Loss of power disrupts hourly employment, disproportionately affecting low-income workers.

Spatial: Decentralised renewable power requires space for photovoltaic panels or wind turbines. Although the space needed for a solar array to supply 100% of the required power for a building typically consumes more space than the building footprint, a building roof may provide sufficient capacity for critical power loads.

in greenhouse gas emissions, and other social benefits. When considering the growing impacts of climate change, the benefits of resilient electricity systems are greater than the costs in most scenarios.[8]

Diesel generators are not an acceptable substitute for renewable, uninterruptible power. Extracting, refining, transporting, and dispensing fuel has direct dangers (hazardous spills, pipeline ruptures) and indirect risks (greenhouse gas emissions, global heating). Generators contribute to poor air quality and increase the risk of carbon monoxide poisoning if improperly operated. Generators run on fossil fuels requiring regular replenishment.

NOTES

1 2021 World Bank data. Accessed at: https://data.worldbank.org/indicator/IC.ELC.OUTG
2 Baggu, M. 2022. Puerto Rico Grid and Recovery Post Hurricane Maria. National Renewable Energy Laboratory. Accessed at: https://www.nrel.gov/docs/fy22osti/82860.pdf
3 Jasper, F.B. et al. 15 September 2022. Life Cycle Assessment (LCA) of a Battery Home Storage System Based on Primary Data. *Journal of Cleaner Production* 366, 132899. Accessed at: https://www.sciencedirect.com/science/article/pii/S0959652622024921
4 National Renewable Energy Laboratory. 2013. Life Cycle Greenhouse Gas Emissions from Solar Photovoltaics. NREL. https://www.nrel.gov/docs/fy13osti/56487.pdf
5 Mabus, R. 2010. Text of Remarks Given to the Clean Energy Economy Forum, 27 July.
6 Department of the Navy. 2022. Department of the Navy Climate Action 2030. Office of the Assistant Secretary of the Navy for Energy, Installations, and Environment. Washington, DC.
7 Dupont, J.L. 2009. *The Role of Refrigeration in Worldwide Nutrition: 5th IIR Informatory Note on Refrigeration and Food*. Institut Internationale de Froid. Accessed at: https://iifiir.org/en/fridoc/the-role-of-refrigeration-in-worldwide-nutrition-2020-142029
8 IEA. 2021. Climate Resilience. IEA, Paris. Accessed at: https://iea.blob.core.windows.net/

assets/62c056f7-deed-4e3a-9a1f-a3ca8cc83813/Climate_Resilience.pdf
9 Venema and Cisse. 2004. *Seeing the Light*. International Institute for Sustainable Development. Winnipeg, Manitoba, Canada. https://www.iisd.org/system/files/publications/seeing_the_light_dre.pdf https://link.springer.com/article/10.1007/s11027-007-9104-7
10 Sanstad, A.H. et al. 2020. *Case Studies of the Economic Impacts of Power Interruptions and Damage to Electricity System Infrastructure from Extreme Events*. U.S. Department of Energy. Accessed at: https://eta-publications.lbl.gov/sites/default/files/impacts_case_studies_final_30nov2020.pdf

RESOURCES

- Climate Resilience. International Energy Agency. 2021. IEA, Paris. Accessed at: https://iea.blob.core.windows.net/assets/62c056f7-deed-4e3a-9a1f-a3ca8cc83813/Climate_Resilience.pdf
- Prioritized rule based load management technique for residential building powered by PV/battery system. Ayodele, T.R. et al. 2017. *Engineering Science and Technology* 20, no. 3, 859–873. https://doi.org/10.1016/j.jestch.2017.04.003.

PART II

Water

Cities and nations are threatened by water ... and the water is rising. The global mean sea level is accelerating and is expected to reach an average 50 cm – 100 cm (1.6–3.2 feet) higher by 2100, threatening low-lying coastal and estuarine zones and placing more people and infrastructure at risk. At these levels, sea level rise will cause the loss of 1.79 million square kilometres of land, property losses on the order of $100 trillion, and the displacement of 187 million people, an unprecedented human migration.[1] This isn't the peak, as sea level rise won't stop in 2100 but continue for millennia, eventually estimated to produce oceans 6 meters (20 feet) higher than current levels.[2] Hurricanes are also getting stronger, and stronger winds typically produce higher storm surge. Intense rainfall events are becoming more common, causing surface water and riverine flooding. Residents in flood-prone communities are cautioned to 'hide from wind but run from water', an emergency manager's adage based on the threats of storm surge, tsunamis, and wild river currents.

Flood risks will increase by 2–3 orders of magnitude, reaching catastrophic levels by the end of the century. Coastal communities are trapped between overflowing rivers supercharged by stormwater from streets, parking lots, and rooftops upstream, and wind-whipped storm surge amplified by advancing sea levels at the water's edge. Riverside communities are experiencing slow-motion encroachment, causing neighbours to question how much longer they can stay or how far inland they must move to remain safe.

Humans cannot 'manage' water. Nature has taken our weak and incomplete attempts at mastery and breached, broken, smashed, overturned, overtopped, and defied the barriers that mankind has placed along the water's edge. However, architects and planners are developing a suite of alternative tools for living with water, managing where and how we build to respond to rising water challenges.

The Protect – Accommodate – Retreat – Avoid framework is a common method of categorising disaster risk reduction activities and adapt to climate change. **Retreat and Avoid** strategies adjust human activity to meet the changing environment, such as avoiding new development in high-hazard areas, and retreat or transitioning out of hazard areas. **Protect** includes modifying the environment to resist change such as constructing floodwalls or levees, enhancing stormwater collection, or other actions to preserve the existing built environment. **Accommodate** finds ways to modify the built environment to allow climate change to occur without impacting human activities, such as altering a site or structure to accept periodic disruption by elevating above the projected floods, or changing uses from residential functions to recreational spaces which can be easily restored after a flood.

At the Community scale, **Topography + Risk** describes flood probability, consequence, risk, and the urgency of incorporating scientific projections in flood risk assessment. **Retreat + Realignment** considers strategies to move people and structures out of high-hazard flood areas. Robust and redundant flood protection for communities includes multiple lines of defence: **Nearshore Breakwaters**; **Modular Revetments**; **Seawalls, Floodwalls, Levees + Berms**; and **Infiltration Zones, Riparian Buffers + Living Shorelines**. **Elevated Roadways** are critical corridors in flood-prone areas, allowing emergency access and evacuation in a crisis.

At the Site scale, **Reconnecting Water** provides options to remove barriers and hard structures and create space to reduce water velocity, allow sediment to settle out, filter contaminants, and cool water temperatures before release. **The Elevated Commons** proposes an alternative to grade-level gathering spaces with aerial connections to neighbours and to higher ground. **Flood Barriers + Gates** offer a catalogue of permanent and temporary barriers to protect sites from intermittent flooding. A **Corniche** presents a continuous line of waterfront buildings linking sites together to intercept storm surge.

The Building scale includes methods of avoiding, accommodating, and protecting against water damage. **Elevation** uses fill or piers to raise a building out of harm's way. **Wet + Dry Floodproofing** offers options for allowing water to enter and exit a ground floor space with minimal damage, or resisting water penetration. **Floating Structures** also have a role in resilient communities, with options for stationary and amphibious structures to accommodate irregular flooding.

Resiliency against rising seas and increasing storms requires a transformation in our approach to design, towards the consideration of water as a regenerative and living force. Water will reshape community form, inspire a reconsideration of the ground plane, and demand adaptation so that buildings will remain imperturbable against the interruption of water.

NOTES

1 IPCC 2019. Working Group 1 Assessment Report 5, Chapter 13, Sea Level Change.
2 Dutton, A. et al. 2015. Sea-Level Rise Due to Polar Ice-Sheet Mass Loss during Past Warm Periods. ***Science*** 349, no. 6244. https://doi.org/10.1126/science.aaa4019

TOPOGRAPHY + RISK 13

ADAPTATION **WATER** SCALE **COMMUNITY**

Global sea levels are changing and each increment measured on a yardstick arrives sooner than the last. Coastlines will experience erosion from higher sea levels and river channels will flood. Houses on stilts that are just high enough now will wake one morning to find that the water has reached the threshold. It isn't a question of if, but when. The only practical refuge is to abandon the lowlands and take advantage of topography, utilising high ground to live, work, grow food, and produce the necessities of life with lower risk of interruption, damage, and casualties.

Figure 13.1: Vintage topographical postcards are overlaid with ink to indicate potential future sea level rise. Postcards from the Future, Kit Boyd.

DOI: 10.4324/9781032702964-16

BACKGROUND

Waterside dwellers in centuries past understood the advantage gained from living on the heights and left stone warnings for future generations. A tsunami stone in Aneyoshi, Japan reads, 'High dwellings are the peace and harmony of our descendants. Remember the calamity of the great tsunamis. Do not build any homes below this point'.[1] Topography determines risk.

Flood risk is determined by a site's relative elevation to the surface of nearby water hazards. Low-relief topography characterises many coastlines and river valleys, with broad plains and flat slopes adjacent to the water. Waves, tides, and storm surge push water higher than the mean sea levels; more intense rainfall inundates land surfaces and rivers. If the land is high enough or the flood protection strong enough, hazard events don't result in flooding; if water surpasses the flood stage, the levee is breached, or tidal inundation exceeds the barriers, the land will flood.

Differences in elevation constitute the primary factor in developing risk maps. Risk is the product of the probability that harm may occur multiplied by the potential consequences. Maps of flood risk categorise land areas based on their *probability* of flooding. In the United States, Flood Insurance Rate Maps (FIRMs) designate areas as A zones if there is a 1% or higher chance of experiencing a flood each year. The maps calculate the *consequence* of flood events by designating V (velocity) zones, where waves and storm surge constitute an additional, dynamic hazard that can sweep away fill materials, scour foundations, and topple structural components. Moderate-risk flood zones (X-shaded) have an annual chance of flooding between 1% and 0.2%. Low-risk flood areas are designated with the letter X (unshaded) depicting areas with less than 0.2% annual chance of flooding. Property

Figure 13.2: Global sea levels are changing and each increment will rise faster than the last, not a question of if, but when. Calculating risk follows a formula: the probability or likelihood of an event multiplied by the consequences or damage from that impact. A 5x5 Risk Matrix is one method of determining risk.

The 5 Probability ratings:

1. Rare
2. Unlikely (but possible)
3. Moderate
4. Likely
5. Almost Certain

The 5 Impact ratings:

1. Insignificant
2. Minor
3. Significant
4. Major
5. Severe

Thus, an Almost Certain event with Significant impacts would result in a very high risk (5 x 3 = 15), equivalent to a Moderate probability event with Severe impacts (3 x 5 = 15).

FEMA Flood Map of Biloxi, Mississippi.

insurance costs, the cost of transferring risk, are calculated based on these maps.

Routine events have a high probability of occurrence but low consequences. Extreme events have a lower probability of occurrence but high consequences. A 1% chance of flooding each year doesn't seem a very high likelihood of occurrence but structures in A zones have a 25% or greater chance of flooding during a 25-year mortgage. These properties have a higher chance of flooding (1.0%) than a person has of drawing a flush in a poker game (0.197%), yet people tend to believe they have a better chance of drawing a flush in a poker game than their property has of experiencing a flood event. This is due to optimism bias, the human tendency to overestimate the chance of a positive outcome and underestimate the chance of a negative experience. Paradoxically, many property owners, having recently experienced a flood event, may believe they are not subject to another for the next 100 years, not understanding that there remains the same 1% chance of flooding every year. Most clients are comfortable planning for a scenario between high and low extremes, resulting in structures prepared for a Design-Level Event with medium probability and medium consequences, or about 10% chance of occurrence over a 50-year period. This may encourage the team to set the design flood elevation (DFE) to slightly exceed the minimum base flood elevation (BFE).[2]

Figure 13.3: The probability of getting a flush in poker in any hand is 0.197%. The probability of flooding in a 100-year flood zone is 1% in any year, with a 25% probability of flooding during a 25-year mortgage term.

Flooding isn't limited to coastal conditions and the FIRM maps include flooding from regulatory floodways along river courses and adjacent land areas. Areas of amplified risk include: proximity to water, including rivers and drainage ways; coastal conditions that may increase storm surge; conditions that may impound water. Flood risk reduction projects such as dunes, afforestation, seawalls, and levees can mitigate flood hazard risks.

Climate change and coastal urbanisation have a compounding effect, with more people moving to cities and more people moving to the coastal edge. The World Bank estimates that 4.1% of the global population currently lives below 5 m (16 feet) in elevation.[3] Over 2 billion people live in the near-coastal zone within 100 km (62 miles) of the coast at elevations of up to 100 m (328 feet) but growth projections show an exponential increase in this number to 2.9 billion people by 2100. Ambitious hazard mitigation efforts may extend the viability of locations for a time and lay the foundation for strong communities beyond 2100 but they will not slow the rate of sea level rise nor eradicate the risks.

Resource-rich coastal cities once turned to land reclamation, a misguided practice

Figure 13.4: The city of Bridgeport, CT allowed river corridors to be infilled with industrial and commercial development throughout the nineteenth and twentieth centuries, creating reclaimed areas that are subject to increasing flood risk. Rebuild by Design: Resilient Bridgeport, WB/unabridged/GCCDS/Yale/Arcadis.

that ultimately exacerbates flood problems in the immediate area and places more assets at risk. Land reclamation directly alters coastal geomorphology in the littoral zone by placing fill material – rock, sand, clay, cement, construction waste, and soils – in waterways. Many sites that were filled for development in the nineteenth and twentieth centuries are expected to go underwater in the twenty-first century. Land reclamation continues across the globe in Singapore, the Netherlands, and Dubai, where construction of artificial islands has consumed more than 750 million tons of sand. The practice of land reclamation places more people and structures in low-elevation coastal zones with high exposure, a classic example of maladaptation.

Maladaptation is the failure to adjust adequately or appropriately to the environment or situation, including climate adaptation actions that deliver the opposite of their intended effect. Maladaptation increases exposure to risks, placing people and investments in dangerous sites and increasing vulnerability. The initial investment of building at an inappropriate site is a sunk cost that locks in poor planning decisions and catalyses more infrastructure to protect, rescue, or replace damaged assets.

Uncertainty in projections can cause architects to question what level of sea-level rise to expect and plan for. Investments that are risk-tolerant and can easily be adapted to unforeseen conditions (temporary structures, lightweight structures that can be disassembled and relocated, and commercial buildings with a short lifespan) can use the likely range of sea level rise projections (a global mean sea level of +0.29 to 0.59 m).[4] Investments with low risk tolerance, particularly those related to public safety and critical infrastructure, should use higher (more conservative) sea level rise projections (a global mean sea level of +0.59 to 1.10 m - although according to the IPCC, a global mean sea level rise of 2 m by 2100 cannot be ruled out). Armed with this knowledge, architects can make clients and communities aware of the long-term implications of their decisions.

KEY DESIGN CONSIDERATIONS

Understand flood risks at the project site and surrounding context. The watershed, a hydrologically-bounded ecosystem, is the logical unit for assessing risks. Consider hazards from increasing development upstream and other cumulative stressors that affect topography, such as land subsidence from groundwater extraction. Use digital terrain models to accurately map the terrain and elevation, water flows, soils, vegetation, and other characteristics. Models generated with data collected by remote sensing techniques can be calibrated with physical land surveys to accurately represent land surfaces.

Use an extended planning time frame when considering sea level rise projections - at this point in the century, projections for 2100 may not align with the expected service life. Identify the likely projected inundation levels using scientific sources with high confidence. Establish DFEs that meet or exceed the projected inundation levels. Use higher sea level rise projections for critical infrastructure or facilities requiring continuity of operations.

Estimate the floodplain boundaries anticipated by the end of the project's service life based on anticipated sea level rise, rate of subsidence, and topography. Overlay sea level rise predictions[5] over topography. If the building's service life is not defined by the client, choose a 75-year timeframe for wood structures and 100-year timeframe for concrete and steel structures. Communities may restrict new development within current and projected floodplains, limiting construction to short-term uses, policies that may be enforced through hazard overlay zoning, coastal setbacks, and other planning tools.[6]

Avoid development on sites where land reclamation has filled former waterways. Land reclamation has been linked to significant increases in the expected annual inundation and populations exposed to coastal flooding.[7] Transform previously 'reclaimed' lands into permanent conservation sites, sites for temporary occupation, or low-impact recreational activities. Prevent placing people and infrastructure in high-risk areas.

Map the assets within the 50-year floodplain that will be exposed to flood risk to understand the potential scope of economic losses. Schedule the relocation of critical assets out of floodplains. The economic engines of the community - industrial and commercial functions - can cripple a city if flooding causes extended interruptions or prevents access.

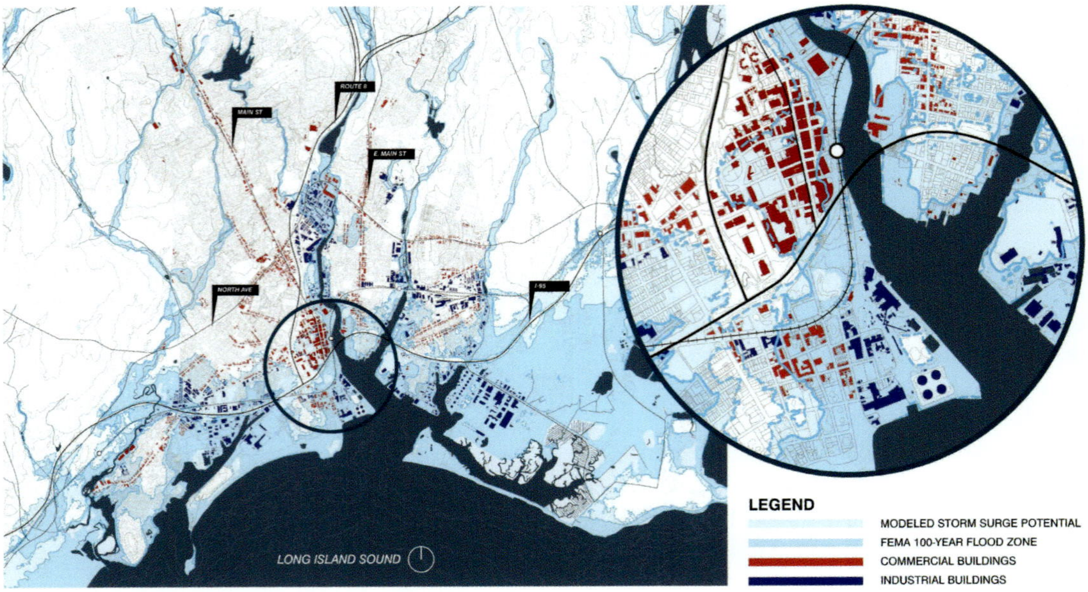

Figure 13.5: Bridgeport, CT has extensive economic assets located within the current 100-year floodplain and the larger area of modelled storm surge potential. Rebuild by Design: Resilient Bridgeport, WB/unabridged/GCCDS/Yale/Arcadis.

Water-dependent functions that are difficult to relocate – shipping, recreation, tourism, seafood industry – can explore flood protection measures such as permanent floodwalls, deployable flood defences, elevation, and nature-based solutions.

Establish neighbourhoods of the future with minimal exposure to flooding. Identify likely receiving areas for populations displaced from the floodplain. Transform less-intensive land use patterns into denser, mixed-use patterns that enhance identity and character with features that make the community more attractive. Compact land planning also conserves land, promotes walkable cities, and creates efficient transportation networks. Invest in resilient infrastructure and improve connections from new neighbourhoods to key economic assets. Work with community stakeholders to envision just transitions that reduce long-term risk, support economic stability, and foster equity.

Develop mechanisms to allow property owners in flood-prone areas to recoup the economic value of sites lost to sea level rise through the Transfer of Development Rights (TDR), buyouts, or incentives for permanent conservation. TDR is a tool that permits higher intensity developments in designated receiving areas in exchange for land preservation or reclamation in designated sending areas.

Reduce the causes of land subsidence through planning and building practices that encourage groundwater recharge: pervious paving, rainwater harvesting, bioswales, injection wells, and the conservation of open space.

IMPACT

Social: Traditionally, the most vulnerable residents occupy the lowest-value lands, which in coastal communities often overlap with the most flood-prone areas. It is important to recognise systemic inequalities and economic barriers, and prioritise re-establishing the most vulnerable residents to lower-risk sites.

Environmental: Understanding topography and risk can motivate communities to abandon highly flood-prone areas, restore them to native ecosystems, and enhance the land's ability to absorb excess flooding.

Economic: Protecting at-risk commercial and industrial assets safeguards essential economic activities. Development on higher ground ensures continued access, uninterrupted services, and reliable housing, all elements of stable economic function.

Spatial: Low-lying and reclaimed lands are likely to be among the first to go underwater. Transforming these at-risk lands into open space, recreation, or temporary uses can buffer the community from flooding.

NOTES

1 Lewis, D. 2015. These Century-Old "Tsunami Stones" Dot Japan's Coastlines. Smithsonian. Accessed at: https://www.smithsonianmag.com/smart-news/century-old-warnings-against-tsunamis-dot-japans-coastline-180956448/

2 American Society of Civil Engineers. 2014. Highlights of ASCE 24-14 Flood Resistant Design and Construction. Accessed at: https://www.fema.gov/sites/default/files/2020-07/asce24-14_highlights_jan2015.pdf

3 World Bank. 2015 data. Accessed at: https://data.worldbank.org/indicator/EN.POP.EL5M.ZS?most_recent_value_desc=false

4 IPCC. 2019. Special Report on the Ocean and Cryosphere in a Changing Climate. Chapter 4.1.2.

5 U.S. Sea Level Rise projections are available at https://coast.noaa.gov/slr/.

6 Smith, G., A. Anderson, and D. Perkes. 2021. New Urbanism and the Hazard Transect Overlay District: Improving the Integration of Disaster Resilience and Design in Coastal Areas. *Landscape Journal: Design, Planning, and Management of the Land* 40, no. 1, 35–47.

7 Xu, L., S. Ding, V. Nitivattananon, and J. Tang. 2021. Long-Term Dynamic of Land Reclamation and Its Impact on Coastal Flooding: A Case Study in Xiamen, China. *Land* 10, no. 8, 866. https://doi.org/10.3390/land10080866

RESOURCE

- Gaul, G.M. 2019. *The Geography of Risk: Epic Storms, Rising Seas, and the Cost of America's Coasts*. New York: Farrar, Strauss, Giroux.

RETREAT + REALIGNMENT 14

ADAPTATION **WATER** SCALE **COMMUNITY**

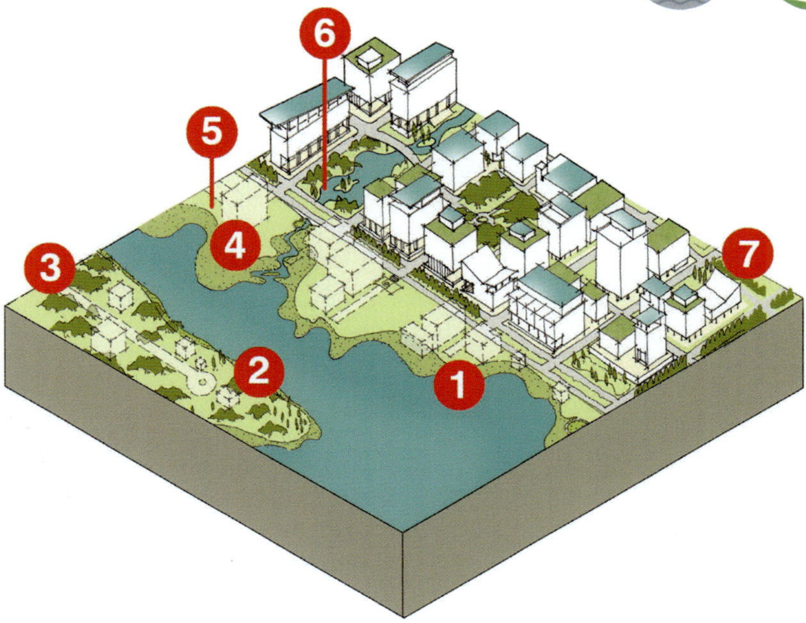

Communities are beginning to recognise that not every neighbourhood can be protected from flooding, making retreat a serious consideration. Managed retreat or realignment plans carefully and incrementally execute the movement of people, structures, and infrastructure out of the flood hazard area to improve safety, avoid losses, and take advantage of new opportunities. Communities designate the boundary of the sending areas where inhabitants and structures will be removed and identify receiving areas where people and commerce will relocate. The lands abandoned by managed retreat are stripped of impervious surfaces, structures, and infrastructure, and restored to natural habitats that can flood without penalty, dampen the force of waves, and provide a buffer to inland sites. Unmanaged retreat is a more haphazard process that leaves a checkerboard of buildings and residents in high-risk zones, often without ready access to essential services.

Figure 14.1: The places where populations leave and structures are removed are known as sending areas. To ensure that these areas provide additional protective barriers for the next front-line communities, the following steps should be taken:

1. Disassemble and relocate structures or salvage materials for reuse.
2. Create living shorelines.
3. Disinvest, remove, and relocate infrastructure.
4. Re-naturalise waterways.
5. Permanently conserve green space.
6. Increase stormwater capacity inland
7. Establish green streets.

unabridged Architecture graphic from the Coastal Hazards Overlay District Guide, 2025.

DOI: 10.4324/9781032702964-17

BACKGROUND

The increase in climate-related disasters and the escalating severity of these events is leading planners to consider how to reduce the number of people and value of assets at risk. Across the globe, nearly 1.4 billion people live in the 100-year floodplain where impacts are accelerating due to climate change.[1] Billion-dollar disasters are increasingly commonplace. And yet the topic of managed retreat is often unwelcome, even in post-disaster recovery, when 'build back better' is a common catchphrase leading to rebuilding housing and infrastructure in high-risk areas. Retreat receives even less attention in pre-disaster mitigation planning, although threat maps illustrate ever-widening hazard-prone areas.

The first and most difficult step in retreat planning is to define the boundaries of sending and receiving areas. Sending, or originating, communities are locations at risk from which the populations need to leave for safety reasons, either following a disaster or in anticipation of hazards. Receiving communities have a lower hazard risk as well as the physical and economic infrastructure to accommodate new residents. These boundaries will determine priorities for buyouts and capital improvements to support a just transition for affected property owners and residents.

The city of Norfolk, Virginia, addressed environmental challenges from flooding and sea level rise with a focus on expanding community involvement in land use planning. PlaNorfolk 2030 guides safe neighbourhood development by identifying four zones:

- New Urban Centres have a low risk of flooding with potential for high-density, mixed-use, and mixed-income development (receiving areas);
- Neighbourhoods of the Future have a low risk of flooding and could benefit from better connections and capital investment (receiving areas);

Figure 14.2: Receiving areas in the city of Norfolk, VA include New Urban Centres (green) and Neighbourhoods of the Future (purple). Areas to consider sending options are identified as Adapting to Rising Seas (yellow). Economic Engines (red) are industrial and military sites to be protected. City of Norfolk, VA: Vision 2100.

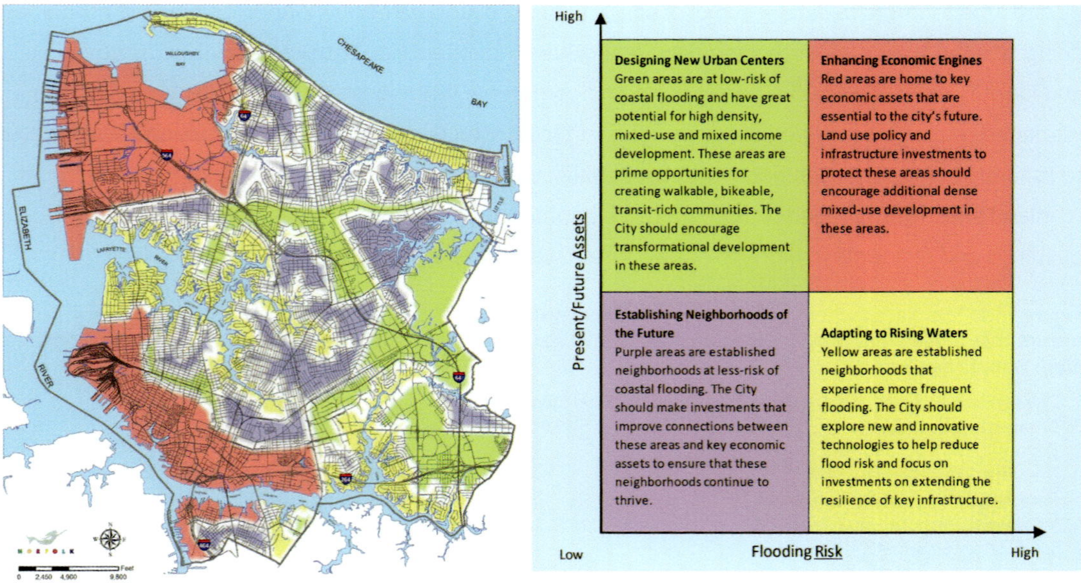

- Economic Engines that are home to key economic assets that should be protected, such as military installations and major commercial centres (protected areas);
- Adapting to Rising Waters establishes neighbourhoods that experience more frequent flooding, where options for reducing flood risk include infrastructure resilience and possible relocation (sending areas).

Resettlement programmes are a mostly voluntary diaspora, scattering people who were formerly neighbours across a broad geographic area. The impetus to move often arises by mutual agreement in a post-disaster period when residents evaluate how the community has been affected. Residents affected by hazards may try to persuade authorities to support relocation but often end up migrating on their own out of necessity.[2] Mandatory resettlement programmes are imposed by a government to protect the entire community. Some residents will overcome their initial opposition due to incentives, while other residents will resist until forced to leave.

One of the greatest uncertainties is knowing when to retreat. A single disaster event rarely causes the abandonment of an established community unless it is truly catastrophic. However, severe weather events can accelerate the process of displacement.[3] Unmanaged retreat creates sunk costs and missed opportunities: the cost of recovery from repetitive disaster losses, market resets, falling real estate prices in at-risk areas, abandoned properties, blight, and the loss of community networks. If retreat is foreseeable, then the time to prepare is now, setting in place the spatial, legal, and financial frameworks to support relocation efforts.

Retreat offers benefits to communities, as well as safety for property owners. Retreat has lower costs than flood protection while permanently reducing the hazard risk to people.[4] Reinvestment in receiving areas can revitalise neighbourhoods that have deteriorated over time. New mixed-use corridors can fill gaps in the urban fabric and enhance safety and economic activity. Expanding mixed-income neighbourhoods can improve social and economic conditions for generations of people. Transforming previously flood-prone properties and infrastructure into parks and waterfront open space can protect the next row of frontline structures and become a recreational amenity for the entire community.

Any discussion of managed retreat must address the primary question: who should pay for it? Retreat will most likely be financed through a combination of sources: government funding for pre-disaster mitigation or post-disaster recovery funding; tax incentives for land conservation; long-term capital improvement plans for infrastructure; grants for data collection, resilience planning, and community engagement; individual reckoning of potential savings from relocation based on insurance costs, business interruption, and avoided losses; and tools such as wetland mitigation banks and transfer of development rights (TDR) that support permanent conservation of the sending areas.

Managed retreat is controversial, with serious consequences for those asked to relocate and for residents of areas where new density is planned. An equitable, community-led process is critically important. Many people acknowledge that retreat will need to happen but fail to recognise that their own neighbourhood is likely to become either an originating area or a receiving destination, both of which change land use planning. Property owners in sending areas will be concerned whether fair market value will cover the cost of an equal property in a non-hazard area; owners in receiving areas will wonder whether property values will be maintained as density increases. Residents of both areas will be concerned about potential impacts from migration: the erosion of social capital, changes to quality of life, the dissipation of memories, and loss of water-based livelihoods. Authorities will be concerned about the potential for lost tax revenue from neighbourhoods that are designated as sending areas. The process of managing retreat must determine how to address the economic and political impediments that inhibit the humane and equitable retreat and how community, communal, and sacred spaces will be preserved after displacement.[5]

Risk isn't just about data but concerns people and their attitude toward uncertainty, unfamiliar situations, and loss. A pervasive history of disenfranchisement is at the heart of any discussion about relocation. Establishing trust between residents and the government enables more productive discussions and can be accomplished by engaging the entire community through trusted third parties with no financial interest in the outcome, such as community leaders, church pastors, and community organisations. Relocation is a long-term process, and people need time to understand their neighbours' plans to maintain community networks. People also need lots of information about their potential destination: living spaces and outdoor spaces, connections to transportation, quality of schools, familiarity with stores and services, and a myriad of individual concerns. One-on-one interactions and visits to the proposed receiving community can also help to foster trust between planners and residents.

KEY DESIGN CONSIDERATIONS

SENDING/ORIGINATING COMMUNITIES

Develop a broad coalition of community leaders to study managed retreat and determine whether relocation is a viable proposition or if protection and accommodation strategies may be effective. Assess the scope of potential impacts from hazards: sea level rise, storm surge, tsunami, surface water flooding, riverine flooding, and seiche. Use high-confidence scientific scenarios to map the potential timeline of effects.

Develop clear criteria for determining which areas are candidates for retreat. This must be a balanced and just ranking system to determine priority. What developed areas are under immediate threat? Where are concentrations of vulnerable populations? What areas have experienced the most frequent interruptions from flooding? Should infrastructure be the priority for investment, or private property? Community agreement about the criteria establishes the positive social factors necessary to build a successful retreat programme.

Create a broad understanding of the mechanisms and incentives for retreat - land swaps, TDR, conservation easements, and eminent domain - to enable buyouts.

A feasible plan for retreat also helps communities develop capital plans that limit investment in communities with a short lifespan. This can divert funding to construct new infrastructure in receiving areas and build capacity in the communities of the future.

Consider whether on-site retreat is a possibility. If there is significant topographic change, existing utilities and access, and appropriate lands are available, it may be possible for some residents to retreat within a site or neighbourhood. Density restrictions may be relaxed to allow duplexes, ADUs, or multi-family occupation to accommodate the influx.

A catastrophic event may support the impetus for retreat, and additional funding and planning resources may be available for implementation in the wake of a disaster. Chronic coastal hazards can sometimes result in less stimulus for retreat, making the problem seem too widespread and daunting, and the options for resettlement less attractive. Individual resettlement may reduce the demand for a mandatory resettlement programme.

Determine the monetary costs for retreat and the funding available to assist property owners. Who will be responsible for the cost of retreat: property owners, the public sector, or a combination? Consider how rezoning, deeper oceanfront setbacks, mandatory disclosures, and land use planning affect property values and make it less viable for owners in sending areas to recoup their investment. In a post-disaster surge of interest in retreat, consider how to offer pre-disaster fair market property values. Consider also the property tax implications for communities who have limited available land to resettle citizens.

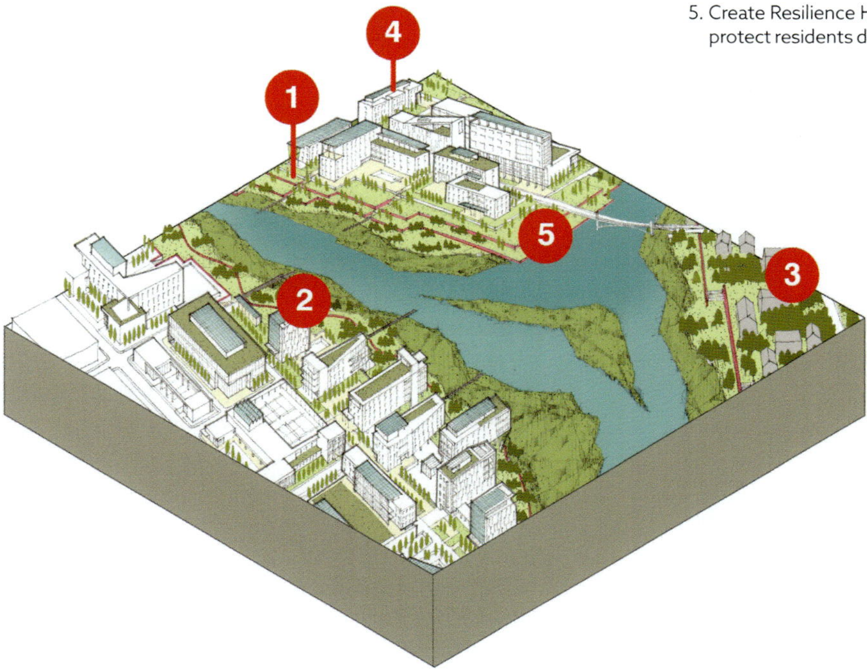

Figure 14.3: Receiving areas are low-risk areas where people and structure can relocate with the physical and economic infrastructure to accommodate new residents, businesses, and supporting services.

1. Cluster development on high ground with floors elevated above the floodplain.
2. Intensify development in areas with existing utilities and road networks.
3. Allow the TDR from the floodplain to increase density at higher ground.
4. Provide deep setbacks from the water to provide more absorptive space for intermittent flooding.
5. Create Resilience Hubs to educate and protect residents daily and in hazard events.

RECEIVING COMMUNITIES

Assess receiving communities to identify areas outside the hazard zone with capacity in the existing infrastructure including roads, water, sewer, and schools, as well as land available for residential development. Review available lands to determine their potential as sites for redevelopment, balancing mixed use development with competing priorities such as agricultural use, conservation and open space, and industrial uses. Consider how existing spatial patterns must be modified to accommodate retreat. Calculate the economic and social resources available to accommodate resettlers; receiving communities may incur startling increases in the cost of providing municipal services in the wake of a disaster, with the cost of housing, water, police, utilities, medical services, transportation, education, and other public services stretched thin after an influx of people. To encourage resettlers to remain within the same tax area, jurisdictions may develop new housing options, amend zoning to allow greater density, or annex unincorporated lands.

Planners must balance the pros and cons of greenfield resettlement versus infill with stronger town planning. Develop options that result in more compact, walkable communities, and preserve environmental resources.

Proximity to the originating property may be important to resettlers who fear losing networks of trusted relationships: teachers, pastors, or healthcare providers. Receiving sites in proximity to originating neighbourhoods offer familiarity, a quality that helps reduce relocation stress. Distant cities seeking to become 'climate havens' may be ready to welcome climate migrants, but they are not nearby.

Consider equity in every land use decision. The neighbourhood where a child grows up influences not only their life expectancy but their socioeconomic status, health, and well-being as an adult. Select receiving communities with the resources to provide for the current and future well-being of residents using the measures found in the Child Opportunity Index: education (early childhood, elementary, secondary, and enrichment), health and the environment (pollution, food access, heat, walkability, safety, and health resources), and social and economic (employment, socioeconomic inequity, broadband, and social resources).[6]

Consider whether the available lands or existing housing stock can encourage family groups and community networks to relocate together. People depend on a network of social capital, and relocation can sever the essential bonds that people depend on for employment, daycare, spiritual support, and other contributions to their well-being.

REALIGNMENT PROCESS

For a smooth transition, residents need to lead the planning and relocation efforts from the beginning, with government entities assisting in their relocation. To fulfil the need for self-determination, members of affected communities must be involved in all aspects of design and implementation of relocation efforts.

Sustained and transparent communication with potential originating communities is critical. Messaging must clearly outline the rationale for relocation. The U.S. National Academies suggests using simple, clear messages by paring down technical information, enlisting caring and trusted messengers, articulating clear objectives, describing risks in clear terms, and conveying the available risk management options and their effectiveness.[7]

Use personalised interactions to alleviate uncertainties and provide extensive details about potential receiving communities. Information that comes from trusted sources must be consistent over time. Take tours of the site or neighbourhood and offer multiple options for resettlers if possible. Information delivered at large community gatherings may need to be reinforced one-on-one with family groups or individual households.

The progressive abandonment of development in the floodplain is inevitable and must be expected and planned in advance. Outcomes for residents are improved if planned retreat strategies are available ahead of a disaster event, rather than following a catastrophic experience.[8] Adaptation is typically planned within local jurisdictions, where capacity and resource constraints impede advance planning. Having a relocation plan in place in the event of a sustained stress or immediate shock is essential to prepare for shifting land uses.

Timing is crucial for planned retreat. While most relocation happens after a precipitating event, practical approaches to prepare for retreat include: providing resources for potential receiving communities to build capacity in advance of migration event; expanding data collection; bolstering coordination between key stakeholders; and setting up a centralised system for migrants to access available services and resources. Relocation campaigns that pop up after an event may be more difficult to execute and more time-consuming to implement.

Zoning policy can discourage rebuilding in high-risk areas. Many structures are 'grandfathered', allowing them to be built back within the same footprint after destruction. Policies supporting retreat may prevent more than one reconstruction of more than 50% of a structure, to prevent repetitive loss in unsafe locations. Limiting reconstruction can trigger litigation and create community opposition if it is not part of a long-term plan for retreat.

Oceanfront setbacks are another policy that requires structures to be removed within a specified time period (usually one year) as the shoreline recedes.[9] Rolling oceanfront setbacks keep pace with sea level rise, preventing the construction of new structures that may be in danger of inundation.

Current levels of funding for managed retreat are woefully inadequate to meet present and future needs. The funding gap in relocation assistance should be addressed now through a variety of means: raising taxes or issuing bonds; allowing the TDR from the floodplain to increase density on higher ground; and establishing a dedicated account for acquisition and buyout programmes. Having a funded programme demonstrates a commitment to retreat which can leverage local funds to obtain grants and loans from other sources.

Despite grave risks such as hurricanes and sea level rise, many coastal residents are reluctant to move inland. Long-term residents may evacuate for a storm but do not consider hurricanes sufficient reason to move permanently if they have the tenacity and wherewithal to rebuild. Industrial, fishing, and tourism communities have livelihoods that cannot be replicated inland. Other residents have strong place-based attachments to landmarks, views, or cultural heritage that

IMPACT

Social: Managed retreat disproportionately affects marginalised communities who lack the resources to relocate or rebuild elsewhere. Ensuring fairness in managed retreat policies and implementation is critical to ensure opportunity for everyone in the community.

Environmental: Sending areas should be managed to restore ecosystem services and create a protective buffer to inland settlements. Receiving areas should consider their carrying capacity to accommodate new residents without overburdening existing infrastructure.

Economic: Managed retreat is a time-consuming and expensive process, with few successful examples. Communities with critical assets at risk should begin preparing a retreat strategy now to plan for the continuation of essential services, to be executed when conditions worsen or a significant event strikes.

Spatial Integration: Good design preserves community cohesion and equitable access to good public space, housing, transportation options, and other city services. Design can also accommodate access to originating lands and suggest alternate community uses that maintain its integrity as a buffer to sea level rise.

makes them unwilling to migrate, even in the face of extreme and sustained risks, until these lands are permanently under water.

The greatest encouragement a design professional can provide to a community considering managed retreat is a clear vision of a proposed community that improves the quality of life for everyone. Migrating residents will be concerned about what they will lose through the relocation process: friends, landmarks, jobs, culture, and history. Those residents need assistance to develop new settlements that assure them a brighter future, with fewer interruptions from flooding, better access to opportunity, and desirable spaces to live, study, shop, and work.

NOTES

1 Devitt, L., J. Neal, G. Coxon et al. 2023. Flood Hazard Potential Reveals Global Floodplain Settlement Patterns. *Nature Communications* 14, 2801. https://doi.org/10.1038/s41467-023-38297-9.

2 State of Hawaii. 2019. Assessing the Feasibility and Implications of Managed Retreat Strategies for Vulnerable Coastal Areas in Hawaii.

3 NASEM. 2024. *Community-Driven Relocation: Recommendations for the U.S. Gulf Coast Region and Beyond*. Washington, D.C.: The National Academies Press, p. 130.

4 Hino, M., C.B. Field, and K.J. Mach. 2017. Managed Retreat as a Response to Natural Hazard Risk. *Nature Climate Change* 7, 364–370.

5 NASEM. 2024. *Community-Driven Relocation: Recommendations for the U.S. Gulf Coast Region and Beyond*. Washington, D.C.: The National Academies Press, p. 97.

6 Noelke, C., N. McArdle, B. DeVoe, M. Leonardos, Y. Lu, R.W. Ressler, and D. Acevedo-Garcia. 2024. Child Opportunity Index 3.0 Technical Documentation. diversitydatakids.org, Brandeis University. Retrieved from diversitydatakids.org/research-library/coi-30-technical-documentation.

7 The National Academies Press. 2022. Engaging Socially Vulnerable Communities and Communicating about Climate Change-Related Risks and Hazards. Box 2, p. 1. https://doi.org/10.17226/26734.
8 Song, J., X. Fu, R. Wang, et al. 2018. Does Planned Retreat Matter? Investigating Land Use Change under the Impacts of Flooding Induced by Sea Level Rise. *Mitigation and Adaptation Strategies for Global Change* 23, 703–733. https://doi.org/10.1007/s11027-017-9756-x.
9 Siders, A.R. 2013. Managed Coastal Retreat: A Legal Handbook on Shifting Development Away from Vulnerable Areas. Sabin Center for Climate Change Law, Columbia Law School. Accessed at: https://scholarship.law.columbia.edu/sabin_climate_change/147.

RESOURCES

- Bittle, J. 2023. *The Great Displacement: Climate Change and the Next American Migration*. New York: Simon & Schuster.
- National Academies of Sciences, Engineering, and Medicine. 2024. *Community-Driven Relocation: Recommendations for the U.S. Gulf Coast Region and Beyond*. Washington, D.C.: The National Academies Press. https://doi.org/10.17226/27213.
- Siders, A.R. 2013. *Managed Coastal Retreat: A Legal Handbook on Shifting Development Away from Vulnerable Areas*. Sabin Center for Climate Change Law, Columbia Law School. Accessed at: https://scholarship.law.columbia.edu/sabin_climate_change/147

NEARSHORE BREAKWATERS 15

ADAPTATION **WATER** SCALE **COMMUNITY**

Nearshore breakwaters are artificial reefs constructed parallel to the shoreline that dissipate wave energy from storm surge. They function like berms or speed bumps to dissipate wave energy, stabilise exposed shorelines, provide scaffolding for sediment deposition, and slow littoral drift. They foster ecological biodiversity within the protected lee of the structure and encourage colonisation of oysters and other aquatic species on the breakwater structure.

Figure 15.1: A partially-submerged breakwater structure is built of stone and ecologically-enhanced concrete reef blocks to reduce the impact of climate-intensified storm events on a low-lying coastal community. Project: Rebuild by Design, Living Breakwaters, Staten Island, New York. Project Designer: SCAPE Landscape Architecture; Project Sponsor: NYS Homes and Community Renewal.

DOI: 10.4324/9781032702964-18

BACKGROUND

Nearshore breakwaters establish a line of defence to break waves offshore instead of at the water's edge. They temper storm surge, reducing both wave velocity and height. Typically constructed in relatively shallow marine environments to reduce the amount of material needed for construction, the structure's geometry, height, rugosity (roughness), length, and distance to shoreline determine its effectiveness at attenuating waves. Breakwaters do not prevent sea level rise and flooding but manage one of the dynamic aspects of flooding from storms: waves.

Breakwaters offer many ecological benefits if they are built with optimal substrates for oysters or corals to thrive. Common materials include traditional concrete and rock, oyster shells in wire gabions, modular reef blocks, bio-enhanced concrete, and geotextile tubes. Stone rubble and bio-enhanced concrete blocks with a low-pH concrete mix have the necessary surface complexity to recruit marine life. This creates a haven for oysters, which accrete on the porous substrate, as well as for juvenile finfish and shellfish, which find food and shelter in the gaps between blocks. These materials also promote the chemical process of biocalcification, utilising the CO_2 molecules present in saltwater to build up calcitic skeletons that remove atmospheric carbon dioxide.[1]

Ecological resiliency helps species and ecosystems withstand disturbances, relying on species richness and completeness to recover from events. Living breakwaters support aquatic vegetation, which thrives in the protected lee, which in turn provides nutrients and hidden nurseries for a variety of marine species. Saltwater marshes thrive in the low-energy environment, allowing plants to take root and flourish. Marine mammals use the exposed uplands to bask and perch. Birds wheel and dive along the teeming edges. Mussels, clams, and oysters assist with water filtration and accrete to keep up with sea level rise.

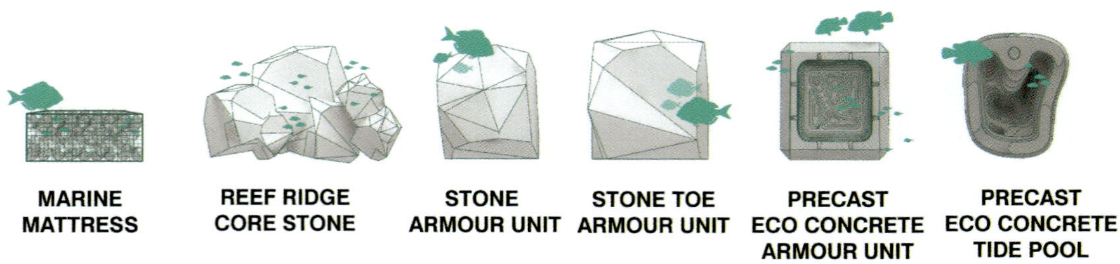

Figure 15.2: Structural and armouring elements used in Living Breakwaters and their dimensions. Project Designer: SCAPE Landscape Architecture; Project Sponsor: NYS Homes and Community Renewal.

Figure 15.3: A double berm or ring-shaped lagoon intercepts wave action offshore, creating calmer water on the leeside of the structure. This proposal for the DARPA Reefense project proposed ring-shaped double berms in the shallow bathymetry of the Gulf of Mexico to protect military installations.

Living breakwaters show promise in protecting critical installations and are currently being tested by the U.S. Defense Advanced Research Projects Agency (DARPA), which developed such innovative technologies such as GPS, stealth airplanes, and the internet. The Reefense project seeks to develop fast-growing, self-healing biological and engineered reef structures to mitigate coastal flooding, erosion, and storm damage.[2] The project employs a base engineered to dampen wave energy and support biological organisms. The pilot projects are accelerating a process that would normally require decades of growth into installations that can be effective in just a matter of months or years.

KEY DESIGN CONSIDERATIONS

BASE STRUCTURES

Coastal engineers, skilled at controlling erosion, designing coastal and marine structures, renourishing beaches, and maintaining navigation, typically define the design parameters for nearshore breakwaters. Solutions must respond to the existing shoreline configuration and determine the distance from shore, breakwater height, geometry, length, permeability, spacing, materials, and textures to enhance accretion.

Understand the prevailing physical processes of working in the marine environment including littoral drift, sedimentation losses, rip currents, and the potential for new construction to have an adverse effect on nearby shorelines. Bathymetry data and computer modelling can reveal potential opportunities and hazards.

The more complex the structure, the more wave energy is expended on it. Nooks and crannies, convoluted geometries, overlapping blocks, scalloped edges, protrusions and gaps ... these jagged profiles mimic the patterns of a natural reef to generate turbulence and knock down wave heights.

High-energy environments require a stable base. Rubble-mound breakwaters are constructed of quarrystone or high-density rocks (basalt, gneiss, granite, or slate) where these are available. The angle of repose is typically less than 1:1. Each layer of stone is sized so that material will not be displaced through the voids of each successive layer, making each layer larger as the wall grows, culminating in the outermost armour layer. Rocks of 3–10 cm (1–4 inches) provide habitat for the youngest and smallest species. Rocks of 20–40 cm (8–16 inches) shelter fish as they grow. Irregular facets in the materials allow them to interlock and settle over time, resulting in slow, progressive weathering rather than sudden, catastrophic failure.

Subtidal (fully covered by water) and exposed (partly covered) breakwaters are capable of dampening wave action, reducing erosion, and providing habitat. Both types can build up biogenically in parallel with sea level rise. Selecting the right type of breakwater for the application depends on specific site features, the nearby community's preferences, and the level of protection required. In a flood event, just a matter of inches can make the critical distinction between flooding and not flooding.

Fingers of rock extending outward on the wave-facing side of the structure create intertidal 'reef streets' for finfish and crustaceans to shelter and forage. Juveniles hide within the pore space between blocks and stones, and larger fish browse the outer edge, attracting recreational fishing.

Specialised marine construction blocks are designed to enhance biological recruitment with bio-enhanced concrete composition, low-pH mixes, complex textures to promote adherence, and cast-in-place terraces to create ecological niches for diverse species.

Figure 15.4: Oyster gardens in wire baskets are suspended from piers and stocked with hatchery-reared juvenile oysters (known as spat) set on oyster shells. Photo by Mississippi Department of Marine Resources.

At sites with excess wave action, a double berm can dissipate higher waves. This can be fashioned into a ring or lagoon in areas with poor water quality to support ecosystems within the circumference.

In shallow-water, nearshore environments, breakwaters can be relatively inexpensive to build. More material is needed in deeper water, resulting in higher construction costs.

BIOLOGICAL ORGANISMS

Living breakwaters support naturally accreting habitats such as corals, oysters, and aquatic vegetation. Regenerating oyster and shellfish habitats can restore the cultural heritage of indigenous people and early settlers, and urban protein sources: oysters, mussels, and clams. Oysters filter 115–190 litres (30–50 gallons) of water a day to improve water quality. Blocks or baskets set with oyster spat give the species a head start.

Plant native aquatic vegetation on and around breakwaters to provide food sources for marine life, trap sediment, and filter contaminants from the water. Aquatic vegetation enhances the drag coefficient of water movement, slowing wave velocity. It also traps sediment at the base of each stalk, encouraging deposition. Leaves and stems provide shelter for juvenile fish and shellfish.

If the site area is home to native marine mammals such as seals and sea lions, include shallow slopes at the intertidal zone to give them space to bask, feed, and mate.

Design points where people can interact with the system and learn more about the marine ecosystem. Invite the community to participate in to defining programming: recreation (walking, hiking, diving, boating, fishing, birdwatching, kayaking), education, exhibits, gatherings, foodways, or tours.

IMPACT

Social: Breakwaters reduce risk from strong wave action which threatens coastal communities. Community access to breakwaters enhances education and environmental stewardship with recreational benefits - kayaking, diving, swimming, walking trails, fishing, and birdwatching - supporting ecotourism and job opportunities for local residents.

Environmental: Ecosystem services provided by breakwaters improve water quality, nutrient cycling, and soil retention and formation. Breakwaters augment production of oysters and finfish and enhance submerged aquatic vegetation, creating a complex and biodiverse marine web.

Economic: Breakwaters absorb wave energy offshore, reducing property damage in extreme weather events. The reduced risk from wave hazards can positively impact property values. Calm water in the lee of the breakwater prevents coastal erosion, replenishes beaches, and reduces beach renourishment frequency and cost.

Spatial: Nearshore breakwaters may modify views to the horizon but they also bring attention to ecological resilience. As breakwaters thrive they become increasingly naturalised, accreting oysters, grasses, and marine species near the shore and bringing people into closer contact with these wonders.

BENEFIT-COST ANALYSIS OF LIVING BREAKWATERS

Nature-based solutions such as living breakwaters have few precedents and may be accompanied by scepticism and permitting barriers. Benefit-Cost Analysis (BCA) is the systematic process of quantifying and comparing the expected costs (including initial construction and lifecycle costs) and the benefits or returns from an investment.

The initial BCA (2014) in the *Rebuild by Design Living Breakwaters: Tottenville Phase 1* pilot project was estimated by the design team, including projected costs:

$51 M in physical infrastructure
$2.7 M in ecological infrastructure
$4 M in social infrastructure
$12 M in maintenance
$69.7 M total lifecycle cost

Projected benefits included:

$263 M avoided damages
$15 M economic activity generated

Plus 52 acres of habitat created, over 30 species supported, and over 24,000 students engaged in education programming annually. The cumulative net benefit (benefits minus costs) for the conceptual design was projected to be $208.3 M, with a BCA of 3.99 (benefits divided by costs).

An updated BCA was prepared in 2017 for the Governor's Office of Storm Recovery using a 50-year planning horizon for the Phase 1 Pilot project. The lifecycle cost to build and operate the Phase 1 Pilot, $62.4 million in 2016 dollars, is expected to generate total benefits of $76.1 million over the same period including:

- Total Resiliency Values: $53.2 million;
- Total Environmental Values: $11.6 million;
- Total Social Values: $8.3 million;
- Economic Revitalisation Benefits: $2.95 million.

The project's cumulative net benefit is $13.7 million, resulting in a BCR of 1.22.[3] Any number over 1.0 indicates a positive return on investment. The project was completed in September 2024 at a final cost of $111 million, with 2,400 linear feet of breakwaters in eight partially-submerged structures to break storm waves, decrease erosion, and stabilise beaches at Tottenville, Staten Island, New York.

Figure 15.5: The Living Breakwaters project completed construction in September 2024 off the south coast of Tottenville in Staten Island, New York. It consists of eight breakwaters designed to reduce risk to the community and provide habitat for oysters, fin fish, and other marine species. Photo by SCAPE/ Ty Cole.

NOTES

1 Sella, I., T. Hadary, A.J. Rella, B. Riegl, D. Swack, and S. Perkol-Finkel. 2022. Design, Production, and Validation of the Biological and Structural Performance of an Ecologically Engineered Concrete Block Mattress: A Nature-Inclusive Design for Shoreline and Offshore Construction. *Integrated Environmental Assessment and Management* 18, 148–162.
2 DARPA Reefense Program Summary. Accessed at: https://www.darpa.mil/program/reefense
3 New York Governor's Office of Storm Recovery. 2017. Breakwaters Project Benefit Cost Analysis. Accessed at: https://hcr.ny.gov/system/files/documents/2023/07/appendix-d_breakwaters-project-benefit-cost-analysis.pdf

RESOURCES

- The Scape Team. 2014. Final Proposal for Rebuild by Design. Accessed at: https://rebuildbydesign.org/wp-content/uploads/2021/12/676.pdf
- Rahim, S. 2024. DARPA Thinks Walls of Oysters Could Protect Shores Against Hurricanes. Wired. Accessed at: https://www.wired.com/story/darpa-thinks-walls-of-oysters-could-protect-shores-against-hurricanes/

MODULAR REVETMENTS 16

ADAPTATION **WATER** SCALE **COMMUNITY**

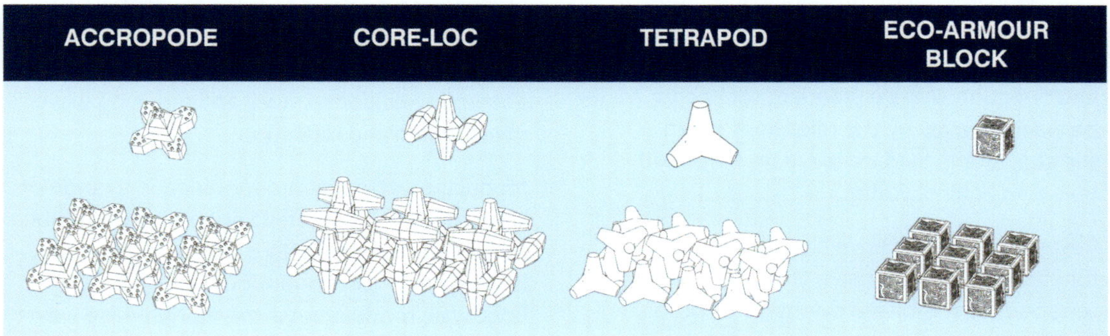

Revetments are impact-resistant armour overlaid on a shoreline, streambank, or seawall to absorb wave energy and protect the natural edge from erosion. The term derives from military terminology for a retaining wall intended to fortify a community. Military revetments were made with readily available materials such as sandbags, chicken wire, wicker, logs, corrugated metal, steel plates, or salvaged building components. Modular revetments deploy small units in geometric or random configurations that can articulate independently and interlock with each other for stability. The revetments conform to changes in the environment while maintaining a protective cover. The elements have a variety of names, some proprietary and others evocative: accropode, armour block, turfblock, riprap, tetrapod, dolosse, tripod, tribar, and gobi block.

Figure 16.1: Modular revetments come in a variety of shapes and sizes: accropode, armour block, core-loc block, riprap, tetrapod, dolosse, tripod, tribar, and gobi block.

DOI: 10.4324/9781032702964-19

BACKGROUND

What deters a marine threat better than a field of spiky, giant-sized jacks positioned along the water's edge? Modular revetments dissipate wave energy by forcing the waves to expend energy on unyielding concrete, absorbing water in the voids between and creating turbulence to dissipate water velocity and direction. Where standard rocks can be washed away by the relentless churn of the sea, interlocked units create hardened bulwarks against water.

Revetment shapes have been engineered for stability and defensive properties. The tetrapod form is based on the *caltrops*, a Roman invention that was fabricated to slow the advance of troops on roadways. It was shaped with four apposite spikes arranged so that no matter how they were positioned, three points always rested on the ground and the fourth was upright. Interlocking barricades derived from this model – Czech hedgehogs – were used in WWII as defences against tanks and landing crafts. The highly-stable shape inspired the first use of tetrapods to fortify essential services in Casablanca, Morocco, in 1950.[1] The permeable revetment proved to be effective in absorbing incidental swell and reducing wave overtopping and reflection.

Modular revetments are moulded in a range of sizes to manage different wave environments, from fist-sized blocks to 8-tonne dolosse. Unlike the single, continuous line of a floodwall, modular revetments minimise wave reflectance. When minor damage occurs, the armour doesn't fail catastrophically due to redundancies from the multiple, overlapping units.

Figure 16.2: The evolution from military obstacle defences to marine coastal armouring relies on a common geometry. From left: a Roman caltrops has four sharp spines arranged so that one spike always points upwards to puncture feet, hooves, or tyres (50 BC); a Czech hedgehog made of bolted steel angles serves as an anti-tank obstacle (1938); a concrete tetrapod has a tetrahedral shape and interlocks to prevent erosion along a coastal edge (1950).

KEY DESIGN CONSIDERATIONS

A coastal engineer will define the design parameters: the maximum breaking wave height, amount of runup, required elevation of the crest, and minimum water level that may scour the base. Consider the tidal range, potential storm surge, sea level rise, and seasonal water levels to determine

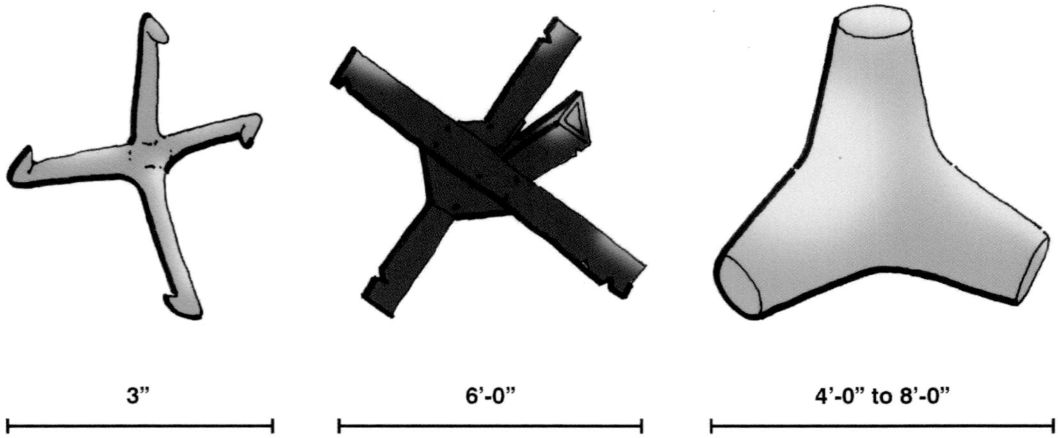

Figure 16.3: Tetrapods interlock to armour a coastline from erosion.

the minimum height of the crest and the maximum height of the base.

Select the armour unit type and size based on performance criteria, availability of local materials, and technical knowledge necessary for construction. Consider the functional and visual characteristics: should the units have uniform shapes, graduated sizes, or rubble? Should edges be rounded or angular? Can units be cast in place using modular moulds? Is a single row of armour stone sufficient or is a double layer more robust?

Install units to ensure maximum stability in a dynamic environment. The angle of repose of the units is normally no greater than 1:2. Use fill material to prepare the grade to a uniform slope or promote interlocking.

It is preferable to determine a height that will prevent overtopping, but prohibitive budgets or the need to maintain access and views may dictate lower structures. Estimate the volume of water that may overtop the structure and design a splash apron, underdrainage, and runoff channels to convey water away without undermining the structure.

Toe protection provides stability against scouring or undermining the bottom of the structure. This may include larger, heavier units at the bottom or a foundation that extends below the base of the structure.

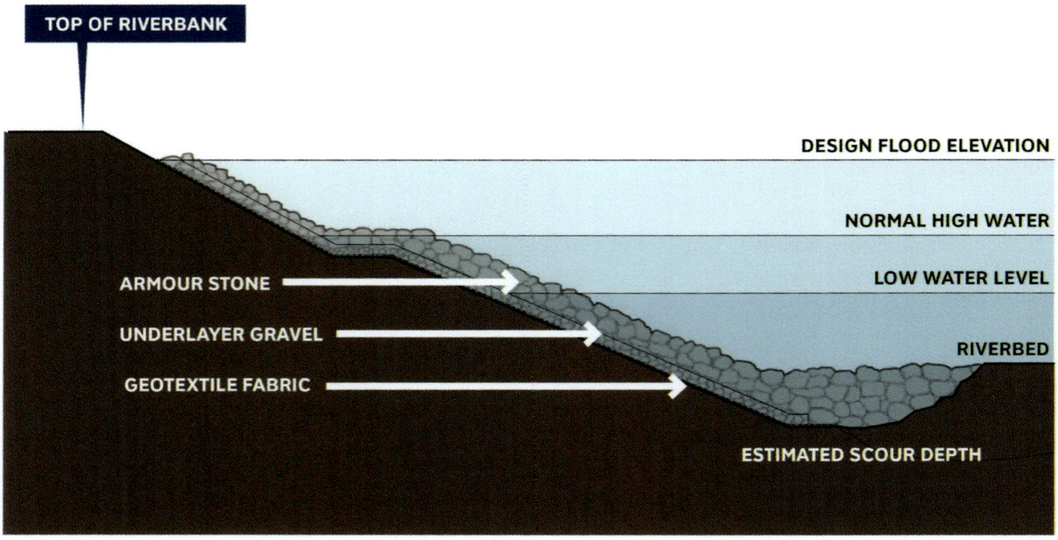

Figure 16.4: Cross-section of modular revetments (riprap) at a riverbank.

Tetrapods are laid so that the first course has three prongs resting on the grade and the fourth pointing upward; the second layer is laid upside down with a prong pointing in the opposite direction, allowing the forms to interlock. The resulting revetment is compact and uniform but exhibits great stability.

Create a filter layer of gravel, small stones, and fabric beneath the structure to distribute the weight of armour units and prevent surface water from eroding soil beneath the units, or fine soil migrating through voids.

Revetments can be combined with vegetation to improve wave dissipation and benefit ecosystem services. Vegetation growing between block units enhances the stability of the blocks, creating greater friction in the wave environment to reduce wave reflectance.[2] The vegetation attracts birds, insects, and fish to support juvenile aquatic species.

Every structure must end somewhere. Provide flank protection at the ends of the armoured structure to return to earth and tie back to the berm. This will reduce erosion and scouring.

Consider how to provide access to water for recreation and working waterfronts. Trying to cross revetments can be dangerous for swimmers, fishermen, and boaters. The units can also cause unpredictable currents around their base, making conditions unsafe for swimmers and kayakers.

IMPACT

Social: Articulated blocks cannot stop extreme events such as tsunamis or seismic waves but delay the full fury by a few seconds, which may be all that is necessary to save lives. Yoshinori Okuyama, Director General of the Sendai Bay South Coast Office, explained after the 2011 tsunami in Japan,

> *We're not trying to completely stop the waves from coming in a tsunami, that's impossible ... Instead, we want to build armor that gives people another 10 seconds to escape. That's what can mean the difference between life and death.*[3]

Environmental: The primary goal of modular revetments is to prevent coastal erosion. Articulated concrete blocks provide interstitial spaces below the waterline which serve as protective nurseries for juvenile finfish and shellfish. Aquatic vegetation may also thrive between blocks. Above the waterline, the units may harbour grasses and forbs that grow in the interstices between the blocks. Woody material should be removed if it volunteers, as the roots can displace blocks.

Economic: Modular revetments prevent erosion from waves and storm surge, and they do this very effectively in communities with steep coasts needing protection from the sea.[4] This allows commerce, shipping, agriculture, and industry to continue operations and protects the economic value of properties behind the armoured edge.

Spatial: Although modular revetments perform well in high-velocity wave environments, they lack the beauty of a beach or marsh. Crossing the revetments is dangerous, which can deter people from the water's edge. Revetment blocks form a distinct and resolute barrier between land and water.

NOTES

1 Danel, P. 1953. *Tetrapods: Conference Proceedings* No. 4. https://doi.org/10.9753/icce.v4.28
2 Rubinate, M., J. Heyworth, and J. Hart. 2020. Protecting Coastlines from Flooding in a Changing Climate: A Preliminary Experimental Study to Investigate a Sustainable Approach. *Water* 12, no. 9, 2471. https://doi.org/10.3390/w12092471
3 Baird, S. 2016. Covering Coasts with Concrete: Japan Looks to Tetrapods to Battle Elements. *Ars Technica*. Accessed at: https://arstechnica.com/science/2016/11/covering-coasts-with-concrete-japan-looks-to-tetrapods-to-battle-elements/#:~:text=Whereas%20rocks%20would%2C%20eventually%2C%20wash,instead%20of%20simply%20blocking%20them
4 In laboratory studies, articulated concrete block systems maintain structural stability in flow velocities conditions exceeding 20 ft/s (6 m/s), where failure was defined as any loss of contact between the block and the subgrade. National Concrete Masonry Association. 2010. *Design Manual for Articulating Concrete Block (ACB) Revetment Systems*. Herndon, VA: NCMA. Accessed at: https://ncma.org/wp-content/uploads/2019/02/NCMA_ACB-Manual.pdf

RESOURCE

- US Army Corps of Engineers. 1995. *Design of Coastal Revetments, Seawalls, and Bulkheads, Engineer Manual 1110-2-1614*. Accessed at: https://www.publications.usace.army.mil/Portals/76/Publications/EngineerManuals/EM_1110-2-1614.pdf

SEAWALLS, FLOODWALLS, LEVEES + BERMS

17

ADAPTATION **WATER** SCALE **COMMUNITY**

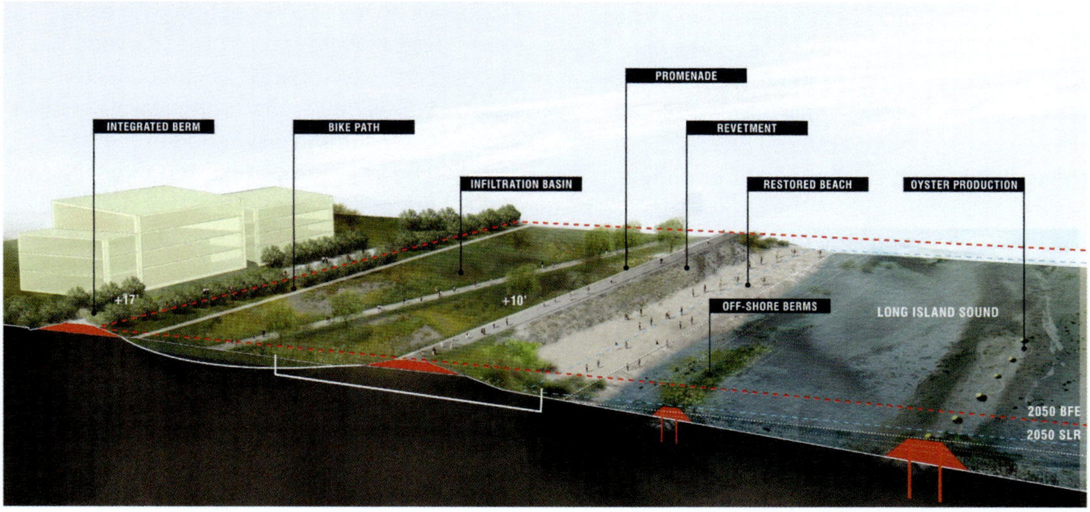

Seawalls, floodwalls, levees, or berms trace a line parallel to the waterway to protect infrastructure and development against flooding. Seawalls and floodwalls are rigid structures installed where there is limited space; they are often integrated into other engineered infrastructure such as roadways, promenades, and rail lines. Berms and levees are primarily constructed of soil mounded up to deter water, although they may have vertical walls extending higher than the embankment to resist overtopping. Their primary purpose is to resist impacts from waves, erosion, coastal, riverine and tidal flooding, and dynamic shifts in watercourses.

Figure 17.1: Multiple lines of defence include nearshore breakwaters, beach renourishment, seawalls with elevated walkways, infiltration zones, and elevated roadways to protect development. Rebuild by Design: Resilient Bridgeport. WB/unabridged/GCCDS/Yale/Arcadis.

DOI: 10.4324/9781032702964-20

BACKGROUND

Embankments are the earliest form of flood defences, utilising natural ridges built from the sediment deposited from rivers or coastal processes. Humans enlarged, extended, and encircled the berms to protect dwellings and farmlands. In the millennia before earth-moving machinery, dykes were constructed by people who dug linear ditches and deposited the soil on top of the embankment, the cut and fill entirely reliant on the strength of the shovel and the determination of the man. These flood defences are found across the globe, from the Indus Valley to the Nile River, the Netherlands to the New World.

Seawalls and Floodwalls: A seawall or floodwall is used in situations where high water hazards are coupled with limited space. The difference between seawalls and floodwalls is primarily location - floodwalls are built in any location prone to flooding but seawalls are constructed at the shoreline of waters subject to wave action. Seawalls are special types of retaining wall that extend above grade and are designed to remain stable when loaded with water on one side. Walls expected to deter water are more challenging to design than soil-retaining walls due to the dynamic forces of water which can cause uplift, impact loads, and erosion at the base. The visible extension above ground is counteracted by the weight of supporting and bracing foundations plus friction and pressure from the underlying soils.

Seawalls have a larger cross-section than floodwalls to resist wave action with extra mass. The seaward face is often curved to dissipate wave energy, as curved faces scatter waves better than vertical walls[1] which can reflect incoming waves and exacerbate flooding nearby. The complexity of reflection, deflection, and dissipation make it necessary to model hydrodynamic forces across a broad area to ensure that impacts on neighbouring shorelines are not compounded. Seawalls present a less structurally complex façade than the natural communities they replace (rocky outcrops and marsh edges) but adding methods to increase complexity and texture at the wall has dual benefits of reducing wave reflectance and encouraging benthic biodiversity. Seawalls typically fail from sliding and erosion at the toe of the seawall, making the design of the toe and interaction with soils a critical challenge.

Floodwalls are categorised by their profile in section. I-walls cantilever from the ground, supported by deep sheet pile footings to prevent overturning. T-walls and L-walls incorporate a reinforced concrete base for stability and additional piles or drilled shafts to prevent

Figure 17.2: A catalogue of common shapes of seawalls and floodwalls. From left: parabolic curved seawall, Galveston curved seawall, I-wall, L-wall, and T-wall. Vertical extensions beneath retaining walls prevent seepage that may undermine foundations.

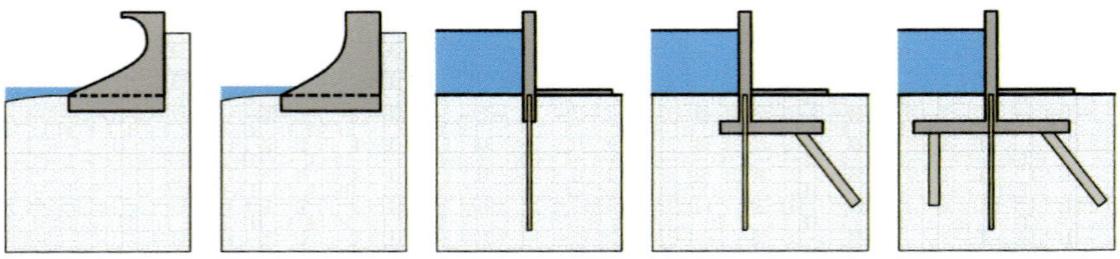

overturning. At fast-moving rivers, floodwalls must design to prevent scouring and erosion along the base of the wall. The conditions that make floodwalls necessary often have poor foundation conditions such as soft soils with fine-grained clay and silt and poor consolidation, low strength, and poor drainage. When the water table is close to the footing, the allowable soil bearing capacity is reduced.

Levees and Berms: A levee or berm is a structure with sloped sides and a flat crest. The waterside slope is typically flatter than the landward side and may feature concrete mattresses or revetments to minimise erosion from wave action. Levees may integrate flood walls extending higher than the embankment to resist overtopping. Levees can be set back from the edge of normal watercourse to provide additional storage capacity for high water conditions. Typically constructed to a consistent height, levees can have a section with a lower crest to allow intentional overtopping at places designated for flooding to occur first,[2] sparing areas with dense development or high-value installations.

The consequences for levee failure are very high. In the catastrophic events of 2005, when Hurricane Katrina broke through New Orleans levees in over 50 locations, levee failures caused tens of billions of gallons of water to spill across the city and remain in the bowl of the city for weeks. The breaches read like a catalogue of failures: at 17th Street, the levee slid away from the canal due to soft soils. At London Avenue, water seeped into sand below the wall and undermined the soils, allowing sand to flow landward with the water and destabilising the wall. At the Industrial Canal, overtopping eroded the land-side base and overturned walls. Several locations failed due to water pressure, which caused walls to tilt, allowing water to fill the gap at the base and reducing soil pressure. Other levee breaches happened when waves overtopped levees, eroding the crest and the embankment.[3]

Construction of any type of flood defence must answer the same question: what level of protection is desired? The height of a seawall or levee is determined by the community's perception of a threat, usually based on experience. Some places may prefer a shorter barrier, which offers lower flood risk reduction but can be combined with land use restrictions that minimise dwelling units in the floodplain. Other communities may opt for higher

Figure 17.3: A floodwall or a levee are the most common ways to control river flooding. Along the Mississippi River, over 3,200 km (2,000 miles) of levees have been built to a height of 4.5–9 m (15–30 feet), in some cases more than 30 m (100 feet) wide at the base. At areas where space is constricted, such as urban areas, a floodwall is preferred to save land for development.

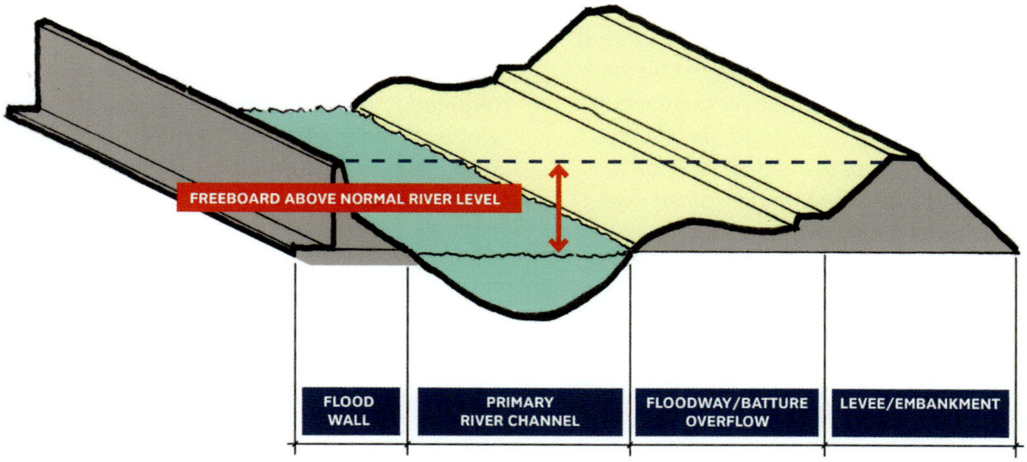

levels of flood risk reduction to protect against interruption and damage to critical facilities or economic engines.

The Netherlands has the lowest tolerance for risk and the highest standard of safety in the world when it comes to casualties and economic damage from flooding. Following catastrophic flooding in 1953, Dutch laws were adopted to protect the coastal zone against an event with a probability of occurring once every 10,000 years.[4] In the river zone, the safety standard was one chance in 1,250 years, with a 6% chance of occurring in an average human lifetime. In 2017, the laws were amended to analyse the Local Individual Risk, which is the annual probability of death occurring at each location due to flooding. The risk is calculated as the product of flood probability, percentage of the population present at the onset of flooding, and the mortality rate.[5] The €1.25 billion expenditure per year is used to protect a country encompassing 16,033 square miles, a coastline of 1,275 km, and 16.6 million people.[6]

In comparison, the United States currently spends $1.5 billion per year on flood risk management (including construction, operations, and coastal emergencies) in a country with a coastline of 19,924 km, and a population of 327 million people. The United Kingdom spent a total of £2.8 billion for flood defences between 2015 and 2021 to protect over 19,717 km (12,245 miles) of coastline and 67 million people. It is not enough. Flood losses for these three nations were substantial in 2021: the Netherlands had no deaths but €1.8 billion in property damage; the United States had seven deaths and $2.8 billion in damage; and the United Kingdom had over £100 million in damage. The annual global damage from flood loss in 2021 was over $82 billion. Floodwalls and levees are an effort to draw 'a line in the sand', but climate change is leading communities to increase flood protection measures. At the current level of investment, it seems that many nations are doing little more than drawing a line in water.

Maladaptation is a crucial drawback to structural flood protection, providing a false sense of security. Static defences can fail. More people now live below sea level in polders in the Netherlands than before the floods of 1953. The population of New Orleans rebounded to almost match pre-Katrina level in the years following the storm, despite the assessment that the flood protection remained inadequate, poorly constructed, and was missing sections that were necessary to form a complete perimeter.

KEY DESIGN CONSIDERATIONS

Consistency is critical to effective flood defences. The barrier height relative to the normal high tide plus storm surge determines its effectiveness. Water finds the path of least resistance: the gap, the crack, or the broken edge of a seawall. In the City of Fort Lauderdale, flooding from king tides regularly exceeded the City's previous requirement for seawalls to be +1.3 feet (0.4 m) above sea level, flooding some areas as many as 180 times per year. In 2023 the City increased the required height of public and private seawalls to a consistent +5 feet (1.5 m) above sea level in an effort to reduce flooding from king tides and manage projected sea level rise over a 50-year planning horizon.[7] Private property owners with seawalls, who are responsible for 98% of the city's flood protection, are required to meet minimum tidal flood barrier elevation standards and if they fail to maintain the seawall may be cited for allowing tidal waters to impact neighbours or the public right-of-way.

Redundancy is a feature of many coastal protection schemes featuring multiple lines of defence. The U.S. Army Corps of Engineers (USACE) adopted the Multiple Lines of

Defense Strategy in 2007 as a methodology for flood protection and wetland restoration in coastal Louisiana, an area with severe coastal erosion and exposure to hurricanes. This approach utilises both natural and manmade features to directly impede storm surge and establish or maintain wetland habitats to provide buffers against erosion and land loss.[8]

Failure can occur, even though coastal and river armour is intended to be impregnable. Currents scour the base to undermine its foundations. Waves attack the face with dynamic, overturning forces. High water overtops the parapet. Joints between the panels shrink and crack, granting access to a trickle, a gush, then a flood. A continuous programme of repair, reinforcement, and upgrading reduces risks for those living behind seawalls and levees.

Determine when construction of a floodwall or levee is warranted. These solutions are necessary where further shoreline erosion could cause serious loss of life or costly damage, and where other erosion protection methods have failed or would be inadequate against accelerating conditions. Flood defences may be necessary to protect concentrated populations, compartmentalise essential activities that must be protected at all costs, or confine areas that might contaminate the environment. However, initial construction costs and maintenance requirements are high. Floodwalls and seawalls can exacerbate erosion and amplify nearby flooding due to wave reflectance. They can permanently degrade habitat and reduce the deposition of sand and. Structures may impede access to the waterway for people. A cost-benefit analysis determines the lifecycle value of flood defences.

A certified civil or coastal engineer will design the floodwall to national, state, and local regulations. As part of an initial feasibility study, they determine the design storm return period, design water level, design wave height, and potential for overtopping. The study takes into account the riparian and littoral processes, investigate the soil's structural properties, determine the optimal wall material and profile to manage load conditions, and ensure no adverse effects are generated.

The coastal engineer will design the seawall height to protect against astronomical tides, compounded by additional wind effects and storm surge levels. They will also incorporate regional and local projections of sea level rise so that flood barriers remain effective over their entire service life. Increases to wave heights driven by climate change should also be considered to ensure the structure is prepared for severe climatic conditions.

The engineer will determine the location and extent of the wall. The closer it is sited to the water, the more likely it is to be affected by flooding, wave action, erosion, scour, debris impact, overwash, and corrosion. To counteract seawall damage, an increasing number of projects integrate nature-based solutions for supplemental flood protection, reinforcing floodwalls with beaches and dunes, living shorelines and oyster reefs on the waterside and infiltration zones on the landward side.

The engineer will estimate the probable construction cost. Maintenance costs are also a factor, including periodic inspections, preventive maintenance, and repair or replacement of deteriorated components. Operational costs include costs associated with its use, such as opening and closing flood gates, maintaining insurance, and providing upkeep for nature-based solutions built in concert with the seawall, such as beach renourishment or replanting.

Floodwalls interrupt the natural flow of drainage of water from land and surface runoff into the watercourse. This condition can create areas where large volumes of water are impounded, causing impacts to neighbourhoods near the floodwall. Pumps or drainage structures can remove water, or infiltration areas can allow water to be retained until it can evaporate or infiltrate the soil.

Design endwall conditions to avoid failure due to flanking. Flank protection is needed to reduce erosion around the ends. Return sections should extend past the point of active erosion and may need to be lengthened if erosion continues. Flank protection consists of sheet pilings, rock revetments, nature-based solutions, and hybrid solutions. Engineers will model conditions beyond the ends of a seawall to determine whether neighbouring shorelines will be subject to higher exposure.

The design will include a safety factor to handle rapid change. Structures must reliably withstand the highest condition for which they claim protection, but the U.S. Army Corps of Engineers requires designs to successfully withstand conditions which have a 50% probability of being exceeded during the project life. In addition, failure of the project during maximum conditions should not result in a catastrophe (i.e., loss of life or inordinate amount of property damage). Note that having a safety factor is not equivalent to an adaptation plan.

Flood barriers should be designed to adapt as conditions change. A proposed floodwall at the Washington Navy Yard has a permanent section at +3 m (9.5 feet) above sea level to manage chronic flooding that threatens the

Figure 17.4: Bio-based seawall tiles have textured substrates to invite marine organism colonisation. Screens such as these can also act as wave deflectors that absorb and redirect wave energy away from the floodwall. Living Seawalls project, University of New South Wales.

installation and two demountable panels that can be added to reach a height of +4.25 m (14 feet), a height which is expected to guard against a 500-year storm and higher sea levels. It is a now-and-later approach that mitigates the visual impact of a tall wall around a site of strategic and historic importance.

Living seawalls use bio-enhanced substrates to encourage a biodiverse marine community to colonise the seawall. Bioengineered tiles or blocks with three-dimensional roughness can be affixed to a seawall, providing habitat for species such as limpets, chitons, snails, oysters, barnacles, mussels, and algae. Seawalls with perforated panels or wave screens placed seaward from the impermeable wall can absorb and deflect wave action. These panels also recruit oysters and other aquatic species to colonise the surfaces, which contributes to further wave dissipation. Modular blocks with internal crevices and gaps can be added to the base to prevent scouring and provide cavities for marine life.[9]

Wave screens in front of seawalls attenuate waves driven by wind or a long fetch area. Wave attenuators can include fixed breakwaters, floating attenuators, and perforated wave screens. Floating wave attenuators are partially submerged polyethylene tubes filled with foam or air chambers to remain buoyant and tethered in front of a seawall. Perforated wave screens allow water circulation and currents to pass through the screen while dissipating the water and flushing the space between. Screens and attenuators require regular maintenance due to their exposure to marine

IMPACT

Social: Floodwalls and levees protect communities in flood-prone areas. Flood protection saves lives and reduces property damage; however, it can establish a false sense of security that encourages more people to live in the floodplain. Floodwalls can restrict public access and views to the waterfront, which may have impacts on equity. New flood protection for existing neighbourhoods may displace the population that lived in the area before the walls were built.

Environmental: Floodwalls and levees affect ecosystems by interrupting natural drainage patterns, accelerating coastal erosion, disrupting ecosystems, and affecting wildlife habitats. They can create barriers to human interaction with nature.

Economic: Although floodwalls and levees involve significant construction costs, property values may increase in areas where they are constructed. Land use within the floodplain may become more concentrated, expanding the potential for future economic damage and loss of life in extreme events.

Spatial: Constructing flood barriers can intensify development in formerly flood-prone areas. They may create physical divisions between protected and exposed zones.

conditions, with special attention needed to maintain coatings and fasteners in good condition.

NOTES

1 Hosseinzadeh, N., et al. 2022. Concrete Seawalls: A Review of Load Considerations, Ecological Performance, Durability, and Recent Innovations. *Ecological Engineering* 178, 106573. https://doi.org/10.1016/j.ecoleng.2022.106573.
2 USACE. 2024. National Levee Safety Guidelines: Draft First Edition. Chapter 2, Understanding Levee Fundamentals. Accessed at: https://mmc.sec.usace.army.mil/NLSP_website/NLSG_Chapter_2_Understanding_Levee_Fundamental_DRAFT.pdf.
3 American Society of Civil Engineers Hurricane Katrina External Review Panel. 2007. The New Orleans Hurricane Protection System: What Went Wrong and Why. Accessed at: https://biotech.law.lsu.edu/katrina/reports/erpreport.pdf.
4 Jorissen, R. et al. 2016. Dutch Flood Protection Policy and Measures Based on Risk Assessment. FLOODrisk 2016 – 3rd European Conference on Flood Risk Management. https://doi.org/10.1051/e3sconf/20160720016.
5 Dutch Water Sector. 2016. Dutch parliament adopts unique risk standards for flood protection. Accessed at: https://www.dutchwatersector.com/news/dutch-parliament-adopts-unique-risk-standards-for-flood-protection.
6 Policy Research Corp. 2009. The economics of climate change adaptation in EU coastal areas: The Netherlands. Accessed at: https://adaptecca.es/sites/default/files/documentos/ue_exective_summary_en_2009.pdf.
7 Bryan, S. 2024. Fort Lauderdale Is Looking at Raising Roads to Battle Rising Seas. Accessed at Physics.org: https://phys.org/news/2024-03-fort-lauderdale-roads-seas.html#:~:text=Last%20year%2C%20Fort%20Lauderdale%20commissioners,anywhere%20from%20%24125%2C000%20to%20%24200%2C000.
8 Lopez, J., et al. 2008. Comprehensive Recommendations Supporting the Use of Multiple Lines of Defense Strategy to Sustain Coastal Louisiana 2008 Report Version 1. USACE, p. 10.
9 Hosseinzadeh, et al. (2022).

RESOURCES

- FEMA P-2181, Hurricane and Flood Mitigation Handbook, Fact Sheet 5.4: Shorelines. Accessed at: https://www.fema.gov/sites/default/files/documents/fema_p-2181-fact-sheet-5-4-shorelines.pdf
- Dutch Water Sector, Room for the River Programme. Accessed at: https://www.dutchwatersector.com/news/room-for-the-river-programme

INFILTRATION ZONES, RIPARIAN BUFFERS + LIVING SHORELINES

18

ADAPTATION **WATER** SCALE **COMMUNITY**

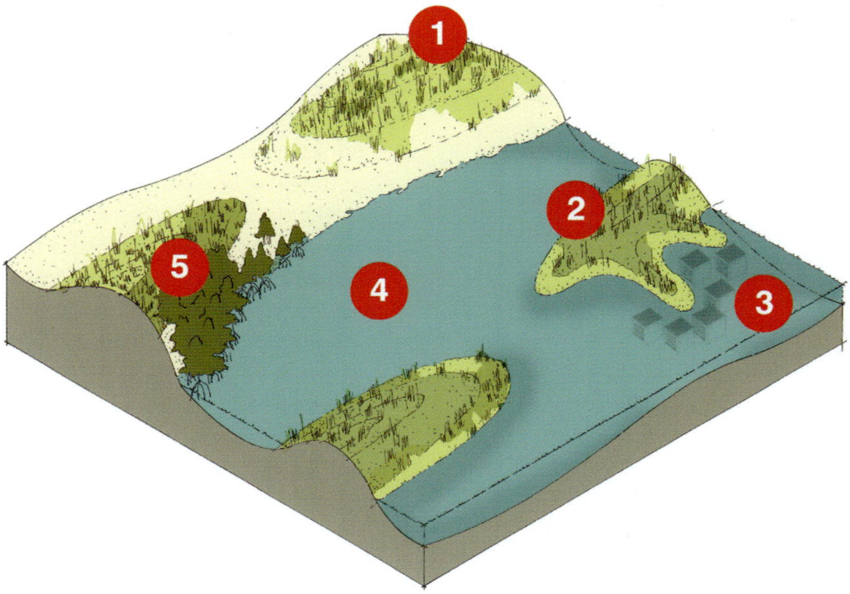

One of the primary methods for tackling flood risk is reducing the volume and velocity of wave action and surface water runoff. Infiltration zones provide extra capacity in bioswales and retention areas, add space for fluvial flooding in riparian buffers, and dissipate coastal flooding. These nature-based solutions act as sponges to protect the built environment with space for water to be absorbed into the ground, utilising vegetation to accelerate transpiration, and adding friction to slow water movement.

Figure 18.1: One of the primary methods for tackling flood risk is reducing the volume and velocity of wave action. Living shorelines dissipate coastal storm surge to protect inland development from the velocity of water. Multiple lines of defence include: (1) Beach and dune restoration. (2) Nearshore breakwater. (3) Offshore armour blocks. (4) Calm water in the protected lee. (5) Mangroves or maritime forests.

DOI: 10.4324/9781032702964-21

- *Infiltration zones* encourage rain and snow to infiltrate soils where it can be stored, with a percentage of water percolating deeper to recharge groundwater aquifers. Along coastal edges, infiltration zones buffer and absorb high tides and storm surge.
- *Riparian buffers* are green belts next to a stream, lake, or wetland containing trees and other plants that filter runoff before it enters the water to improve water quality and provide absorptive capacity to deter riverine flooding.
- *Living shorelines* stabilise the coastal edge with a sill of plants, sand, and rock, which grows over time as vegetation spreads, plants collect sand at their roots, and marine organisms colonise subtidal surfaces.

BACKGROUND

The edge between land and water offers rich rewards: the tangled roots of mangroves, high dunes fringed with sea oats, maritime forests, and swathes of grassy wetlands. In too many places, humans have stripped away this variety, building structures close to the water's edge and installing hard bulkheads and defiant concrete walls. In addition to reducing the spectacular variety of the original condition, this manmade infrastructure may be less effective against severe flooding than the original contours.[1]

Infiltrative buffers protect both terrestrial and marine ecosystems: first, by defending human settlements from flooding; and second, by preventing human incursions - effluent, fertilisers, pesticides, petrochemicals - from entering waterways. These intermediary zones adapt over time, unlike traditional coastal defence structures, forming a regenerative and biodiverse ecosystem to address flooding from minor events and critical hazards.

Riparian buffers are a transition between the extent of human control and the dynamic waterway. Buffers minimise the effect of human activities on adjacent wetlands and waterways; they also intercept floodwater and waterborne debris before it can reach developed areas. Buffers are recommended at the edge of agricultural fields to re-naturalise edges where croplands or grazing lands abut water bodies and prevent fertilisers, pesticides, and animal waste from entering the stream. In forested areas, riparian buffers preserve a ribbon of trees along waterway edges to prevent stream erosion and stop logging road debris from entering the stream. In urban environments, riparian buffers intercept litter, septic system releases, and petrochemicals from parking areas and roadways. They absorb fertilisers and pesticides from lawns and structures, keeping contaminants out of the waterway. Buffers can improve the site microclimate in adjacent fields and create new habitats along the land-water ecotone.

Living shorelines restore ecosystem services and protect from erosion in places where saltmarshes, oyster reefs, mangroves, or freshwater vegetation have been lost or compromised. These living edges are most effective at sites with low wave energy - estuaries, bays, rivers, and sheltered shorelines - rather than the open oceanfront exposed to waves. They also work best in areas without high fluctuations in tidal levels, which are subject to extreme conditions on a daily basis. As sea levels rise, these intersectional zones will continue to move inland unless they are prevented by infrastructure and development.

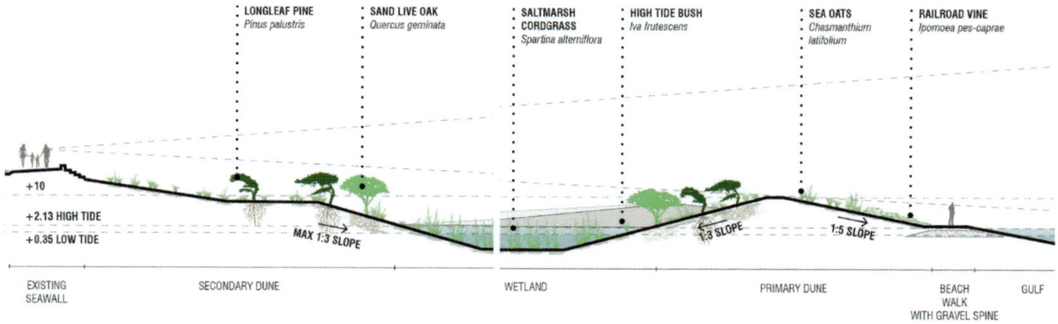

Figure 18.2: An existing seawall is strengthened by adding a secondary dune, an interstitial wetland to slow, cool, and filter stormwater, and a nearshore breakwater to form multiple lines of defence. unabridged Architecture and Local Office Landscape and Urban Design.

KEY DESIGN CONSIDERATIONS

RIPARIAN BUFFERS

The optimal width for a riparian buffer is highly dependent on local conditions. Factors that determine buffer width include the intensity of overland flow, the length and angle of the slope, the roughness coefficient of the surface, the amount of water infiltration, and the soil absorption capacity.[2] Roughness in the ground plane creates depressions for water to pond and infiltrate. The slower the stormwater travels over vegetation in the buffer strip, the longer the residence time, which creates more opportunity for vegetation to remove nitrogen and sediment and retain it to support growth within the buffer. A riparian meadow or sawgrass marsh can uptake significant amounts of phosphorus, reducing the chance of explosive algal growth.

Jurisdictional requirements for riparian buffers vary widely. One study analysed 60 communities in the United States and Canada; minimum buffer requirements ranged from 15.5 m (50 feet) adjacent to intermittent streams to 43.8 m (144 feet) at streams containing fish.[3] Regulatory standards should be considered minimum requirements while actual conditions may recommend wider buffers. To protect against flooding, the U.S. Department of Agriculture recommends buffer widths correspond to the width of the floodplain. A narrow buffer may be frequently inundated and subject to high fluctuations in flow, which can cause stress to vegetation materials. Wider buffers protect against unusually wet years, catastrophic weather, and disturbances in upland areas.

The Sustainable SITES Initiative[4] recommends minimum widths for wetland buffers depending on context: estuarine and tidal ecosystem buffer of 30 m (10 feet) from mean high tide; perennial riverine buffer of 30 m; intermittent riverine buffer of 15 m (50 feet); and palustrine ecosystem buffer of 15 m.

Where existing development encroaches on wetland buffers, ecological restoration can protect and maintain aquatic ecosystem functions. Remove impervious surfaces to restore groundwater infiltration, eliminate non-native species, plant native vegetation,

Figure 18.3: Recommendations for riparian buffers for estuarine, tidal riverine, perennial riverine, intermittent riverine, and palustrine conditions. unabridged Architecture and SCAPE Landscape Architecture.

and develop a maintenance regime that protects inherent ecosystem values.

Identify the appropriate plant species and planting density to match objectives. In migration corridors, provide a diverse mix of native species to provide sustenance for migratory birds in season. For airborne pollutant control, create a mix of heights from tall trees to an understory of shrubs and groundcover to diversify the plant structure, spatial arrangement, and biodiversity. To cool streams, maintain existing forest growth and restore tree canopies along streambanks to reduce water temperatures by 6–8°C (10–15°F). Improve biodiversity with a dense, layered forest canopy to supply twigs, branches, and leaves that form a complex matrix in the watercourse to capture organic matter as it travels downstream. This creates a variety of pools, eddies, and riffles, establishing spawning, feeding, and overwintering habitat.

Riparian buffers can divide a single, concentrated channel into multiple, smaller channels or spread sheet flow across the ground plane. This diffuses the velocity and impact of runoff, increases contact with soils and vegetation, and reduces erosion.

Design spaces and activities for people within buffer zones to add social, recreational, mobility, and educational benefits. Limit the use of impervious surfaces that inhibit absorption within the buffers. Provide interpretive signage to describe the objectives of the buffer zone and share safety and water quality outcomes.

Harvest buffer strips periodically to remove accumulated material and keep buffers in a young successional stage.

LIVING SHORELINES

Analyse the site conditions to determine whether a living shoreline is appropriate. Consider the prevailing wind and wave direction, normal and potential wave energy, the geologic conditions (soils, depth, and bathymetry), and native habitats. Determine the potential for sea level rise and other water level changes, and estimate the capacity of the system to migrate in response.[5] Some coastal wetlands can adapt to rising seas through landward migration, a process where wetlands move into adjacent upslope or upriver ecosystems in response to changing inundation and salinity. However, other wetlands are prevented from migrating by established agricultural lands, infrastructure, or urban development.[6]

Living shorelines are an environmentally-sensitive option for protection. Design the proposed shoreline using the softest approach possible in order to function as a close approximation of the natural system. A soft approach uses geotextile fabric, coir logs, sand dunes, mangroves, and freshwater or saltmarsh vegetation; instead of a hard approach using rocks, concrete, or steel gabions. Be mindful that a soft approach may be subject to damage from predators, invasive species, and human activity.

Design dunes and vegetated islands to trap sediment and accrete naturally. Shape and orient the constructed features to trap sediment from the prevailing wind and waves using chevrons, boomerangs, and similar shapes to amplify natural processes and assist with sand collection.

Utilise a diverse mix of native and adapted vegetation. Low profile plants – shrubs and

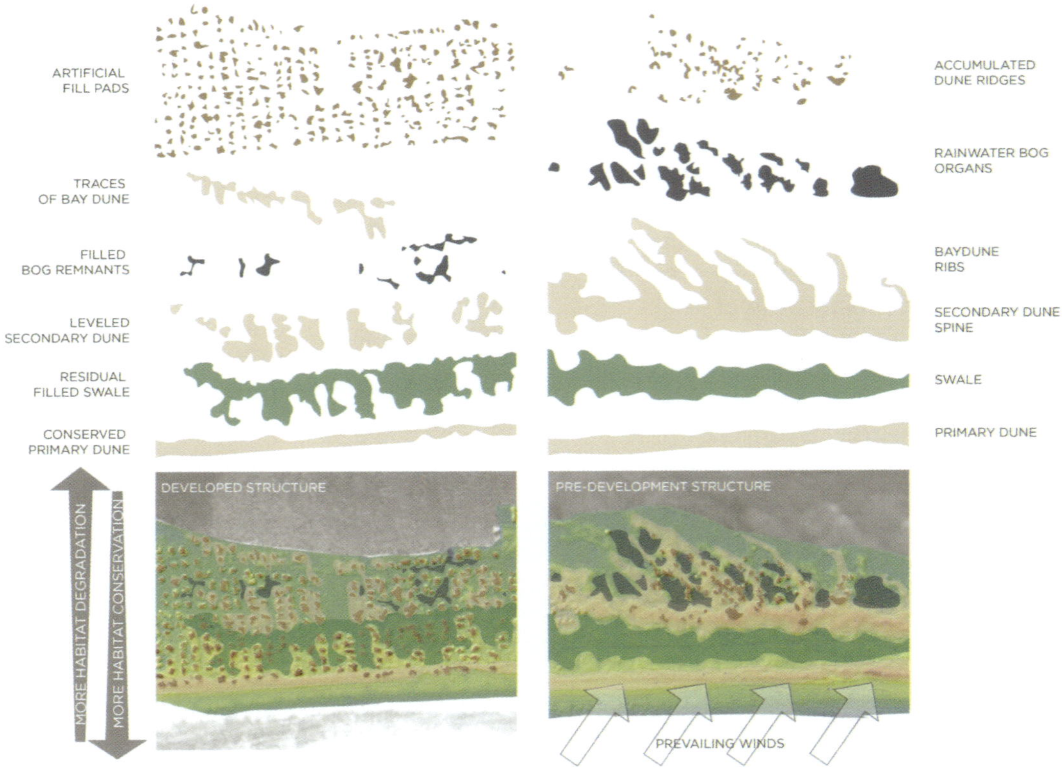

Figure 18.4: Resilient shorelines accommodate dynamic processes at the water's edge with swales and bogs between layered dunes to encourage stormwater to infiltrate, sediment to settle, and supply freshwater to plant roots. Local Office Landscape and Urban Design.

grasses - spread extensive root to form a mat of roots and high-friction surfaces. High profile plants - trees with vertical taproots and woody plants - can fix dunes in place and be planted in clusters to collect windblown sand or sediment. Closely spaced tree trunks (within 1.5 m or 5 ft) with an understory of salt-tolerant shrubs attenuate storm surge while stabilising the soil against erosion. Woody plants can be planted into existing stands of beachgrass and herbaceous plants. In high-sand environments, mix organic material into planting locations at a 1:2 ratio to support new vegetation. Consider local climate conditions to determine the best planting schedule to avoid drought, heat, and storms.

Each stalk of a salt-tolerant plant is a marsh-building mechanism that strips sediment from air or water and deposits it at the base of the plant; over time, the soil grows thicker, the plant's roots form a stabilising mat, and the marsh grows. Along coastal edges, even a narrow fringe of marsh attenuates waves. Spartina salt marshes have been shown to dissipate wave energy by 50% within the first 2.5 m.[7] Protect and support native habitat and propagate new areas adjacent to existing marshes to expand vegetation.

Map current stormwater runoff channels through the site and reshape these to provide more contact with vegetation.
A long, meandering pathway slows and cools runoff, using biological, chemical, and physical processes to absorb contaminants.

Increase roughness in the subtidal zone by sculpting parallel sandbars, berms, and troughs, which dissipate wave energy better than a flat bottom surface.

Incorporate other living materials to stabilise the shoreline until it becomes established. Sills made with rocks, oysters in gabions, mattresses, or prepared cultch provide low-elevation stabilisation at the base of the shoreline; these components accrete sediment on the landward side of the sill.[8] A 1:10 slope maintains stability and promotes healthy vegetation.

Figure 18.5: The Hancock County Marsh and Living Shoreline Project installed nearly 10 km (6 miles) of living shoreline and restored 18 hectares (46 acres) of subtidal oyster reef to reduce shoreline erosion and create marsh habitat for oysters, birds, and other organisms. This $65.5 million restoration project was funded by the BP Deepwater Horizon settlement from the 2010 oil well blowout in the Gulf of Mexico. Photo by Allison Anderson.

Oysters deliver multiple benefits at living shorelines, providing a source of protein and economic value. Oysters attach at or below the Mean Low Water line, as they cannot remain out of water for long, but accrete on a substrate to maintain the same elevation relative to sea level rise.[9] A single oyster can filter up to 50 gallons of water per day to improve water quality.

Incorporate breaks in living shorelines to facilitate water flushing, increase dissolved oxygen in water along the edge, and allow aquatic organisms to migrate freely.

Coordinate with regulatory agencies early in the design process to establish the requirements for permitting. Project compliance may require approval from federal, state, and local agencies.

Minimise impacts to aquatic habitats or animals living along the shoreline by timing construction to avoid critical times of year such as spawning or migration. Clearly mark site boundaries, existing features, and vegetation to be preserved.

Prepare the site by clearing debris and unstable trees and removing bulkheads and other structures. Protecting the site may restrict the number of entry and exit points for construction equipment. Do not permit temporary hard-surface roadways in the construction area but use beach mats or other temporary sand covers that can be removed, leaving no trace.

Provide ongoing maintenance including debris removal, replanting vegetation, and periodic renourishment.

IMPACT

Social: Infiltration areas reduce flooding and impacts on agriculture and urban development. Recreational uses may enhance these spaces for social interaction. Riparian buffers in urban environments can reduce the heat island effect and may improve equity if they pass through historically disenfranchised neighbourhoods.

Environmental: Infiltration zones improve water quality for marine and terrestrial ecosystems by removing organic matter, nutrients, and other chemicals from stormwater runoff; filtering the amount of sediment entering the waterway that causes turbidity; increasing soil permeability and extending the contact time between water and soils; and harvesting nutrients through contact with vegetation. Marshes also sequester carbon through plant photosynthesis and sediment trapping - one square mile of saltmarsh stores 675 metric tons of CO_2 equivalent.[10]

Economic: Infiltration areas protect human settlements by intercepting floodwaters and creating more space for water storage. The avoided losses from flooding and improvements to water quality for drinking water, aquaculture, and recreation can be quantified in a Benefit-Cost Analysis. More research is underway to quantify the value of ecosystem services; for example, a single acre of marsh can filter pollutants from water runoff with an ecosystem services value of $35,000 to $150,000.[11]

Spatial: Buffers and infiltration zones following waterways throughout an urban or suburban environment enhance and identify the path of the watercourse through the city and provide more opportunities to encounter nature.

Plan for post-construction monitoring to evaluate the costs and benefits of the system. Monitor biodiversity and identify the species that thrive or decline. Measure how the system attenuates waves in storm events. Evaluate the richness and population of marine life and other species that regularly use the shoreline. Monitor human use and assess impacts from littering, vandalism, and other negative behaviours. Assess structural materials after severe weather events and repair or replace as appropriate.

NOTES

1 Gittman, R. 2014. The Living Shoreline approach as an alternative to shoreline hardening: Implications for the ecology and ecosystem service delivery of salt marshes. UNC. https://doi.org/10.17615/c87p-tj13
2 Mander, U., V. Kuusemets, K. Lohmus, and T. Mauring. 1997. Efficiency and Dimensioning of Riparian Buffer Zones in Agricultural Catchments. *Ecological Engineering* 8, no. 4, 299–324. https://doi.org/10.1016/S0925-8574(97)00025-6
3 Lee, P., C. Smith, and S. Boutin. 2004. Quantitative Review of Riparian Buffer Width Guidelines from Canada and the United States. *Journal of Environmental Management* 70, 165–180. https://doi.org/10.1016/j.jenvman.2003.11.009
4 SITES is a program of Green Building Certification Inc. Information can be accessed at: https://www.sustainablesites.org/about
5 Osland, M. et al. 2022. *Science Advances* 8, no. 26. https://doi.org/10.1126/sciadv.abo5174
6 Bernhardt, E. 2022. Coastal Freshwater Wetlands Squeezed Between Migrating Salt Marshes and Working Lands. *Science Advances* 8, no. 26. https://doi.org/10.1126/sciadv.add162
7 Knutson, P.L., R.A. Brochu, W.N. Seelig, and M. Inskeep. 1982. Wave Damping in Spartina Alterniflora_Marshes. *Wetlands* 2, 87–104.
8 Currin, C., P.C. Delano, and L.M. Valdes-Weaver. 2008. Utilization of a Citizen Monitoring Protocol to Assess the Structure and Function of Natural and Stabilized Fringing Salt Marshes in North Carolina. *Wetlands Ecology and Management* 16, 97–118. https://doi.org/10.1007/s11273-007-9059-1
9 Sutton-Grier, A.E., K. Wowk, and H. Bamford. 2015. Future of Our Coasts: The Potential for Natural and Hybrid Infrastructure to Enhance the Resilience of Our Coastal Communities, Economies and Ecosystems. *Environmental Science & Policy* 51, 137–148.
10 NOAA Habitat Blueprint: Living Shorelines. 2023. Accessed 27 May 2023 at: https://www.habitatblueprint.noaa.gov/living-shorelines/
11 Ruggeri, A. 2018. Louisiana Is Disappearing Under Water - Can Oysters Save It? *BBC.com*. Accessed 27 May 2023 at: https://www.bbc.com/future/article/20180822-recycled-shells-of-louisiana-oyster-reef-protect-new-orleans

RESOURCES

- Establishment and Restoration of Riparian Buffers. Accessed at: https://climate-adapt.eea.europa.eu/en/metadata/adaptation-options/establishment-and-restoration-of-riparian-buffer-s
- Watershed Management for Potable Water Supply: Assessing the New York City Strategy. 2000. Chapter 10: Setbacks and Buffer Zones. National Academies of Sciences, Engineering, and Medicine. Washington, DC: The National Academies Press. https://doi.org/10.17226/9677. https://nap.nationalacademies.org/read/9677/chapter/12#438

ELEVATED ROADWAYS 19

ADAPTATION **WATER** SCALE **COMMUNITY**

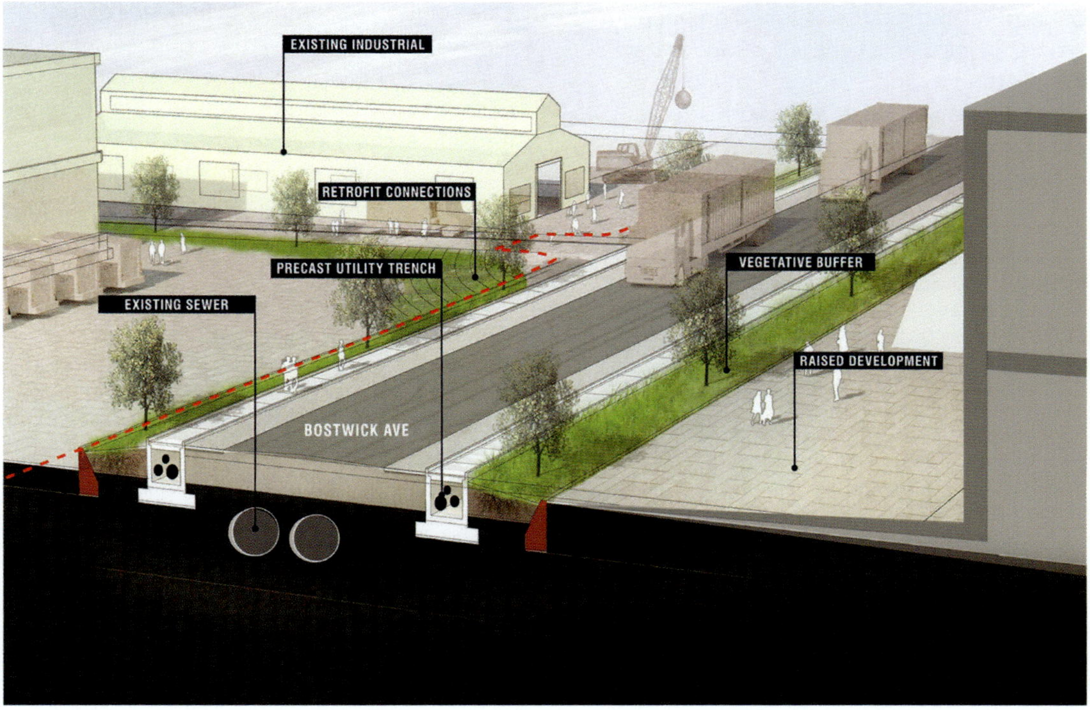

Roadways and utility infrastructure in low-lying coastal areas face regular interruptions from nuisance flooding and major flooding from storm events. Road closures impede access to school, work, home, deliveries, and emergency services, with cascading social and economic impacts to people and communities. Elevating critical roadways ensures continuity along high-traffic arteries and serves as one measure in a comprehensive flood solution that promotes evacuation, provides continuous access during and after an event, and alleviates public safety concerns.

Figure 19.1: Elevated roadways maintain access along critical corridors for evacuation, emergency access, and commercial traffic. Raising roadways and utility connections prepares for higher tides driven by rising sea levels and more intense storms. Rebuild by Design: Resilient Bridgeport. WB/unabridged/GCCDS/Yale/Arcadis.

DOI: 10.4324/9781032702964-22

BACKGROUND

Flooded roadways are killers. As little as 15 cm (6 inches) of fast-moving flood water can knock over an adult and 30 cm (12 inches) of rushing water can move a car. Over half of flood-related deaths occur when people are trapped inside a vehicle by flood waters. People tend to underestimate the force of water, but as sea levels rise, more streets are plagued by stormwater impoundment, subjected to tidal flooding, and inundated by higher storm surges. Road closures and detours are disruptive and motorists regularly dismiss flood hazards, even as campaigns such as 'Turn Around, Don't Drown' bring awareness to the potential risk.

One solution to commonly flooded roadways is elevating them above the flood elevation to maintain dry access for vehicles and pedestrians. Elevating streets ensures they will remain passable in all weather for decades, serving as critical connectors for public safety, commercial activity, and an interconnected traffic grid. However, elevated roads can also displace floodwaters to other locations, cause water to impound on adjacent property, and create new problems in harmonising connections to existing lots and structures.

A substantial component of the difficulty and cost of elevation is harmonisation with adjacent properties. Ideally, the crown of the

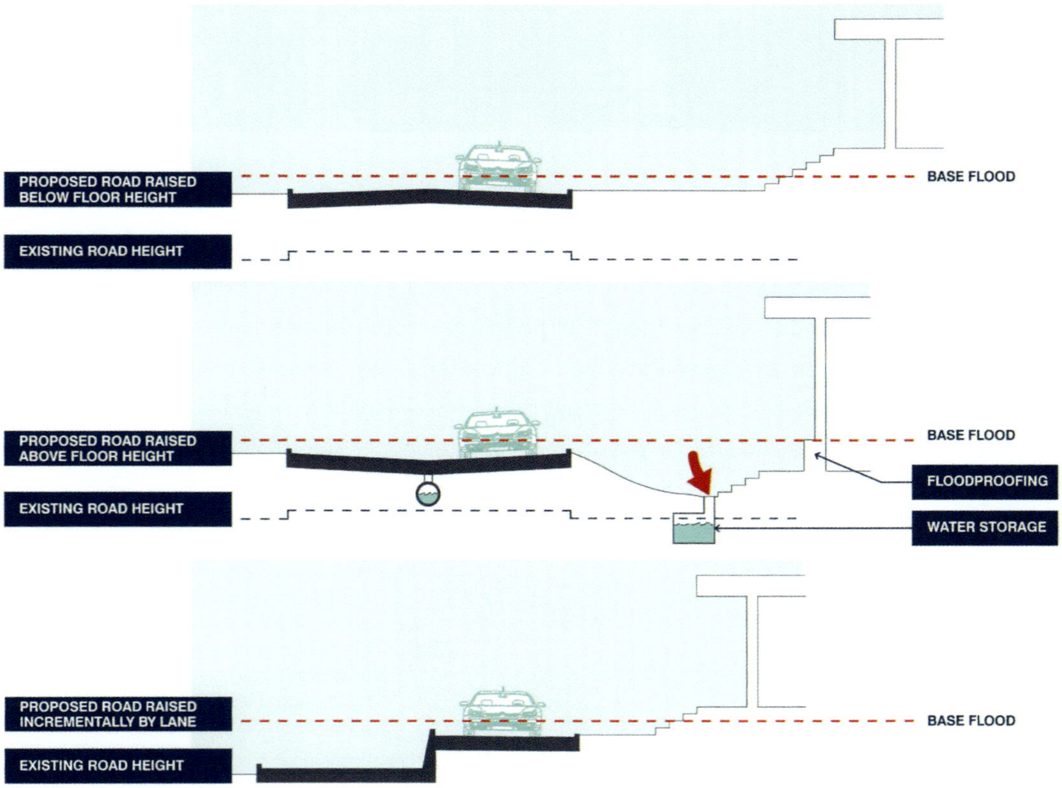

Figure 19.2: Harmonisation accounts for adjacent properties that have been built to different flood heights. Older structures may be lower than the Base Flood Elevation while recently raised homes may be built above. If the crown of the roadway is above the finish floor elevation of the structure it may impound water at the site and flood the structure. If conditions on opposite sides of the street are different, it may be possible to raise lanes incrementally.

street should rest below the finished floor elevation (FFE) of adjacent structures, allowing the roadway to flood before the buildings. The street essentially provides temporary storage capacity for excess stormwater. Buildings are constructed, renovated and replaced over time, and not all buildings are elevated to a safe flood elevation or are raised to a consistent height. If a roadway crown is higher than the finished floor of a building, it may worsen flood impacts for low-lying neighbours unless other solutions - wet or dry floodproofing, sump pumps, and other drainage improvements - are incorporated.

The difficulty and cost of elevating roadways is also increased by the need to improve other infrastructure in the right of way. Water supply and wastewater piping, power conduits and communications cables, and gas utilities are usually routed along road corridors. When a roadway is raised, these community lifelines must be evaluated for their capacity to withstand the load of additional soil, gravel, and concrete, plus extensions to utilities. Utility conditions in many communities are compromised by years of deferred maintenance and a lack of capacity. The American Society of Civil Engineers (ASCE) Committee on America's Infrastructure prepares a report card[1] every three years with letter grades ranging from A: 'exceptional and fit for the future' to F: 'failing and unfit for purpose'. The most recent reports are damning, with significant funding gaps to comply with current regulations, and even higher retrofitting costs to address flooding and climate change.

A comprehensive resilient transportation plan will decrease reliance on individual motor vehicles, mitigate climate change by shifting to zero-carbon transportation options, and ensure emergency access. Roadway elevation must address compounding risks from sea level rise, tides, and wave action, establishing criteria for near-term and short-term needs. The plan must also enable system-wide linkages to promote safe access throughout the community. It may outline other measures to reduce street flooding, such as stormwater improvements, tidal check valves, to prevent backflow of seawater into streets, and raising perimeter seawalls.

The ten criteria for road elevation developed for Fort Lauderdale, Florida by the Urban Land Institute Task Advisory Services Panel include[2]:

1. Is the roadway an evacuation route, critical connector, or serve essential public facilities? Public health, safety, and welfare are of paramount importance to community safety during hazard events and everyday emergencies.
2. Is the road within the 100-year floodplain? These areas are susceptible to higher flooding now and in the future.
3. Have adjacent buildings been damaged by flooding? This is a good predictor of whether flood damage will continue or accelerate if no action is taken.
4. Does the road experience frequent or intense flooding from king tides? These locations have a history of flooding and are likely areas of future inundation.
5. Are bridges along the roadway below the 100-year floodplain? Many bridges are old, low, or structurally compromised and should be included in the consideration of roadway elevation.
6. Have other flood solutions been installed? Stormwater improvements, tidal valves, and higher seawalls may delay the need for road elevation. If these solutions have addressed flooding intensity or frequency, road elevation may not be a priority, but if they have not yet been tried, they may be effective.
7. Are a high number of people served by the roadway? More people living, working, or using a roadway indicates these are higher priority for elevation.
8. Does the roadway serve a disadvantaged community? Vulnerable populations may have fewer resources to address temporary displacement, interruptions to work, or the ability to work remotely.

9. Do a majority of adjacent property owners support road elevation? Local acceptance of this solution is essential and local resources may contribute to funding the solutions.
10. Can road elevation catalyse associated benefits? A project may be able to leverage funding to provide bike lanes, beautification, sidewalks, or other benefits to residents.

KEY DESIGN CONSIDERATIONS

Public safety is the number one criterion to determine whether a road should be elevated. How critical is the roadway? Does it serve as an evacuation route away from hazard zones or access to critical care facilities? Is it a critical commercial corridor or a connection between neighbourhoods? Does it experience high traffic volume?

How high should the roadway be elevated? It depends on the criticality of the roadway.

Critical roadways should be established at elevations above the 100-year flood elevation to allow travel during a storm event: at least BFE +30 cm (1 foot).

Collector roadways should establish a surface above king tides + sea level rise + 20-year rain event: or about at the BFE.

Local roadways may remain below the finished floor level of flood-compliant properties: about BFE –30 cm.

Anticipate climate change by determining the historic king tide height, adding sea level rise over the extent of the road's service life (typically 30 years), and adding 12 inches for the road base, drainage, and cross-slope. Ensure the bottom of the road base is above groundwater levels plus rising tides, or mean higher high water (MHHW) for the extent of its service life.

Ideally, the roadway height should be set below the FFE of adjacent structures to provide storage capacity for floodwaters in severe storms. However, the FFE of adjacent structures may not be uniform, leading to the possibility of impounding water on adjacent properties. Use a combination of solutions to prevent flood damage: stormwater drains, backflow preventers, sump pumps, and wet or dry floodproofing to protect the structure.

Investigate buried utilities and determine their structural capacity to withstand additional fill and increased loading and replace if necessary.

Figure 19.3: In addition to reducing interruptions, elevating roadways on piers allows continuous surface water flow to prevent impoundment.

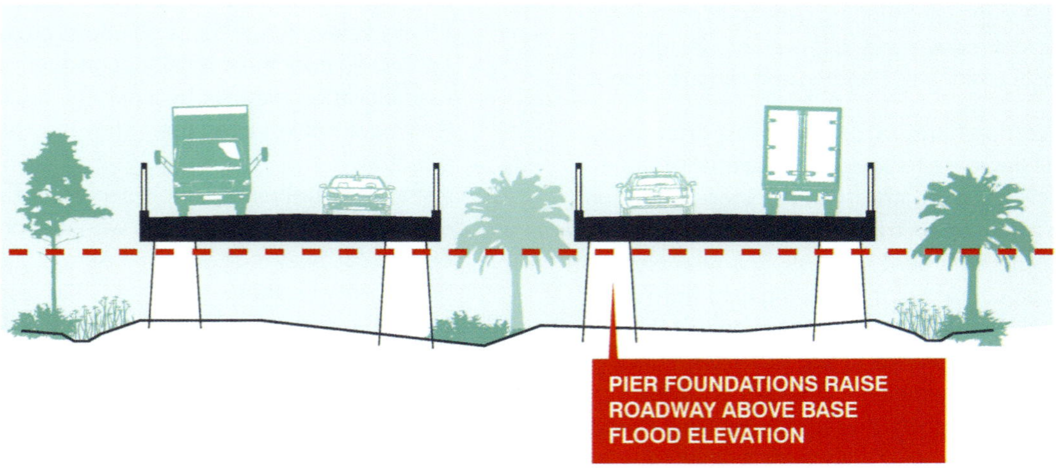

Extend and reconnect buried utilities to new street elevations. Adjust the height of overhead utilities to maintain required clearances.

Roadways may be elevated on piers to improve the margin of safety for essential traffic access and allow unimpeded water movement at the at the grade level. Elevated roadways should be built to prevent disturbance of the ground below, preserve wildlife habitats, and maintain connectivity at the floodplain. Elevated roadways are required to conform to high safety, loading, capacity, and impact standards, similar to bridges.

Engineering and economic analysis will determine the logical time to construct an elevated roadway. The threshold for road elevation may occur when: 60% of adjacent properties have been raised to the BFE; roadway flooding of 30 cm or more occurs more than 60 days per year; or another metric determined by the community. Economic analysis may suggest elevating roads in coordination with associated capital improvement projects, such as significant maintenance on roads or major upgrades to water or wastewater lines; this reduces inconvenience and interruption from multiple construction activities. A community may also keep track of the economic burden from roadway flooding: commercial activity losses, early school dismissal, and emergency service interruptions and compare these in a Benefit-Cost Analysis.

Roads can be elevated incrementally. The edge of the road with the highest exposure to hazards or the side adjacent to elevated structures might elevate the travel lane(s), sidewalks, and utilities, separating the new lanes from the original elevation with a sloped median or retaining wall. The opposite side can be elevated when the conditions warrant additional investment, but in the meantime a single elevated lane allows emergency access.

The available right-of-way (ROW) space can limit the potential roadway height and accessory uses. A large ROW can provide additional space for bicycle lanes, gentle transitions to private property, improved drainage swales, and planting a tree canopy for shade. A narrow ROW curtails many of these opportunities and makes harmonisation with private lots more difficult. Additional easements may be necessary in some areas to elevate roadways, adding time and expense to the process.

When harmonising new road elevations with existing properties, design a maximum driveway slope of 12.5% for residential properties and 10% for commercial properties, if space permits. If slopes are steeper than this, add fill materials to existing properties, or lower the sidewalks to improve driveway grade.

If lots are lower than the elevated street, they have the potential to impound water. Rainfall that strikes lots and roadways should be treated prior to release. Depending on soil and groundwater conditions, stormwater can be diverted to temporary water storage areas, allowed to percolate in infiltration zones, fed into an injection well for deep recharge, captured in above-ground cisterns, or channelled through the storm drain system to municipal pumping stations.

Elevated roads must stabilise road shoulders and embankments with edge treatments including retaining walls, terraces, and vegetated slopes to prevent erosion.

Floating roadways are another option in places with intermittently flooded areas or areas permanently subjected to floodwater. Standard components of a floating roadway include: modular pontoons, typically aluminium or steel boxes filled with polystyrene foam; a roadway platform of wood, metal grate, or concrete planks fastened to the pontoons; anchors, piles, or mooring lines to stabilise the roadway; and approach ramps that manage changes in relative height from dry land to the roadway height. More flexible than bridges in adjusting to changes in water levels, floating roads can be quickly assembled for emergencies, then demounted and reassembled elsewhere.

Road elevation is typically the solution of last resort due to cost, complexity, and difficulty. Paradoxically, having a larger number of adjacent properties can make elevation more economical, as higher property taxes and more owners can support the costs. For this reason, it is essential to consider road elevation and other transportation improvements in conjunction with land use planning as higher density and traffic may improve the Benefit-Cost Analysis of elevating roadways.

IMPACT

Social: Roadways are community lifelines to maintain connectivity and access essential services. Inundated roads isolate neighbourhoods and interrupt school and work schedules; extended interruptions can cause displacement and relocation, disrupt social networks, and lead to economic instability. Engaging local residents in the planning process can mitigate some negative impacts and make sure local concerns are addressed.

Environmental: Elevated roadways can alter drainage systems, affect ecosystems, and impound floodwater. Environmental justice considerations are essential to ensure that vulnerable communities and sensitive habitats are not disproportionately affected by the consequences of road elevation.

Economic: Elevated roadways affect property values in both positive and negative ways. Properties near elevated roads risk fewer interruptions to access, potentially increasing their value. Low-lying properties adjacent to elevated roads may flood more often, negatively affecting their value and exacerbating disparities.

Spatial: Elevated roadways may require additional ROW space to harmonise with adjacent properties. In some cases, this may require displacement of existing structures, with economic and social consequences.

NOTES

1 Report Card for America's Infrastructure. https://infrastructurereportcard.org/
2 ULI Advisory Services Panel. 2024. Building a Resilient Fort Lauderdale: Developing Criteria for Road Elevation. Accessed at: https://knowledge.uli.org/en/videos/2024/uli-panel-presentation-fort-lauderdale-fl

RESOURCES

- Jacobs Engineering. 2020. Road Elevation Strategy and Neighborhood Project Prioritization, City of Miami Beach, Florida. Accessed at: https://www.miamibeachfl.gov/wp-content/uploads/2020/01/Jacobs-Engineering-Final-Presentation-Tasks-2-3.pdf
- ULI Advisory Services Panel. 2024. Fort Lauderdale Florida: Building a Resilient Fort Lauderdale: Developing Criteria for Road Elevation. Accessed at: https://www.fortlauderdale.gov/home/showpublisheddocument/85580/638659041083030000

RECONNECTING WATER 20

ADAPTATION **WATER** SCALE **SITE**

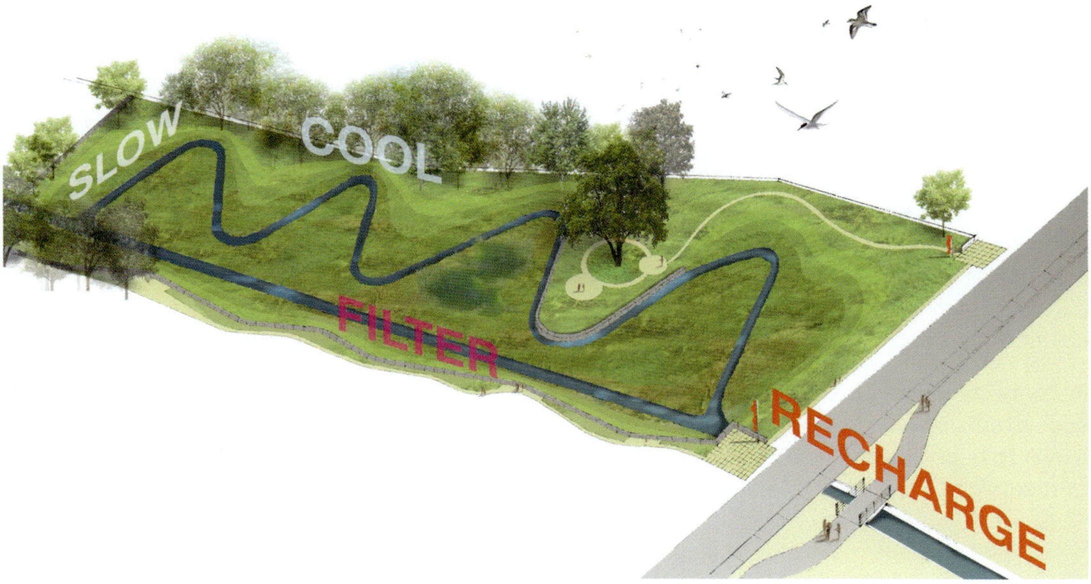

Few, if any, waterways remain in a pristine, natural state. Humans have imposed barriers to prevent water from moving naturally: directing rivers through culverts, burying them beneath roadways in slender pipes and into hard concrete channels to thwart meandering, detaining them in dams. At a localised scale, disconnected floodplains interrupt the natural functions of the watershed and impede hydrologic flow. Barriers - culverts, pipes, channels, and dams - impound water and create conditions that exacerbate flooding. Daylighting and reconnecting waterways eliminates the constrictions formed by channels, pipes, and culverts, allowing a previously confined stream more room to flow and pool, and slows water velocity to reduce flood risks for downstream communities.

Figure 20.1: Renaturalising floodplains and rivers creates meandering channels with shade and vegetation to slow the velocity of water, cool runoff temperatures, and filter contaminants before release. This approach reduces the rate of flow to larger channels that may be overwhelmed with runoff and allows water to be released slowly once the risk of flooding has passed.

DOI: 10.4324/9781032702964-23

BACKGROUND

Urban areas depend on freshwater sources for drinking water, but as cities develop roadways, infrastructure, and buildings, waterways are redirected, channelised, or buried to create more valuable land space. Changes in precipitation from climate warming are straining the limits of these confined systems, causing overflows into areas that were once broad floodplains but are now residential and commercial neighbourhoods. Increases in impervious surfaces require more infrastructure to control floods and protect development, in a vicious circle. Reconnecting and daylighting natural streambeds and floodplains are solutions to reduce urban flooding.

Reconnecting water is critical to healthy ecosystems. A wide floodplain allows a river to deposit water, sediment, and nutrients into the alluvial zone in support of healthy ecosystems. A wider floodplain also accommodates spatial changes and periodic realignments of waterways without having to relocate infrastructure and people. Reconnection involves removing or retrofitting the infrastructure that disengaged the river from the floodplain or created barriers to free flow. Droughts caused by climate change are likely to become more severe in many regions, and the impacts are exacerbated where impervious surfaces interfere with the floodplain's capacity to recharge aquifers.

Natural and renaturalised floodplains offer benefits beyond flood protection for communities: for example, a restored

Figure 20.2: McCoy's Creek recreation and restoration plan in Jacksonville, Florida, reconnects the channelised river to the floodplain, allowing the river to meander through a re-vegetated plain to improve stormwater capacity and water quality. SCAPE Landscape Architecture.

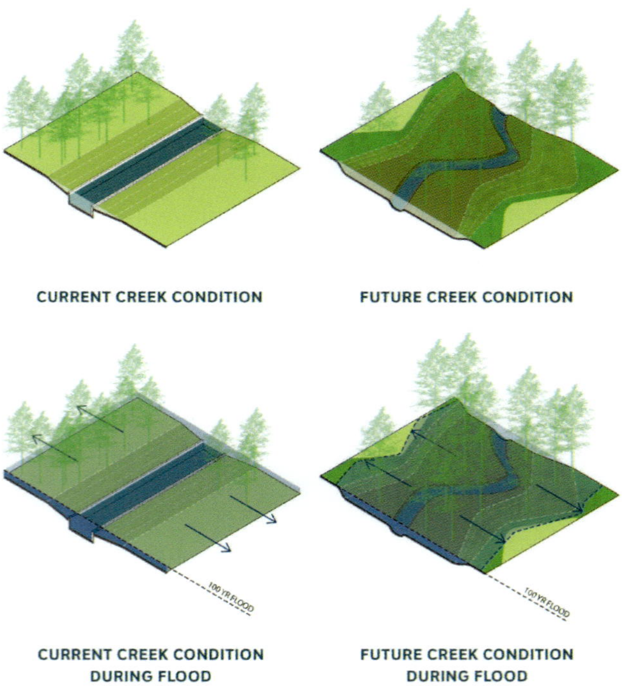

streambed allows stormwater to infiltrate the soil and recharge the aquifer. Plants within the waterway filter pollutants and collect sediment to improve drinking water quality; improved water quality requires less treatment for human consumption. Renaturalisation also supports fish and wildlife, provides a variety of habitats for spawning and juvenile development, and attracts food sources, invertebrates, amphibians, and other creatures. Improvements in the watershed divert stormwater from urban systems, which can otherwise overflow into wastewater collection, requiring additional treatment or causing accidental sewage releases.

Daylighting waterways at a site enhances urban revitalisation and attractiveness, benefits commercial areas by creating active outdoor spaces, and increases property values in the vicinity. Restoring urban waterways reconnects adults with the historic landscape condition and introduces children to nature in the city. These projects create recreational space, urban greenways with bike trails and walking paths, and blueways for kayaking, tubing, and wild swimming.

KEY DESIGN CONSIDERATIONS

RECONNECTION

An ecologically functioning floodplain depends on four elements that are essential to produce a web of complex interactions and processes.[1] Is flowing water able to access the floodplain? Is the river channel large enough support both high and low flows? Does the floodplain have adequate space to accommodate all possible stage of inundation? Are there diverse habitat conditions? Identify the condition of each of the four floodplain functions and determine how to enhance the missing attributes.

A reconnected floodplain invites frequent, seasonal overflows to catalyse sediment deposition, recharge groundwater, increase healthy vegetation, and support the food web. Remove obstacles - levees, groins, roadways, buildings, fences, and infrastructure - within the floodplain to encourage the free movement of water and activate the floodplain with each flood pulse. Set levees and other lines of flood protection back from river channels to increase flood capacity. Where levees are no longer necessary, breach segments or remove vertical embankments.

Consider flood bypass areas to accommodate floodwaters in wet seasons and support ecosystems. Provide a notched weir or designated overflow in the channel edge to safely divert water to safe detention areas or alternate waterways.

Structural diversity leads to biological diversity. Establish new features within the floodplain by enhancing log jams and allowing woody debris

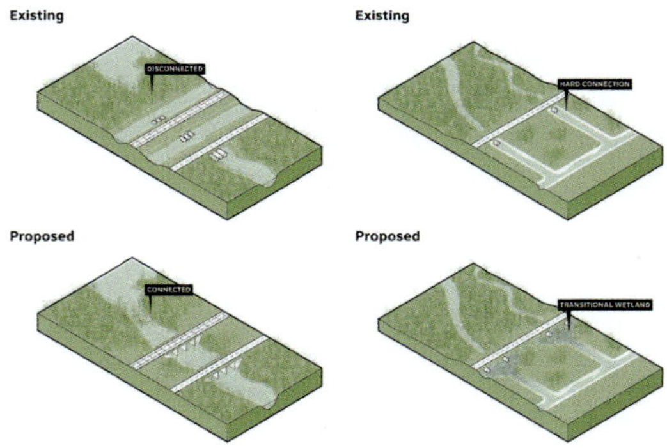

Figure 20.3: Instances where lines of infrastructure cross waterways should be designed to minimise hydrologic disruption. Left: Causeways and precast concrete box culverts are preferable to pipes because they allow more hydrological and ecological connectivity through the crossing. Right: Pipe connections can become bottlenecks for water but an alternative strategy is to allow the water to spread in a transitional wetland and divert it to forested areas for filtration and sheet flow. unabridged Architecture and SCAPE Landscape Architecture.

to remain in-stream. Create topographic diversity with small depressions and hills to mimic a variety of microclimate conditions.

Where high-velocity flows are concentrated, such as at culverts that must remain, transform channels into transitional wetlands to diffuse the flow and allow water to spread more evenly. This can be accomplished by excavating wet basins or level spreaders, which dissipate point flow into sheet flow. A rock or grass channel distributes stormwater across a broad area, where the length of the channel depends on the type of vegetation. Thick ground cover needs 13 linear feet for every 1 cubic foot per second to reduce erosion and a forested buffer needs 65 linear feet for every 1 cubic foot per second to allow stormwater to infiltrate.[2]

Paved paths and trails should be carefully planned not to conflict with floodplain habitats or infiltration. Do not use wood treated with chemicals that are toxic to aquatic life. Use unconsolidated trail surfaces. Design trails to follow the existing grade and avoid steep slopes and washouts. Remove as little of the existing vegetation as possible and weave trails around specimen trees, boulders, and other features.

DAYLIGHTING

Stream restoration should enhance the stream to 'the least degraded and most ecologically dynamic state possible given the regional context'.[3] A restored stream has a pervious streambed to allow infiltration and reduce 'flashier' hydrographs (more frequent and large events with extreme high and low flows).

In ideal conditions, restored streams can be reestablished to follow the original contours of the channel but there may be places where development is in the way, requiring a new path. Only manmade channels follow straight lines, while natural channels meander, braid, and curve in complex geometries. This animated geometry stores more water than a linear channel and also requires more space; the restoration process may necessitate the acquisition of open space to create a dynamic, healthy river that is self-sustaining and resilient to external disturbance.

A dynamic and ecologically healthy system is varied in biological abundance and distribution, with a composition that adapts to changes over time. The channel shape and configuration should respond to natural variability and seasonal cycles. Proposed waterway hydrology and geomorphology may reference prior conditions or relatively undisturbed sites near the site.

Daylighting reconnects fragmented habitat corridors, giving resident and migratory species contiguous pathways to travel between hunting areas, dens, food sources, and mating spots. The resulting increase in biodiversity helps species adapt to change and recover from disturbance.

Reduced mowing schedules enhance the passive restoration of the streambed by encouraging diverse vegetation, including grasses, sedges, ground covers, and herbaceous plants. Allow vegetation growth to give cover for insects, birds, and small mammals. Annual mowing still achieves the goal of limiting woody growth but promotes a healthy ecosystem.

Daylighting an urbanised channel is another method to expose a stream while still confining the channel within floodwalls and an impervious streambed. Cheonggyecheon is a 11-km (6.8 mile) stream restoration in Seoul,

Figure 20.4: A daylighted urban river in Cheonggyecheon, South Korea.

South Korea. A ten-lane covered expressway and four-lane road were demolished to make way for a deep channel to manage urban stormwater. The stream cross-section in the upstream portion is 100 m wide, narrowing to 20 m wide in the downstream section, with multiple access points for pedestrians to step down and explore the watercourse. To ensure water quality in this highly-visible location, the water is sourced from subway tunnels and the nearby Han River. Water depth is maintained at 40 cm deep and moves at a rate of 0.25 m/second. The popularity of the project with the public demonstrates the economic value of daylighting and the benefits to urban revitalisation, recreation, and tourism.

Cultural restoration is the practice of placing surface markings along the former courses of now-buried waterways on streets, paths, and buildings. Documenting the original extent of streams through mapping and interpretation is a first step toward raising awareness of what lies below the urban basin. Watercourse markings can be used to develop policies for daylighting and restoration.[4]

Planners must acknowledge regulatory limitations. Some rivers may have regulated flow due to water rights, hydropower, or other legal considerations that prevent high and low flows, requiring negotiation to modify or restore rivers.

Decisions to remove infrastructure to create more room for the river can be justified through a cost benefit analysis that quantifies the associated benefits, weighed against financial and other costs.

IMPACT

Social: The primary benefit of reconnecting hydrology is in mitigating flood risk. Excess water is absorbed, stored, or slowly conveyed to reduce the severity of flooding downstream. Managing hydrological flow enhances community resilience to natural disasters such as floods, droughts, and erosion.

Environmental: Improving surface hydrology can also improve the availability of water resources through enhanced infiltration; however, in very dry climates, a daylighted river may evaporate more quickly than in a pipe. Restored streambeds and floodplains improve water quality and support greater biodiversity.

Economic: A naturally preserved or restored floodplain is more valuable than a disturbed one due to the ecosystem services provided by flood attenuation, water supply and quality improvements, greenhouse gas mitigation, nitrogen mitigation, and carbon sequestration. The site of a restored stream may increase property values and offer new commercial and tourism activities.

Spatial: Increasing the area reserved for floodplains in urban areas equates to more open space, with accompanying benefits. Access to natural spaces improves physical and mental well-being, and at the site, can integrate blue and green infrastructure with the building.

NOTES

1 American Rivers. 2016. Reconnecting Rivers to Floodplains: Returning Natural Functions to Restore Rivers and Benefit Communities. Accessed at: https://www.americanrivers.org/wp-content/uploads/2016/06/ReconnectingFloodplains_WP_Final.pdf

2 North Carolina State University and North Carolina A&T State University Cooperative Extension Program. Urban Waterways: Level Spreaders: Overview, Design, and Maintenance. Accessed at: https://chesapeakestormwater.net/wp-content/uploads/2022/07/3272-3.pdf

3 Palmer, et al. 2005. Standards for Ecologically Successful River Restoration. *Journal of Applied Ecology*. https://doi.org/10.1111/j.1365-2664.2005.01004.x

4 American Rivers. 2016. Daylighting Streams: Breathing Life into Urban Streams and Communities. Accessed at: https://www.americanrivers.org/wp-content/uploads/2016/05/AmericanRivers_daylighting-streams-report.pdf

RESOURCES

- European Environment Agency Report No 24/2019. Floodplains: A Natural System to Preserve and Restore. Accessed at: https://
- www.eea.europa.eu/publications/floodplains-a-natural-system-to-preserve-and-restore
- Regeneration: Wildlife Corridors. Accessed at: https://regeneration.org/nexus/wildlife-corridors#:~:text=Today%2C%20wildlife%20habitats%20are%20becoming,species%20room%20to%20move%20naturally

THE ELEVATED COMMONS

21

ADAPTATION **WATER** SCALE **SITE**

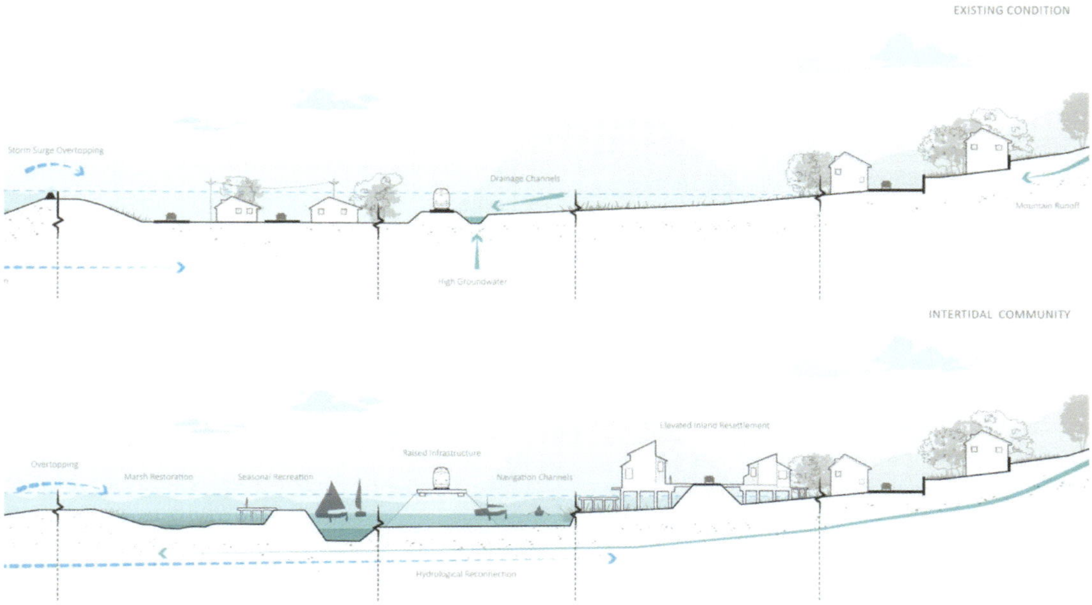

Persistent flooding affects an increasing number of communities, interrupting the movement of people and supplies and preventing emergency access. In periods of flooding, an elevated walkway is a flood-adaptive asset, connecting individual structures to one another for communal support and to safe ground for emergency access and supplies. In a dense urban fabric, an elevated walk links residences across property lines so narrow lots can share vertical circulation that won't fit on individual lots. At larger structures, raised plazas provide alternative entry and exit points above the waterline and host activities along the promenade. An elevated path allows occupants to circulate, evacuate, or obtain supplies during inundation but an elevated common space accommodates activities, social gathering, and exchange. If grade level networks are no longer reliable due to persistent flooding, architects must work to recreate vitality, inclusion, and interest at the raised level.

Figure 21.1: Sited on stilts above the floodplain, structures are connected to an elevated intertidal commons that allows residents unhindered access during flood conditions. Beyond Retreat: Occupying the Intertidal Edge, Megan Spoor.

DOI: 10.4324/9781032702964-24

BACKGROUND

A rapid rise in the extent of flooding makes it impractical to relocate all affected residents and buildings before rising sea levels become persistent or permanent. Transforming existing buildings into flood-resistant structures may require decommissioning the grade level or elevating the structure so that primary entrances and exits discharge above floodwaters to mitigate disruption. The comfort of knowing there is an alternative pathway to safety can reduce the mental and physical stresses from living with flood conditions. A well-connected urban environment enhances mobility at all times of day and night, and in all seasons, independent from tides and flooding.

In places with perennial flooding where access is interrupted several times a week, elevated walkways are necessary community lifelines that extend neighbourhood viability. Elevated walkways can create inundation districts where clusters of structures are elevated on piers and connected to one another with walkways, canals, and elevated transit lines. This releases the ground plane from having an impervious cap and restores ecological services to manage intermittent flooding, intercept storm surge, produce food, remediate pollution, sequester carbon, and generate energy.

Designing the elevated commons must solve two distinct problems: decommissioning the first level and creating a continuous elevated path with at least one endpoint above the waterline. Both issues must navigate complex legal, regulatory, and transportation restrictions.

Figure 21.2: Connecting houses with elevated walkways promotes cooperation with neighbours across site boundaries to share stairways and elevators. Mississippi Renewal Forum, Gary Justiss.

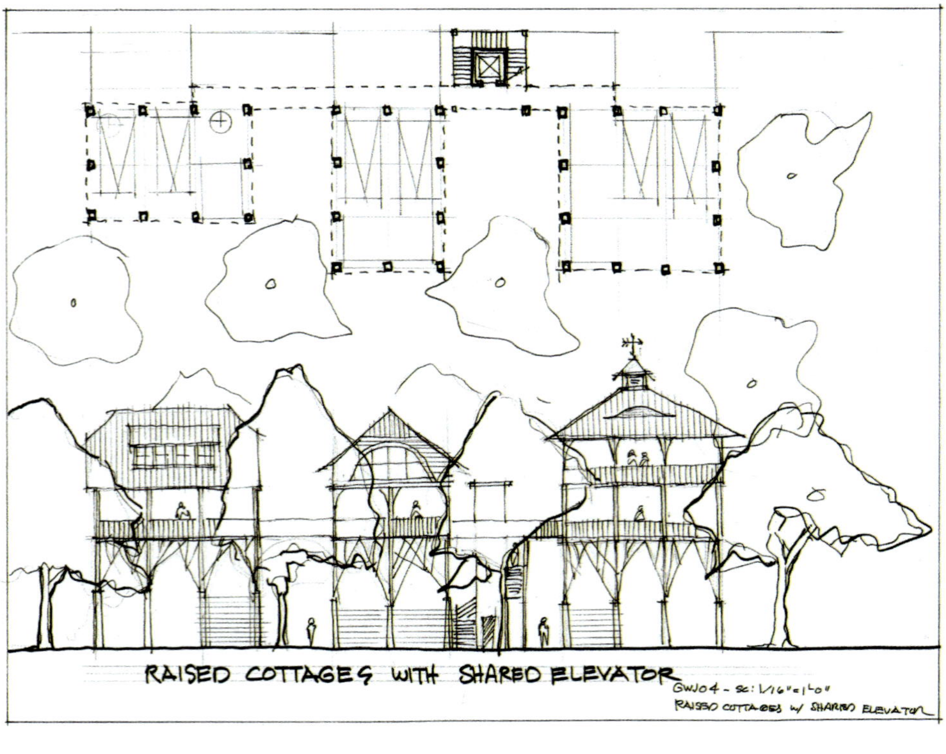

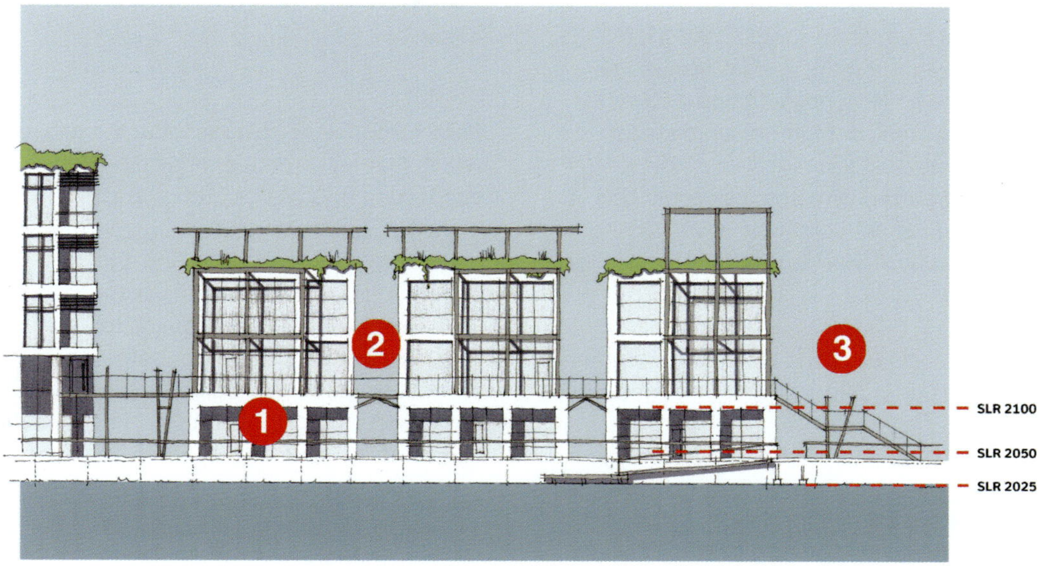

Figure 21.3: Elevated walkways connect structures to each other and to safe access points. (1) The grade level is decommissionable when the water rises, inviting movable items to activate the public frontage. (2) A continuous elevated walkway links to (3) multi-level connections to the grade, accommodating a range of water height.

KEY DESIGN CONSIDERATIONS

DECOMMISSIONING THE FIRST LEVEL

Remove walls and other barriers that might damage the structural frame in a flood event. Deconstruct walls and finishes and salvage for reuse if possible. If screening the area below the flood elevation is desired, use louvers or flood vents that permit water to equalise on both sides.

Strengthen foundations to support the structure against increased loads and dynamic forces generated by water such as storm surge, standing water, scour, waterborne debris, and high-velocity wakes. Disengaging the floor slab from vertical columns may be required to prevent dynamic load from being transferred throughout the frame. A structural assessment can determine if additional bracing or reinforcing is required.[1]

If steel or other materials susceptible to corrosion will be exposed, finish with high-performance coatings or replace with long-life materials. Create a plan for ongoing maintenance to maintain structural integrity.

Water can damage concrete by affecting the spacing of cement grains, which are forced apart when water is present; after the water dries, the remaining space is filled with air, reducing the structural integrity of the concrete. If saltwater covers concrete that was not designed for the marine environment, magnesium sulphate present in seawater reacts with calcium hydroxide and hydrated calcium aluminate to mount a chemical attack on concrete structures. Foundations designed for marine inundation should have a low water-to-cement ratio, special admixtures, air-entraining elements, additional cover for reinforcing steel, or high-pressure steam cured elements. Existing concrete piers can be retrofitted with epoxy-filled jackets supplemented with cathodic protection to reduce chemical reactions at reinforcing steel.

Move all mechanical and electrical equipment above the ground floor to ensure continuous operation.

Install waterproofing, insulation, and soffits at the underside of the new lowest inhabited floor to prevent moisture intrusion from below.

Remove asphaltic pavements at the ground, which may leach petrochemicals when exposed to floodwater. Design the ground plane to absorb and store water, promoting infiltration using porous paving and vegetation. Plant trees to shade the raised walkways. Use the ground plane for functions that can tolerate periodic (or permanent) inundation, such as food production, recreation, energy generation, bioremediation, and temporary functions.

Figure 21.4: Communal spaces elevated above grade level can help communities adapt to sea level rise and flooding. Salty Urbanism, Brooks + Scarpa/Florida Atlantic University/University of Southern California.

CREATING THE ELEVATED COMMONS

Accessibility is the most important consideration. Walkways should invite use by the entire community: elderly, children, wheelchairs, strollers, and walkers. Include designated lanes for scooters and bicycles. The clear walking zone should be at least 1.5 m (5 feet) wide in low density areas, 1.8 m (6 feet) in medium density areas, and 2.5 m (8 feet) at public facilities. Walkways can grow wider to accommodate railings, furniture, frontage, and activity zones, similar to traditional complete streets.

Raised walkways also provide a solution for universal access to elevated units. Many single-family lots in urban areas are too narrow to build individual ramps in the front or side yard, but shared ramps can be placed in the public right-of-way or at easements. The cost of building stairs and elevators can be amortised across multiple households, making access more affordable.

Plan the walkway to allow space for a variety of activities. Integrate complementary mixed uses where appropriate: retail and food services, recreation, shade, seating, and gardens.

At least one end of the walkway should connect to safe ground that is not subject to inundation. Provide stairs and ramps at regular intervals along the length for access at critical points, street intersections, and endpoints. Ramps and stairs both provide variable access for different levels of inundation but must be maintained to prevent slippery surfaces caused by algal growth, sediment deposits, and marine debris that may be left from rising and falling tides.

Locate elevators beyond flood-prone areas where the travel distance is reasonable. Equip elevators with controls to prevent cabs from descending into floodwaters. Use a hole-less hydraulic elevator and ensure that machine rooms are located above the flood level. Enclose elevators to reduce maintenance and weathering.

Create distinctions at entries from the walkway with materials, screens, overhead planes, or physical barriers to distinguish public from private zones. The traditional architectural language of porches and stoops may be lost but the concept of creating transitional spaces remains important for identity and privacy.

Use durable materials that maintain walkability in wet, freezing, or intense heat conditions: non-slip tile, rubberised coatings, recycled concrete planks, or FSC-certified hardwoods. Materials at elevated decks should have extended lifecycles to reduce maintenance and the need for replacement.

Open-jointed decks or grates may be used for private sections to allow sunlight to penetrate and maintain vegetation below. Alternatively, walkways elevated at least 1.8 m (6 feet) above grade allow sunlight to reach beneath a solid deck so vegetation can grow.

Walkway foundations should be constructed with materials designed to withstand the marine environment and prevent leaching chemical that affect aquatic ecosystems. The treated wood preservatives Ammoniacal Copper Zinc Arsenate (ACZA) and Chromated Copper Arsenate (CCA) have the lowest aquatic toxicity of any metal-arsenate preservatives.[2] Treated wood piers exposed to water can be sealed with an inert wrapping or coating (industrial-grade plastic, fiberglass, polyurea, or epoxy coating) to encapsulate the treated wood and minimise leaching of preservatives. Coatings should extend from below the waterline to above the high-water level. Avoid the use of coal tar epoxy coatings, as they leach polycyclic aromatic hydrocarbons, with high toxicity for aquatic life.

Take advantage of shade provided by trees at grade level or in raised planter boxes to reduce heat on elevated walkways. Provide vegetated areas along the walkway with native plants and plants adapted to container growing conditions: drought-resistant trees, grasses, shrubs, and wildflowers. Elevated gardens are the equivalent of a green roof system, requiring a waterproof membrane, drainage mat, gravel, subsoil, mulch, and mesh to prevent soil erosion from wind.

Collect rainwater from walkways and neighbouring roofs and funnel into planting beds or cisterns for irrigation and reuse.

Illuminate pathways with low-level LEDs to invite robust nighttime use. Conform with dark sky guidelines, guidelines for glare prevention, and reducing light trespass into dwelling units.

IMPACT

Social: Elevated walkways improve safety and provide emergency access in flood events. They enhance liveability, create space for social interaction, and invite neighbours to get to know one another. This flood adaptative infrastructure can reduce the need to evacuate during floods.

Environmental: Relieving the ground plane of impervious surfaces devoted to circulation assists in reconnecting hydrology. Elevated walkways promote better groundwater infiltration, potentially reducing flood events.

Economic: Raised paths permit uninterrupted access and commerce when the ground plane is compromised by flooding. Although construction and maintenance costs are higher for elevated paths than grade-level corridors, they can extend the viability of existing structures in flooded areas.

Spatial: Public acceptance of elevated walkways varies, making engagement and communication about the long-term benefits important. An elevated walking path separates people from the ground and highlights the difficulty of creating vitality at two levels, the ground and the elevated level.

NOTES

1 Federal Emergency Management Agency. 2011. P-55 Coastal Construction Manual, Fourth Edition. Washington DC. Accessed at: https://www.fema.gov/sites/default/files/2020-08/fema55_voli_combined.pdf
2 Metz, V. 2019. Use of Preservative-Treated Wood and Alternative Materials for Building Overwater and Waterfront Structures. Marinas Interagency Coordinating Committee. Accessed at: https://documents.coastal.ca.gov/assets/water-quality/marina-boating/meeting-notes/Marinas%20mtg%20notes%20&%20materials%202019/May%202019%20mtg%20agenda%20&%20materials/Treated%20Wood%20&%20Alternative%20Materials%20in%20Overwater%20Structures%20(Factsheet)_Metz_May%202019.pdf

RESOURCE

- Huber, J. et al. 2024. *Salty Urbanism: A Design Manual for Sea Level Rise Adaptation in Urban Areas*. ORO Editions.

FLOOD BARRIERS + GATES 22

ADAPTATION **WATER** SCALE **SITE**

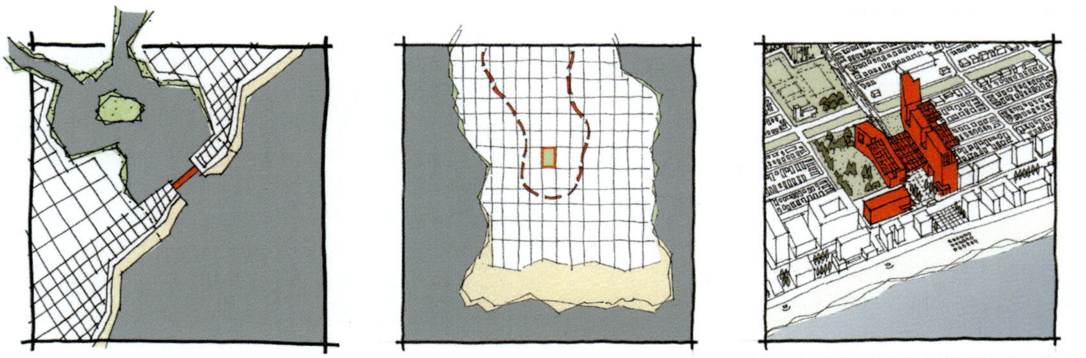

Flood barriers are used to restrict water from entering an area or control the direction of water flow. Flood barriers should be easy to deploy or have automatic operation. Temporary deployable barriers are installed when and where they are needed and removed when the floodwaters recede. Permanent deployable barriers are always in place but are moved into position when floodwaters threaten. Permanent passive barriers remain in place and deter flooding without human intervention.

Figure 22.1: Flood barriers occur at three scales: city-scale barriers protect cities and neighbourhoods, site-scale barriers surround a site, and building-scale barriers are installed at the building edge.

DOI: 10.4324/9781032702964-25

BACKGROUND

There are a variety of demountable and fixed flood barriers and flood gates designed to protect at-risk sites and buildings from inundation. Floodgates work at multiple scales scale as part of a comprehensive flood protection system: at the building edge, around the perimeter of a site, and at the city scale.

Building-scale floodgates are installed at the building edge to create a water-resistant base and minimise damage from flooding. Barriers can be integrated into façade systems so that fasteners and hardware do not detract from the building's aesthetic or impede operations during non-flood conditions. Operable floodgates include permanently-installed doors, windows, and drop-down panels. Removable floodgates include panel systems and flood logs. Building-scale floodgates use pumps and drainage to remove water that enters the protected area, and backflow valves to prevent the influx of water through pipes.

Site-scale flood barriers are installed in conjunction with floodwalls around the perimeter of a site to protect against flooding. Low retaining walls can sculpt terraced edges that weave between trees, buildings, and other site features to form a continuous perimeter but the walls must also permit the access of vehicles and people. Active barriers at access points have a mechanical component that opens and closes on demand to protect streets, driveways, and sidewalks. Removable barriers are installed prior to flood events using modular units filled with water or sand. Heavy, concrete modules must be placed by crane and are typically used around critical infrastructure and at sites where the equipment necessary to place the barriers is already available. Automatic gates deploy when water levels rise beyond a predetermined threshold; the action of the barrier is controlled by the height of the waterway, with floating barrier panels that rise along with the water level.

Figure 22.2: The Thames Barrier in London, UK, protects 1.25 million people who would otherwise be at risk from flooding.

City-scale barriers are installed to protect neighbourhoods and larger geographic areas. As part of a comprehensive flood protection system, flood barriers work in tandem with levees and floodwalls but these structures must have gaps or other accomodation to protect waterway access, roadways, and pedestrian pathways. In advance of a storm event, operable barriers are deployed to form a continuous line of defence. Coastal cities may install operable barriers to close in extreme high tides, triggered by three conditions: height of the tide, height of the accompanying tidal surge, and river flow behind the barrier. They open at the ebb tide to release water from precipitation and fluvial floods.

Large-scale floodgates come in multiple types and variations: bulkhead gates with movable or removable sections between permanent vertical floodwalls; hinged gates that rotate from horizontal to vertical to provide flood protection (MOSE Barrier in Venice); hinged gates that close like a pair of doors; guillotine sluice gates that lower into flood defence position; and radial gates that rotate horizontally (Maeslantkering in South Holland, stretching 360 m wide) or vertically (Thames Barrier in London, rising 20 m high) to protect against tidal surge.

KEY DESIGN CONSIDERATIONS

GENERAL CONSIDERATIONS

Evaluate barrier types by their robustness to resist the volume of flooding and maintain stability at a predetermined performance level. Consider a system's resistance to damage, the likelihood of localised damage (punctures or wind-blown debris) to impact the overall assembly, and the ability to repair damage while deployed.

Identify the capacity to deploy flood protection and how fast systems must be fixed in place. Where human intervention is required to deploy flood barriers such as installing gates or shields, develop a Flood Emergency Operations Plan to ensure measures can be implemented promptly. Practise deployment regularly so facilities personnel are familiar with the procedures.

Determine the type of flooding that is most prevalent or most consequential and select the appropriate system. Temporary deployable systems don't work well for pluvial flooding because the window of time to deploy them may be too short; permanent deployable and passive systems are more effective. Flood doors and windows work for any type of flooding.

Evaluate the timing of flood alert systems in the area; the earlier the flood alert, the more time is available for mobilisation and closure processes. Compare this to the time required to deploy temporary or demountable barriers, based on the organisational resources (economic and personnel), availability of the barrier, transportation requirements, and the site preparation required. A building must be evacuated when flood barriers are installed, which may affect the timing for deployment. Temporary or demountable barriers can be stored onsite if space is available but it is essential to consider the timing of deployment and potential interruptions if barriers are stored offsite.

Identify the desired protection height based on scientific predictions of tides, king tides, sea level rise, storm surge, riverine, and storm flooding. Design to allow the barrier height to increase over the service life, as sea level rise will make today's high tides commonplace in the future.

Determine the length of the barrier needed to close gaps in the flood protection. Consider the structural compatibility of the barrier to withstand anticipated loading and potential overtopping. Identify appropriate connections and end fixings, and evaluate the integrity of existing structures to serve as stanchions.

Consider the existing terrain conditions and the barrier's ability to match soil bearing capacity and conform to uneven ground. If the soil bearing capacity is insufficient for temporary installations, use systems with pre-installed foundations or permanent frames with demountable barriers.

Determine the desired alignment of flood defences and how the barrier turns corners, adjusts to adjacent structures, or navigates vertical plane changes. Can modular units define a radius, avoid fixed obstacles, or make a 90-degree turn? Select a system that matches the installation conditions.

Select flood barriers that are appropriate for the site's climate conditions. In cold climates, snow and ice may have to be cleared before an activated barrier can be closed. In environments with windblown sand, the fine grains can be trapped in the housing and cause system failure.

The authority having jurisdiction may prevent the use of temporary deployable barriers on public rights of way or installations that conflict with urban patterns. Notify the fire department prior to deployment so they are aware of limited access to the building. A flood operations plan is necessary in case someone is in the building and needs to leave.

Lightweight frame buildings may be incapable of resisting flood loads or supporting permanent barriers. At these structures, an independent, perimeter protection system may be used to protect the site.

TEMPORARY DEPLOYABLE BARRIERS

Prefabricated geotextile or PVC tubes are filled with air or water to form a dam. They are prevented from rolling with anchors; for air-filled tubes, this is a weighted skirt held in place by pressure from the floodwaters but it must be secured prior to flood impacts to prevent blowing away. Tubes are used to create continuous lines of flood protection that bend to match horizontal or vertical conditions, although they need a relatively flat ground surface to create a tight seal. Tubes are filled using an air pump or fire hydrant and are susceptible to punctures and tears (like a tyre). The units may be difficult to connect end-to-end.

Filled cellular containers are constructed of permeable geotextile fabric and filled with sand or aggregate. Some containers use wire mesh or frames to maintain a rigid shape while others are wider at the base to

Figure 22.3: Temporary deployable barriers include sandbags, open-topped cellular gabions, inflatable or water-filled geotextile tubes, and freestanding interlocking barriers.

prevent overturning or sliding. These barriers are refined sandbags, and the height of the barrier can be increased by stacking multiple containers. They adapt to uneven terrain and can use any readily available fill material, collapsing for storage when emptied after an event. However, disposal of contaminated fill material may pose difficulties; the fabric cover may absorb effluents, and frames can buckle from stacking and service loading, so potential reuse may be limited.

Flexible, freestanding barriers are made with reinforced membranes held in an acute angle position by tension straps or baffles. The cover material is impermeable, with a weighted skirt on the floodwater side to ensure stability. Although they may be susceptible to high winds prior to the flood peak, they are easy to deploy, clean, and store.

Flexible frame barriers have a rigid metal support frame covered with a waterproof fabric; the obtuse angle uses a skirt at the bottom to hold water in place. Rigid frame barriers have a similar shape but are constructed with rigid panel elements that span between the frames. Both types adapt well to uneven surfaces and are easy to stack and store between events. However, any fabric barrier is susceptible to punctures or tears.

Impermeable containers are formed with rigid plastic or polyethylene walls and filled with water or sand to stay in place. A tapered or prism shape uses gravity to resist overturning and the ends interlock to fill a gap of any size. Units are washable and can be reused many times but their rigid bottom may not conform to uneven terrain. This type of barrier requires significant storage space when not in use.

Rigid barriers come in a variety of shapes and designs, from 2-tonne precast concrete 'Jersey' barriers to hinged panel barriers with internal supports. The barriers interlock to form a continuous wall. Because they use their weight for stability, they require heavy lifting equipment to transport the barriers and put them in place, potentially making deployment more complex and time-consuming.

Horizontal flood barriers can be used to cover below-grade access points such as basement stairs, subway entrances, and window wells. The New York City subway system uses a waterproof textile cover stretched across a structural frame, similar to a window shade with a confined edge condition. The Kevlar cover can withstand 4.9 m (16 feet) of head pressure, using a fabric that weighs only 33 kg (72 lb).[1]

When selecting a barrier system, also consider also the tasks necessary in the aftermath: cleanup, storage, disposal of fill material, and restoration of the bedding surface. Include the regular maintenance and operational testing required for deployable systems. These calculations inform whole life cost benefit analysis.

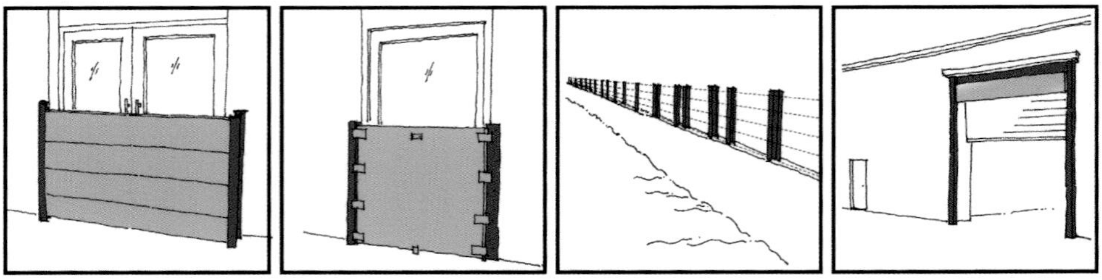

Figure 22.4: Permanent deployable barriers include systems with permanently-mounted components that can be deployed quickly, including flood log panels, door shields and bund gates, floodwalls with extension channels, and drop-down barriers.

PERMANENT DEPLOYABLE BARRIERS

Hinged or sliding flood gates are permanently installed and stored alongside a floodwall to slide or swing into place when it is necessary to complete the perimeter protection system. These gates are typically made of steel and engineered to form a seal with the floodwall under water loading conditions.

Frame and panel barriers have demountable rigid panels (or flood planks) slotted into place between posts with pre-installed foundations or permanent connections. These systems are engineered to respond to predicted flood conditions and have higher resistance to loading than temporary systems. They can be designed to increase in height by adding panels up to the height of the frame for long-term adaptation. When barriers are not in use, the base remains flush with the ground to allow accessibility.

Flood panels at doors and windows are designed to protect standard doors and windows from flooding. The metal composite panels are stacked or hinged to cover openings from hydrostatic and hydrodynamic loads, wave loads, and debris impact. They mechanically anchor into the structural frame and allow pressure from the floodwaters to compress perimeter gaskets and obtain a tight seal.

Stackable flood logs protect openings using vertical posts with pre-installed foundations or C-shaped channels mounted at the jamb, with horizontal planks that slot between the supports and interlock to form a tight seal. Each aluminium plank is typically light enough for one or two people to lift and install. This system can be extended as needed to meet future flood challenges, to the height of the vertical posts or channels. If the assembly is open at the top, allowing rainwater to get into the space between the flood planks and the building, a sump pump is necessary to evacuate water from the base.

Drop-down flood barriers are used at oversized vehicular entrances to protect standard roll-down doors from hydrostatic loading or debris impact. A steel panel, usually 1 m (3 feet) high, travels up and down along a channel mounted outside the standard door jamb. An electronic control system locks the barrier into place, with backup power to allow deployment and release in the event of power interruptions.

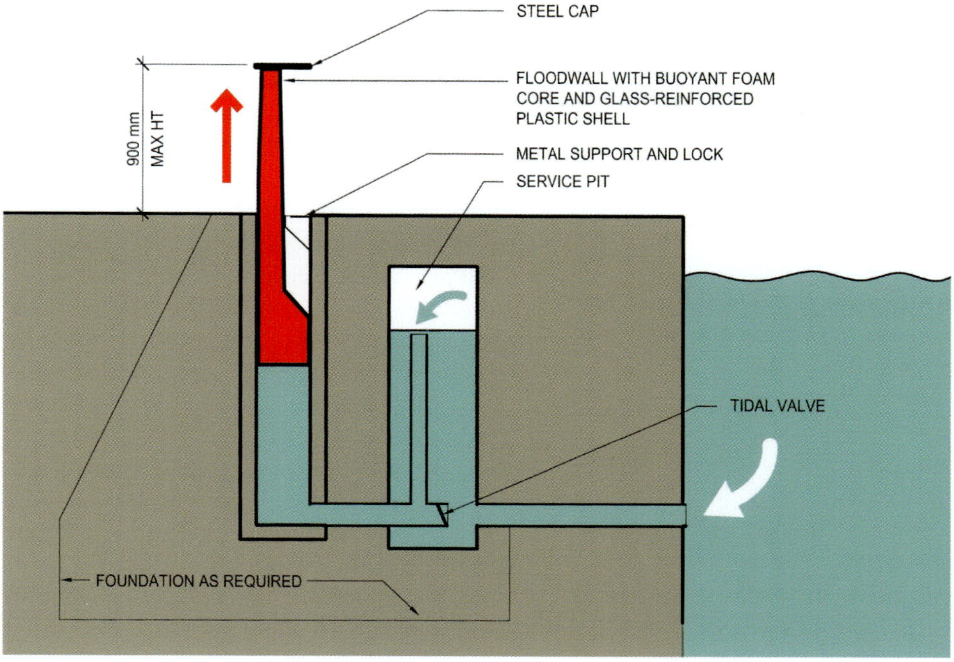

Figure 22.5: Permanent passive barriers resist flooding without requiring additional installation at critical times. A self-closing flood barrier uses floodwater and buoyancy to raise the barrier into position; when the water recedes the barrier lowers automatically.

PERMANENT PASSIVE BARRIERS

Automatic or passive flood barriers use hydrostatic pressure to deploy. Fibreglass and foam core gates can be either horizontal or vertical in orientation, using the hydraulic power of the approaching floodwaters to raise the barrier without electricity, and without human intervention. In its resting position, the barriers are stored underground with a cover panel to allow level crossings.[2] In cold climates, the flood barrier may need to be connected to a heat source to prevent snow and ice buildup.

Sectional barriers are pre-installed underground at driveways, launches, or other gaps in flood defences. These can be passive barriers to significantly improve deployment time but may accidentally deploy under unanticipated conditions, such as fire hydrant testing, with impacts to egress and emergency access. In cold climates, the flood barrier may need to be connected to a heat source to prevent snow and ice buildup.

Floodproof doors are designed and tested to protect against floodwater, typically to a maximum height of 1 m (3 feet), the standard height of dry floodproofing measures for walls. Flood doors are a passive solution that remain in place at all times, and are designed to resist hydrostatic and hydrodynamic loading, debris impacts, breaking wave loads, and wind loads. The weight of water on the steel door compresses the perimeter gasket to form a complete seal and thresholds are anchored in place. Flood doors may be single swing (outwards toward floodwaters) or paired swing doors with a removable mullion.

IMPACT

Social: The primary benefit of on-site floodwalls and barriers is protection and safety for communities at risk of flooding. However, inequitable deployment of barriers to protect high value properties may exacerbate economic disparity. Ensuring equitable access to flood protection prevents marginalised communities from bearing disproportionate risks.

Environmental: Flood barriers can impede the natural hydrological flow, disrupt habitats, prevent welcome sediment deposition, and harm aquatic ecosystems. Balance flood protection with environmental conservation to minimise negative effects.

Economic: Flood barriers are one part of a comprehensive flood risk management strategy that encourages long-term adaptation and land use planning to prepare for future flood events.

Spatial Integration: The temporary deployment of flood barriers is a stark reminder of the potential extent of flooding. Protection at the perimeter of a site can create unwelcome barriers to access and use by the community.

Floodproof windows are engineered to resist specific flood requirements, preserving views and daylighting in a passive protection system. The assembly uses reinforced framing components mounted with steel anchors to the structural frame, along with structural glazing and sealants, employing construction methods similar to aquarium walls. Floodproof windows can be individual windows or storefront systems constructed with tempered glass and laminated coatings at each interlayer to prevent breakage from water pressure.

To ensure the safety of occupants, at least one exit door should be at or above the Design Flood Elevation to provide ingress and egress during flood conditions. This is located above the wet or dry floodproofing extent or at the level above.

NOTES

1 Shaw, B. 2017. Time to Rethink Floodproofing. *Construction Specifier*, August. Accessed at: https://www.constructionspecifier.com/time-to-rethink-floodproofing/7/

2 Floodproofing.com website: Passive Automatic Flood Barriers. Accessed at: https://www.floodproofing.com/passive-automatic-flood-barriers

RESOURCES

- Ogunyoye, F., R. Stevens, and S. Underwood. 2011. Temporary and Demountable Flood Protection Guide. U.K. Environment Agency. Accessed at: https://assets.publishing.service.gov.uk/media/603376bce90e0766021bf14f/_flood_protection_guide.pdf
- 2018. Climate Resilient Design Standards & Guidelines for Protection of Public Rights-of-Way: Section 7: Deployable Flood Barrier Guidance. Boston Public Works Department. Accessed at: https://www.boston.gov/sites/default/files/file/document_files/2018/10/section_7.0_deployable_flood_barrier_guidance.pdf

CORNICHE 23

ADAPTATION **WATER** SCALE **SITE**

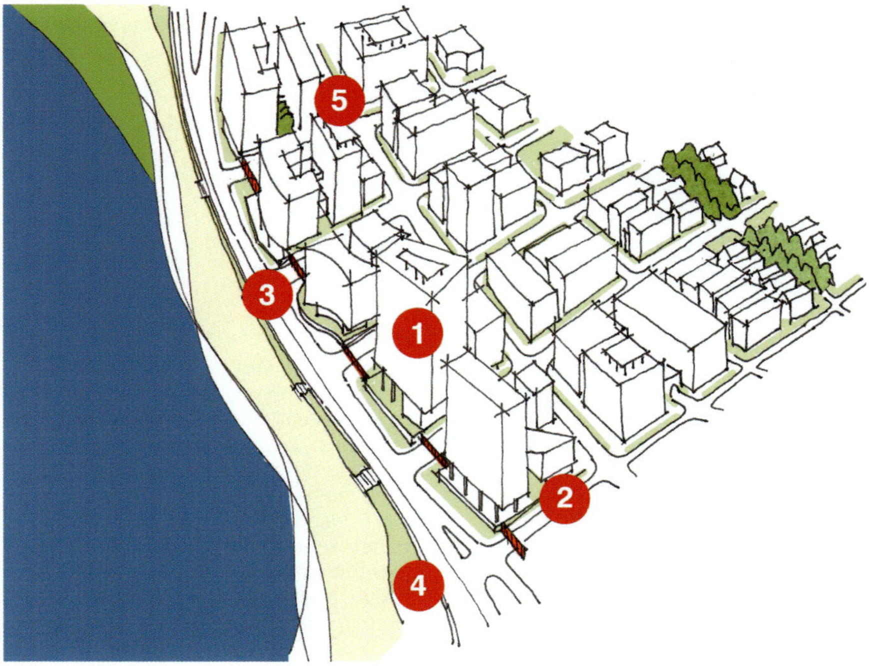

Downtown waterfronts feature tall mixed-use structures designed to withstand higher wind pressures and storm surges, effectively shielding smaller structures behind them. A continuous line of floodgates and street barriers seals the gaps between buildings, helping to deter flooding.

Figure 23.1: A continuous line of hardened structures deflects the impact of water, protecting smaller and more vulnerable structures inland from exposure.

1. High-investment front-tier structures are built to higher standards for exposure and risk category. Buildings have zero setbacks at the street and meet a minimum height requirement to shield the buildings behind.
2. A street grid perpendicular to the water minimises the length of flood barriers at street openings.
3. Buildings exceed minimum floodplain requirements for the first inhabited floor, employing a plinth, floodwall, or dry floodproofing.
4. The waterfront boulevard is elevated and hardened with a seawall or modular revetments, and may also be protected with a beach, marsh, or other natural lines of defence.
5. Open spaces are located at the rear of buildings for stormwater infiltration and storage.

DOI: 10.4324/9781032702964-26

BACKGROUND

The devastation from Hurricane Katrina exposed an unanticipated benefit from a relatively new building type along Mississippi coast beaches: multi-story casino developments. The Beau Rivage, a 28-story hotel tower, intercepted Category 3 winds and about 22 feet of storm surge in Biloxi, diminishing the storm's impact on wood-framed cottages behind the structure. Outside of the tower's protected lee, buildings were shifted off their foundations, roofs torn off, and structures reduced to matchsticks by the storm surge and windborne debris. The staunch structure redirected the storm around the building but had there been a linked chain of these coastal linebackers there may have been less destruction to inland structures.

The word *corniche* comes from the French term for a road along a coast at the bottom of a natural cliff, but in an architectural context, the cliff may be constructed rather than natural. Multi-story waterfront structures are built to higher standards than small residential or commercial buildings because of their construction type (fire-resistive concrete and steel). They have a higher risk factor based on the number of occupants, whether people sleep in the buildings, whether a significant percentage of residents have family relationships, and whether the occupants may be vulnerable population groups.[1] The increased building strength demands a higher initial investment, which is more easily borne by commercial and institutional investors than by small property owners.

Figure 23.2: A view of Marine Drive in Mumbai, a 3 km esplanade of art deco structures featuring housing, hotels, nightclubs, restaurants, and sports clubs. Mumbai has been declared one of the most vulnerable cities to sea level rise and although the structures are not currently linked with flood protection at the bases, this adaptation method might protect from coastal flooding in the near future.

KEY DESIGN CONSIDERATIONS

Risk Category: The International Code Council (ICC) Risk Category measures the risk to human life, health, and wellbeing, requiring buildings that represent substantial hazard to human life in the event of failure be designed to higher standards. Risk Category I applies to low-hazard agricultural facilities, temporary structures, and incidental storage facilities. Risk Category II includes offices, shops, single-family housing, duplexes, and other low-occupancy buildings. Risk Category III applies to buildings containing public assembly with occupants over 300, schools, institutions, other high-occupancy loads, and public services. Risk Category IV includes critical facilities, first-responder stations, hospitals, and public utilities.[2]

Exposure Category: The exposure category measures variations in surface roughness of adjacent conditions including ground irregularities from topography, vegetation, and constructed features. Open areas enable winds to accelerate before they interact with a structure and Exposure Category measures the conditions that prevail in the upwind directions. Surface roughness B is terrain with closely spaced obstructions such as urban or suburban sites or forested areas. Surface roughness C is open terrain with scattered obstructions. Surface roughness D includes unobstructed areas and water surfaces, marshes, and flat plains. A waterfront site is typically Exposure D, with the highest wind pressure.

Figure 23.3: A section through a corniche illustrates the first level on a plinth with a 4–6 m (13–20 feet) high commercial and parking base. Structures are linked with a continuous line of site floodwalls and floodgates. The corniche establishes a consistent datum for flood protection and a minimum height to block winds from inland structures.

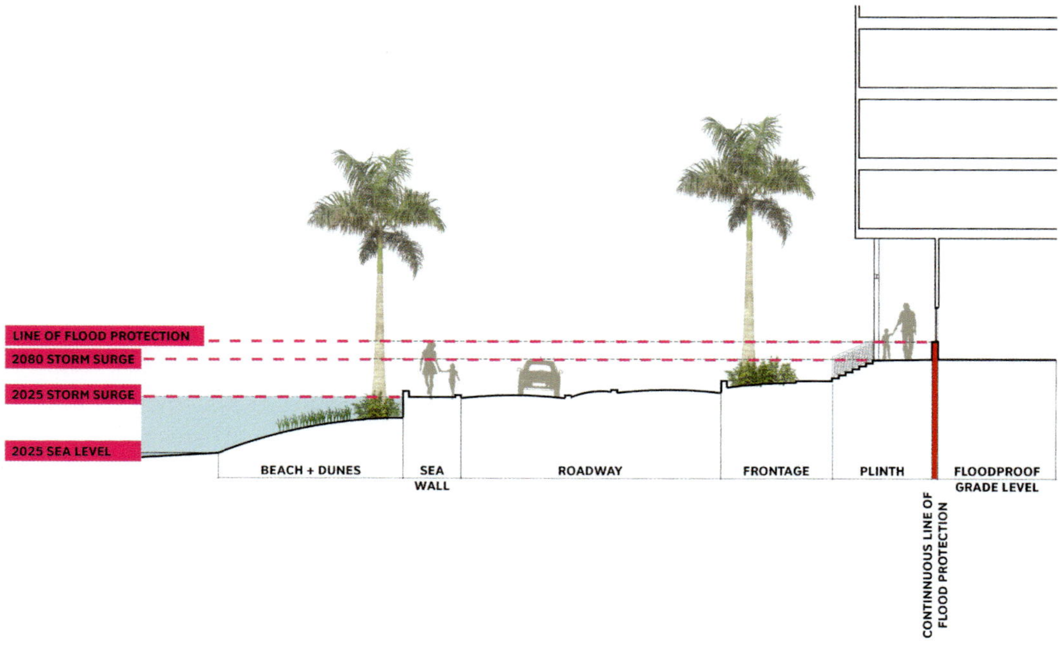

A corniche establishes a consistent setback, typically along the property line in high-density waterfront locations to form a barrier against water. The corniche should establish a consistent flood protection datum and a minimum parapet height of at least three stories. Wind pressures behind the frornt line will be reduced, with a wind shadow lower than the corniche height.

The building base must meet the height of the required base flood elevation, at a minimum. It may be set on a plinth of fill or a commercial base of shops, restaurants, offices, or parking to raise the first level of dwelling units above potential flooding. The extra height of a commercial grade level may be useful if it is later decommissioned due to sea level rise, leaving space for an intermediate floor to be built or leaving space for temporary activities that enliven the street edge: pop-up markets, social and recreational spaces, food kiosks, and special events.

Incorporate a floodwall at the waterfront perimeter of each site or within the base of each structure to resist flooding. Protect street openings and gaps between buildings with floodwalls and flood gates. Align floodwalls on both sides of the street; the street grid should run perpendicular to the waterfront boulevard to minimise the length of flood gates at street openings.

Buildings should be designed to foster lively social interactions along the corniche at the street. Retail, restaurants, and other commercial functions at the ground level enhance both social and economic value and ensure the building remains useful and well-maintained. Robust buildings integrate public functions and community spaces - post offices, banks, public toilets, health clinics, and other functions - which can be used as public spaces to shelter-in-place during emergencies when there is limited time for evacuation. Common areas can also support short-duration public services: communications and charging hubs, cooling or warming centres, or temporary accommodations.[3]

Place surface parking, open spaces, and courtyards behind the buildings, leaving no gaps in the floodwall. Gaps from construction and demolition may be filled with temporary flood barriers.

Incorporate resilient landscaping elements along the corniche: densely-planted dunes, deep-rooted alleés and clusters of trees, medians and berms to disrupt wave action.

The roadway along a corniche can be hardened with multiple layers of protection: road elevation, a seawall, elevation, beaches, marshes, or modular revetments.

Structures in the lee of the bulky waterfront structures may transfer development rights to allow waterfront developers to construct buildings with higher Floor Area Ratios (FAR).

Maintaining an intricate system of private and public floodwalls and gates requires a dedicated agency to plan, test, and maintain the system. Development of a flood-resistant corniche is therefore limited to dense waterfronts with high economic value.

IMPACT

Social: Reinforcing large buildings along the waterfront edge against water and wind protects smaller, privately-owned structures in their lee. Structures that remain viable after disaster can provide essential services for nearby residents, giving them places to shelter, gather, get provisions, and share food and information.

Environmental: Although the primary materials of a corniche are high-embodied carbon concrete and steel, the potential to remain intact, operational, and capable of protecting weaker structures may offset the carbon investment.

Economic: A continuous floodwall protects residents within its perimeter. If the cost of constructing the barrier is shared among multiple private developments, it can reduce the cost burden for taxpayers. The benefits to developers are minimal flood and wind damage, fewer interruptions to productivity, reduced recovery costs and time, and economic stability.

Spatial: The historic pattern of higher density structures along the waterfront to take advantage of coastal breezes and scenic views supports the development of a flood-resistant corniche and draws a clear spatial line of defence.

NOTES

1 International Code Council (ICC). 2021. Performance Code for Buildings and Facilities, Appendix A.
2 ICC. 2021. International Building Code, Table 1604.5. Country Club Hills, IL.
3 State of California. 2022. Public Buildings: Shelter in Place Guidelines. Government Operations Agency.

RESOURCE

- FEMA 549: Hurricane Katrina in the Gulf Coast: Building Performance Observations, Recommendations, and Technical Guidance. 2006. Accessed at: https://basc.pnnl.gov/library/fema-549-hurricane-katrina-gulf-coast-building-performance-observations-recommendations-and

ELEVATION 24

ADAPTATION **WATER** SCALE **BUILDING**

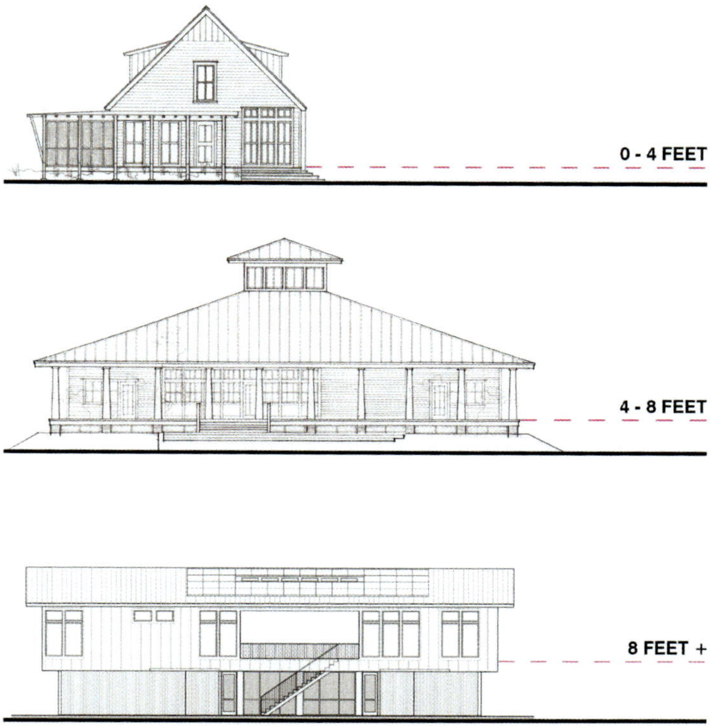

Elevating a structure above the anticipated flood height is a common flood defence to avoid inundation. There are a handful of standard methods: build up the ground with fill, raise the structure on a closed foundation, or use open foundations such as piers, pilings, and columns. Hybrid methods combine elements of the three options. Elevated structures reduce flood damage but may create difficulties in access, affect neighbourhood appearance, impede the potential for social interaction, and have the capacity to strand people within the structure during extended flooding.

Figure 24.1: Elevating 0–4 feet is a traditional height above ground in hot, humid climates to allow air circulation and reduce flooding. Elevating 4–8 feet is an in-between zone, using a hybrid of fill and piers. Elevating 8 feet or more allows multiple uses below the structure.

DOI: 10.4324/9781032702964-27

BACKGROUND

Elevated structures that are prepared for flooding withstand minimal damage during an inundation. Elevating a structure does not transform the hazard risk; rather, it simply provides a measure of adaptive capacity, a characteristic that helps avoid loss from damage to the structure and contents of the building. Will floods still interrupt access, utilities, and services? Probably. Will a small flood event inundate the first floor? Likely not. Is a flood higher than the base flood elevation (BFE) possible? Yes, it is still possible over the life of the structure. These are the risks that clients must consider to determine their tolerance for the inherent risks of building in a floodplain.

Determining an appropriate elevation strategy requires deciding on the appropriate elevation height. While regulatory maps can provide useful information about flood risk, they use historical flood data from river and tidal gauges without accounting for current or future environmental changes such as sea level rise and more intense storms. Flood maps are often outdated, leaving more people and properties at risk than are shown within boundaries that may have been delineated decades ago. The worst-case scenario might be uncomfortably high, with a corresponding price tag. The most appropriate design flood elevation (DFE) may be somewhere in between.

There are two types of Special Flood Hazard Areas (with 1% annual risk of a major flood) in the United States: those that are subject to dynamic water loads (V-zone and some Coastal A-zones) and those that receive still water loads (A-zone). In the United States, the BFE is the minimum requirement for the finished floor elevation of the lowest level of inhabitable space. A-zones require the top of the finished floor elevation meet the BFE, while V-zones require the bottom of

Figure 24.2: The National Flood Insurance Program (U.S.) has minimum elevation requirements but individual communities may add freeboard above these minimum requirements. A zones must elevate the top of the lowest inhabited floor to the Base Flood Elevation or above. V-zones must elevate the bottom of the lowest horizontal member to or above the BFE. Federal Emergency Management Agency.

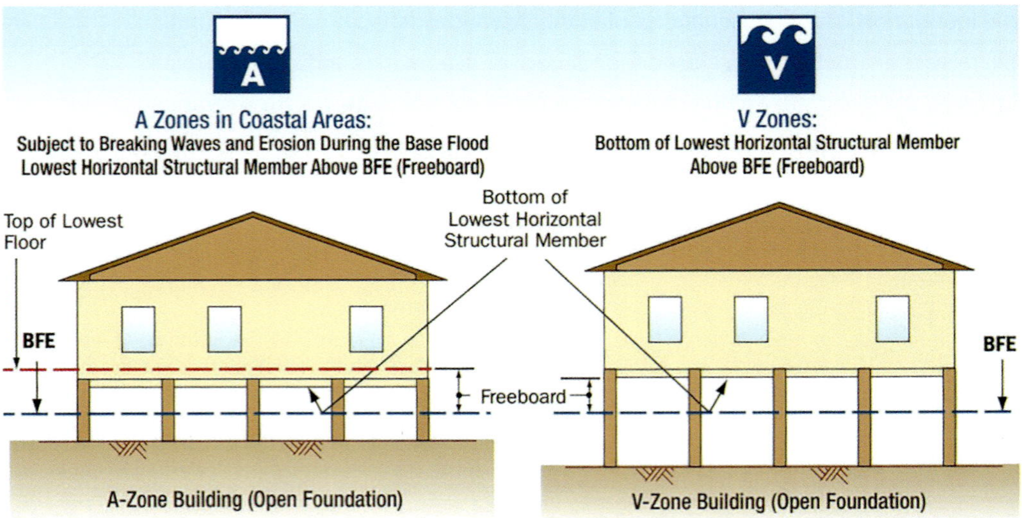

the lowest horizontal floor member meet the BFE. The V-zone requirement is designed to keep the entire building structure above the anticipated breaking wave height of a storm surge. Horizontal structural members are obstructions to moving water and beams or joists can transmit the force of wave impacts to rest of the structure, causing failure.

Designing the foundation system for a raised structure requires understanding soil bearing capacity, the loads generated by the form and function of the structure, and potential flood loading conditions. Flood loads are calculated with three types of loads: hydrostatic forces from elements submerged in water at rest; hydrodynamic forces resulting from the movement of water against a structure; and waterborne debris impacts. The effects of floods on buildings are exacerbated by erosion and scouring, which occur when waves erode the soil surrounding the supports and causing the loss of load-bearing capacity.

There are three methods for elevating a structure: fill, fill with enclosed foundations, and open foundations. Hybrid foundations, such as a compacted fill pad with open pier foundations, may minimise the apparent height of the structure and provide gentle transitions. Selecting the right foundation depends on regulatory requirements, existing site conditions, and the difference in height between the existing grade and the proposed finished floor level.

Fill: Compacted fill is often the simplest and least expensive method of elevation. Fill material is installed in layers, compacted, and shaped into a pad or confined within an enclosed foundation. A pad typically extends 2–5 m (5–15 feet) outwards from the building walls to create a stable angle of repose for the soil; this method may not work on small, narrow sites or to elevate structures more than a few feet. Fill can dramatically alter hydrological patterns. It is not allowed in V-zones susceptible to erosion, and at sites where fill can displace stormwater onto neighbouring sites.

Enclosed foundations: Structures within a flood zone rarely have basements. Retaining walls are built of reinforced concrete or masonry. Within the stem wall perimeter, fill material can be placed and compacted to support a concrete floor slab or alternately, the space can remain open as a crawl space, as long as it has sufficient flood vents. Flood vents allow water into the enclosed space to equalise water on both sides of a foundation wall. Flood vents need one square inch of opening in the foundation wall for every square foot below the structure, so a 2,000-square-foot crawl space requires 2,000 square inches of opening. (These U.S. standards don't convert quite so memorably to the metric system.) Accessory screens, grates, grilles, or fixed louvers are not allowed to hinder the flow of floodwaters into and out of the enclosed area.

Open foundations: Pile supports may be wood or concrete, poured or precast concrete, or reinforced masonry columns. The foundations must be deep enough to resist scour, with adequate spacing to support gravity loads, numerous enough to provide a measure of redundancy, and braced to resist dynamic lateral forces from moving water.

Buildings with open foundations are allowed to have breakaway walls or screens between the posts to enclose storage or entry spaces; breakaway walls are designed to detach under wind or water loads to maintain structural integrity. Decks and porches below the BFE must also be built with breakaway detailing to prevent load transference to the main structure.

Existing structures: Raising an existing structure is one way to ensure a longer life and lower risk. Raising a house that is already on pier foundations is a straightforward process: ensuring that the existing foundations can handle the additional height and weight, jacking up the floor diaphragm, and either adding new material between the new floor elevation and the original foundation

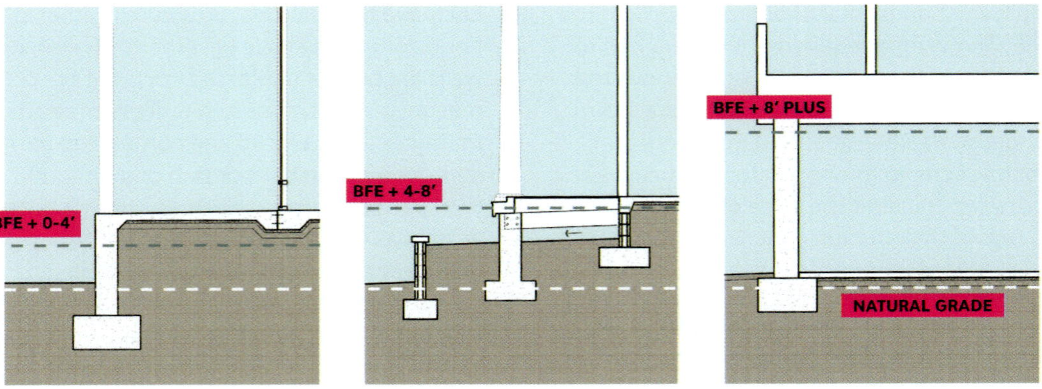

Figure 24.3: Foundation systems to elevate the floor level above BFE: fill with retaining walls, a hybrid system with part of the required elevation accomplished with fill and the remainder with pier foundations, and open piling foundations. Each foundation typology is suited to a range of heights and site conditions.

or replacing old columns with new ones. However, when a building is constructed on a slab foundation, it is a bit more complicated, requiring the contractor:

- excavate below the slab and identify joints in the existing slab;
- disconnect the utilities;
- place beams below the slab approximately 2 m (5 feet) apart;
- jack up the beams to the required height, lifting the slab evenly as a single, monolithic load;
- install new foundations beneath the beams and lock together in place;
- reconnect the utilities;
- add fill or screening around the base as desired.

It may not be possible to elevate a structure if it is too big or has an under-sized foundation. Another alternative is to reinforce the existing structural frame and abandon the first level, extending the walls upward, replacing the roof, and building a new elevated level within. Walls below the BFE may be removed or flood vents inserted. The original floor slab below may be left in place for parking, storage, and access.[1]

Benefit-Cost Analysis shows that mitigation measures for flooding save money, increase occupant safety, reduce business interruption, and create beneficial economic impacts for the community. A 2019 study by the National Institute of Building Sciences[2] shows that natural hazard mitigation for new projects saves $5 for every $1 spent to prepare for riverine flooding beyond the code requirements, and building retrofits return $6 for every $1 spent. The return on investment for hurricane surge is even higher, with new project benefits returning $7 for every $1 spent.

KEY DESIGN CONSIDERATIONS

There are four key problems to solve related to elevated houses: access, aesthetics, underside functions, and urban sensitivity.

- **Access:** Navigating the vertical transition from the street to the elevated first floor can be difficult, especially when universal accessibility is desired. Stairs present challenges for young children, strollers, elderly people, pets, and deliveries; they create insurmountable barriers for people in wheelchairs. Ramps require a significant amount of space, 3.7 m (12 feet) of ramp to traverse every 30.5 cm (1 foot) in height, plus space for landings, turns, and platforms. Small lots may not have

Figure 24.4: This house in coastal Mississippi is elevated with stepped terraces and fill enclosed with retaining walls. Designed for aging in place, there is a ramp from the car parking (not shown). The accessory structure on the right is allowed to have a floor level below the BFE because it is not an inhabited structure.
Photo by Drew Tarter.

enough space to accommodate a ramp and elevators are expensive and require significant maintenance, placing raised homes literally out of reach. Some functions, such as retail and restaurants, don't create adequate return on investment when they are located above grade because they rely on foot traffic, and a level change of even a few feet may deter customers. Access and vertical circulation is highly context-dependent, but good transitions can be made through a series of gentle level changes, an inviting stair, a landscaped incline, a series of terraces, or a shared elevator. Clustered structures make shared vertical circulation elements more affordable. (Chapter 21: The Elevated Commons.)

- **Aesthetics:** A small structure can look ridiculous when elevated high above the floodplain as the proportions become exaggerated and awkward. New patterns for designing these underside and interstitial spaces are necessary to visually link buildings to their site and context. Shutters, slats, and screens create a sense of enclosure for the grade level. Apparently 'solid' walls with breakaway connections can make a structure look grounded but maintain structural integrity in case of surge. Berms and retaining walls (where permitted) plus landscaping improve screening and minimise the visual distance between the grade and the floor. A hybrid solution of fill and piers can minimise the apparent elevation change.
- **Underside functions:** Create uses for the space beneath the raised structure so that

it doesn't become cluttered with excess junk. A full floor between the grade and the underside of a house can be used for: parking cars, boats, golf carts, kayaks, and bikes; recreational equipment storage for fishing, boating, and tinkering; a screened outdoor living space; storage; outdoor dining and kitchen area; swimming pool, fountain, outdoor shower and bathing; murals, sculpture, and other durable art; a plant nursery and greenhouse area; a place for a suspended hammock or sleeping porch. When the vertical separation is compressed to a crawl space, cabinets or oversized drawers allow storage for recreational games, outdoor furniture, pool toys, or other items. Do not store items that may be damaged by moisture below the structure. Create separate screened areas for trash, lawnmowers, equipment, and other service items.

- **Urban sensitivity:** It is difficult for elevated homes to contribute to street life and sociability. Neighbourly houses are traditionally placed close to the street, making the front door and porch accessible for socialising, but placing the front door above eye level immediately severs the visual connection to the street. Create entrances that offer social infrastructure at or near the ground level - front stoops where the stairs land near the street, grade-level or half-raised porches, and a clear path with wayfinding to the front door. Enclosed entrances at the grade level with foyers and stairs are limited to 28 m^2 (299 ft^2) within the floodplain and must have breakaway walls or flood vents.

Ensure that critical equipment is also elevated: air conditioning, ductwork, electrical panels, generators, inverters, etc. This can be screened from view in an unconditioned enclosure, behind shutters, or with a railing that hides equipment from view.

Follow cues from the context to avoid an inconsistent street elevation. Structures elevated at different times - and to different heights - can create a gap-toothed street frontage, with some houses close to the ground and others high in the air. Infill must meet minimum elevation requirements but can use detailing to extend datums from neighbouring structures.

Consider constructing retaining walls at the property line with a gradual slope up to the BFE. On large lots, this strategy may require significant amounts of fill, so it may be more appropriate at small lots.

Support the adoption of policies requiring disclosure of previous flooding in real estate listings. A transparent policy requires disclosing whether flooding has ever been experienced, the flood zone classification (and the source and date of the information), if there is a flood elevation certificate, if there is flood insurance on the property, and whether there are requirements to maintain flood insurance on the property. Many floodplain homes exceed the intrinsic value if the cost fully reflected information about flood risk.[3] Severe floods can trigger price adjustments that can affect property value.[4]

IMPACT

Social: Elevating a structure to a safe elevation above the BFE reduces the risk of flood damage to the structure and contents. Low-income residents may not have access to resources for elevating their homes, exacerbating socio-economic disparities.

Environmental: Elevating structures may have environmental implications, alter the local landscape, and affect wildlife habitats. Elevation may increase energy consumption if additional resources are needed to heat or cool elevated structures.

Economic: The cost of elevating a structure can vary significantly depending on the size of the building, the elevation required, and the construction methods used. Sources of funding for elevation can come from property owners, government agencies, or insurance companies, and may impact property values and affordability in the area. Elevating beyond the code-requirement has a return on investment of 5:1 for mitigating beyond code and may create immediate discounts for insurance.

Spatial: Incremental elevation in a neighbourhood can create an uneven datum of floor levels, resulting in a disordered street elevation. The height of the floor relative to the sidewalk can inhibit social interaction. The additional space necessary to gain access through stairs and ramps can devour ground space and require larger, consolidated lots.

NOTES

1 Federal Emergency Management Agency. 2014. FEMA P-312, Homeowner's Guide to Retrofitting: Six Ways to Protect Your Home from Flooding; Chapter 5, Elevating Your Home. Accessed at: https://www.fema.gov/sites/default/files/documents/fema_elevating-your-house-chapter-5.pdf
2 National Institute of Building Sciences. 2019. Natural Hazard Mitigation Saves: 2019 Report. Accessed at: https://www.nibs.org/projects/natural-hazard-mitigation-saves-2019-report
3 Hino, M. and M. Burke. 2020. Does Information About Climate Risk Affect Property Values? *National Bureau of Economic Research: Working Paper 26807*. DOI: 10.3386/w26807
4 Hino and Burke (2020).

RESOURCES

- Federal Emergency Management Agency. 2014. FEMA P-312, Homeowner's Guide to Retrofitting: Six Ways to Protect Your Home from Flooding; Chapter 5, Elevating Your Home. Accessed at: https://www.fema.gov/sites/default/files/documents/fema_elevating-your-house-chapter-5.pdf
- Urban Design Associates. 2005. A Pattern Book for Gulf Coast Neighborhoods. Mississippi Renewal Forum, Governor's Commission on Recovery, Rebuilding, and Renewal.

WET + DRY FLOODPROOFING 25

ADAPTATION **WATER** SCALE **BUILDING**

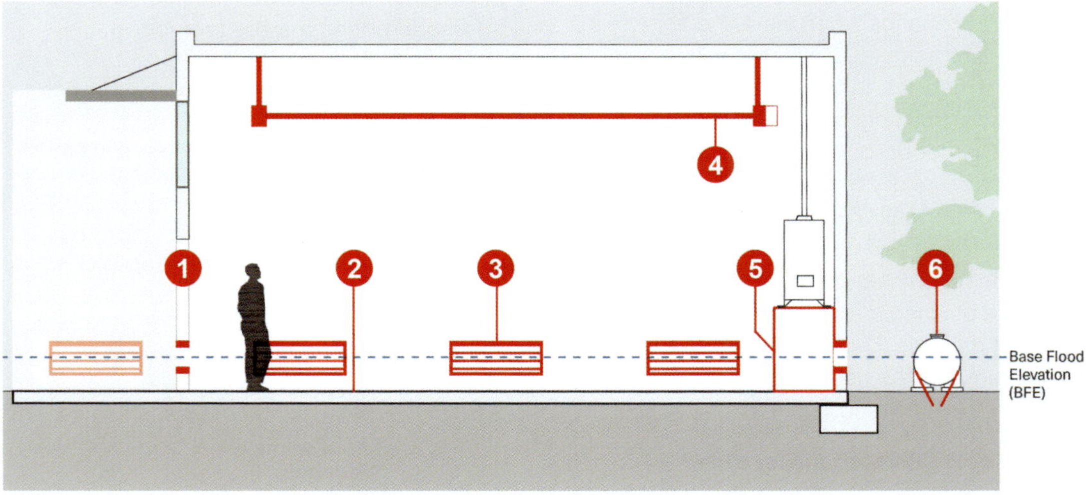

Wet and dry floodproofing provide a measure of protection for a structure to resist flood damage when the finished floor is below the base flood elevation. Wet floodproofing allows floodwaters to enter areas that are below the flood level and exit without leaving permanent damage to non-porous wall materials and finishes. Dry floodproofing creates a substantially impermeable barrier to water and prevents floodwaters from entering a building. Selecting the appropriate floodproofing measure depends on site conditions, building functions, and regulatory restrictions.

Figure 25.1: Wet floodproofing allows floodwaters to enter and exit a structure when the finished floor is below the BFE. The space can be cleaned by washing down walls and floors without damaging materials and systems.

1. Flood damage resistant wall construction.
2. Water-resistant flooring.
3. Flood opening with bottom no more than 30 cm (12 inches) above exterior grade.
4. Elevated electrical outlets.
5. Equipment elevated above BFE.
6. Anchor exterior equipment to prevent floating

Mississippi State University, Gulf Coast Community Design Studio.

DOI: 10.4324/9781032702964-28

BACKGROUND

Floodproofing a building is another tool to protect occupants, structures, and sometimes contents, during a flood event. There are scenarios when elevating a building isn't advised, such as in existing or historic structures, industrial structures, and commercial buildings where accessibility is critical. Dry floodproofing keeps the interior of the structure dry by placing a barrier at the exterior of the wall. Wet floodproofing allows water to flow in and out so that occupants can flush out any residue left behind and allow the building materials to dry out with no inherent damage. Deciding which approach to use requires the design and client team to consider the following options:

Desired Flood Protection Elevation: Codes and standards set minimum height requirements, but a risk assessment may indicate the merits of exceeding the minimum requirements. Floodproofing above the Base Flood Elevation provides contingency for errors and accelerated changes in water levels due to sea level rise or subsidence. However, dry floodproofing is generally economical only to about 1 m (3 feet) high; beyond that, the structural frame and reinforcing will need significant reinforcing. In locations where the base flood elevation plus freeboard is greater than 3 feet above the floor, the cost of dry-floodproofing may be prohibitive.

Figure 25.2: Dry floodproofing creates a substantially impermeable wall at the building base but exposes the structure to higher hydrostatic pressure.

1. Waterproof construction to about 1 m (3 feet) high.
2. Standard wall construction above base.
3. Watertight doors and windows.
4. Backflow valve prevents floodwater from entering through pipes.
5. Flood panels to cover door and window openings.
6. Mechanical and electrical equipment raised above flood protection level.
7. Emergency power for sump pump.
8. Paints, gaskets, and sealants to reduce water seepage at joints and utility penetrations.
9. A sump pump is used to remove water that enters the building.

Mississippi State University, Gulf Coast Community Design Studio.

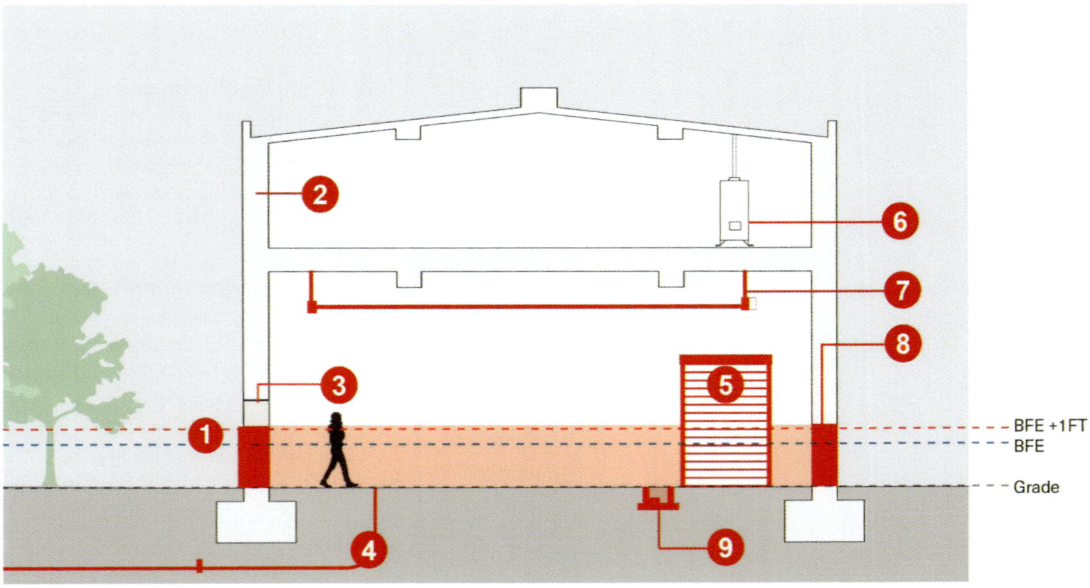

Site Exposure: Velocity zones cannot have wet or dry floodproofing as both create barriers to flowing water. A-zones with still-water flooding may use dry floodproofing if the building and foundation are adequately anchored against flotation, lateral movement, and collapse. Residential structures in A-zones must be constructed with their lowest floor level elevated to or above the BFE, and floodproofing is typically not allowed as a substitute for meeting the requirement.

Flood velocities in excess of 5 feet per second are not generally acceptable for dry floodproofing.[1] Sites where the anticipated BFE (in feet) multiplied by the velocity (in feet per second) has a product greater than 4 pose a hazard to anyone attempting to evacuate or access the site. As an example, a site with a BFE of 3 feet multiplied by a low-velocity flow of 4 feet per second would produce 12, indicating hazardous conditions.

Building Function: Buildings with any function may use wet floodproofing but it is not recommended for functions where the contents may be damaged by water, such as housing. Dry floodproofing is limited to non-residential buildings in the United States; non-residential portions of mixed-use buildings are allowed to be dry floodproofed provided that all residential units, as well as the building systems and service equipment that serve residential units, are elevated above the required elevation.

Type of Construction: Cast-in-place concrete or concrete masonry unit assemblies are the most common - and impervious - wall systems used for dry floodproofing. Wood-frame construction is not recommended for use with wet floodproofing due to high moisture seepage rates and potential damage to the structure from wetting (including mould growth).

Figure 25.3: Forces exerted by water include: hydrostatic loads, exerted by standing or slowly moving water (less than 10 feet per second), which increase as the water becomes deeper. Hydrodynamic loads are exerted by moving water, including frontal impact on the seaward face, drag along sides, and negative pressure on the downstream façade. Buoyancy pressure is the vertical upward force from water-saturated soils.

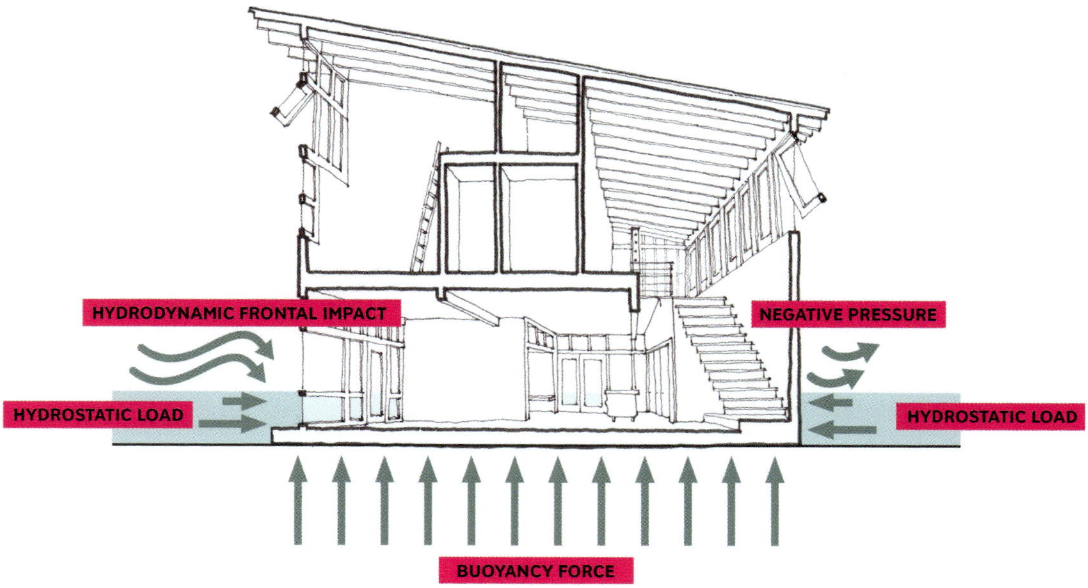

To select the right floodproofing system, it is important to understand flood loads. Flood loads are orders of magnitude stronger than wind loads, with three critical types of loads to consider: hydrostatic, hydrodynamic, and buoyancy forces.[2]

Hydrostatic: Loads are exerted by standing or slowly moving water (less than 10 feet per second). Hydrostatic loads cause less structural damage when flood depths on both sides of the wall are equalised, explaining the rationale for wet floodproofing. Dry floodproofing intended to keep floodwaters outside the building must withstand hydrostatic forces acting on one side of a wall, which can fail if the loads are underestimated.

Hydrodynamic: Loads from high-velocity flow are capable of destroying solid walls, dislodging buildings, and moving large quantities of sediment and debris. Hydrodynamic loads are exerted by moving water, including direct pressure on the seaward face, drag forces along facades perpendicular to water movement, and suction or negative pressure acting on the downstream façade.

Buoyancy: Loads occur when the vertical upward force (buoyancy) is greater than the downward force exerted by gravity. Structures must resist buoyant forces to prevent floating and uplift from foundations.

KEY DESIGN CONSIDERATIONS

WET FLOODPROOFING

Wet floodproofing allows floodwaters to enter and exit to minimise structural damage, using water-resistant materials. This approach reduces repair costs and facilitates faster recovery.[3] Wet floodproofing is practical for spaces that are not used for living and working, which may contain finish materials susceptible to water damage and furniture, appliances, or contents that are easily damaged by floodwaters.

Flood damage-resistant materials are resistant to floodwater damage, can survive wetting and drying, and are easily cleaned after a flood. These materials include non-porous materials such as stone, concrete, tile, steel, glass, terrazzo, and others. Materials that are not acceptable include wood, fibreglass, linoleum, gypsum board, and particle board.

Exterior walls below the BFE must have openings to equalise loads with flood vents in order to balance hydrostatic pressure on both sides of the wall. In the event of a flood, automatic flood vents have internal floats that lift to release a flood door, which rotates open to allow bi-directional water flow. If there are interior walls, these may also need to have through vents and waterproof construction. Each individual space within the floodplain requires a minimum of two flood vents to be located on opposite walls.

The number of flood vents needed to equalise the loads is determined by the size of the building footprint, approximately 1 square inch of opening per 1 square foot of building footprint. A 1,500 square foot house would therefore require 12 vents (1500 ÷ (16 x 8) = 11.72). The size of a flood vent is based on the size of a concrete masonry unit, nominally 16″ wide by 8″ high in the United States (20 × 20 × 40 cm in Europe or 440 × 215 mm in the United Kingdom).

Flood vents must be located with the bottom of the vent no more than 30 cm (12 inches) above the adjacent grade to promote free flow during flood conditions.

Figure 25.4: Dry floodproofing at a mechanical room, using a spray-applied waterproof coating over a reinforced base to a height of about 1 m (3 feet).

In order to protect vulnerable service equipment, building utilities and sanitary facilities - including heating and air conditioning, electrical service, water supply, and sanitary sewage - must be located above the BFE, completely enclosed within the dry floodproof envelope, or have a watertight housing.

Floodwater is assumed to be 'black water' containing pollutants such as sewage, solvents, oil, pesticides, fertilisers, and other chemicals that are potentially hazardous to humans. Consider the potential exposure to flood-borne contaminants when selecting flood damage-resistant materials and determine the protocol for removing contaminants after an event.

Cleaning up after a flood event may involve not only removing mud and debris but also washing, disinfecting, and decontaminating walls, floors, and other surfaces.

DRY FLOODPROOFING

Dry floodproofing is watertight construction with walls substantially impermeable to a certain height, usually 1 m (3 feet).[4] Substantially impermeable is defined as allowing no more than 4 inches of water to enter during a 24-hour period.[5]

The structure must be reinforced to manage water loads acting on one side of the wall, typically requiring reinforced cast-in-place or concrete masonry unit construction. A standard masonry wall can typically withstand the pressure exerted by water to a height of 1 m (3 feet).[6] When flood depths exceed 1 m, unreinforced masonry walls are more likely to crack or collapse. As a result, FEMA does not recommend use of dry floodproofing systems in areas where the depth of water under base flood conditions is greater than 1 m, although custom-engineered solutions are possible with an engineer's certification.

The waterproofing membrane is the key determinant of success or failure in dry floodproofing. Standard waterproofing membranes can fail against hydrostatic loads that remain in place for extended periods. A liquid-applied asphaltic membrane with consistent application of an adequate thickness can perform well if diligent construction administration is practiced on-site during installation. Industrial spray-applied coatings used for wastewater infrastructure (the pink material in Figure 25.4[7]) have a long life and robust impermeability.

Fewer joints in a wall assembly lead to better hydrostatic resistance. The difference between minor infiltration and critical failure may be redundancy. Poor construction in dry floodproofed assemblies can develop critical leaks, as hydrostatic pressure forces water through very small cracks.

Concrete admixtures and penetrating surface treatments such as siloxane can improve concrete imperviousness for situations in which frequent inundation will occur.

It may be practical to floodproof only certain core areas, such as mechanical or electrical equipment rooms. These spaces may require additional reinforcing at the base, as well as waterproofing, flood gates, and sump pumps to evacuate seepage.

Spaces that are dry floodproofed should have drainage to the outside that remains viable during a flood or an automated sump pump. The sump pump must have backup power to enable operation during a power outage.

Backflow valves or non-return valves are one-way flow regulators placed on sewage, drainage or waste effluent piping. In normal use, the valve allows wastewater and effluent to flow out of the property into the mains drainage system. However, when flooding causes the pressure in the main drainage to rise and effluent to back up towards the property, the valve closes, preventing contaminated water flooding the property through a toilet, sink or shower. However, when backflow valves are closed, sewerage collection in the building cannot be used, requiring the effluent be stored temporarily or forced around the valve. It is important to know that sewage can back up into buildings due to surcharged sewers at locations distant from the site.

A site that floods frequently may not be a good candidate for dry floodproofing, as the cumulative wear-and-tear on a building's external components as a result of recurring inundation may damage the materials. The cost of repeated business interruption and frequent cleanup activities, as well as the effects of having to repeatedly implement a flood emergency plan, should be considered and balanced against the cost of relocation or elevation.[8]

IMPACT

Social: Wet and dry floodproofing enhances resilience against flood events by safeguarding structures, reducing the impacts of flooding, protecting lives, and enabling faster recovery from disasters. Floodproofing may reduce the temporary displacement of residents from nuisance flooding and more consequential events.

Environmental: Floodproofing measures often have high embodied carbon in the reinforced structure, petrochemical coatings, or waterproof finish materials. It is essential to balance the embodied carbon, costs, and anticipated service life of mitigation methods in flood hazard areas against possible relocation to less-hazardous sites.

Economic: Floodproofing can mitigate financial losses for homeowners and businesses, and preserve the economic stability of communities. Floodproofing measures can lead to lower insurance premiums for property owners in flood-prone areas, encouraging owners to protect their properties. Floodproofing can extend the service life of existing structures, keeping them viable against changing climate conditions.

Spatial Integration: Floodproofing measures can support the retention of historic or existing buildings in the floodplain. Mixed use structures are allowed to use dry floodproofing at the grade level, which can encourage retail and commercial spaces and contribute to complete communities.

NOTES

1 FEMA. 1993. Non-Residential Floodproofing – Requirements and Certification for Buildings Located in Special Flood Hazard Areas in accordance with the National Flood Insurance Program. FIA-TB-3. Accessed at: https://www.fema.gov/sites/default/files/2020-07/nfip_t3_04011993_0.pdf. This publication cites a 1987 Colorado State University study of human stability in flood flow conditions. That study is published: Abt, S.R. et al. 1989. Human Stability in a High Flood Hazard Zone. *Journal of the American Water Resources Association*.

2 FEMA. 2021. NFIP Technical Bulletin 3: Requirements for the Design and Certification of Dry Floodproofed Non-Residential and Mixed-Use Buildings.

3 FEMA. 2008. Flood Damage-Resistant Materials Requirements: Technical Bulletin 2. Accessed at: https://www.fema.gov/sites/default/files/2020-07/fema_tb_2_flood_damage-resistant_materials_requirements.pdf

4 FEMA. 2021. Requirements for the Design and Certification of Dry Floodproofed Non-Residential and Mixed-Use Buildings: NFIP Technical Bulletin 3. Federal Emergency Management Agency. Accessed at: https://www.fema.gov/sites/default/files/2020-07/fema_p-936_floodproofing_non-residential_buiildings_110618pdf.pdf

5 Title 44 Code of Federal Regulations (CFR) 60.3 Flood plain management criteria for flood-prone areas. Accessed at: https://www.ecfr.gov/current/title-44/chapter-I/subchapter-B/part-60/subpart-A/section-60.3

6 FEMA. 2014. Homeowner's Guide to Retrofitting: FEMA P-312, 3rd Ed., Chapter 3. Accessed at: https://www.fema.gov/pdf/rebuild/mat/sec3.pdf

7 SpectraShield is a polymeric lining system designed specifically for wastewater structures – and it is pink. https://spectrashield.com/about-us/

8 FEMA. 1993. Non-Residential Floodproofing – Requirements and Certification for Buildings Located in Special Flood Hazard Areas in accordance with the National Flood Insurance Program. FIA-TB-3. Accessed at: https://www.fema.gov/sites/default/files/2020-07/nfip_t3_04011993_0.pdf.

RESOURCES

- FEMA. 2021. Requirements for the Design and Certification of Dry Floodproofed Non-Residential and Mixed-Use Buildings: NFIP Technical Bulletin 3. Federal Emergency Management Agency. Accessed at: https://www.fema.gov/sites/default/files/2020-07/fema_p-936_floodproofing_non-residential_buiildings_110618pdf.pdf
- Perkes, D. 2011. *Floodproof Commercial Construction: Working for Coastal Communities*. Oak Ridge National Laboratory. Accessed at: https://www.gulfcoaststudio.msstate.edu/sites/www.gulfcoaststudio.msstate.edu/files/2023-11/SERRI%2BReport%2B80024-01_Floodproof%2BConstruction%2B%28Sept%2B2011%29.pdf

FLOATING STRUCTURES 26

ADAPTATION **WATER** SCALE **BUILDING**

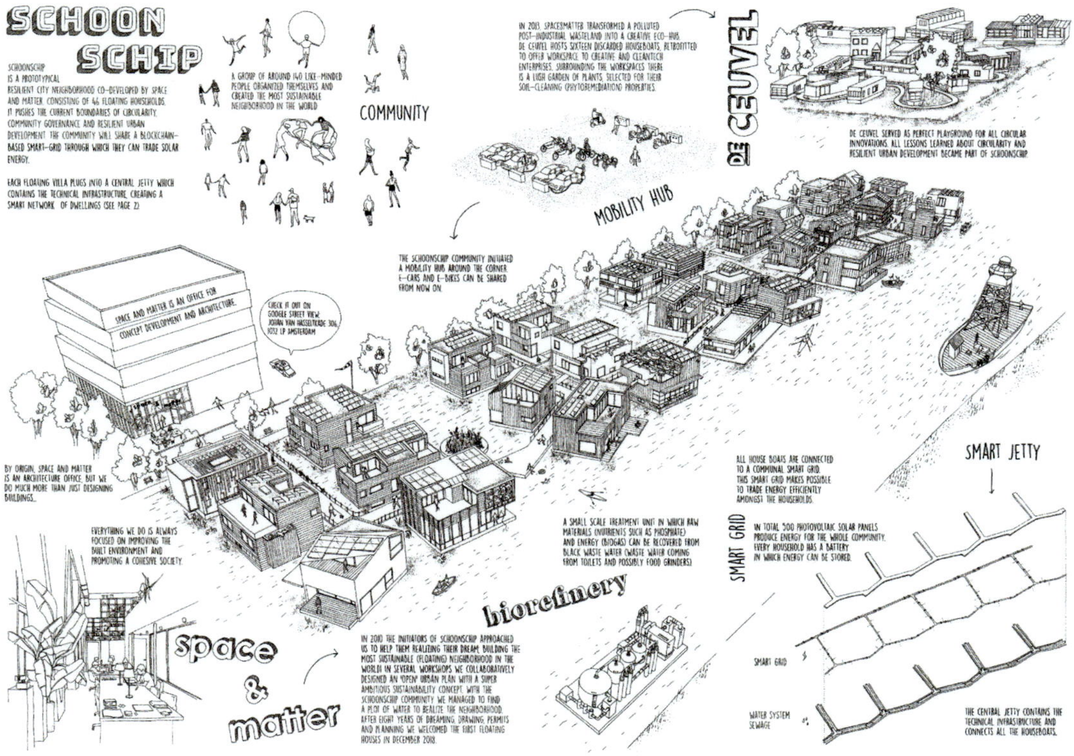

Floating structures have a buoyant base that rises in tandem with the water level during flood conditions. There are two types of floating structures: stationary and amphibious. A stationary structures towed into position and docked; it isn't stationary at all but the hull is distinguished from hulls designed for seafaring. Amphibious structures have a vertical guidance system that allows the structure to rest on dry ground most of the time, only floating when water inundation occurs. Floating structures rely on a flexible, permanent link to shore for utility services and waste processing. Neither of these types of floating structures is considered a houseboat, as they cannot move under their own power.

Figure 26.1: Elements of the floating community at Schoonschip in Amsterdam include 46 floating households connected with a smart jetty, smart grid, biorefinery unit, mobility hub, and adjacent workspaces. Space & Matter.

DOI: 10.4324/9781032702964-29

BACKGROUND

Coastal cities continue to grow even as flooding regularly inundates low areas and waterfronts. Land reclamation is difficult, time-consuming, expensive, and risky. Is it time to develop new models for floating structures and entire neighbourhoods that remain safe in flood conditions?

A stationary floating structure has a buoyant base and superstructure, moored in place within a waterway using a multi-point mooring to prevent rotation and provide redundancy in case of failure. An amphibious structure not only rests on the ground but also has a buoyant base to provide flotation as needed. It is connected to a vertical guidance system that directs the structure to return to exactly the same place after the flood recedes.

The Netherlands has become the leader in design, engineering, and construction of floating structures. The country's navigational skill, experience in boatbuilding, approach to living with water, and willingness to experiment has encouraged the use of waterways for multiple purposes. Couple this with a high demand for housing, little available land for development in Rotterdam and Amsterdam and low-wave energy environments, and the demand for floating structures was born.

Schoonschip began as an idea in 2008 when Marjan de Blok assembled a group of people interested in living on sustainable houseboats. In 2013, the collective development applied to build 46 private households on 30 floating structures in the Johan van Hasselt Canal in Amsterdam. The project meets ambitious social and sustainability goals, including food and energy production, cooperative living and working conditions for around 140 residents, and an ongoing demonstration of sustainability through the use of heat pumps that extract warmth from the canal water, solar hot water heating, green roofs, and a shared pool of electric bikes and cars.

Amphibious houses are built at sites that transition from land to water. The Float House in New Orleans was designed by Morphosis after Hurricane Katrina destroyed the Ninth Ward, at a time when many architects responded with innovative solutions to rebuilding in a flood-prone city. The floating chassis uses expanded polystyrene foam (EPS) modules coated in glass fibre-reinforced concrete. Two steel mooring piers supported

Figure 26.2: An amphibious house rests on the ground when conditions are dry but can float above the adjacent grade to cope with flooding extremes. Flexible service piping allows services to remain operational during a flood event.

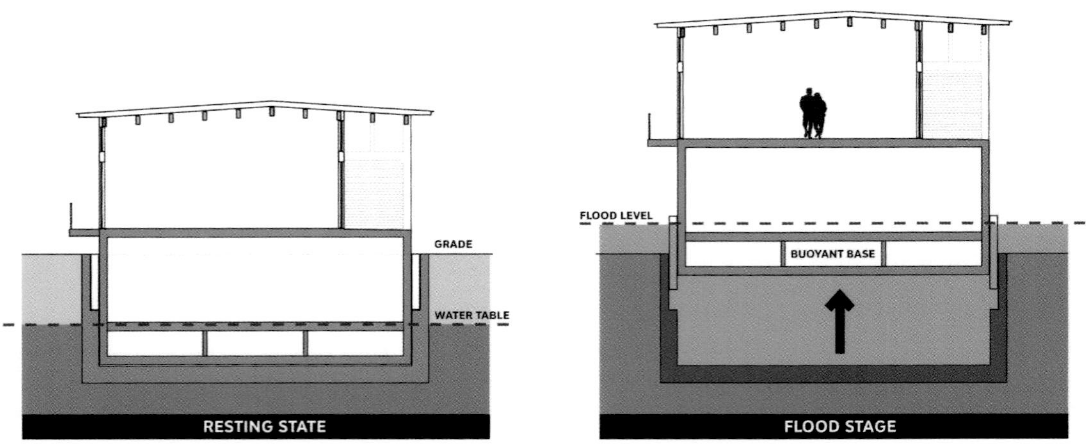

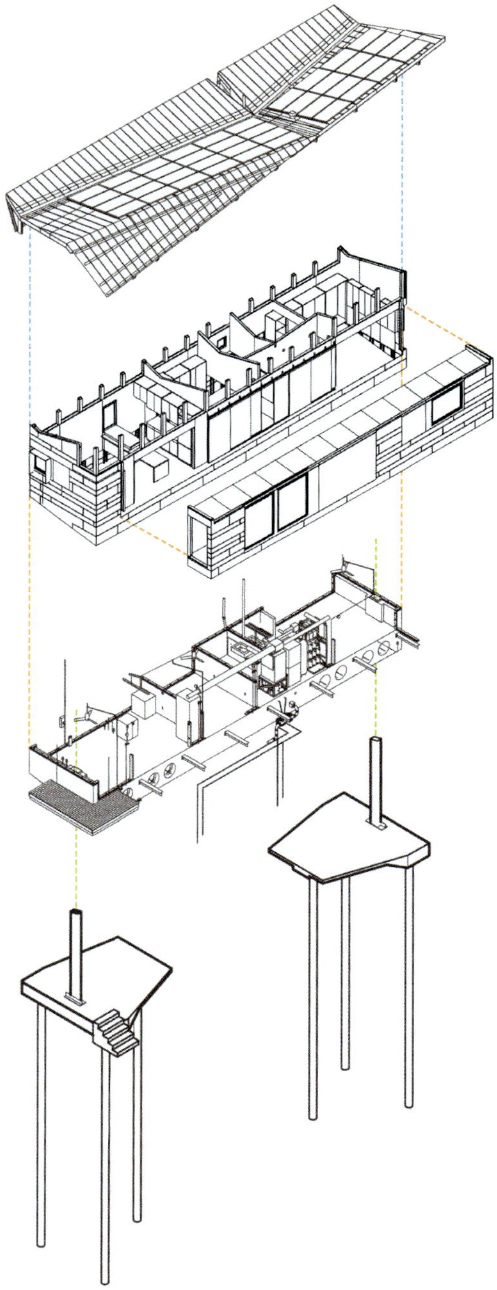

Figure 26.3: An amphibious house was built in the Ninth Ward of New Orleans following the failure of levees. The buoyant foundation sits on the normal grade until a flood occurs, when it rises with floodwaters to an extent of 3 m (12 feet) above normal elevation. Float House, Morphosis.

by 14 m (45 feet) deep pilings, anchor the house to the site and prevent horizontal displacement. Panelised walls were assembled on-site to reduce waste in the 88 m^2 (945 square foot) residence. The amphibious foundation allows the shotgun-style house to rest 1.25 m (4 feet) above grade, a traditional relationship with the ground in New Orleans. When a flood occurs, the house rises up to 3 m (12 feet) to protect the structure and contents from flooding, maintaining utility connections through flexible piping. Sustainable features include a solar photovoltaic roof, rainwater harvest system, ground-source heat exchange, and a highly-insulated building envelope, achieving LEED Platinum certification.

Floating communities can create space for social cohesion along the docks and jetties or in land-side green spaces, clubhouses, and allotments. Jetties should invite visitors to explore the site and interact with the residents, and must be wide enough to accommodate trolleys, bicycles, conversations, strollers, and water-dependent recreation. The following considerations affect the design of floating structures: location, harmonising connections, materials, shape, mooring options, regulatory, and environmental concerns.

KEY DESIGN CONSIDERATIONS

LOCATION

Mooring sites for floating structures should have calm water anchorage, usually found in lakes, canals, or inland waterways. Surface waters are allowed to flow and ebb due to tidal or seasonal changes but a smaller vertical fluctuation places less stress on docks and mooring connections. Site selection should avoid potentially dangerous situations or uncomfortable movement due to currents and waves.

Figure 26.4: Schoonschip in Amsterdam has 30 water plots, 46 floating households, and around 140 residents. The development is planned around a smart jetty that integrates access, utilities, and social spaces. Space & Matter + Alan Jensen.

Stationary floating structures require a minimum water level depth of 1 m at all times to remain afloat; if water levels drop so that floating homes rest on the bottom at low tide it can create stresses that can contribute to cracks or damage to the floats.

Amphibious houses can be placed at sites that would not be suitable for conventional homes, and places that are strategically allowed to flood during periods of heavy rain.

HARMONISING CONNECTIONS AND UTILITIES

Floating structures require connections to land for multiple services, including utilities, deliveries, access to land-based transport, and waste processing provided in a jetty with flexible utility connections below. Fixed height jetties on pile foundations are often damaged more substantially in storms than the adjacent structures designed to float. Ensure that all connections are designed to withstand the maximum expected conditions.

Floating structures are often unshaded by trees or other structures, making the rooftops useful for photovoltaic arrays to offset electricity use. Include battery systems for self-sufficiency and uninterruptible power in an emergency.

Most floating structures obtain potable water from municipal sources on land. In some locations, fresh water from the waterway may be used as greywater. Check local regulatory requirements to see if alternative potable water sources are allowed and obtain water samples to determine if the source water is suitable for treatment to become potable through reverse osmosis, sand, and UV filters.

Hot water is generated using solar thermal systems to capture heat energy generating water temperatures of 70–80°C.

As with conventional construction, water and wastewater pipes above the waterline should be insulated in cold climates. Condensate drainpipes that discharge outdoors should also be insulated.

Insulation on pipes below the waterline can absorb water and become non-insulative and is therefore not recommended.

Wastewater processing is a little different in a floating structure. A residential floating structure will have a macerator with a mechanism that grinds sewage to about 1/16-inch, and a 30- to 50-gallon tank and pump to transport waste through a flexible hose to a land-based treatment site. Wastewater service connections may require backflow preventers or check valves to prevent sewage backup into the floating structure.

A floating biorefinery can serve a cluster of floating residences. This equipment collects wastewater, filters and reuses greywater for non-potable uses, and pumps the effluent to a living machine on a barge for tertiary treatment before releasing the water back to the natural waterway.

MATERIALS

Floating houses are heavy but are able to float because of the large amount of water they displace. Typical floats are large blocks of EPS encapsulated with another material, either concrete, steel, or high-density polyethylene (HDPE) to prevent disintegration from abrasion or animal interactions. Steel floats may require dry-docking for inspection and repair every 15–25 years.

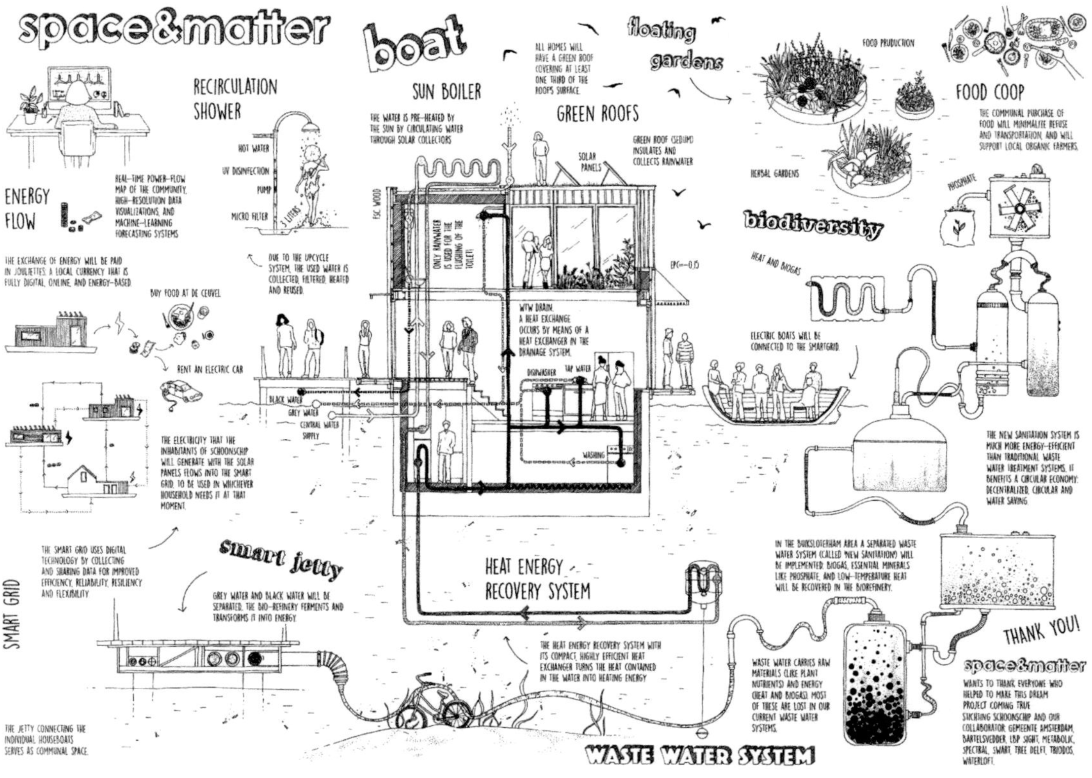

Figure 26.5: A diagram of building services at the floating households at Schoonschip illustrates the unique technical challenges of living sustainably on the water. Solar water heating, heat recovery systems, and renewable energy are treated as common goods, their use tracked by an electronic dashboard. Space & Matter.

Concrete floats may have long life spans. A concrete hull is built with 4,000 PSI concrete and steel reinforcement, typically a grid of #4 (1/2-inch diameter) epoxy-coated rebar in the walls and bottom, and #5 (5/8-inch) rebar at the bottom, corners, and parapet wall.[1]

In regions where timber resources are plentiful, logs, or logs wrapped in polystyrene, may be used as floats. Logs can last up to 75 years underwater; since water contains little oxygen, the underwater portions of logs deteriorate much more slowly than the portions above water. Log floats use pressure-treated wood or steel stringers above the waterline to support the decking and walls.

The superstructure must be lightweight and able to withstand environmental conditions, especially corrosion. Standard cladding materials include treated or close-grained wood, fibre-reinforced concrete board, insulated aluminium panels, or other lightweight materials. Steel at the superstructure should either be 430 stainless steel or have a high-performance coating for corrosion protection. Stainless steel fasteners with rubber washers are preferable to galvanised metal, which can deteriorate.

Exteriors can be painted with polyurethane epoxy to resist the accelerated weathering from the harsh environment - sun, salt spray, corrosion, abrasion from blowing sand, and chemical and other types of weathering. The epoxy coating will deteriorate but offers better protection and is more durable over time.

Ensure the hull has documented positive flotation, so even if a breach of the hull develops, the structure will not sink. Additional flotation may be added to level out the floor once the interior fixtures and belongings have been introduced, using EPS blocks to 'trim' the structure and adjust the angle relative to the water's surface to maintain a level, dry floor.

Railings along jetties allow accessibility under all weather conditions and also invite children to play safely. Low-level lighting at night and non-skid surfaces help people of all abilities navigate walkways safely. Decks that regularly go underwater may use grating to allow water to pass through without resistance. Safety equipment along jetties should include lifebuoys and steps or ladders leading out of the water.

SHAPE

A rectangular shape is the most stable floating shape. When loads shift or a float element rotates, a rectangular shape displaces more water than a circular or triangular shape.

One example of the importance of shape stability is found at the Floating Farm in Rotterdam, which hosts 34 dairy cows on a 450 m^2 (4,843 SF) platform. The rectilinear floating farm never tilts more than 280 mm (11 inches), 'even in winds topping 70 mph or if the herd crowds the stern'.[2]

MOORING OPTIONS

There are generally two options for mooring a floating structure to allow the structure to rise and fall with the water levels. The first, used for both stationary floating and amphibious structures, embeds two or more wood pilings, steel trusses, or concrete posts into the seabed for fore and aft tie-off points. The second option runs cables to anchors permanently embedded in the seabed. These cable anchors - metal chains or composite mooring hawsers made with reinforced rubber and stainless steel - are fixed in a triangulate or X-braced pattern, and can extend to depths of 90 m (295 feet).

The design for floating structures must consider the ramifications of working in an extreme environment, as a permanently moored floating structure should not be allowed to move significantly, even in a storm. Moorings for marine structures are designed for storm events that happen more frequently than those for wind loads on land-based structures. Wind loads on a mooring system are applied to the surface area of the fixed mooring structure (anchorage points), whereas environmental loads (surge force, sway force, and yaw movement from wind, waves, current, tidal variations, tsunamis, and passing vessels) apply to the superstructure and subsurface areas of the vessel, typically much larger areas.

Regular maintenance of connections is essential. Mooring connections that are too loose may allow the floating structure to rub against the dock or slip, abrading the surfaces, causing damage to lead to low cycle fatigue, and accelerated wearing on the hawsers.[3] Braided polyester rope can wear and lose strength over time, and metal fasteners can weather and corrode, needing periodic replacement.

REGULATORY CONSIDERATIONS

Mooring locations are controlled by local jurisdictions to maintain waterway access for all residents. Communities will determine appropriate locations, density, and the availability of municipal utilities for floating structures, which will still be required to meet minimum separation between units for fire safety.[4] Projections may not be allowed over docks or walkways, or beyond the limits of the mooring site.

The minimum freeboard (the space between the waterline and the lowest level of the structure) may vary by jurisdiction but is often between 300 and 400 mm (12–16 inches).

The maximum list (tilt) may also be established by the jurisdiction but is usually in the range of 6 degrees or 50 mm (2 inches) overall.

A jurisdiction may set a maximum height limit for firefighting or zoning conformance. Height limits also preserve viewsheds for land-based residents.

Gangways, jetties, and ramps must meet slope and width requirements to maintain accessibility. Walkways should be sufficiently wide and connected to multiple exit ways to allow residents and visitors to escape a fire without having to jump into the water, which may be freezing or dangerous. Ramps to building entrances should be of sufficient length to meet accessibility standards, no matter the water level.

Floating structures are typically required to display an identification number, mooring number, and a record of inspections. Depending on the jurisdiction, they may be treated as immovable property (the same as landside construction) or movable property (such as a houseboat). This status may affect insurance, mortgages, taxation, and legal compliance.

The US National Flood Insurance Program (NFIP) requires buildings to be constructed using methods and materials that minimise the potential for flood damage affecting the building under construction and nearby buildings. In addition to potential wave and floodwater diversion effects, obstructions such as floating structures can break free and become floodborne debris that may strike and damage other buildings. Therefore, floating structures may not be allowed in Velocity Zones where wave action is anticipated.

ENVIRONMENTAL CONSIDERATIONS

Floating developments are growing in popularity due to growth along coastal edges, the need for additional housing inventory, the desire for a deeper connection with nature, and adaptation strategies to respond fluvial flooding and sea level rise. Floating structures are more environmentally-responsible than land reclamation, which can cause significant environmental damage, demand increasingly scarce fill materials, and can cause permanent changes to waterway ecosystems.

Floating structures may contribute to anaerobic conditions, allowing the growth of invasive species such as mussels on mooring posts. Stationary floating structures can reduce aquatic grasses due to shading, where the presence of a structure covering the water surface influences the penetration of light, although only slight ecological differences were measured below floating structures in the Netherlands.[5]

Floating structures with a minimum 1 m water depth below the structure maintain water quality; lower dissolved oxygen concentrations are found beneath structures floating in less than 1 m due to a lower rate of water renewal and less water movement below the structure.[6]

Floating structures offer many environmental benefits. They contribute to water cooling through shading. Structures with green roofs and dockside plantings attract birds to nest and provide habitat and food for aquatic life.[7] They can also reduce development pressure on sensitive land sites by offering an alternative space for housing and commerce.

IMPACT

Social: Floating communities foster social cohesion among water dwellers, who seek out a deeper connection to nature and find interaction among the members of a close-knit community with similar interests.

Environmental: The initial embodied carbon of a structure made to float may be the same as one constructed on land but the attenuated life span and increased maintenance may result in higher embodied carbon over the structure's life cycle. Negative environmental impacts must be addressed promptly to maintain good water quality in the waterway, quickly correcting leaks or releases.

Economic: The cost of building a floating house is about 8% more expensive than building on land.[8] However, utilities and roadways already serve most waterfront areas, reducing the cost of providing infrastructure to new developments.

Spatial Integration: Floating developments may expand the utilisation of water bodies that have traditionally been off-limits to urban planning. They are not constrained by the same geographical limits as land-based developments and can be located in areas where land is scarce and expensive.

NOTES

1 Gromicko, N. and K. Shepard. Inspecting Floating Homes. International Association of Certified Inspectors (InterNACHI). Accessed at: https://www.nachi.org/inspecting-floating-homes.htm#:~:text=Houseboats%20must%20have%20a%20seaworthy,an%20on%2Dboard%20sewage%20system
2 Mallonnee, L. 2020. Floating Farms Point the Way to Alternative Food Ecosystems. *Wired Magazine*, February 18. Accessed at: https://www.wired.com/story/floating-farms-global-food-ecosystem/
3 Percher, M. 2023. How to Design Permanent Moorings for Nearshore Floating Structures. *Civil Engineering Magazine*. Accessed at: https://www.asce.org/publications-and-news/civil-engineering-source/civil-engineering-magazine/issues/magazine-issue/article/2023/09/how-to-design-permanent-moorings-for-nearshore-floating-structures
4 City of Portland, OR. 2024. City Code, Title 28 Floating Structures. Accessed at: https://www.portland.gov/code/28/05/010
5 Lima, R., F.C. Boogaard, and R. deGraaf. 2015. Innovative Dynamic Water Quality and Ecology Monitoring to Assess about Floating Urbanization Environmental Impacts and Opportunities. Conference Paper: Amsterdam International Water Week Volume 2015. Accessed at: https://www.researchgate.net/publication/283502521_Innovative_dynamic_water_quality_and_ecology_monitoring_to_assess_about_floating_urbanization_environmental_impacts_and_opportunities
6 Lima et al. (2015).
7 Lima, R., R. deGraaf, and F.C. Boogaard. 2022. Impacts of Floating Urbanization on Water Quality and Aquatic Ecosystems: A Study Based on In Situ Data and Observations. *Journal of Water and Climate Change* 13, no. 3, 1185–1203. Accessed at: https://iwaponline.com/jwcc/article/13/3/1185/87023/Impacts-of-floating-urbanization-on-water-quality
8 Charalambides, D. 2022. How Are Floating Houses Priced in Relation to Comparable On-Land Housing? Evidence from Portland, USA. University of Groningen, Netherlands. Accessed at: https://frw.studenttheses.ub.rug.nl/4027/1/Master%20Thesis%20RES%20Final%20-%20Demetrios%20Charalambides%20%20%28s4733215%29.pdf

RESOURCES

- Floating Amsterdam: The Development of IJburg's Waterbuurt. Municipality of Amsterdam, Projectbureau IJburg. Accessed at: https://www.ansa.it/documents/1334931625986_AmsterdamFloating.pdf
- Gromicko, N. and K. Shepard. Inspecting Floating Homes. International Association of Certified Inspectors (InterNACHI). Accessed at: https://www.nachi.org/inspecting-floating-homes.htm#:~:text=Houseboats%20must%20have%20a%20seaworthy,an%20on%2Dboard%20sewage%20system
- Schoonschip: A Sustainable Floating Community. Space & Matter. Accessed at: https://www.spaceandmatter.nl/work/schoonschip

PART III

Wind

The extreme weather of the future is not the extreme weather of the past. Unimaginable storms now travel inland for hundreds of miles, causing devastation in areas once considered safe. Storms have doubled in size since 1980, and so-called '500-year storms' arrive with terrifying regularity. By 2100, catastrophic hurricanes are expected to double in frequency, with an increase of 25–30% per 1°C of warming. In addition, the paths of tornadoes are getting longer and wider as the thunderstorms that spawn them increase.

Protecting occupants and reducing property damage from high wind events at the Community scale requires architects to understand the forces of wind and their interactions with buildings through **Wind Analysis**. The effects of **Spatial Texture** in cities can help to dissipate winds. Solutions for **Temporary Housing** assist those displaced by storms.

At the Site scale, **Defensible Landscape** reinforces efforts at the building edge with windbreaks and screens.

At the Building scale, understanding the principles behind **Continuous Load Path** and **Envelope + Breach** leads to more robust structures. Designing to withstand **Collateral Damage** addresses falling debris and laydown hazards at the roof. **Safe Rooms** provide near-absolute protection against tornadoes and hurricanes. The ancient protection strategy of **Earth Shelter** is gaining credence as a solution against wind and debris-impact. Architects also need to accommodate an **Emergency Cache** in residential units, offices, and gathering places to store essential water and food.

There are winds we can manage and winds we cannot control. How much of the built environment succumbs to wind damage is a factor of materials, connections, site exposure, and the skill employed in design and construction. It has always been the architect's responsibility to build for the future, even if the future seems more uncertain than the past.

WIND ANALYSIS 27

ADAPTATION **WIND** SCALE **COMMUNITY**

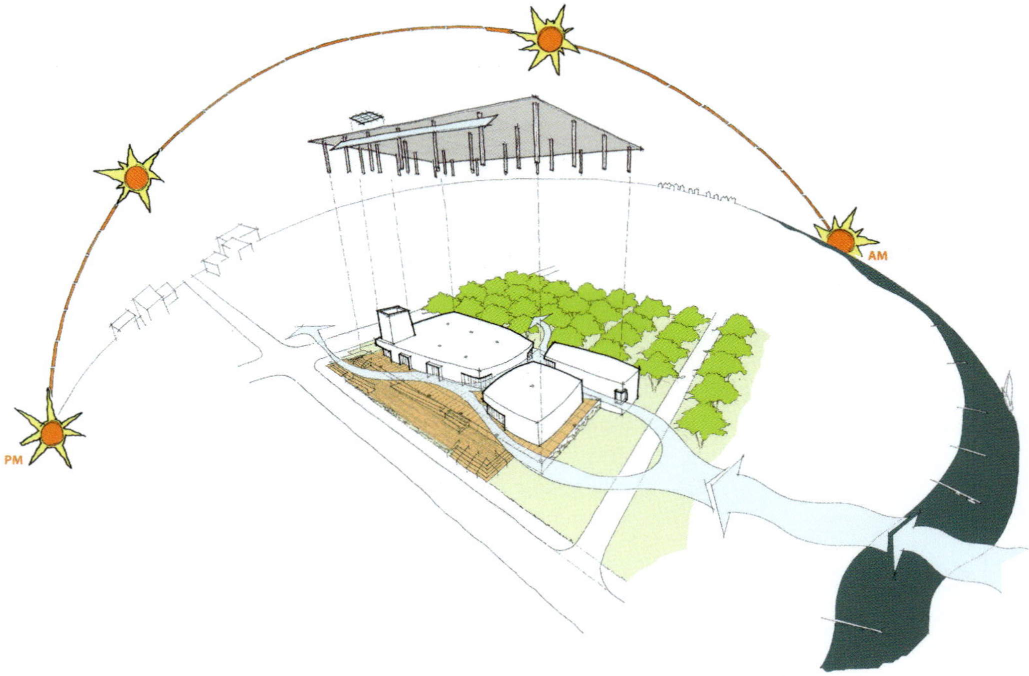

Wind analysis distinguishes the desirable effects of wind upon the built environment, such as improving natural ventilation and dispersing pollutants, from the negative impacts that can be addressed through design: areas of concentrated wind, damage from wind loading and windborne debris, and decreased thermal comfort. Sophisticated wind analysis can: (1) optimise building form, height, and orientation to mitigate wind damage; (2) reduce wind gusts, downdraughts, and eddies in the spaces between buildings to improve pedestrian comfort; and (3) admit airflow to promote natural ventilation.

Figure 27.1: Sun and wind analysis at Studio Waveland. Exterior circulation between enclosed programme areas reduces heating and cooling and invites access from all sides of the building. Prevailing winds come from the south, water side of the project. A double roof system protects pedestrian circulation from rain and direct sunlight.

DOI: 10.4324/9781032702964-31

BACKGROUND

Wind affects every location on the globe with individual characteristics of wind speed, direction, and frequency. Global increases in water temperatures are very likely to generate stronger tropical cyclones, with 5% faster winds (3% for the Atlantic basin). Although the overall global frequency of tropical cyclones will likely decrease, the frequency of Category 4–5 hurricanes is projected to increase. Severe thunderstorms and increased downdraughts will increase under stronger warming scenarios.[1] Designing for wind resistance is becoming increasingly critical to ensure the safety of occupants and neighbours and create durable structures that can resist higher wind pressures.

A wind rose illustrates the wind speed and direction, and the frequency that wind blows from a particular direction. The circular format corresponds to the compass directions, the spoke length indicates the amount of time the wind blows from that direction, and the colours indicate wind speeds. Wind rose diagrams help designers visualise wind patterns at a site and recognise seasonal patterns, but designers should pay close attention to the frequency and direction of the strongest winds affecting the site in the design of the main wind force resisting system. A good understanding of the wind conditions

Figure 27.2: Wind direction, speed, and frequency is summarised in a wind rose. In this example from Fort Dodge, Iowa, the strongest winds blow from the south and north-northwest (crimson and orange). This wind rose shows evenly distributed low wind speeds, which may be ideal for natural ventilation. Iowa University Mesonet.

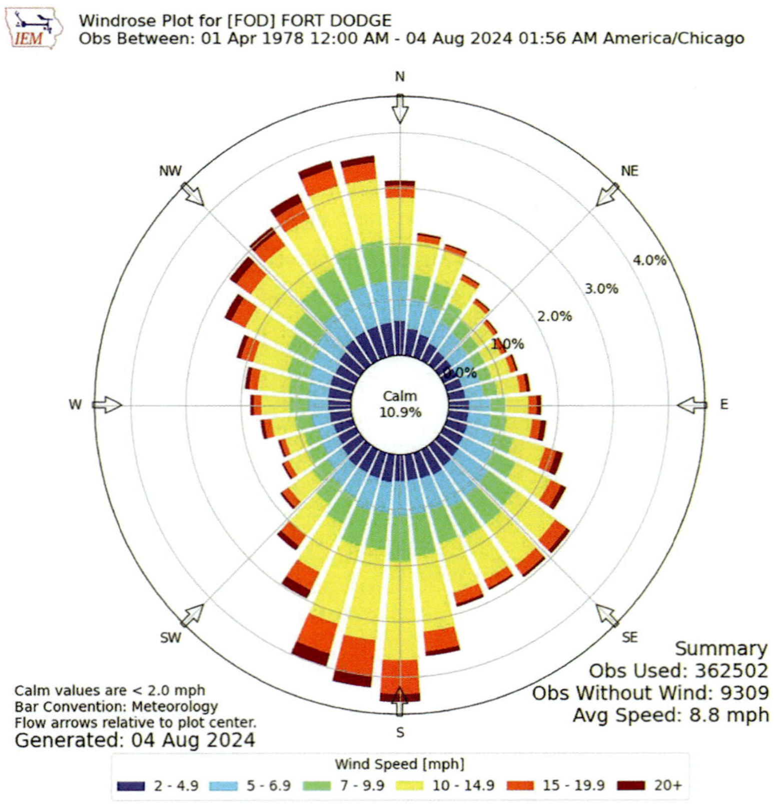

over the seasons can improve site and building design and performance.

Fluid dynamics describes the flow of liquids and gases around any object that obstructs their path. When applied to building design, wind analysis simulates the airflow interacting with the building and its context, illustrating where air separates and becomes turbulent and develops pockets of high and low pressure. As the wind separates around a building, it generates three types of forces: along-wind forces, which acts in the direction of the airflow and transmits positive pressure on the upwind side and negative pressure on the downwind side; cross-wind forces, which act perpendicular to the sides of the building; and torsional forces, which encourage the building to rotate.

To understand wind loading on a structure, designers must understand the way air moves across the terrain and interacts with nearby obstacles.

Terrain and surface roughness. The International Code Council measures variations in surface roughness of adjacent conditions including ground irregularities from topography, vegetation, and constructed features. Exposure categories indicate the conditions that prevail in the upwind directions and are used to determine the amplification of wind to calculate design wind pressures. Open, unobstructed areas (such as large bodies of water, grasslands, or fields) enable winds to ramp up before they interact with a structure. The resulting design wind pressure influences the shape, orientation, height, and design of openings in a structure.

Turbulent drag or friction occurs when Earth's surface, vegetation, or objects cause resistance to airflow and reduce wind speed. Drag is lower in the high atmosphere where there are no objects, causing winds to speed up. Surface roughness B is characterised by terrain with closely spaced obstructions such as urban or suburban sites or forested areas. Surface roughness C is open terrain with scattered obstructions. Surface roughness D includes unobstructed areas, marshes, flat plains, and open water surfaces, where wind speeds can increase up to 200%.[2]

Natural landforms have a marked effect on wind exposure. Wind accelerates at the top of a hill, so sites at the top of a ridge, escarpment, or head of a valley facing into the prevailing wind will be subject to higher winds. Elevated sites experience a greater frequency of windy days, while sites in a depression are usually more sheltered. Part of this acceleration is explained by the pressure gradient force, which accelerates airflow from high to low pressure following the path of least resistance. Air pressure is greatest at low elevations and decreases with altitude where there are fewer gas particles per unit volume, encouraging air to rise. Higher wind speeds can also be tempered by landforms: a windward berm creates a sheltered zone in its lee and a terrace wall can deflect winds past the occupied zone.

The interface between terrain and water causes air movement due to temperature differentials. Water has a higher heat capacity than soils, and it takes much more energy to raise the temperature of water, causing soils to heat much faster than large bodies of water. During the day, land is heated by solar gain, causing warmer air to rise. Because air flows from an area of high pressure to low pressure, the cooler air over the water flows toward the land mass, resulting in onshore breezes after sunrise. After sunset, the airflow reverses, flowing from land toward the water. Regions experiencing warmer ocean temperatures from climate change have a lower temperature differential between land and water, resulting in weaker or altered onshore breezes.

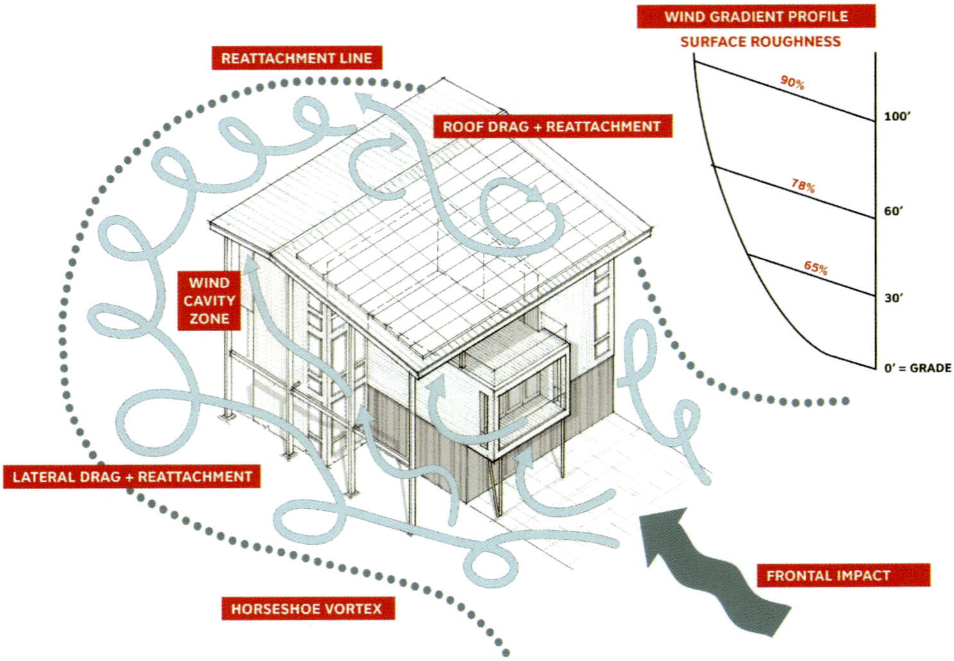

Figure 27.3: Flow diagrams can simplify an architect's understanding of flow patterns, wind and thermal comfort, and pollutant dispersal or concentration. If wind is perpendicular to the building face, it is slowed by the windward façade and accelerates along the side walls and roof, oscillating between flow separation and reattachment. Wind speed and turbulent drag are affected by surface roughness at the earth's surface. A wind shadow is the location where separated flows are reattached at the downwind side of the building.

Interference from nearby obstacles. Wind speed increases when air movement is restricted by an object in its path, channelled through a narrow gap, or compressed by surrounding landforms, a principle called the Venturi effect where pressure rises and velocity increases. Air currents are affected by a building's orientation to wind direction, shape in plan and profile, dimensions, surface roughness, and porosity (percentage of openings). The impacts from surrounding buildings and vegetation are exponentially complex, requiring increasingly sensitive modelling to calculate airflows.

Wind flow around a building is divided into four distinct zones. Upwind from the obstacle is the *displacement zone*, where the air is slowed by the windward face, and a stagnation area occurs where the flow splits; as airflow separates it accelerates around the corners of the windward face, subjecting the side walls and roof to suction. The *separated flow* along the building sides and the roof may reattach and separate again, creating eddies and turbulence. The separated flow has a point of *eventual reattachment* beyond the *wind shadow* of the downwind facade.[3]

Modelling offers valuable information for architectural design, but there are concepts which can be applied intuitively once the general principles of airflow are understood.

- Orientation: If long street canyons are oriented parallel to the wind direction the airflow is channelised and accelerates; when air flows over building-lined streets at a 45-degree angle, the bar effect creates a localised area of accelerated wind speed.
- Shape in plan and section: A pyramidal object tends to create a smaller wind shadow than a rectangular shape because it has less cornering effect, similar to the effect found in buildings with multiple setbacks. Curved or oblong plan shapes reduce turbulent airflow in their wake and decrease wind pressures on the structural frame. A curved roof directs airflow over a structure, reducing acceleration and uplift.
- Dimensions: The taller and wider the structure, the larger the wind shadow. A solid, rectangular building casts a wind shadow approximately four times its height.[4]
- Surface roughness: Abrupt changes in the city fabric, from a variety of building heights or setbacks, create a rougher surface area in contact with the wind, leading to greater turbulence. A multi-faceted or deeply indented façade may slow winds slightly due to increased friction.
- Porosity: The denser the obstacle, the more pronounced the wind shadow and the greater the downwind turbulence. A semi-porous object such as a screen diffuses airflow with an effect that extends over a larger area than the shadow from a solid object.

Figure 27.4: Computational fluid dynamics (CFD) simulations can be used for many applications. External CFD simulations are used to determine pedestrian wind comfort, wind loads, wind-driven rain, façade ventilation, or water surface level and stormwater behaviour in sewage systems. In indoor environments, CFD simulations resolve temperature distribution and thermal comfort, and contaminant dispersion such as CO_2 concentrations or relative humidity. Sweco.

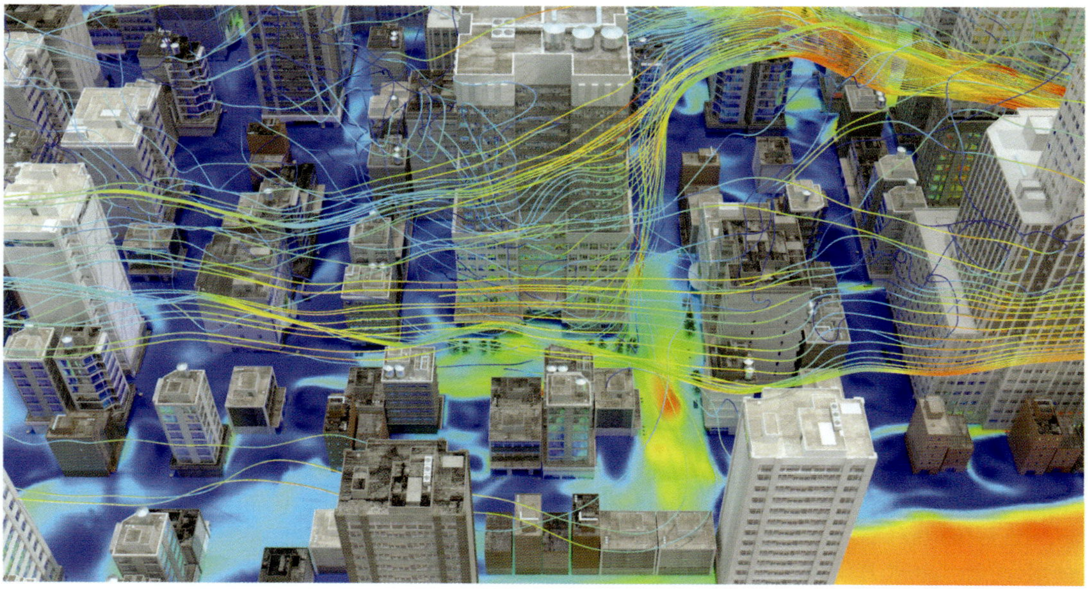

The wind analysis process should identify the targets for design performance, as determined by the answers to several questions: What is the sustained design wind speed at the site? Does high wind constitute a high priority hazard at this site? Are unusual wind conditions possible due to mountainous terrain, promontories, or other landforms? What is the ICC Risk Category for the project? Does the facility need to support continuous operations during and immediately after a high-wind event? How might cascading consequences such as the loss of overhead power service affect the site, occupants, and community? What is the potential for changes in wind exposure? What are the future projections for wind in the project area?

Computational fluid dynamics (CFD) modelling has transformed wind analysis with increased precision, allowing architects to test refinements instantaneously: mapping peak high and low pressures on the building that require additional reinforcement; influencing parametric design by testing strategies to adapt to winds; developing wind comfort studies for pedestrians around buildings; and optimising natural ventilation. CFD models simulate wind flow using a computer-based numerical analysis, producing more accurate results than those possible with wind tunnel testing apparatus. The computer models incorporate accurate terrain and meteorological data to identify wind directions, flows, turbulence, and shear.

Urban CFD analysis uses local wind data from a worldwide database[5] and runs simulations from 16 wind directions, corresponding to a wind rose with each quadrant divided into four sections. CFD models include buildings within 400 m of the centre of the project site, although they can include taller buildings outside that radius if the buildings have a potential influence on wind conditions at the site. Large mature trees are included, but landscape features under 8 m (26 feet) in height are often excluded. A CFD model includes a detailed 3D representation of the proposed building, including all features projecting more than 0.5 m. The model breaks up the environment into small cells (called a mesh) measuring 0.3 m, with a smaller mesh at critical locations such as corners and entrances. The resulting model is used to optimise the building form and structure, design for pedestrian comfort, and promote natural ventilation.

KEY DESIGN CONSIDERATIONS

OPTIMISE BUILDING FORM AND STRUCTURE

Orient buildings with the smallest area facing into the wind and the longest dimension parallel to the predominant wind direction to mitigate the impact of wind loads on the structure. This will minimise loads on the Main Wind Force Resisting System (MWFRS): shear walls, roof trusses, diaphragms, cross-bracing, and other structural elements that work together to resist wind forces. The MWFRS distributes wind loads evenly to reduce the risk of structural failure.

When designing a new building, wind impacts can be moderated by keeping the height of the building as low as possible to take advantage of surface roughness near the ground. Average wind speed increases with building height with possible effects including: turbulence buffeting (strong, repeated assaults of wind); galloping (self-induced vibrations produced as an effect of wind load); and vortex shedding (a pattern of swirling vortices created as the wind flows past the building creating alternating low-pressure zones on the downwind façade. When wind speed increases, the vortex shedding frequency attempts to match the building's natural frequency, leading to building sway and potentially dislodging windowpanes). These effects are mitigated by aerodynamic modifications of the building, by elements on the façade to disrupt turbulence,

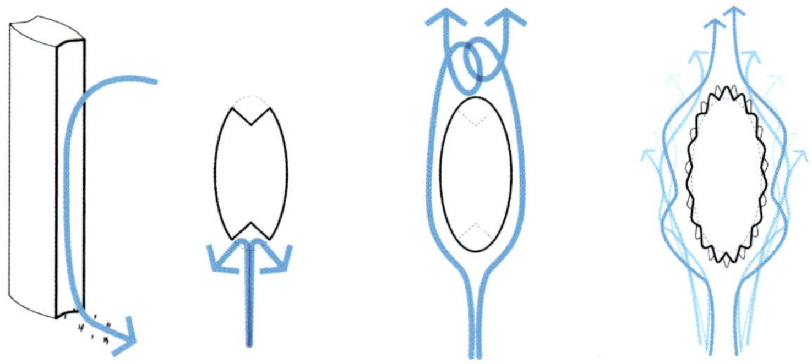

Figure 27.5: Wind analysis revealed that filling in the missing 'ends' of the existing tower's shape, as well as adding a textured façade of bay windows, would greatly reduce wind forces to improve pedestrian comfort at ground level. Studio Gang, Tour Montparnasse Competition Entry, Paris, France, 2017.

or tuned mass dampers to calm galloping and vortex shedding.

Keep building heights relatively uniform along the street so wind can flow uninterrupted over rooftops. Abrupt differences in the height of structures can result in higher gusts and strong downdraughts.

Test design options to find the aerodynamic form and optimal orientation and height of a proposed new building. Design modifications might include creating baffles, deflectors, or spoilers; softening corners; tapering the height or varying the cross-section with setbacks; and adding openings, bleed slots, or other methods of adding porosity to the mass. CFD analysis can optimise the shape to reduce the materials needed to resist the expected forces. For example, walls curved in plan to direct wind around the structure could reduce the amount of concrete in the structure by 20% due to the curved wall's ability to resist overturning.

Adaptive or kinetic building facades are composed of louvers, plates, screens, or origami-shaped panels, which act as flow-altering mechanisms to help combat vibration in tall buildings. A smart façade system responds with configurations programmed to specific wind conditions. The controller must be able to measure wind conditions, measure the orientation between each of the façade plates, and be programmed in advance to set a plate angle that minimises vibration amplitude.[6] Artificial intelligence may soon be able to control wind-deflecting and solar-shading plates more rapidly and with greater precision.

Roof geometry also has a significant effect on wind loads. Aerodynamic roofs have little overhang to catch winds and exert uplift forces. Roofs curved in section offer less resistance to wind pressures. Similarly, hip roofs offer better performance due to lower overall surface area than gable roofs, fewer sharp corners, and a more stable pyramidal shape. Steeply pitched roofs usually perform better than flat roofs because uplift on windward roof slopes is reduced. Flat or low-pitched roofs may increase leeward turbulence, especially in low-rise construction.

In suburban areas, maintain distances between buildings in the range of 1.5–2.5 times the overall building height. Create wind barriers between structures with fencing or vegetation.

Create wind shelter zones within a subdivision by arranging the buildings in an irregular pattern to disrupt direct wind paths. This site planning method increases the ground roughness and contributes to lower wind speeds. (Chapter 28: Spatial Texture.)

On sites where the wind always comes from one direction and very exposed sites, align buildings to follow the wind direction, allowing each building to shelter the one in its lee.

Wind flows upward at a sloping or hilly site. Updraughts can be reduced by locating the building as far back as possible from the edge of the slope, terracing the slope to form sheltered zones, or adding decks to deflect the wind.[7]

OPTIMISE PEDESTRIAN COMFORT

Wind speeds below 5 m/sec (below 18 km/hr) are comfortable and safe for pedestrians. In winds of 5–8 m/sec (18–30 km/hr), dust and debris is suspended and blows about. Sharp corners and intersections create accelerated air speeds and intensified wind gusts, a phenomenon known as the cornering effect. This effect can be mitigated by orienting the street grid parallel to the prevailing wind direction to streamline airflow. At the building scale, chamfered or rounded building edges reduce the cornering effect.

Step façades back as the building rises to reduce the effect of downdraughts at ground level. Introduce roof canopies, balconies, covered walkways and arcades to provide shelter from downdraughts at lower levels.

Design wind-shelters using the building form and accessory structures to protect pedestrians, seating areas, alcoves, and entrances from wind gusts and downdraughts. Design outdoor spaces to reduce wind velocity. Courtyards were developed in ancient times to improve the microclimate by deflecting wind, trapping sunlight, and moderating temperature through thermal mass walls. A courtyard buffers wind if the length of the courtyard does not exceed six times the height of the walls.[8] The wind speed inside a courtyard is about 55–85% less than external wind speeds[9] although the precise value of the shelter depends on courtyard geometry and wind characteristics. The best wind protection is found in smaller courtyards with limited opportunities for air circulation.

Introduce or restore urban landscapes to disrupt winds and turbulent downdraughts with an allée of street trees that offer side benefits such as trapping pollutants and providing shade. Vegetation screens can protect pedestrian areas and reduce eddies at intersections.

Avoid wide, straight streets that can channelise winds and accelerate wind speed. Many traffic calming measures – curved streets, narrow lanes, overhanging trees – are also wind calming measures.

Construct wind breaks with fences and freestanding elements. Fences and screens provide the simplest and most immediate form of shelter from the wind, reducing wind speed and volume. A solid fence that completely blocks the wind will provide protection immediately adjacent to the fence but will create downwind turbulence. Paradoxically, a permeable fence is better at reducing wind speed. A fence with about 40–50% open area provides a sheltered lee area with a width of four to five times the fence height.[10] Angling the top of a fence toward the wind direction can further reduce turbulence downstream.

In suburban areas, landscape shelter belts provide optimum shelter when the average porosity is about 50–60% solid, with dense planting at the ground level. Trees allow some wind to pass through, reducing turbulence on the lee side. Trees can be grouped in a convex arc to deflect wind around a building rather than a concave arc to dam the wind. The optimal shelter belt has a length at least 15 times its height, with continuous plant density and consistent spacing. A Leyland cypress shelter belt with 15 m (50 feet) high trees should be about 230 m (750 feet) long.

PROMOTE NATURAL VENTILATION

Orient the building so that the shorter axis aligns with prevailing winds to provide the greatest opportunity for natural ventilation; orienting the long axis parallel to prevailing winds provides the least opportunities for passive ventilation.

Buildings and open spaces can be organised to preserve the neighbouring building's access to cooling breezes but this may conflict with the spatial distribution intended to reduce wind loads. To promote cross-ventilation, buildings should be separated by a distance five to seven times the building height to ensure adequate airflow. If buildings are irregularly distributed without a consistent setback, airflow between buildings as greater and the distance may be decreased.

Natural ventilation depends largely on air movement to cool occupants. An open building relies on its connection to the outside wind environment for ventilation. An open/closed building operates in different modes at different times of day based on a balance point, where the building must be cooled when the outside temperature reaches a certain degree, and heated when it reaches temperatures below the balance point.

A typical cross-ventilation configuration depends on a pair of windows located on opposite walls but the precise location and angle between the windows varies by climate and wind direction. Spaces with windows on only one side will not circulate air farther than two times the floor to ceiling height into the building; they have an average velocity of 3.3–4.7% of the outside air velocity. Spaces with windows on opposite sides can expect the natural ventilation effectiveness limit to be less than five times the floor to ceiling height into the building; interior velocity can be 35–65% of outside air velocity.[11] Maintain an unobstructed path between the inlet and the outlet for adequate airflow.

Cross ventilation requires minimum opening sizes to maintain air movement through the building. In general, the required inlet size is a percentage of the floor area based on outdoor wind speed and desired cooling effect. A wind speed of 3 mph can remove 75 Btu/hour/square foot if openings comprise 20% of the floor area. At 8 mph, the openings need only be 8% of the floor area.[12] If the temperature differential between inside and outside is less than 3°F, openings must be proportionally larger.

Buildings with natural ventilation typically have a narrow floor plate to promote cross-ventilation. The 2030 Palette recommendation for daylighting[13] is also useful for natural ventilation. Use the 4.5/9 m (15/30 foot) rule-of-thumb for developing building shapes and floor plates with: a 4.5 m (15 foot) perimeter zone depth for task daylighting and access to natural ventilation;

IMPACT

Social: Incorporating wind analysis in design can resist building collapse or dislodged components; address downdraughts and eddies to ensure pedestrian comfort and safety; and promote airflow for natural ventilation. These measures enhance the safety, utility, durability, and convenience of the built environment.

Environmental: Actions resulting from wind analysis can reduce soil erosion and increase planting of shelter belts and wind breaks. These wind-resistive measures have multiple benefits, reducing urban heat islands, expanding habitat for birds and other species, and managing stormwater.

Economic: Wind analysis can identify solutions to pedestrian discomfort and enhance street-level activity. Design modifications can decrease initial construction costs by optimising the building form and the structure. Analysis can also reduce operational costs effective natural ventilation.

Spatial Integration: A wind-responsive city is altered in many ways. At the city scale, new streets are oriented to align with or protect from winds. Building shapes and structural frames are streamlined, with added elements to create drag such as baffles, deflectors, or setbacks. Building forms and openings are organised and oriented to promote natural ventilation.

and an adjacent 4.5 m (15 foot) zone with ambient daylighting and incidental air movement.

Stack ventilation uses low inlets to admit cool, fresh air, and high outlets for exhaust. The effect is enhanced by increasing the vertical distance between inlet and outlet, along with proper sizing and orientation of the openings. Using an elevated stack or tower that exhausts above the roof plane increases efficiency, as does placing the outlet in a negative pressure zone (downwind).

NOTES

1 The National Academies Press. 2023. *Fifth National Climate Assessment, Chapter 2: Climate Trends*. Washington, DC. https://doi.org/10.17226/26757.
2 Building Research Association of New Zealand (BRANZ). 2018. *Managing Wind Effects Around Buildings*. Judgeford, Porirua, NZ. Accessed at: https://d39d3mj7qio96p.cloudfront.net/media/documents/BU620-Managing-wind.pdf
3 Bensalem, R. 1991. *Wind-Driven Ventilation in Courtyard and Atrium-Type Buildings*. Sheffield: University of Sheffield, p. 51. Accessed at: https://etheses.whiterose.ac.uk/3000/1/DX197102.pdf
4 Spirn, A.W. 1986. *Air Quality at Street Level: Strategies for Urban Design*. Boston, MA: Boston Redevelopment Authority, p. 20.
5 Copernicus Climate Data Store can be accessed at: cds.climate.copernicus.eu
6 Abdelaziz, K., A. Alipour, and J. Hobeck. 2021. A Smart Façade System Controller for Optimized Wind-Induced Vibration Mitigation in Tall Buildings. *Journal of Wind Engineering and Industrial Aerodynamics* 212.
7 BRANZ (2018).
8 Bensalem (1991).
9 Bensalem (1991).
10 BRANZ (2018).
11 Brown, G.Z. 1985. *Sun, Wind, Light: Architectural Design Strategies*. New York: John Wiley and Sons, p. 138.
12 Brown (1985, p. 91).
13 2030 Palette is a project of Architecture 2030. Accessed at: https://2030palette.org/form-for-daylighting/

RESOURCES

- Building Research Association of New Zealand (BRANZ). 2018. Managing Wind Effects Around Buildings. Judgeford, Porirua, NZ. Accessed at: https://d39d3mj7qio96p.cloudfront.net/media/documents/BU620-Managing-wind.pdf
- Wind Rose Data (U.S.): Midwestern Regional Climate Center, cli-MATE Database: https://mrcc.purdue.edu/CLIMATE/ Wind Rose Data (EU): Climate Data Store Toolbox: https://cds.climate.copernicus.eu/applications
- Yoon, N. et al. 2020. Optimization of Window Positions for Wind-Driven Natural Ventilation Performance. *Energies* 13, no. 10. https://doi.org/10.3390/en13102464

SPATIAL TEXTURE 28

ADAPTATION **WIND** SCALE **COMMUNITY**

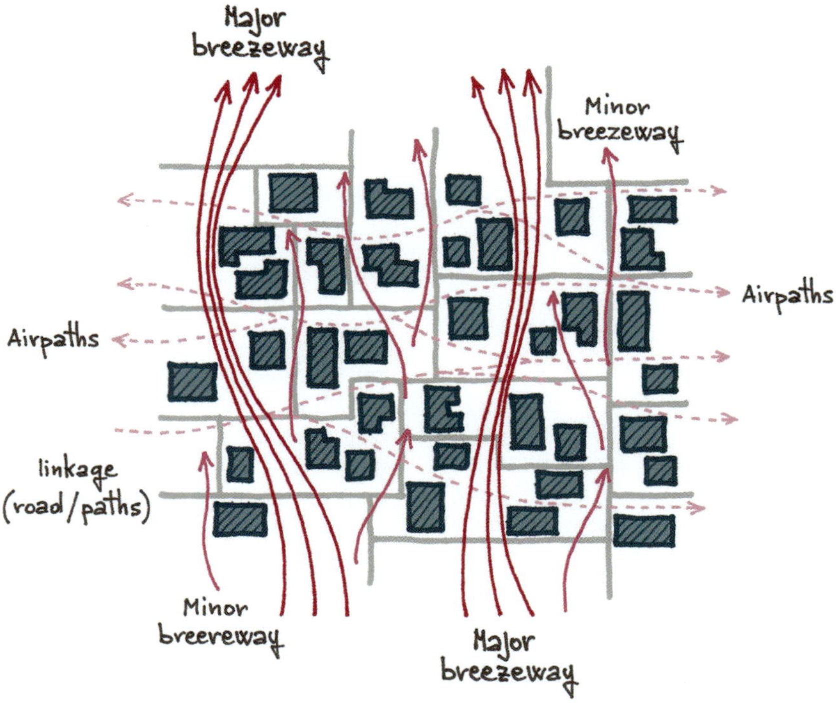

Ordered cities with regular grids generate urban street canyons that channelise and amplify winds, resulting in greater exposure to wind. Disordered cities with low density, irregular geometry, random spacing, and mixed orientation, offer better protection from winds as nonuniform buildings create friction to dissipate wind strength and send smaller flows in multiple directions. These disordered patterns reduce overall damage from high wind events, making the practice of increasing spatial texture in the urban environment a strategy for hazard mitigation.

Figure 28.1: A city plan marked by disorder diffuses wind instead of channelising it along urban street canyons. Federico M. Butera, Energy and Resource Efficient Urban Neighbourhood Design Principles for Tropical Countries: A Practitioner's Guidebook. UN-Habitat.

DOI: 10.4324/9781032702964-32

BACKGROUND

Buildings interact constantly with the wind, directing airflow patterns, creating turbulence, and establishing pockets of wind-resistance. As wind moves through low density, high disorder environments such as those found in medieval cities, wind speed is reduced as wind is channelled into dead ends, deflected by buildings in its path, and exhausted by twists and turns. In highly ordered, high density cities, wind speed accelerates down street canyons and around corners.

Urban texture measures the probability of finding a building within a certain distance from another building. It is calculated by drawing a radius (typically 0.5 km) around each building in a city and counting the number of buildings within the circle. The higher the probability, the more ordered and regular the local texture is, while the lower the probability, the more disordered and unpredictable. The greatest wind load reductions occur in locales with low density and high disorder.[1]

Figure 28.2: Wind loads are amplified in high density, low disorder environments, such as New York City's gridded street canyons. Allison Anderson.

This interference of neighbouring structures is accounted for in the International Code Council's exposure categories. The surrounding terrain determines the exposure factor at the mean roof height, where the surface roughness is derived from the average height and area density of nearby obstructions: Exposure A (urban), Exposure B (suburban), Exposure C (open terrain), and Exposure D (water surfaces). Comparatively denser terrain classes, such as Exposure A, correspond to lower wind loads.

Adapting to the potential for higher winds and stronger hurricanes suggests that coastal cities might enhance disorder within existing communities and plan new neighbourhoods with irregular geometries to trap and deflect winds. A disordered urban environment is distinguished by variety in mutual positioning: the shape and geometry of the buildings and interstitial spaces, and the orientation of a building to its neighbours. This approach to city planning conflicts with much of the current planning canon, which prioritises broad, straight boulevards, high connectivity, uniform building heights, and continuous setbacks. Drawbacks to a disordered city plan include difficulties in navigating the city, with associated traffic and emergency access issues. Urban districts with narrow streets and irregular patterns may restrict the potential to tap into natural ventilation in periods of heat stress, as spatially confined locations have a smaller volume of air at slower velocities. Spaces with reduced air penetration may also develop higher particulate concentrations.

KEY DESIGN CONSIDERATIONS

Plan for disorder at the city scale to dissipate high winds. Prioritise variety in street layouts by establishing asymmetrical and non-orthogonal patterns. Design narrow roadways that change direction frequently. Where wider boulevards are needed to manage traffic, incorporate a tree-lined median.

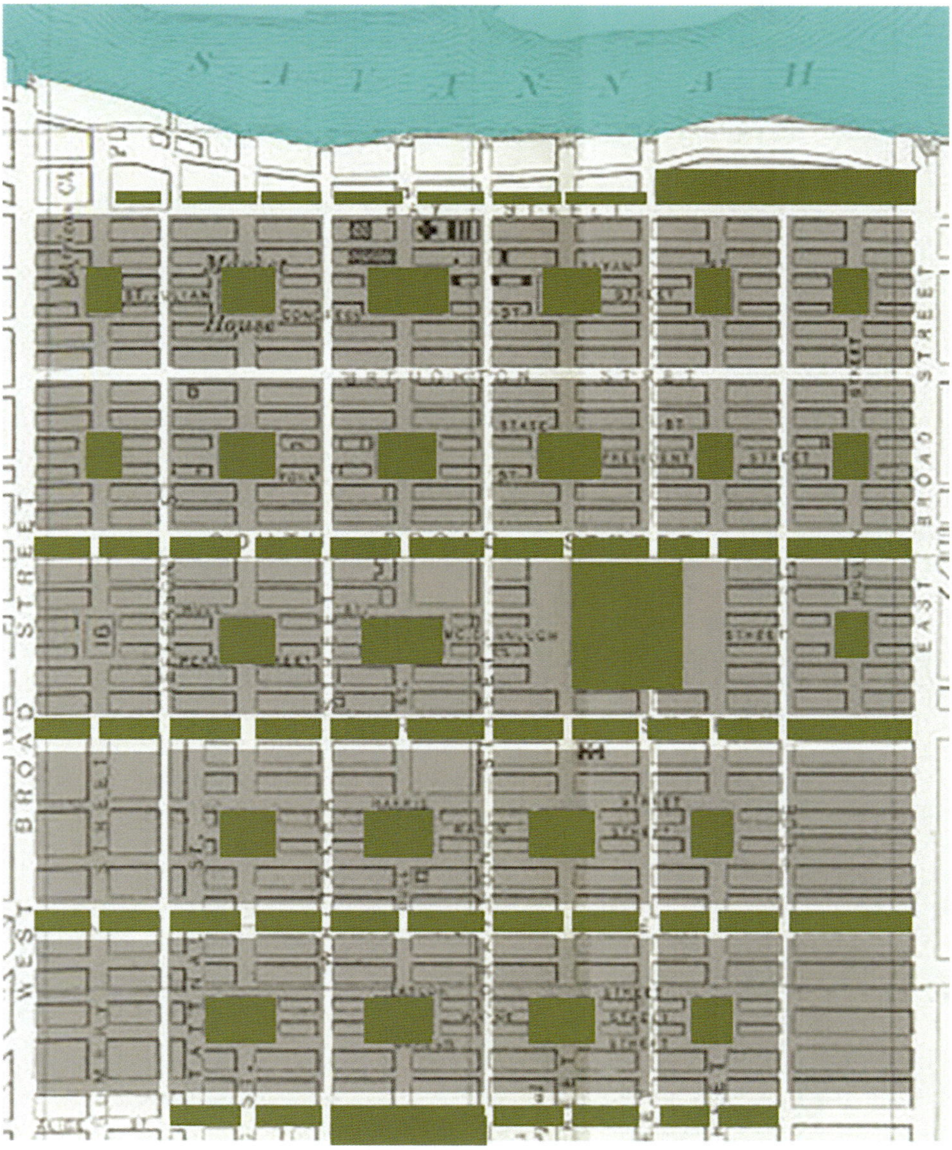

Figure 28.3: Savannah, Georgia's city plan, developed by James Edward Oglethorpe in 1730, has a network of repetitive grids with a mix of residential and commercial lots surrounding a green square. Originally designed with 24 squares, the open spaces have a standardised dimension of 61 m (200 feet) measured north to south, with the east-west dimension between 30 and 90 m (100 and 300 feet)

Establish small city blocks with multiple intersections to spread out airflow. Offset streets if possible.

Street grids can follow the natural line of topography and waterways, or change direction to avoid features such as existing buildings and specimen trees.

Incorporate void spaces along the length of the street to reduce the dominant wind canyon effect. Stagger setbacks at the street level and in the envelope of the building above to create isolated roughness, which more rapidly dissipates overall wind strength.[2]

Interrupt the grid with open spaces. Create voids along the street for pocket parks, gardens, and sheltered plazas.

Create more penetrations along the edge of the city facing the predominant wind direction to relieve pressure. A permeability of 20–30% open disperses winds broadly if the streets behind the city façade maintain a disordered pattern.[3] Wind-facing structures must be reinforced to resist higher exposure).

Avoid uniformity in building height. Irregular building heights and misaligned placement create local turbulence and downdraughts, dispersing wind energy into diffuse, smaller pockets within the urban environment.

Orient substantial buildings at angles to regular street grids to break up channelised patterns but note this may cause isolated roughness. Use CFD modelling to determine the optimum orientation to deflect wind patterns and identify critical points of reinforcement in the structure.

Wind accelerates in large, open spaces 400 m (1/4 mile) or greater. Walls taller than four stories high can shelter a courtyard space up to 50–60 m (165–200 feet) wide; to invite winds, create smaller courtyards where wind may slip into the open space.

Restore clusters of trees to the built environment to deflect winds. Install windbreaks, plant medians and cul-de-sacs, exposed ridges and roadside verges. Plant densely, with layers of groundcover and shrubs.

To manage high particulate concentrations and protect sensitive users of disordered and narrow streets, designate pedestrian-only pathways and restrict high emission vehicles.

Adjust zoning ordinances to deliver a city texture that will reduce wind loading. Allow a variety of lot sizes and setbacks to create low density, high disorder environments.

Provide wind mitigation for existing buildings in communities with high density and low disorder. In wood-framed buildings, use hurricane strapping or tie-downs, provide hurricane shutters at windows and doors, improve roof deck attachment, and install secondary water resistance.[5]

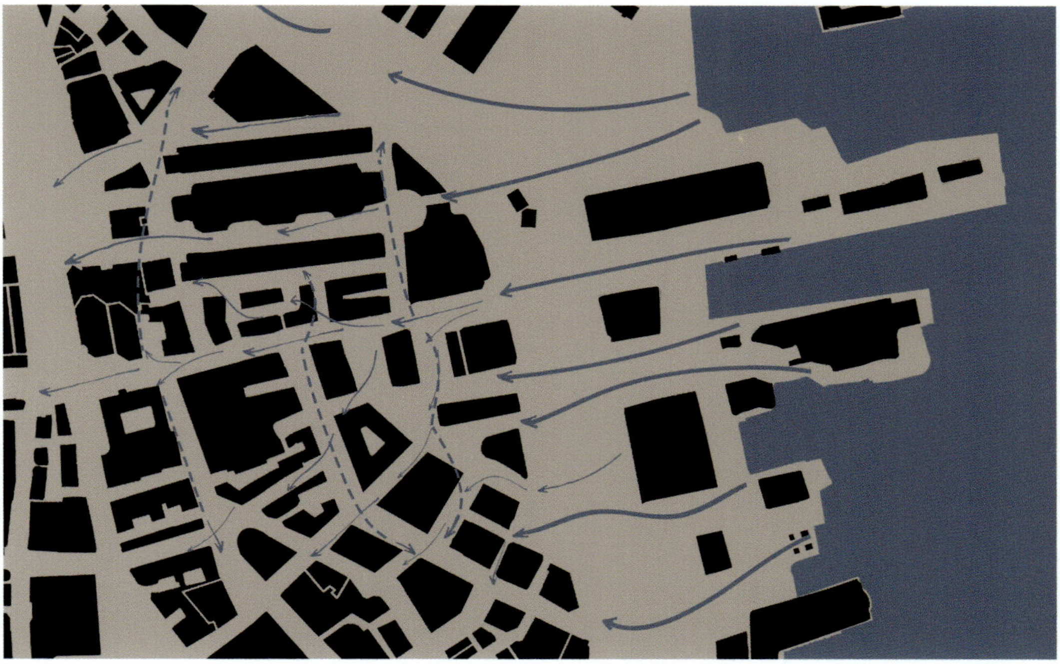

Figure 28.4: In waterfront cities with low surface roughness at exposed edges, permeability of about 20–30% openings will help to dissipate winds if the street grid is disordered, as in the old section of Boston near Faneuil Hall Marketplace.

Figure 28.5: An example from the MIT Concrete Sustainability Hub, showing city texture on the left and expected annual benefits of mitigating homes across the selected area. The tool (analysing selected east coast regions of the U.S. only) can be accessed at: https://cshub.mit.edu/city-texture-dashboard/ Dr. Ipek Bensu Manav, MIT Concrete Sustainability Hub.

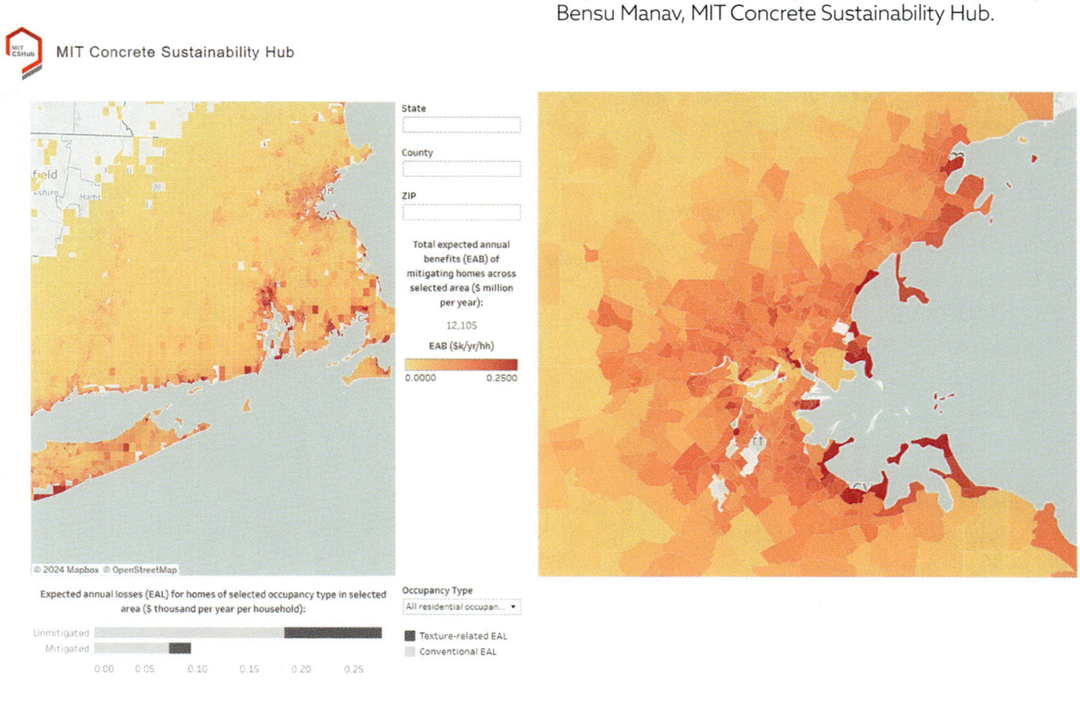

IMPACT

Social: In addition to reducing wind exposure, a more disordered street pattern may lend itself to providing space for social interaction along pedestrian-friendly paths and in parks, gardens, and squares.

Environmental: A disordered city plan can integrate nature in the interstitial spaces. Retain existing trees, build windbreaks and plant clusters of trees, and enhance urban forests.

Economic: Cities with highly ordered spatial texture can magnify hurricane winds from a Category 3 to a Category 4 wind speed.[4] Modelling city texture can identify cities and neighbourhoods that are highly susceptible to hurricane and high wind damage, and target buildings for retrofitting to become more resilient.

Spatial: A city with irregular streets and a large number of open spaces invites exploration and promotes walkability.

NOTES

1 Logan, A. 2020. Discerning the Texture of Urban Resilience. *MIT News*, March 30, 2020. Accessed at: https://news.mit.edu/2020/discerning-texture-of-urban-resilience-0330

2 "Sustainable Neighborhood Design in Tropical Climates". Federico M. Butera, in *Urban Energy Transition* (Second Edition), 2018.

3 Chinese University of Hong Kong, 2005.

4 Logan (2020).

5 Manav, I.B. 2021. *Texture-Informed Approach for Hurricane Loss Estimation: How Discounting Neighborhood Texture Leads to Under-Valuing Wind Mitigation*. MIT.

RESOURCE

- MIT Concrete Sustainability Hub, City Texture Dashboard: https://cshub.mit.edu/city-texture-dashboard/

TEMPORARY HOUSING 29

ADAPTATION **WIND** SCALE **COMMUNITY**

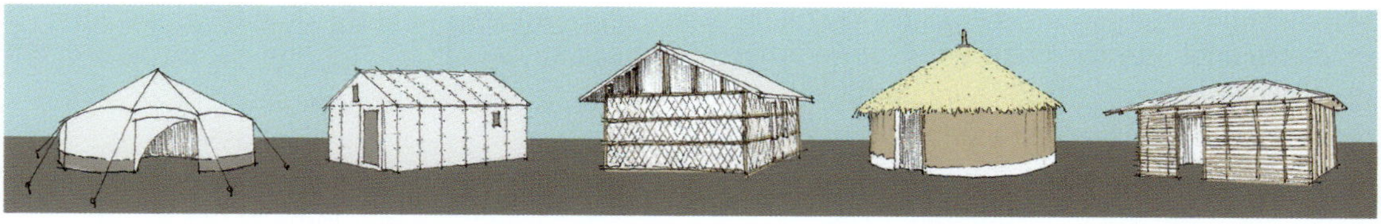

After a disaster, damage to housing units can render them uninhabitable, displacing residents and labourers, and slowing the recovery of jobs, schools, and services. Temporary shelters supplement the existing housing inventory for a period of a few weeks or months by accommodating survivors in improvised shelters, tents, trailers, or hotels. As the recovery continues, temporary housing provides an intermediate place to reside while people resume normal daily activities, with living quarters ranging from rental housing, prefabricated unit, or a small structure that can suffice for a period of six months to three years. Permanent housing is a long-term replacement concerned with reoccupation, repair, or rebuilding.

Figure 29.1: A catalogue of temporary shelters for immediate housing, from left: tent, prefabricated UNHCR Refugee Housing Unit, bamboo and reed mat house in Bangladesh, mud and thatch tukul in Sudan, and wood frame with mud infill and corrugated metal roof, Mozambique.

DOI: 10.4324/9781032702964-33

BACKGROUND

The number of natural disasters has dramatically increased since 2008, causing an average of 24 million people per year displaced by flood, windstorm, earthquake, or drought. Disasters damage housing units, making many unusable until they can be repaired, while other units experience more significant damage and require demolition and replacement. Housing is the fulcrum upon which community recovery is possible - without housing, there is no labour to reconstruct necessary infrastructure, no children to reconstitute schools, and no workers to provide services, or restart production.

TEMPORARY SHELTER: IMMEDIATE

There is a humanitarian imperative to provide victims of disaster with basic shelter as soon as possible, in tandem with ensuring access to water, sanitation, food, and healthcare. Losing a house deprives its former occupants of safety and shelter, destroying dignity, identity, and privacy. The temporary shelters provided by relief agencies are widely used after large scale disasters, but they have also been criticised for being unsustainable and culturally indiscriminate, a one-size-fits-all response to emergencies. Such universal designs neglect cultural values by ignoring cultural needs, family size, and climatic variation, a factor that becomes more important the longer the 'temporary' shelter remains in service. However, this timely support can save lives in the initial stages of a crisis.

The parameters for a 'basic' shelter are developed by aid workers, NGOs, and the IFRC, and have coalesced into the Sphere Project's international guidelines for humanitarian aid. These guidelines define the minimum standards to ensure lifesaving, protective, and accountable responses to crises. When the resources of the affected community are unknown or constrained, temporary shelters are provided from supply chains beyond the immediate area.

- Hosted arrangements allow survivors to live with family members, friends, or strangers willing to take in displaced people. Host communities near the disaster areas often swell in population for months and years after a disaster, with increased competition for resources, jobs, and infrastructure.
- Rental units may also be available and offer a sense of freedom of choice and integration within a community. However, in a widespread disaster there may not be sufficient capacity to house all victims. Post-disaster billets have utilised apartments, hotels, and even cruise ships. A competitive market may result in price increases or the unscrupulous rental of units that require upgrades or repairs. Rental units may be remote from work, school, or community networks, adding to social isolation.
- Tents are the most basic form of emergency shelter; they are stockpiled by the UN and other humanitarian aid groups throughout the world and are ready for use in disasters, migrations, and conflicts. They are lightweight, quick to install, and can be winterised. However, tents may be unstable in high winds or heavy snow, and are difficult to heat. Tents are not the most sustainable solution, requiring frequent patching over the period of use; they are almost never reused.
- Plastic sheeting or tarpaulins requires additional materials to provide overhead shelter, such as wood posts or metal frames, which may not be available.[1] They may be insecure in windy conditions or insufficient in wet climates. Tarpaulins are often part of a shelter kit given to displaced people to construct shelter for themselves under self-help schemes.

Basic designs for immediate shelter have room for improvement. Ian Davis points out in Shelter After Disaster, the design of emergency response shelters has no shortage of ideas:

Having visited various relief agencies in Geneva and Washington I found that a familiar pattern was for the officials to say "Emergency Housing", and walk over to a filing cabinet which virtually overturned as it was opened. The drawers were bulging with "57 varieties" of shelter types. The vast majority of these concepts mercifully never left the drawing board or filing cabinet, but this seems no deterrent to the ingenuity and persistence of designers. The reason for this is perhaps that architects and industrial designers have seen this problem (wrongly) as relatively simple and well-defined. And it uniquely combines many of the preoccupations of students and designers: social awareness; advanced technology; mobility and impermanence.[2]

There are five questions that relief agencies must ask about any temporary shelter:

- How quickly can it be occupied? Anything beyond a week may be too slow.
- How much work will its construction generate? Labourers must be available and onsite.
- How universal is the shelter design? Unfamiliar and unaccommodating options may be rejected.
- Is it a group or individual shelter? Individual family shelter is preferred over communal accommodation as it provides the necessary privacy, psychological comfort, and emotional safety.
- How much does it cost? Materials, labour, and transportation costs for imported solutions may be comparable to what the same currency could purchase locally.[3]

To find answers to these questions, designers must work with the affected population, beginning with the cultural, climatic forms and the indigenous materials and skills of the place.

TEMPORARY HOUSING: INTERMEDIATE

Temporary housing indicates a cautious return to household responsibilities and normal daily functions. The desire to return home, regroup the family, and begin the process of reconstruction is particularly powerful in times of stress, and people will endure great discomfort to achieve these goals. Temporary housing includes larger and more durable units, such as trailers, prefabricated shelters, modified shipping containers, or a kit of parts that is small, lightweight, easy to handle, and can be assembled on site.

In disasters with widespread damage, such as Hurricane Katrina, temporary units may be installed at group sites with multiple units staged on public or private lands. Group sites may take 3–4 months to build after a disaster. Some sites are constructed in peripheral areas, distant from the disaster area, which can cause social isolation and increase the difficulty of returning to work or home sites. The rows of homogenous units, spaced close together on unfamiliar sites, are a mismatch to the original community form, increasing stress and discomfort, often resulting in higher crime rates, fighting, and domestic violence.[4] Some group sites remain open for two years or more following a significant disaster.

Ready-made units such as trailers are useful but they can also have problems. The units may use materials with high VOCs, which caused unhealthy levels of formaldehyde in the 120,000 trailers distributed after Hurricane Katrina.[5] Prefab units are often rejected by local authorities who know that once placed, they will be difficult to remove. Cost is also a factor; according to the United Nations Disaster Relief Coordinator, a temporary house unit can cost more than a permanent one, even though temporary units lose value quickly and are unlikely to be reused in the next disaster.

Figure 29.2: The original Katrina Cottage was designed by Marianne Cusato during the Mississippi Renewal Forum in October 2005. It is delivered as a kit of parts with instructions for assembly, similar to the Sears & Roebuck Houses sold through catalogue in the United States from 1908 to 1942.

Often, the schedule to deliver intermediate solutions takes a very long time, as in Mississippi's alternative housing programme following Hurricane Katrina. Six weeks after the storm, a group of volunteer architects and planners convened in the ballroom of a flooded casino in Biloxi, Mississippi for the Mississippi Renewal Forum, to envision a more walkable, dense, and mixed-use pattern for redevelopment along the coast. The problem of temporary housing was pervasive, with the loss of over 130,000 homes and apartments in south Mississippi affecting the pace of recovery. Designer Marianne Cusato sketched out a simple, gable-roofed cottage on piers that could be prefabricated or sold as a kit of parts through large hardware retailers. The state of Mississippi rushed to adopt the design and contracted with six manufacturers of modular housing to produce units ranging from small, one-bedroom to three-bedroom accessible cottages. The units were anchored to the ground in order to withstand 150 mph winds and they were elevated on concrete block piers to meet flood elevation requirements. The first two units were installed 22 months after the storm; 36 months after the storm about 2,800 units had been installed. The temporary housing programme ended 48 months after the storm, at which time the units were either sold to eligible households, transferred to local governments or community partners for affordable housing, or sold at public auction.[6] Temporary housing units are suitable for long-term occupancy when major disasters result in extended recovery periods and can serve as permanent housing if housing needs continue.

HOUSING RECONSTRUCTION: LONG-TERM

Housing reconstruction is often interpreted as a developmental responsibility rather than a humanitarian responsibility, limiting the role of government in permanent housing reconstruction. Individual houses affected

Figure 29.3: A Seed Cottage is a small house that can be built inexpensively and immediately, with options to expand incrementally, adding spaces as resources permit. Eric Moser, Mississippi Renewal Forum, 2005.

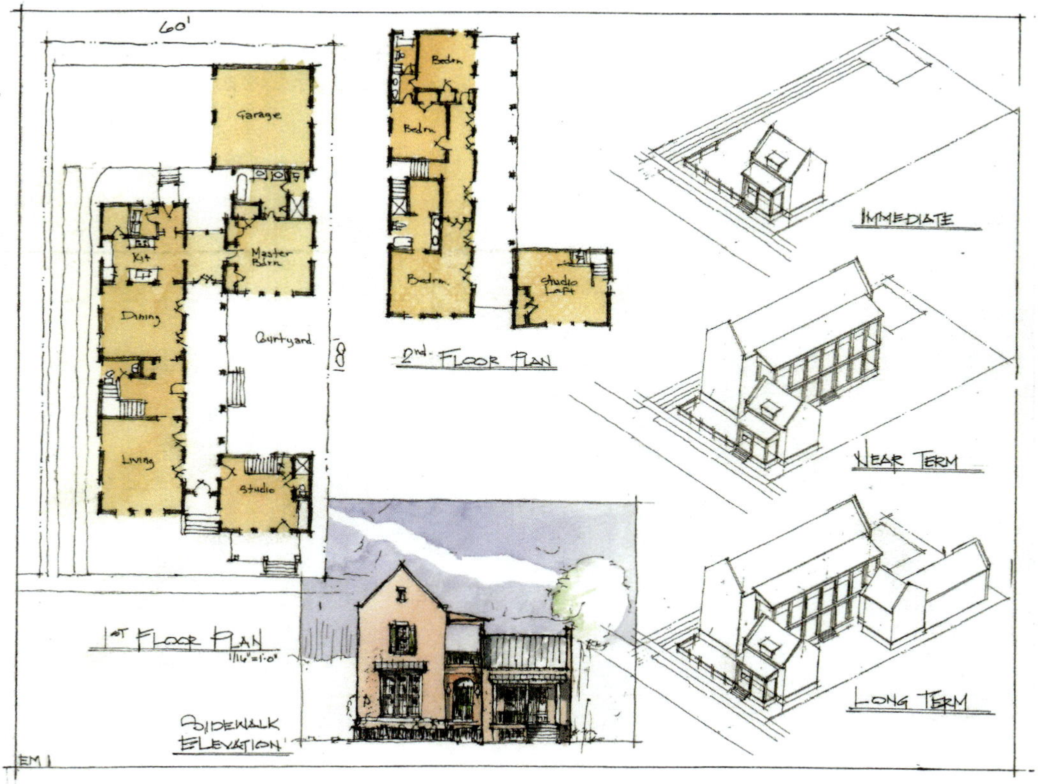

by disaster are typically remodelled by their occupants, and multifamily units by their owners. A community reconstruction plan sets out to re-establish or improve lost housing and its aim must not be limited to alleviating immediate threats but also to address climatic and social resilience challenges.

The Mississippi Renewal Forum spawned other temporary and incremental housing prototypes, notably the 'seed cottage' by architect Eric Moser. A small cottage could be constructed as an immediate housing solution, leaving room to extend or add onto the structure as resources permitted. The original structure could remain a separate Accessory Dwelling Unit with housing for extended family members or be integrated into the overall form of the house. The seed cottage could be delivered as a modular unit, a panelised kit of parts, or be built using traditional methods.

The City of Houston responded inadequately following Hurricane Ike in 2008 when the first round of disaster recovery projects focused on multi-family sites and ignored the residents of single-family homes who were displaced by the storm flooding. The Disaster Recovery 2 Programme corrected that oversight, developing a catalogue of single-family designs for six highly-impacted neighbourhoods. The design team assessed the historic context and neighbourhood patterns to identify consistent materials, features, and forms to re-establish familiar neighbourhood patterns. The architects involved neighbourhood residents, community leaders, and local design architects in preparing diverse design options and sizes, then worked closely with individual homeowners to select and site the house on their family property.[7] The programme constructed over 300 new housing

Figure 29.4: City of Houston Disaster Recovery 2 project replaced about 300 flood-damaged properties on family lots in six neighbourhoods near downtown Houston. Architects: buildingcommunityWORKSHOP, MSU Gulf Coast Community Design Studio, and unabridged Architecture.

units on family sites within established neighbourhoods, which were built to current codes and flood elevations, and addressed family sizes, preferences, and site parameters. The project was recognised with the 2016 HUD Secretary's Award for Community Informed Design.

Many of these examples are appropriate for rural or suburban sites where resources and labour are limited. In dense, urban environments, where do communities temporarily house residents after a disaster? After Hurricane Sandy, over 56,000 people in New York, New Jersey, and Connecticut were eligible for housing repairs or temporary rental assistance. The City of New York and the U.S. Army Corps of Engineers constructed an urban post-disaster housing prototype designed by Garrison Architects in Brooklyn. The prototype is a three-story structure with two, three-bedroom units 75 m^2 (813 square feet) each, and a one-bedroom unit 45 m^2 (480 square feet). Every unit features a living area, bathroom, kitchen, and storage space. Units are built with zero formaldehyde, an energy-efficient building envelope, large windows, and can be equipped with photovoltaic panels for passive survivability.[8]

Figure 29.5: A prototype to test replicable, panelised units for rapid construction in urban disasters was built by the City of New York and the U.S. Army Corps of Engineers. The prototype was designed by Garrison Architects with Mark Line Industries and Anastos Engineering Associates.

Relief can be the enemy of reconstruction, as funds for recovery are always limited. More resources invested in shelters for immediate assistance means that fewer resources are available for intermediate housing or permanent reconstruction. The growing number of displaced persons is increasing faster that the world can respond.

KEY DESIGN CONSIDERATIONS

TEMPORARY SHELTER: IMMEDIATE

Public officials and NGOs will document the number of people displaced, the scale of the damage, and the need for immediate housing. They will identify available resources: available housing units within a defined radius of the disaster, pre-positioned tents, trailers, or construction materials. Under perfect conditions, government agencies and disaster-recovery consultants will determine eligibility and distribute resources quickly so that NGOs can deliver humanitarian assistance.

The international standard for temporary shelter provides a minimum of 3.5 m^2 (37.7 square feet) covered space per person in warm climates, excluding cooking facilities or kitchen. Units should have a minimum height of 2.6 m (8.5 feet) at the lowest point, a height to aid air circulation and ventilation. In cold climates, a minimum of 4.5–5.5 m^2 (43–53 square feet) is allowed per person, as more time will be spent inside the shelter and more space is required to store warm clothes and blankets. A maximum ceiling height of 2 m reduces the volume of heated space. In arid climates with both cold and hot seasons, use the cold climate standards.[9]

In the United States, architects can help local governments assess the safety of existing dwelling units in the aftermath of a disaster. Professionals trained in the California Governor's Office of Emergency Services Safety Assessment Program (SAP) survey damaged facilities to determine if there are safety hazards to building occupants or to the general public, and then tag buildings with placards representing the damage as follows: Green may be damaged but is still safe; Yellow is restricted use; and Red poses an immediate threat to life safety. This programme allows people to re-occupy safe homes and businesses and prohibits people from entering unsafe structures after a disaster. For more information, go to the American Institute of Architects Safety Assessment Program website: https://www.aia.org/resource-center/safety-assessment-program.

Aid organisations may provide materials and tools for construction (shelter kits). The International Federation of Red Cross and Red Crescent Societies (IFRC) distributes a shelter kit consisting of two tarpaulins and a set of tools including: a handsaw, shovel, hoe, machete, shears, rope, nails, roofing nails, and tie wire, packaged in a woven sack.[10]

Disaster survivors can fashion immediate shelter from local materials that are culturally appropriate and familiar. However, this approach requires time, training, and labour to erect structures. Architects can apply these skills directly in reconstruction teams or train residents and volunteers. Using low technology solutions are more likely to come within the price range of disaster victims, are probably better suited to local cultural patterns and climate, and will generate local employment.[11]

Mass shelters in existing buildings such as schools, gymnasiums, and community shelters are a short-term stopgap but schools need to be able to reconvene soon after a disaster to provide a sense of normality and continuity for their students. New options for mass shelters include large, portable buildings such as inflatable structures or hangar-sized tents requiring only a concrete slab and source of power. These shelters can be installed in 4–6 weeks but this delay may miss the period of greatest need for immediate housing.

Architects can collaborate with local communities and relief organisations and plan for more durable solutions beyond the emergency phase. They can provide design assistance to help the community envision a more resilient and equitable future, taking into account climatic conditions, local building knowledge, and community factors. They can illustrate energy-efficient and culturally-appropriate designs that can be shared with people in the affected area, like the collection of homes for Lahaina after the wildfire in August 2023.

Architects can work with communities to set up sorting and storage areas for material reuse. In the aftermath of a windstorm or flood, many materials are sent to the landfill that could otherwise be used for reconstruction, including dimensional lumber, metal roofing sheets, doors, and decorative hardware. Avoid reusing materials contaminated with hazardous substances: hydrofluorocarbons, asbestos, lead paint, fibreglass insulation, and others.

Figure 29.6: FEMA group site of trailers in Hancock County, Mississippi after Hurricane Katrina.

TEMPORARY HOUSING: INTERMEDIATE

Trailers may be delivered and installed on private sites, depending on available space and the presence of utility hookups. In many jurisdictions, these trailers must be permitted and meet local codes for wind-resistance. The trailers may be required to be removed after a certain length of time or after the permanent housing is rebuilt.

Emergency management agencies may develop group sites with trailers or prefabricated housing units. These are staged at sites near the disaster area while cleanup and reconstruction begins. Many of these sites eventually serve as the footprint for new developments, so the implications of initial decisions regarding site and planning can be significant. Ideally, the temporary sites have not historically been affected by natural disasters. Engineers can minimise environmental degradation by avoiding the use of heavy machinery to clear and grade the lot. Ensure that the spatial distribution of units conforms to emergency response standards, local and national codes, and cultural norms. Consider clustering the units in small groups to foster community connection or accommodate extended family groups or displaced neighbours together. Integrate green buffers in multi-family sites to reduce

Figure 29.7: After the devastating fire in Lahaina, Maui, prefab (foldable) units were customised by Hawai'i Off-Grid with a private kitchen and bathroom, plus a private lanai to create additional living space.

problems of stormwater, erosion, wildfire, shading, and privacy. For more information on group site master planning, see: https://emergency.unhcr.org/sites/default/files/UNHCR%20Master-Plan-Approach%20to%20Settlement%20Planning_2019.pdf.

'Quick-assembly modular homes' can be assembled in three to five minutes by a single person and a forklift. Prefab units can withstand local climatic conditions but have a high unit cost, long lead time, and may face transport challenges in getting to the affected area. They cannot be easily modified and may not fit all cultural preferences. Look for manufacturers operating in the region of the disaster, especially if they have developed vernacular design options and use locally-sourced materials. Consider placing the units with space between to allow individually-constructed additions, storage, and outdoor living area. These structures may serve as a home for 3–5 years or longer.

Design government-supplied modular units to have long-term reuse potential. A sustainable programme must include multiple planning and logistical steps: initial manufacturing with durable materials, transportation, and installation; maintenance during recovery operations; demounting and transportation to a site for cleaning, refinishing, and storing for the next disaster; and transportation and re-installation when the units are redistributed.

A prefabricated 'seed cottage' may be built or installed on a private lot as an intermediate solution, offering greater permanence than a tent or trailer. Small structures, often one bedroom and one family room, can be used as sleeping quarters for the entire family. Over time, additional resources may make it possible to expand the number of rooms and add accessory uses so that the single cottage becomes a permanent family dwelling. Extended use requires the original structure to be structurally sound and capable of supporting extensions or additions.

Consider incorporating renewable energy in temporary housing units to reduce common post-disaster interruptions. Some UNHCR Shelter Kits include solar panels to power lights and devices.

HOUSING RECONSTRUCTION: LONG-TERM

Link humanitarian responses to forward-thinking design and planning. Recovery settlements should address increasing climate risks to strengthen local resilience capacity. Design principles should facilitate the long-term development priorities of the community, such as appropriate density, mixed uses, transit-oriented design or other goals. Communities must restore the displaced population in a respectful manner and support coexistence with an influx of temporary volunteers and new residents.

Use a strong community participation process to develop new solutions or modify existing community plans. The appropriate timing of the engagement effort is crucial - too soon and many people will still be in survival mode, unable to participate; too late and many decisions will have already occurred. Design teams must recognise the delicacy of asking people to make major decisions soon after a traumatic event. They must also accept that a community that has undergone a catastrophic event may find it difficult to accept further change. Do not treat the community as a blank slate; respect existing property boundaries and surviving historic landmarks.

Rebuild on previously-occupied lots where advisable. After a severe weather event, some sites may be abandoned due to erosion, increased flooding, or other hazards; these should be identified quickly, providing certainty to property owners and the affected community about areas that will be abandoned or restricted. If new restrictions or guidance (especially flood maps) arrive too late, some people will have already rebuilt what they lost, new homes that may not be as robust against hazards as units rebuilt to match improved standards. The best time for a re-mapping effort is in advance of a hazard event; the second-best time is in the immediate aftermath when memories of the event are still keen.

Rebuilding on previously developed lots requires debris removal, restoration of utility service, and access to construction materials and labour. However, it restores the community form much more quickly and can sometimes reuse existing foundations and salvaged materials. It also avoids expansion into greenfield sites and urban sprawl, an example of maladaptation that causes urban and habitat fragmentation and may extend development in proximity to hazard areas.

Existing structures that are still partially extant and can be restored, should be restored. These survivors serve as a direct connection to the past, protect community memories, and act as landmarks in an utterly changed landscape.

Public reconstruction programmes may construct durable, permanent housing on existing (private) sites. This is possible where the site of the disaster has been cleared, the site has no increased risk from future disasters, local materials and labour are available, and the required technical skills are common. However, these programmes can be costly, need time to plan, and require adherence to local ordinances and codes.

IMPACT

Social: Restoring safe housing for residents is at the heart of disaster recovery. In the short-term, temporary shelters keep people safe and meet immediate needs; temporary housing allows residents to return to the community and resume daily activities in the intermediate term. The goal of long-term recovery is to restore permanent housing that responds more robustly to hazards.

Environmental: The embodied carbon of temporary housing units may be significantly higher than that of permanent housing due to the use of steel in the framing and chassis, as necessary for transportation. In the operations phase, if heating, hot water, and cooking are provided by fossil fuel sources, operational carbon emissions will also be elevated, contributing to a high overall carbon footprint.[12]

Economic: The cost of housing displaced people after a disaster is significant, whether the source of the funds comes from individuals, relief organisations, or governments. It is more economical to get people back in their homes as quickly as possible, which depends on a programme of short- to long-term solutions for restoring housing in the affected area.

Spatial: Post-disaster housing include a wide range of potential spatial impacts: extended development along the periphery of the affected area, with associated impacts to ecosystems and infrastructure; the temporary displacement of people to intact areas, placing a strain on roadways and utility services; and temporary or permanent abandonment of high-hazard areas. Unfortunately, temporary settlements are not temporary, and there are many displaced residents who never return home after a disaster.

If rushed, the process may expose inadequacies. In Lice, Turkey, 1,500 permanent prefabricated houses were completed by the Turkish government only eight weeks after the 1975 earthquake, an unarguably quick recovery. However, the houses had many deficiencies for the rural residents: they were unsuited to the climate and culture, had no provision for animals, were too small, and did little to generate local construction work.[13]

Use local materials and construction techniques to build housing quickly and economically, reduce transportation costs, utilise the local workforce that may have had income disrupted, and ensure long-term sustainability and ease of maintenance and repair and extension. Use simple construction systems that are easy to assembly and dismantle, and small elements that are easier to handle without cranes and heavy equipment. Use materials with lower embodied carbon and high insulation value to reduce heating/cooling demands. Choose materials with zero VOCs.

Allow residents to customise and personalise their units, making additions or modifications according to their needs and possibilities. After disasters, housing often serves as a workplace for families and a school for children; flexibility in the design can allow the unit able to accommodate multiple functions or nontraditional families.

NOTES

1 For a full list of shelter solutions, see: https://emergency.unhcr.org/emergency-assistance/shelter-camp-and-settlement/shelter-and-housing/emergency-shelter-solutions-and-standards
2 Davis, I. 1978. *Shelter After Disaster*, Oxford Polytechnic Press: Oxford. p. 49.
3 Davis (1978, p. 60).
4 Lohr, K. 2006. Drugs and Crime Plague FEMA Trailer Park Residents. NPR, July 19, 2006. https://www.wuwf.org/2006-07-19/drugs-and-crime-plague-fema-trailer-park-residents
5 The CDC tested trailers in December 2007 through January 2008, finding about 77 parts per billion (ppb) of formaldehyde in the air (the National Institute for Occupational Safety and Health recommends a limit of 16 ppb for workers exposed more than ten hours). By the time of the study, people had already lived in the trailers and mobile homes for two years; the formaldehyde level was probably higher in newer trailers and mobile homes and when the weather was warmer. U.S. Centers for Disease Control and Prevention. 2008. Fact sheet: final report on formaldehyde levels in FEMA-supplied travel trailers, park models, and mobile homes. https://stacks.cdc.gov/view/cdc/26757
6 Abt Associates and Amy Jones and Associates. 2009. A Case Study of the Mississippi Alternative Housing Program. Accessed at: https://www.fema.gov/pdf/about/programs/ahpp/ahpp_ms_cs.pdf
7 City of Houston. Technical Guide Appendix: DR2 Housing. Disaster Recovery Round 2 Design Guidebook. Accessed at: https://static1.squarespace.com/static/5248ebd5e4b0240948a6ceff/t/55b7fd32e4b081f691b08cf1/1438121266990/TG02_DR2-01.pdf
8 Selected drawings of the Prototype for Urban Interim Housing Units are available at: https://www.nyc.gov/assets/whatifnyc/downloads/pdf/oem_prototype_dwg_set.pdf
9 Sphere Project. 2018. The Sphere Handbook: Humanitarian Charter and Minimum Standards in Humanitarian Response. Accessed at: https://handbook.hspstandards.org/en/sphere/#ch008
10 IFRC. 2009. The IFRC shelter kit. Accessed at: https://www.ifrc.org/sites/default/files/2021-08/IFRC_shelter-kit-guidelines-EN-LR.pdf
11 Davis, I. 1978. *Shelter After Disaster*, Oxford Polytechnic Press: Oxford. p. 53.
12 Atmaca, A. and N. Atmaca. 2016. Comparative Life Cycle Energy and Cost Analysis of Post-Disaster Temporary Housings. *Applied Energy* 171, 429–443. Accessed at: https://www.sciencedirect.com/science/article/pii/S0306261916303786
13 Global Shelter Cluster Case Studies: https://www.shelterprojects.org/shelterprojects2009/ref/C.20-Turkey-Lice-1975-Earthquake.pdf

RESOURCES

- After the Storm: An Urban Design Case Study for Post-Disaster Interim Housing. Accessed at: https://www.nyc.gov/assets/whatifnyc/downloads/pdf/urban_design_playbook_interim_housing.pdf
- Barakat, S. 2003. Housing Reconstruction After Conflict and Disaster. Humanitarian Practice Network, Network Paper No. 43. Accessed at: https://www.files.ethz.ch/isn/95619/networkpaper043.pdf

DEFENSIBLE LANDSCAPE 30

ADAPTATION **WIND** SCALE **COMMUNITY, SITE**

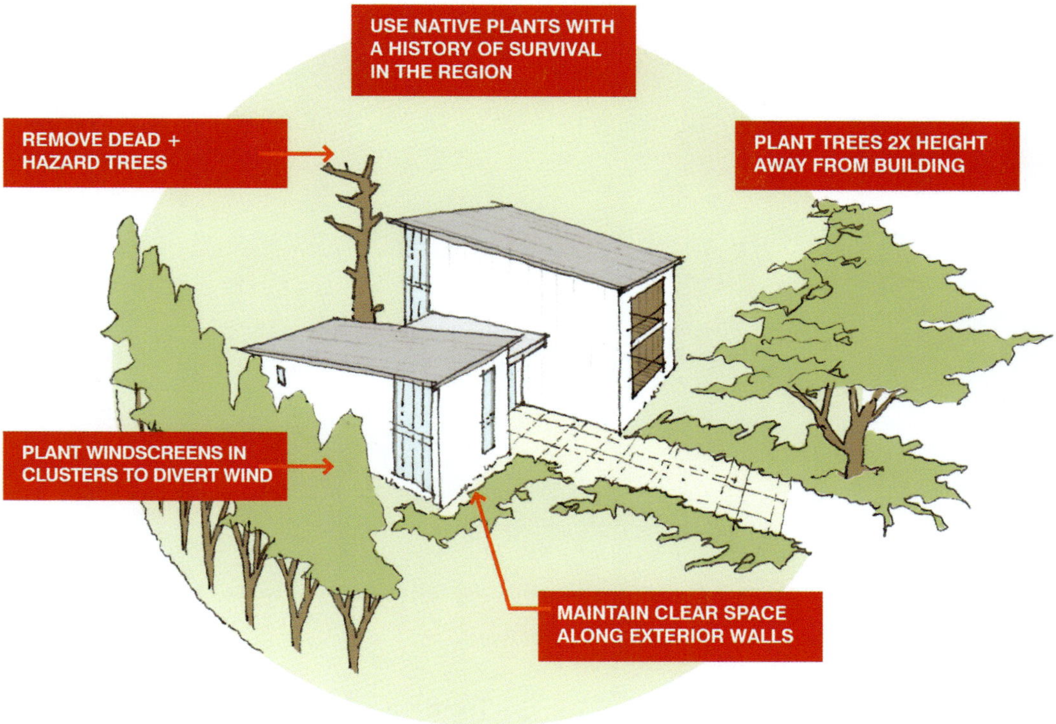

Landscape elements can both help and harm the built environment in a windstorm, protecting structures or shedding branches that become wind-borne debris. Landscaping that is properly selected, placed, and maintained can provide windbreaks, with benefits that increase as the trees and shrubs mature. Insufficient consideration of landscaping materials and design can threaten structures with windborne branches, broken limbs, and uprooted trees. Designing a defensible landscape in high wind regions requires an understanding of landscape forms and the selection of species that perform well under local climate conditions.

Figure 30.1: Defensible landscaping includes the removal of hazardous trees and overhanging limbs, the selection of native plants with a history of survival in the region, planting windscreens to divert wind, and maintaining clear areas along exterior walls.

DOI: 10.4324/9781032702964-34

Figure 30.2: A house in Bay St Louis was protected from waterborne and windborne debris in Hurricane Katrina by a row of small trees along the waterside property line. Allison Anderson.

BACKGROUND

A spindly row of trees with 4- to 6-inch trunks protected our house from near-certain failure in Hurricane Katrina. The self-seeded pine trees, volunteers along a chain link fence on the windward side of the structure, were the remnants of wooded pine savannahs in the coastal plains. Close spacing and deep taproots helped the trees survive the Category 3 winds and prevented waterborne debris – including the entire roof of a neighbouring house – from crashing into the side wall and breaching the envelope.

There is a mutual relationship between the landscape and the climate. Trees in high winds can become hazardous and pose risks to personal safety and property damage but they can also deflect and filter winds to provide a measure of protection. Windspeed is the most likely determinant of tree losses; the higher the wind speed of a storm, the more likely trees will fall, although conditions accompanying the storm and the time it takes to move through the area also determine losses.[1]

Understanding the conditions under which trees may fail in a windstorm is useful, as they typically fail at their weakest point. Larger trees may have less flexible trunks and older trees may harbour more decay. An asymmetrical canopy may cause overturning toward the centre of gravity. Shallow root systems are more susceptible to toppling and trunks are more easily uprooted by high winds, especially in saturated soil. Branches with rotten wood, cracks, diseased areas, and hollows can split and fall. Uneven wind loading can cause twisting or torsional stress resulting in reaction wood, causing abnormal trunk tapering and an increase in buttressing. If winds are too strong for the trunk, the tree oscillates until the roots or trunk fail.

Native trees and plants have adapted to survive wind conditions over centuries of exposure, evolving in morphology, physical structure, and even chemical composition. Strong winds can create bending in the stem, reorient the canopy, and induce the tree to shed needles, leaves, and branches to reduce drag. Juvenile wood, spiral grain in plant stems, and small leaves are adaptations designed to increase flexibility and reduce the impacts from wind. Wind-exposed trees may reduce the length of wood fibres to increase compressive strength and allow bending and elongate wood fibre on the windward side to increase tensile capacity. Trees that defoliate easily in a storm may have developed this capacity as a survival tactic, allowing the tree to resist winds with less surface area.

The amount of rainfall in a windstorm matters, too, as most trees can only tolerate between 24 and 36 hours of flooding, with broadleaf trees managing floods better than conifers. Middle-aged trees usually withstand inundation better than seedlings and older trees. Trees are more likely to recover from flooding if it occurs in the final stages of the growing season, when energy has already been stored in the tree's crown and roots for the next growing season.

Insurance companies are increasingly concerned about the damage that trees can do to structures. Swiss Re, one of the global leaders in insurance and re-insurance, reports that the two largest loss-making perils are tropical cyclones (including hurricanes) and severe convective storms (including both tornadic and straight-line winds, also known as derechos).[2] As a result, insurance companies are demanding proactive landscape maintenance, requiring property owners to cut back limbs that overhang structures and remove trees within 15 feet of structures. However, underwriters offer no credit for the wind deflection benefits of landscapes.

After high winds have passed, trees need care to recover. They may appear healthy but can decline or die rapidly in the aftermath of a storm, even if wind damage is not immediately apparent. If leaves have been swept away by strong winds can temporarily impair a tree's ability to photosynthesise and make it less able to survive other stresses, such as drought or excessive heat. Storms may cause bending or twisting, leaving hidden damage to the internal wood structures and the vessels in the wood that deliver water from the roots. It is also possible for a tree to be partially uprooted and then settle back into place, leaving it with broken roots that no longer support the tree effectively. Provide immediate maintenance and give the landscape time to recover, as trees that lose some or all of their leaves are not necessarily dead.

KEY DESIGN CONSIDERATIONS

Plant trees with a proven history of wind resistance in the region.[3] Native species that have withstood climate conditions for decades are survivor trees, rather than victim trees. Wind-resistant trees bend rather than break. They may have a deep tap root or a slender trunk with few leaves, like palm trees. Become familiar with native species and assess how they perform in high winds, floods, and other severe weather conditions.

Consider removing hazardous trees or species that have demonstrated poor survival in high winds and replacing them with more wind-resistant species.

Cluster trees in groups to survive winds better than individual trees. To encourage mutual sheltering, space trees closely with each trunk growing within 10′ of another, in groups of five or more. Ensure that there is adequate rooting space so that trees can develop a strong supporting root system. Interplant shrubs and diverse trees to maintain airflow screens at ground level.

Soil wetness can contribute to uprooting and overturning. Provide adequate rooting area, reduce soil compaction, and drainage at roots. This is often a problem in dense, urban environments with large areas of impervious surface surrounding confined root zones.

Plant trees an adequate distance away from structures, utilities, and power lines so that roots can develop and canopies will not contact overhead wires. If a tree is anticipated to reach a height of 18 m (60 feet), the appropriate planting distance from a structure is at least 36 m (120 feet) away.[4] Trees and power lines have a history of hazardous interactions, downing wires, interrupting service, and sparking fires. Some electricity providers regularly trim trees to ensure clearance of 12′, which can leave the canopy oddly scalped or divided.

Prune trees as a form of risk management. Improperly pruned trees become weaker but an arborist can prune overhanging limbs and re-shape trees so that the centre of gravity is located above the trunk. An arborist can also assess older and much-valued trees using specialist technology to test storm resistance and strength, and recommend corrective action or removal.

Figure 30.3: Prophylactic pruning removes branches that may interact with power lines, causing power outages, downed lines, or fires but may be detrimental to tree health and appearance.

Select salt-tolerant species for coastal areas with the potential for wind-blown salt spray. A variety of species are relatively tolerant to salt, although no plants are immune to salt injury. The list varies by climate hardiness zone but a list of species with good salt tolerance can be found here: https://www.nswooa.ca/uploads/5/9/6/9/59690537/salt-tolerant-trees.pdf.

In addition to tall windbreaks of trees, plant shrubs, bushes, and vines near structures to filter winds and create dead air space that can help to insulate in hot and cool seasons. Allow at least 30 cm (1 foot) of space between mature plants and the exterior wall to prevent moisture buildup and reduce insect damage.

Use soft mulch (pine straw or bark) rather than gravel, river rock, or landscape glass, which can become windborne in high winds. Gravel and other hard materials become small missiles that can breach window glazing or dimple wall cladding.

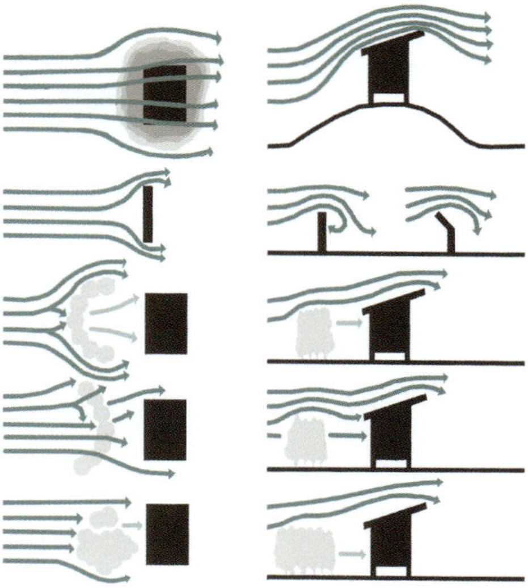

Figure 30.4: The shape, composition, and height of landscape features can dissipate wind effects on buildings.

Before expected windstorms, which are often accompanied by intense rainfall, clear storm drains and gutters of leaves and maintain bioswale paths to direct stormwater away from structures.

Fences and screens have a localised effect on reducing wind speed. For maximum shelter, a fence should maintain about 40–50% of its face porous with 50 × 50 mm apertures. This type of fence provides a sheltered lee area four to five times the fence height.[5] Angling the top of the fence toward the wind direction reduces turbulence on the lee side.

Figure 30.5: Following Hurricane Katrina, many signature live oak trees (*Quercus virginiana*) along the coast were covered in debris, had lost leaves and long, spreading limbs, their soil eroded and heavy salt deposits left at exposed roots. The Land Trust for the Mississippi Coastal Plain restored over 500 trees, removing debris and salt deposits and restoring soil and mulch. Allison Anderson.

IMPACT

Social: Defensible landscape strategies reduce wind damage and protect homes, businesses, infrastructure, and public spaces, enhancing community safety.

Environmental: Windbreaks and shelter belts improve human comfort by sheltering occupants from wind and sun. Proper design and selection of species can provide long-lasting ecosystem services.

Economic: Following the recommendations for defensible landscapes can avoid costly damage from wind and provide savings for property owners. Noncompliance with insurance requirements can lead to higher premiums or the loss of insurance.

Spatial Integration: Landscaped windbreaks, groupings of trees, and enhanced landscaping improve aesthetic appeal and vegetated buffers in urban and sub-urban areas. Defensible landscape is a proactive approach to mitigating wind.

Coastal sand fencing is used to reduce wind speed at the surface of the dune, to trap sand, enhance dune formation, and slow dune migration. The success of sand fencing depends on the ratio of solid-to-void in the fence material (wood slats or geotextile), the amount of blowing sand, the frequency of overwash from waves, and whether vegetation helps to stabilise the sand. To protect from wind erosion, a single row of porous sand fencing provides the deepest sheltered area.[6]

Provide swift maintenance after a high-wind event to reduce tree mortality. Remove broken branches. Remove salt deposits from seawater that may have penetrated the soil at the roots, as increased salt levels in soil can displace the nutrients that trees need to survive. Remove compacted soil and debris that can suffocate the roots. Replace soil above exposed roots with new layers of soil and mulch but do not fill the area higher than the original soil level. Damaged trees need regular watering to provide essential moisture and protect against drought.

NOTES

1 Duryea, M. and E. Kampf. 2007. FOR 118: Wind and Trees: Lessons Learned from Hurricanes. University of Florida IFAS Extension. Accessed at: https://hort.ifas.ufl.edu/woody/documents/FR173.pdf

2 Swiss Re Institute. 2024. Sigma 1/2024: Natural Catastrophes in 2023: Gearing Up for Today's and Tomorrow's Weather Risks. Zurich, Switzerland, p. 13. Accessed at: https://www.swissre.com/institute/research/sigma-research/sigma-2024-01.html

3 A list of recommended tree species for the southeastern coastal plain, tropical, and subtropical climates can be found in Duryea and Kampf, 2007: https://hort.ifas.ufl.edu/woody/documents/FR173.pdf
4 U.S. Department of Energy. Landscaping for Windbreaks. Accessed 8 August 2024 at: https://www.energy.gov/energysaver/landscaping-windbreaks
5 BRANZ. https://d39d3mj7qio96p.cloudfront.net/media/documents/BU620-Managing-wind.pdf
6 Cornelis, W. and D. Gabriels. 2005. Optimal Windbreak Design for Wind-Erosion Control. *Journal of Arid Environments* 6, 315–332.

RESOURCE

- Building Research Association of New Zealand (BRANZ). 2018. Issue 620 Bulletin: Managing Wind Effects Around Buildings. Judgeford, Porirua, NZ. Accessed at: https://d39d3mj7qio96p.cloudfront.net/media/documents/BU620-Managing-wind.pdf

CONTINUOUS LOAD PATH 31

ADAPTATION **HEAT** SCALE **BUILDING**

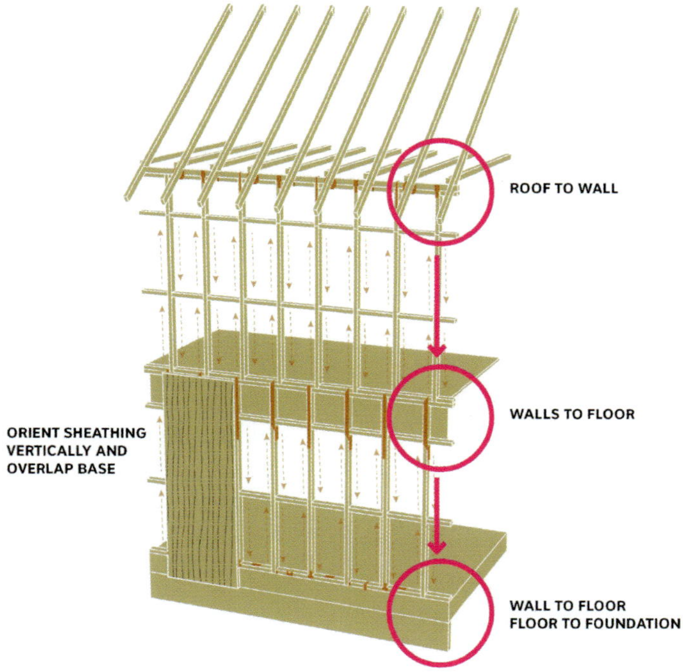

Buildings must be constructed with a strong, continuous load path from the roof to the foundation to avoid structural damage during hurricanes, high winds, and earthquakes. The term continuous load path describes the structure necessary to resist all loads acting on a building: vertical loads from gravity, compression, and uplift forces from wind; and the horizontal, lateral loads from wind or seismic movement. A building's continuous load path transfers all vertical and horizontal loads to the ground to avoid uplift, sliding, racking, overturning, deflection, or collapse. Structures fail at their weakest connection, and the connections between the roof, walls, floors, and foundations are typically the weakest links in the load path.

Figure 31.1: A continuous load path uses structural connections to transfer horizontal and vertical loads from the roof to the foundation to help the building remain intact in high-wind and seismic events. Sheathing acts as a shear panel to prevent racking. This example shows the addition of plywood sheathing oriented in the vertical direction and fastened at studs. LSU Ag Center.

DOI: 10.4324/9781032702964-35

BACKGROUND

Buildings are designed to withstand a range of forces: prescriptive live and dead loads, anticipated winds, and sometimes extreme forces from conditions over and above those expected in daily use. A continuous load path is critical in regions prone to hurricanes, high winds, earthquakes, tornadoes, and floods to reduce the risk of structural damage and failure by helping the building transfer extraordinary loads to other structural members and reduce the chances of failure. If structural members and connections are not strong enough, an alternative load path will form, finding a new route through the structure to transfer the load. The factor of safety is a margin of security against risk, and indicates how much stronger a member or connection is than its usual loading. If the building is designed with adequate redundancy, this alternate route may utilise nearby members that are capable of carrying the load but if alternative paths are inadequate, the excessive loading may lead to structural failure or progressive collapse.[1] Facing a future with unknown risks makes it critical to meet or preferably exceed the anticipated loading conditions and establish redundant paths for transferring loads.

The external wind forces acting on a building are uplift, sliding, racking, and overturning.

- **Uplift:** wind flowing over a roof creates a strong lifting force that can cause the roof to break away from the deck or roof structure. Wind uplift loads generally originate beneath an overhang and from negative pressure creating suction on the roofing and decking. This load is then transferred through the truss or rafter to the top plate via the most direct route. Structures which sustain wind damage have a tendency to fail close to where the load originates, which is most often the roof level. To prevent uplift, strengthen connections between the roofing material and the deck, between the deck and the framing. Reduce overhang dimensions and brace them against uplift.
- **Sliding:** the lateral force of wind blowing against the side of a structure can cause the structure to slide off its foundation. To prevent sliding, strengthen connections between walls and foundation.
- **Racking:** the lateral force of wind blowing against the side of a structure can cause the structure to lean over to one side. To prevent racking, strengthen roof-to-wall and wall-to-foundation connections. Strengthen load paths around window and door openings. Brace the frame and corners with diagonal members or solid sheathing to create a diaphragm.
- **Overturning:** the lateral force of the wind can cause the structure to rotate or overturn. To prevent overturning, provide hold-downs between floor-to-wall,

Figure 31.2: Structural failures resulting from wind forces acting on a building: uplift, racking, sliding, and overturning.

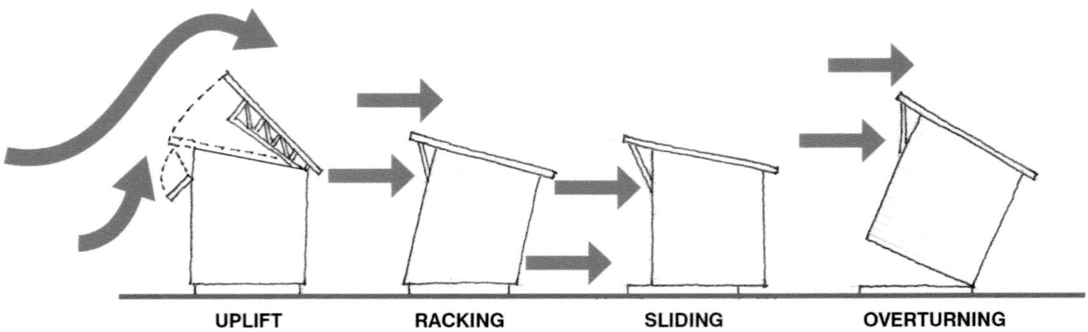

roof-to-wall, and wall-to-foundation connections.

Wind resistance capable of managing extreme weather often exceeds the code-required minimum standards. The Fortified Home program was developed by the Insurance Institute for Business and Home Safety (IBHS) to reduce loss and damage caused by hurricanes and high winds (less than or equal to 115 mph) by improving wood-frame construction methods and establishing continuous load paths. There are three levels of the standard: Fortified Roof focuses on minimising roof damage, water intrusion, and associated damage; Fortified Silver focuses on minimising damage at roof overhangs, protecting openings, and bracing gable ends; and Fortified Gold focuses on tying all components of the structure together through a continuous load path.[2] Certification in the IBHS programs can avoid damage from high wind events and reduce insurance costs, often with a payback period of only 2–3 years.

KEY DESIGN CONSIDERATIONS

Determine the wind design velocity and whether the structure is located in a high-wind or hurricane-prone region. For hurricane-prone regions, a licensed structural engineer should determine appropriate load path connections.

Specify elements to constitute a continuous load path, ensuring the building has positive connections from the roof to the foundation to resist and transmit wind uplift and lateral shear loads to the ground. This includes: roof sheathing-to-framing connections; roof-to-wall connections; wall-to-floor and wall above-to-wall below; and wall-to-foundation connections. Typically, metal straps and threaded connectors are suitable for the

Figure 31.3: Minimum requirements for wood roof sheathing and fastening for FORTIFIED Home™ certification. Insurance Institute for Business & Home Safety..

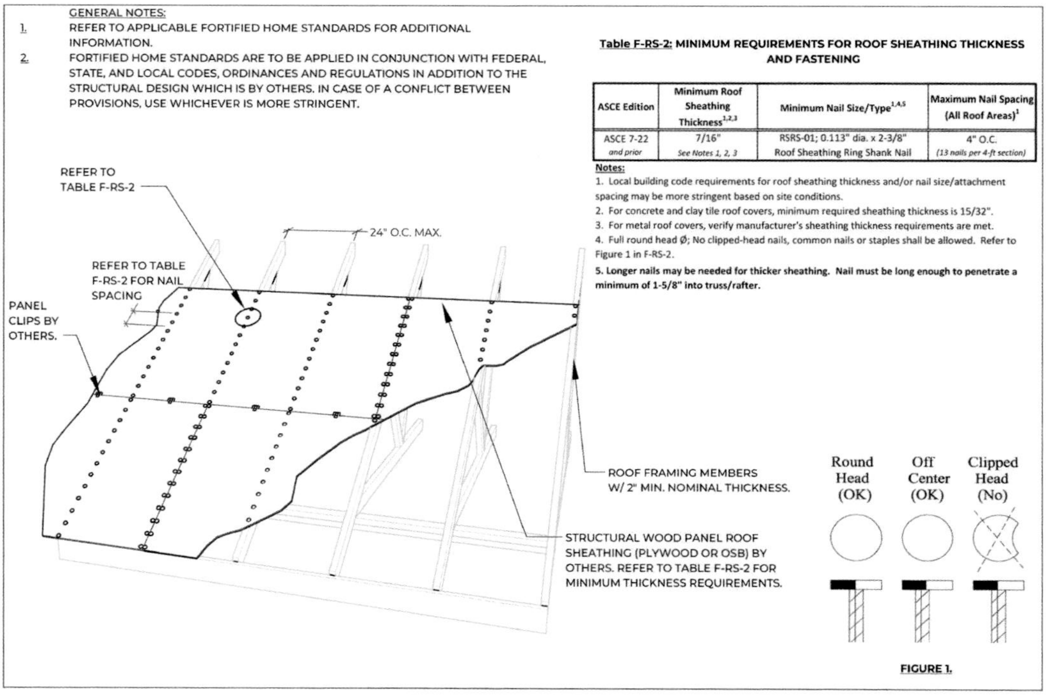

GENERAL NOTES:

1. REFER TO APPLICABLE FORTIFIED HOME STANDARDS FOR ADDITIONAL INFORMATION.
2. FORTIFIED HOME STANDARDS ARE TO BE APPLIED IN CONJUNCTION WITH FEDERAL, STATE, AND LOCAL CODES, ORDINANCES AND REGULATIONS IN ADDITION TO THE STRUCTURAL DESIGN WHICH IS BY OTHERS. IN CASE OF A CONFLICT BETWEEN PROVISIONS, USE WHICHEVER IS MORE STRINGENT.

Table F-RS-2: MINIMUM REQUIREMENTS FOR ROOF SHEATHING THICKNESS AND FASTENING

ASCE Edition	Minimum Roof Sheathing Thickness[1,2,3]	Minimum Nail Size/Type[1,4,5]	Maximum Nail Spacing (All Roof Areas)[1]
ASCE 7-22 *and prior*	7/16" *See Notes 1, 2, 3*	RSRS-01; 0.113" dia. x 2-3/8" Roof Sheathing Ring Shank Nail	4" O.C. *(13 nails per 4-ft section)*

Notes:

1. Local building code requirements for roof sheathing thickness and/or nail size/attachment spacing may be more stringent based on site conditions.
2. For concrete and clay tile roof covers, minimum required sheathing thickness is 15/32".
3. For metal roof covers, verify manufacturer's sheathing thickness requirements are met.
4. Full round head Ø; No clipped-head nails, common nails or staples shall be allowed. Refer to Figure 1 in F-RS-2.
5. **Longer nails may be needed for thicker sheathing. Nail must be long enough to penetrate a minimum of 1-5/8" into truss/rafter.**

cumulative uplift (tension) and shear loading requirements.[3]

Pay close attention to roof sheathing and fasteners, especially at corners where wind pressures are higher. Deck nailing or screwing patterns range from 4 inches on centre to 6 inches on centre (100–150 mm). Solid roof sheathing with a minimum thickness of 7/16″ to 15/32″ (11–12 mm) in hurricane and high wind zones can span roof members spaced at 24″ (609 mm) on centre. For more information, see the IBHS Fortified standard listed in the resources below.

A sealed deck system has an engineered wood panel with built-in roof underlayment that replaces the need for building felt. Flashing tape is fully adhered at all panel seams, preventing water intrusion.[4]

If there are extensions through the roof (such as chimneys), specify sufficient block-out framing and continuous load path connections to support roof members.

Exterior walls transfer lateral wind forces to the adjacent shear walls, which transfer the forces to the foundation through a sheathing diaphragm and hold-down connections. Shear walls must have the strength to transfer forces from each edge to the opposite edge, balancing forces on all four edges of the shear wall to prevent racking.

Continuous, interior shear walls from the foundation to the roof help to stabilise a building and optimise load distribution by providing an alternative load path. Sheathed on both sides with structural plywood, these are often placed at the core of a multi-storey structure to provide stiffness but can also be placed perpendicular to exterior walls to act as a buttress. Regular, close-spaced nailing of the sheathing to the studs and purlins produces effective shear resistance; nailing patterns at the perimeter are particularly important.

The need for solid shear walls often conflicts with the design of more openings, larger windows, or corner windows. Sheathing at exterior walls resists lateral wind pressures but continuous, interior shear walls may contribute to the overall stability and rigidity of a building and optimise load distribution by providing alternative load paths. A structural engineer can offer recommendations for alternative bracing methods.

Solid corners manage a significant amount of structural bracing in two directions. Corner windows are a common casualty in high-wind environments but they are not necessarily proscribed. If a corner dematerialises to allow daylight and views, the shear strength bracing that would normally be provided at the corner must be accommodated another way.

Hold-downs resist uplift loads imposed on wood framing elements in vertical applications with: cast-in place straps, embedded in the concrete foundation and attached with nails or screws to wood framing; hold-downs with threaded anchors to the slab; or a threaded rod from the top of the beam through the base plate to the foundation. Tension ties are engineered to resist lateral loads in horizontal applications. Elements to resist both vertical and horizontal loads are critical to provide secure connections in high wind zones. More information is available from Simpson Strong-Tie at: https://seblog.strongtie.com/2016/07/select-connector-series-holdowns/.

Post-and-beam structures use a single structural column that spans between the roof

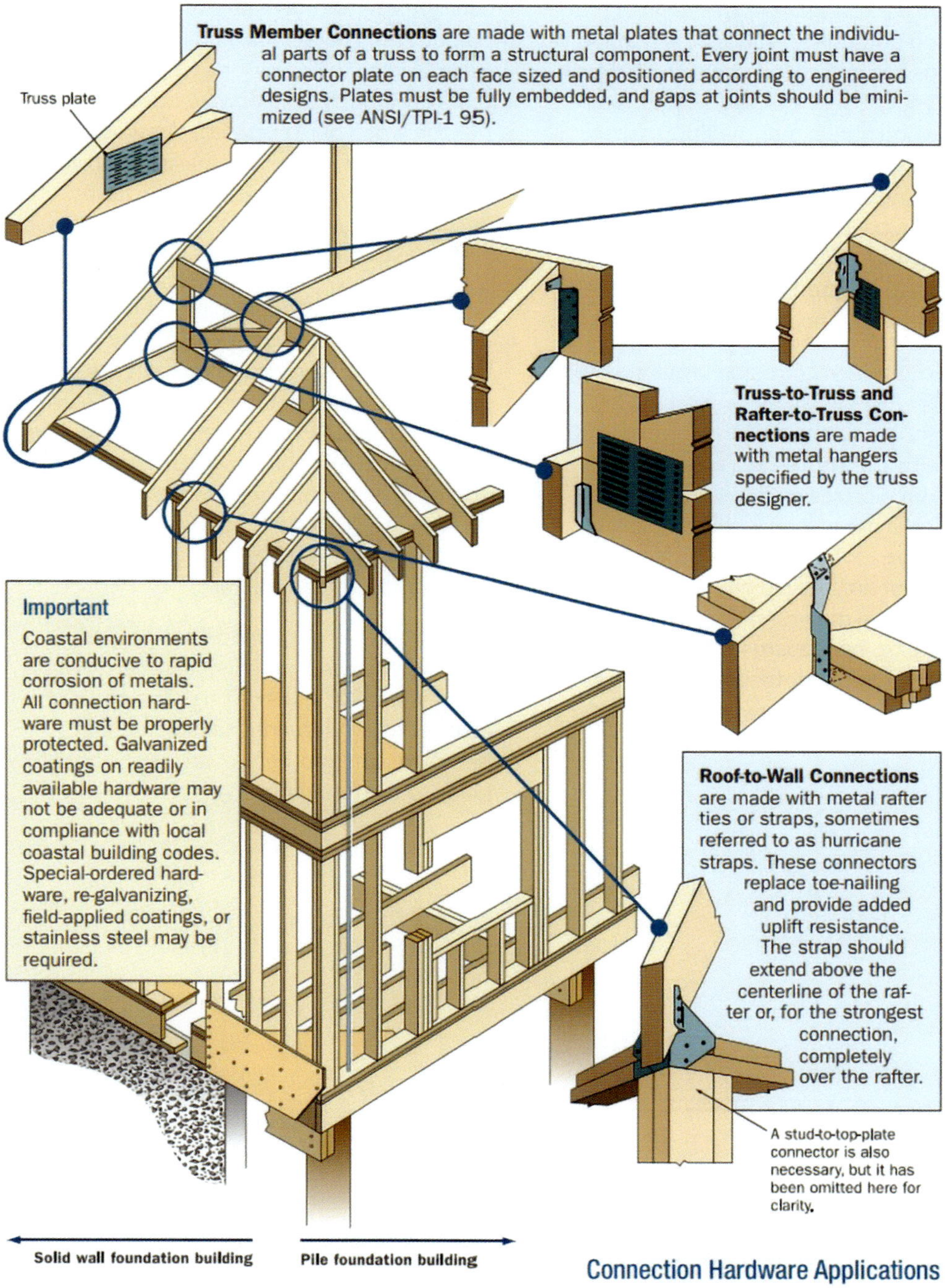

Figure 31.4: Connection hardware is applied at roof members, roof-to-wall connections, wall-to-floor connections, and floor-to-foundation connections. FEMA P-499 Homebuilder's Guide to Coastal Construction.

framing and the foundation. This approach to construction potentially reduces the number of connections but makes the strength of these members critical. Select high-grade lumber with high wood fibre strength (8,000 psi or greater) for the poles, so they can resist the natural bending moment. A post-and-beam system with a continuous load path uses integrated (interlocking) truss-to-column connections that fasten to both sides of the column, with uplift anchors at foundations.

The highest grade of corrosion protection for fasteners is type 316 stainless steel (ASTM A316), typically used at structures within 300 feet of a saltwater shoreline. Fasteners with medium corrosion resistance have a ZMAX finish, which is galvanised with 1.85 oz. of zinc per square foot total on both sides of the fastener, or are hot-dip galvanised after fabrication so the minimum average coating weight is 2.0 oz. per square foot total for both sides. Low corrosion protection is provided by standard galvanised, powder coated, or painted finishes.

Screws provide much greater strength against pull-out than nails, with values at 700 lbs for a screw versus 250 lbs for a nail. Nails initially push the wood fibres downward while screws pull the wood fibres upward, but wood fibres tend to return to their original position when a fastener is driven inside, so as the fibres return to their original position, they push nails out and pull screws tighter.

A unique detail to resist uplift has been developed in communities along the Gulf Coast, using a steel chain between a reinforced pier footing and a perimeter support beam. The chain replaces the nailed-on light-gauge galvanised steel connectors to restrain the floor from lifting off the foundation. This detail is often used in historic renovation projects but its use may be subject to approval by the authority having jurisdiction.

Verify that the construction has properly installed the wind-resisting fasteners. Follow shear and uplift loads through the chain of load-resisting elements and ensure that tie-downs and moment connections transfer loads to the foundation.

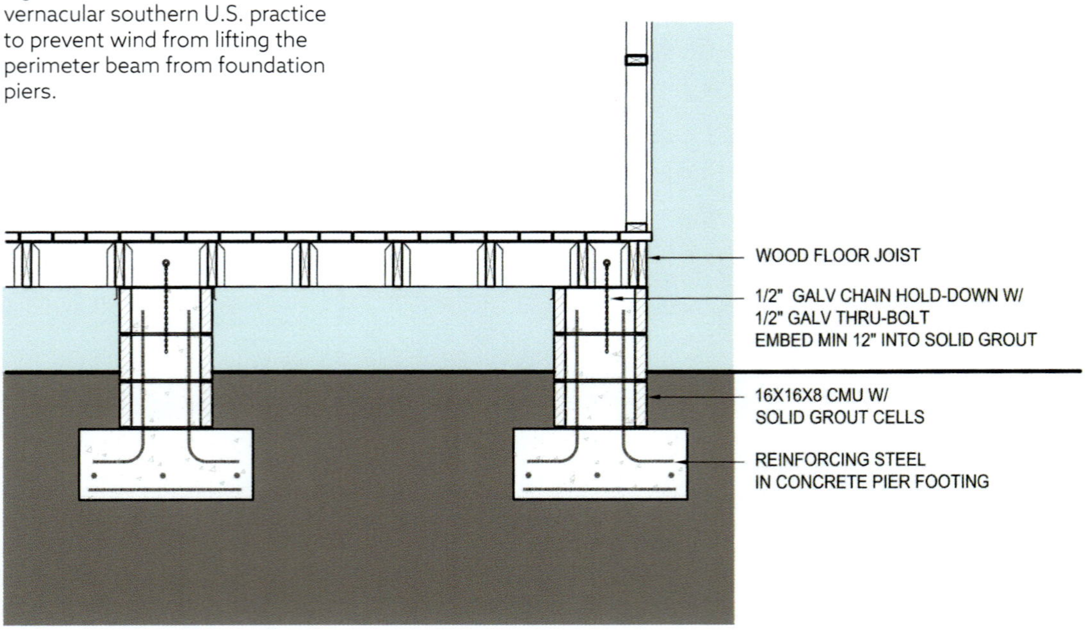

Figure 31.5: A chain hold-down is a vernacular southern U.S. practice to prevent wind from lifting the perimeter beam from foundation piers.

IMPACT

Social: A structure with continuous load path has a much greater chance of surviving high wind events, keeping occupants safe, and reducing property damage. Reinforced structures also reduce the chance of building elements being detached from the building, becoming windborne debris with a detrimental effect on nearby structures.

Environmental: There is embodied carbon in the steel hold-downs, straps, and additional nailing required to ensure a continuous load path; however, the use of these fasteners improves the longevity and survival of the structure, balancing the life-cycle cost.

Economic: Estimates of the cost for providing a continuous load path for a single-family wood-framed home range from $1 to $2 per square foot. However, annual discounts on home insurance may be between 20 and 60%. The value of the home may also be increased by 2–4%.[5] The break-even period for Fortified Gold certification is typically about five years, with more benefits accruing over time.

Spatial: There is no spatial impact from integrating a continuous load path.

NOTES

1 Whole Building Design Guide. 2024. Natural Hazards Mitigation. Accessed 7 September 2024 at: https://www.wbdg.org/design-objectives/secure-safe/natural-hazards-mitigation

2 Institute for Business and Home Safety. 2020. Fortified Home Standard. Accessed at: https://fortifiedhome.org/wp-content/uploads/2020-FORTIFIED-Home-Standard.pdf?v=1725380613459

3 IBHS (2020).

4 Huber Engineered Woods. 2020. ZIP System Roof Sheathing Brochure. Accessed at: https://www.huberwood.com/uploads/documents/technical/ZIP-System-Roof-Brochure-REV-1_20-SEC.pdf

5 Petrolia, D., S. Ishee, S. Yun, R. Cummings, and J. Maples. 2023. Do Wind Hazard Mitigation Programs Affect Home Sales Values? *Journal of Real Estate Research* 45, no. 2, 137–159.

RESOURCES

- High Wind Retrofit Solutions: Simpson Strong-Tie. Accessed at: https://ssttoolbox.widen.net/view/pdf/dwco5akzcw/S-C-HWRGUIDE22.pdf?t.download=true&u=cjmyin
- Institute for Business and Home Safety. 2020. Fortified Home Standard. Accessed at: https://fortifiedhome.org/wp-content/uploads/2020-FORTIFIED-Home-Standard.pdf?v=1725380613459
- U.S. Department of Energy. 2024. Continuous Load Path Provided with Connections from the Roof through the Wall to the Foundation. Accessed at: https://basc.pnnl.gov/resource-guides/continuous-load-path-provided-connections-roof-through-wall-foundation#edit-group-scope

ENVELOPE + BREACH 32

ADAPTATION **WIND** SCALE **BUILDING**

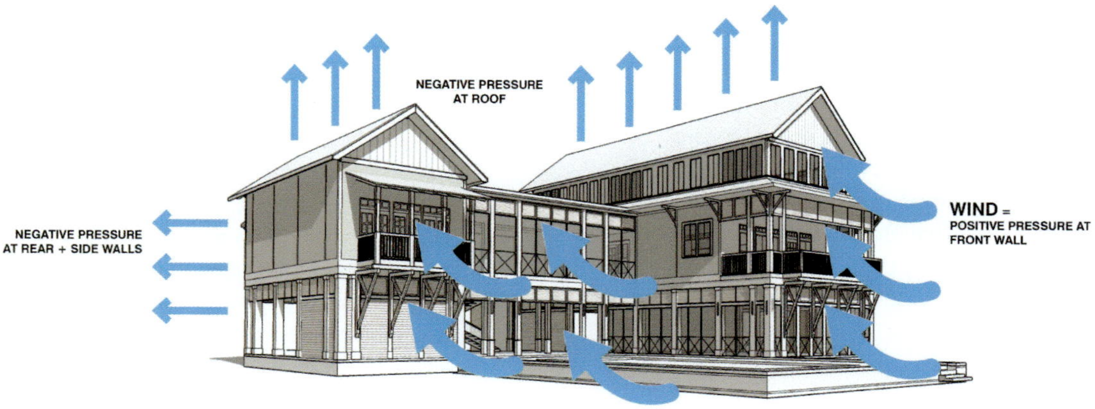

A wind-resistant building has a strengthened envelope to protect against wind and flying debris. High wind speeds increase the risk of breaching the building envelope, either by wind forces acting on the structure or by windborne debris penetrating the building envelope. The building envelope includes everything that separates the interior of a building from the outdoor environment: roof, walls, and floor. When wind interacts with a building, positive pressure and negative pressure (suction) occur simultaneously at different points on the building. If the envelope allows wind through windows and doorsair infiltration through walls that are not airtight, or debris penetration, it can increase the pressure within the building, with disastrous results: broken glazing, roof detachment, and water damage from the rainfall that typically accompanies windstorms.

Figure 32.1: Wind pressures exert both positive pressure and negative pressure (suction) on areas of the building. If there is a breach in the building envelope, the interior and exterior pressures compound and can dislodge the ceiling and roof or overturn the walls.

DOI: 10.4324/9781032702964-36

BACKGROUND

When wind strikes a building it exerts a positive pressure on the windward wall, forcing air through any openings in the wall. At the same time, the opposite and side walls, along with the roof, experience negative (suction) pressure that draws air out of openings in these planes. This results in the interior of the building becoming pressurised as internal pressure pushes upwards on the roof and outward on the side and rear walls. When a building becomes fully pressurised, the high internal pressure load is compounded by negative wind pressure outside, which can shift walls out of alignment, blow ceiling tiles out of their support grid, and detach sections of the roof.

Wind pressures affect the roof in a variety of ways. Higher uplift pressures occur at roof corners, while the roof perimeter has a slightly lower load. This is the reason that nailing patterns for wind-resistive construction are more closely spaced at the corners. Uplift loads on a low-slope roof are larger than a gable or hip roof. The steeper the slope, the lower the uplift load – one reason for the vernacular tradition of steep-slope roofs (8:12 and above) in high-wind regions.

Wind pressure on exterior walls typically generates lower pressures than on the roof, but the ends and corners of the building develop higher suction pressures than the centre of the facade. When a wall faces the wind, the entire wall is uniformly loaded. Irregular features such as re-entrant corners, projecting windows, and towers cause localised turbulence with associated wind speed-up.

In extreme high wind events such as hurricanes and tornadoes, missiles can puncture roof coverings, wall cladding, and glazing. In hurricane regions, significant missile-induced damage is expected over the life of the structure, which has led to advancements in windows, doors, and envelopes that can resist small and large missiles. Missile testing determines an assembly's resistance to penetration and failure.

- Small missiles are small pieces of debris such as gravel. Impact-resistance is tested against 30 solid steel balls, typically 2 grams in weight and about 8 mm (5/16 in) diameter, shot at an assembly in groups of ten at a speed of 40 m/s (130 feet/sec). Small missiles generally strike envelopes above 9.1 m (30 feet) in height, either because they originate from neighbouring roofs or their small size allows the debris to fly farther.
- Large missiles are larger debris specimens, generally lumber or cladding boards that generally strike between 0 to 9 m (30 feet) above the ground. The standard impact test uses a 2 × 4 weighing 4.1 kg (9 lbs) and is launched at a speed of 15.2 m/s (34 mph). Approved units do not allow penetration through the window membrane and do not fail when subsequently subjected to 4,500 cycles of cyclic pressure loading; failure is any crack longer than 127 mm (5 inches) and 1.6 mm (1/16 inch) through which air can pass.
- Large missile testing at essential facilities use a 2 × 4 weighing 4.1 kg, propelled at 24.4 m/s (50 mph).
- Critical facilities designed to meet ICC 500 standards for impact-resistance use a 2 × 4 weighing 6.8 kg (15 lbs) launched at a speed of 44.7 m/s (100 mph) towards vertical surfaces and 67 mph for horizontal surfaces (see Chapter 34: Safe Rooms).
- Although the differences between missile testing protocols sound inconsequential, the difference in protection is exponential; standard large missile tests resistance at 348 ft-lbs, while critical facilities are tested for resistance at 5,017 ft-lbs.

The following considerations for wind loading and the building components affect the envelope illustrating the likelihood of failure in a wind event: exterior walls, windows, doors, and roofs.

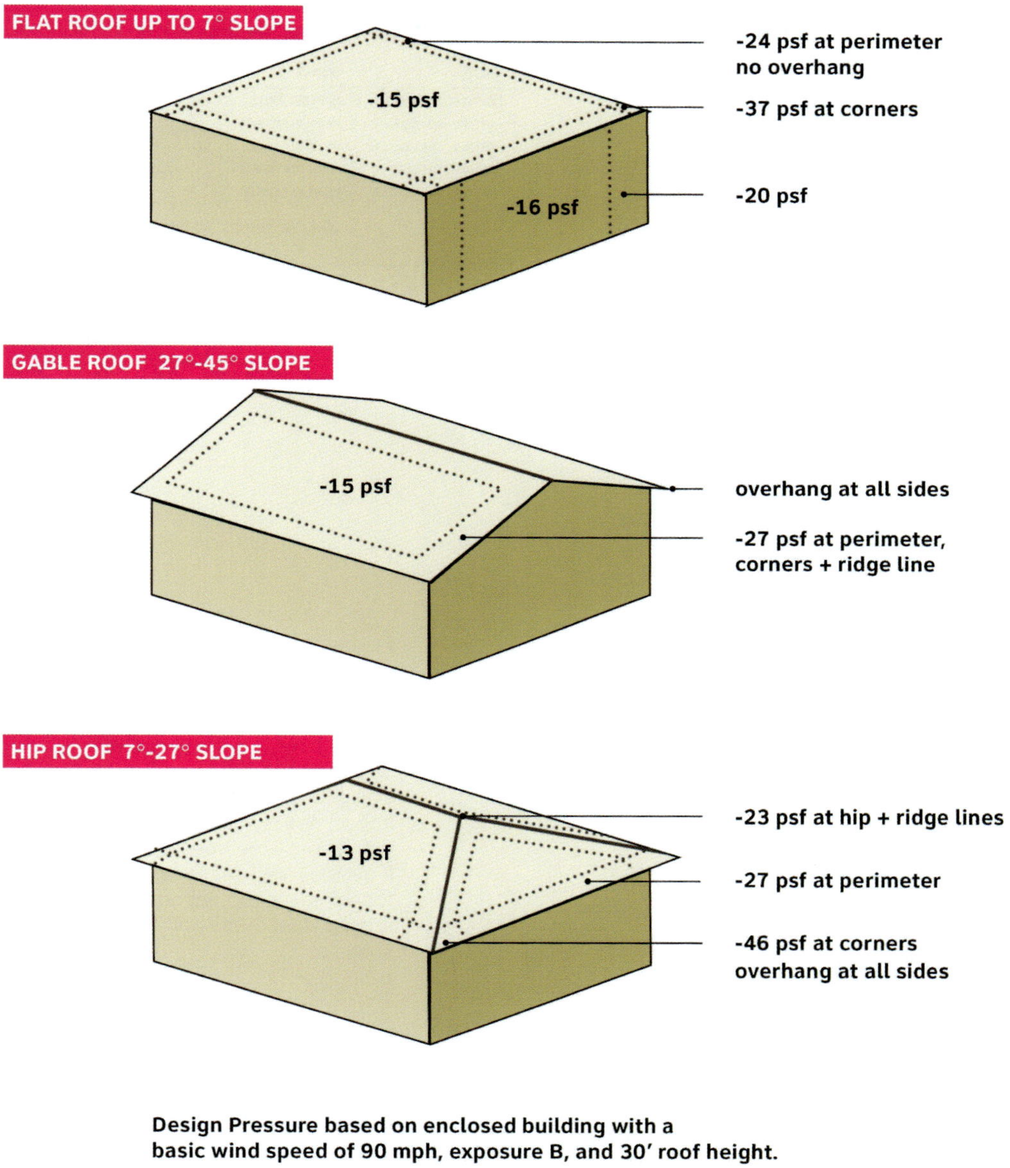

Figure 32.2: Uplift forces at roofs vary widely depending on roof pitch and location, with corners having the highest uplift pressure, and edges higher values than the centre of the roof.

IMPACT TEST REQUIREMENTS

TEST	MISSILE	PASS
ASTM E-1996 LEVEL A	2g STEEL BALL	MISSILE PENETRATES GLASS
ASTM E-1996 LEVEL B	2# AT 50 FT/SEC	NO TEAR PERMITTING A 3" SPHERE TO PASS THROUGH
ASTM E-1996 LEVEL C	4# AT 40 FT/SEC	
ASTM E-1996 LEVEL D	9# AT 50 FT/SEC	NO TEAR LONGER THAN 5"
ASTM E-1996 LEVEL E	9# AT 80 FT/SEC	
FEMA P-361	15# AT 147 FT/SEC	NO TEAR GREATER THAN 5" LONG X 1/16" WIDE

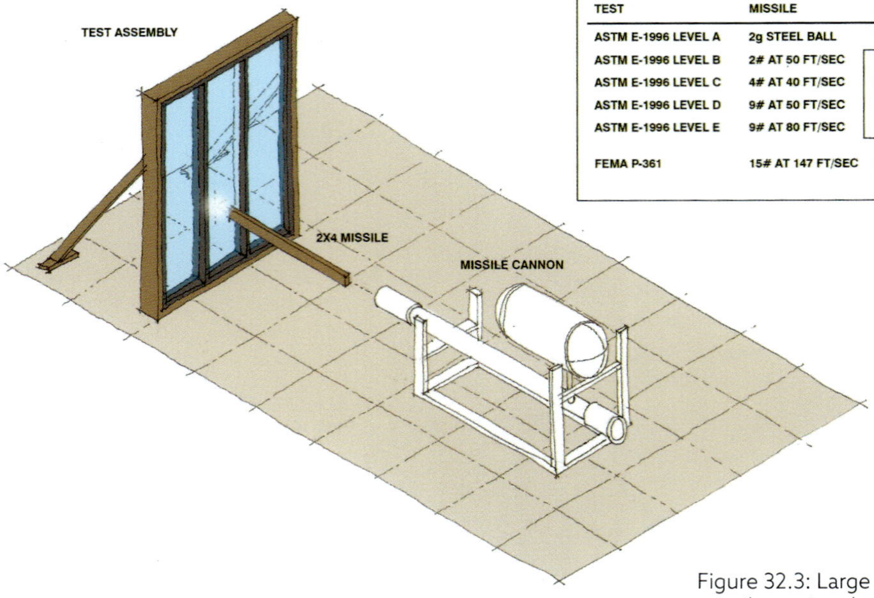

Figure 32.3: Large and small missile testing determines the impact-resistance of wall, door, and window assemblies to windborne debris. Level A is small missile impact above 30′. Level B is used for skylights. Level C is 'medium' missile impact and is not often used. Level D represents large missile impact. Level E missiles are used to test assemblies for enhanced protection. FEMA P-361 is used for tornadic and hurricane shelters.

KEY DESIGN CONSIDERATIONS

GENERAL

Determine the basic wind speed using ASCE 7 (U.S.) or local codes. In adaptive reuse of existing buildings, compare the current basic wind speed with the loads for which the building was originally designed. If the original design loads are significantly lower than current loads, consider upgrading the wind resistance of the building envelope and/or structure. This is especially critical if the basic wind speed exceeds 90 mph, as the risk of damage is increased.

For adaptive reuse projects, perform a field investigation to evaluate the primary building envelope elements, rooftop equipment, and structural system elements, to determine if the facility was generally constructed as indicated on the original contract drawings or according to best practices. Check the condition of the structure, fasteners, flashing, and other elements of the building envelope for deterioration.

Ensure load path continuity is adequate in new construction and adaptive reuse of existing buildings (see Chapter 31). A window depends on a chain of supporting members: glass lites strong enough to resist the wind pressure, secure anchors to the window frame, the frame adequately anchored to the wall, the wall to the foundation, and the foundation to the ground. Load path connections are designed to transfer positive and negative loads applied to the roof and exterior bearing walls, down to the foundation and into the ground.

During the Design Development and Construction Documents phases, the design team will determine which elements are critical to ensuring high-wind performance. The analysis includes the structural system, building envelope, and exterior-mounted equipment. After determining the critical elements, identify the need for any special inspections and develop a schedule for Construction Observation.

Wind resistance at caulking, flashing, and fasteners will degrade over time due to exposure to weather unless critical elements are regularly maintained and repaired. After several years of exposure, scratches and chips on glazing can become extensive enough to weaken the material, making it more susceptible to cracking or missile impact.

In preparation for a high wind event, close and lock all exterior openings to resist building pressurisation. Closing all interior doors and windows reduces excess loading on the roof by up to 30%.[1]

Building damage can occur if the envelope has inadequate design, poor installation, or material deterioration.[2] A status inspection is recommended following unusually high winds, to assess whether the storm caused damage that needs to be repaired to maintain building

Figure 32.4: The yellow house in Bay St Louis experienced a breach in Hurricane Katrina, causing roof failure and associated water damage. The blue house slid off its foundations as a result of lateral pressure from storm surge and the lack of a continuous load path. Allison Anderson.

integrity. In addition to inspecting for obvious signs of damage, determine if cracks have developed that may allow water infiltration.

EXTERIOR WALLS

Reinforced wall assemblies provide exemplary performance against breach. This is typically achieved with minimum 6-in thick concrete, 8-in thick concrete masonry, or insulating concrete forms, assembled with full reinforcing. However, a 2 × 4 stud wall can also pass the ICC500 missile impact test provided the outer face has concrete infill between studs and either 1/2-in. expanded metal sheet or 14 gauge steel on the impact side.[3] Wood siding and panels rarely blow off in high wind events,[4] making them a good choice for wind-resistant construction, although they may face challenges from moisture or insects.

Metal wall panels exhibit a wide range of wind performance, depending on the strength of the specified panel (material, thickness, panel profile, and panel width) and the strength of the attachment method, either concealed clips or exposed fasteners. Excessive spacing between clips/fasteners is the most common reason for detachment in high wind events. Exposed fasteners are more vulnerable to deterioration over time and are often associated with thinner gauge metal panels. Concealed fasteners are more weathertight and require fewer replacements.

Exterior insulation finish systems (EIFS) and stucco finishes often exhibit poor wind performance. A widespread example is EIFS detachment, where expanded polystyrene was attached to gypsum board, which in turn was attached to metal studs. If the exterior gypsum board sandwich detaches from the studs, it is common for interior gypsum board to also be blown off, allowing wind-driven rain to enter the building.

Brick veneer has a high rate of failure in wind events, with the most common failures related to brick ties (fasteners) including pull-out, embedment failure, poor bonding between ties and mortar, poor quality mortar, and corrosion. Other types of veneers, such as ceramic tile, stone veneer, and cement-fibre panels, are subject to blowing off. The Brick Industry Association provides guidance on securing brick veneer in high wind zones at: Technical Notes 28: Anchored Brick Veneer, Wood Frame Construction (2002).

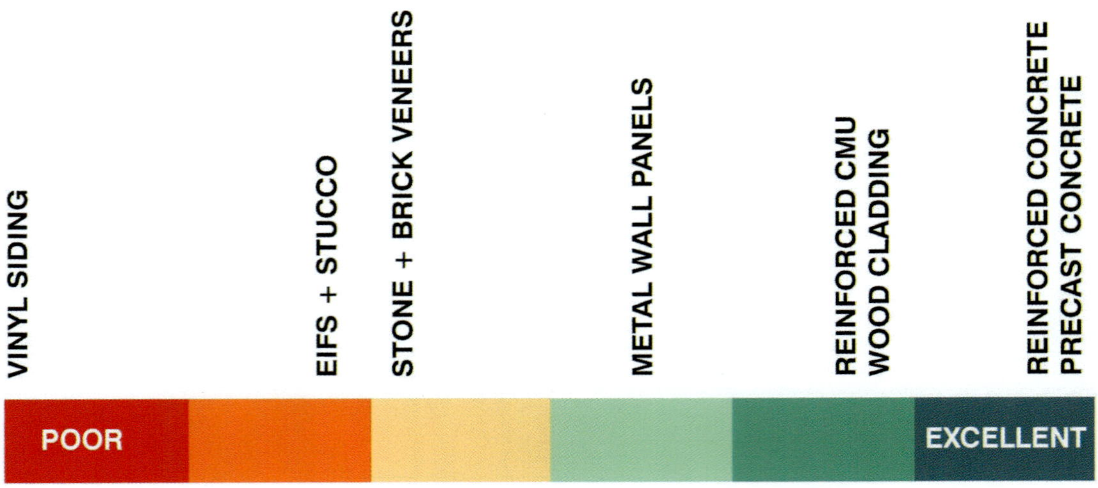

Figure 32.5: Relative wind performance of exterior cladding and construction systems.

Exterior non-load-bearing masonry walls are not intended to carry gravity loads but they must resist external and internal loading to avoid collapse. If these types of walls collapse in a wind event, they represent a severe risk to life because of their weight.

Vinyl siding strips are lightweight and generally have inadequate wind resistance. Blow-off is often caused by nails spaced too far apart.

Almost all wall cladding permits the passage of water past the exterior surface, particularly when the rain is wind-driven. For this reason, most wall cladding should be considered water-shedding, rather than water-proofing. A moisture barrier and flashing around door and window openings provides a secondary line of protection to prevent moisture intrusion. Specify the moisture barrier be installed so that the bottom of the wall allows drainage.

Preventing building collapse and structural damage is the primary goal of wind-resistant design but minimising water intrusion also reduces major damage to the building. Non-load-bearing walls may be designed in accordance with rain-screen principles, to intercept water in an air-pressure equalised cavity that provides drainage from the cavity to the outer surface of the building.

WINDOWS AND DOORS

The IBC requires that window and door assemblies, including glazing, frames, doors, hardware, and frame attachment to the wall, be of sufficient strength to resist both positive and negative design wind pressures. Windows and doors have a published design pressure (DP) rating that quantifies how much loading they can resist; higher DP ratings indicate stronger window or door assemblies. The height of the opening plays a role in determining the design pressure, as winds increase with height above the ground but missile sizes decrease. Ensure that the DP rating meets the code requirements for the site location, site exposure, and risk category.

The site location determines whether impact resistance is required. Coastal areas, windborne debris regions, hurricane-prone regions, and other areas with a significantly open exposure may be required to have impact-resistant windows and doors. Impact glass may add protection in wildfire regions. Alternatives to impact-resistant glazing include hurricane shutters, storm panels, and precut plywood covers.

Impact-resistant windows are constructed with an exterior pane of annealed (standard) glazing and an interior pane comprised of two sheets of annealed glass laminated with a vinyl interlayer such as Lexan™. When the glass receives an impact, the exterior pane may break but the interior pane will deform and bounce back due to the vinyl interlayer. The interior glass may also crack but the pieces will remain bonded by the vinyl, preventing penetration and stopping glass shards from entering the building. The impact rating is based on the thickness of the glass and interlayer sheets, the strength of the metal frame, and the embedment of the glass in the frame which allows the pane to flex. Proper installation of these windows, which may be heavier than standard units, is critical to ensure they are properly seated and attached to the wall.

Out-swinging doors are preferable for wind resistance, as high winds push out-swinging doors closed. Weatherstripping is located on the interior side of the door, where it is less susceptible to degradation, and wind forces compress the weatherstripping and making it less susceptible to moisture intrusion.

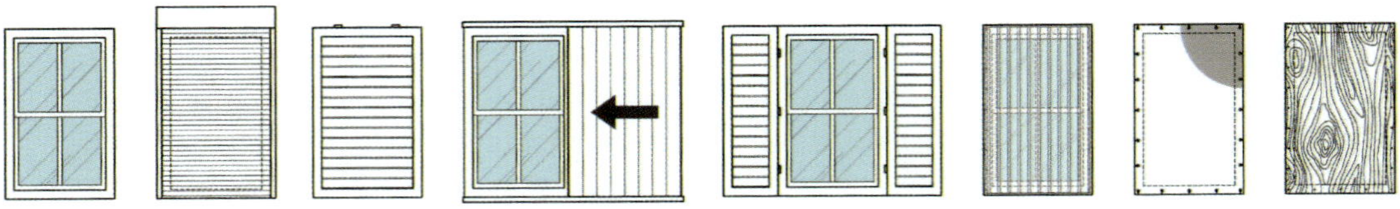

Figure 32.6: Catalogue of impact-resistant window coverings. Plywood panels must have a minimum thickness of 11.1 mm (7/16″) and a maximum panel span of 24 cm (8′), and be precut, labelled, and predrilled as required by the anchorage method.

Hardware also affects how a door performs in high winds. Exit door hardware is often recommended to minimise the possibility of the doors being pulled open by wind suction. Exit hardware with three-point locking systems and top and bottom rods is more secure than exit hardware that latches at only one point at the jamb. Other recommended hardware includes: sill pan flashing with end dams, rear leg, and turned-down front leg; door shoes to minimise the air gap between the door and the threshold; an overlapping astragal with weatherstripping; and door closers and hinges that are rated for high winds.

Overhead sectional and rolling doors commonly fail in high winds, usually as a result of door and track assemblies that have insufficient wind resistance. Reinforcing struts and heavy-duty brackets, rollers, hinges, and tracks can prevent damage to the door. For essential facilities, vertical lift doors, bifold doors, and airplane hangar doors may be more reliable (albeit more expensive) choices.

Wind-driven water infiltration can occur between a door and its frame, the frame and the wall, and between the threshold and the door. When wind speeds approach 120 mph, some leakage should be anticipated because of the very high wind pressures. A vestibule designed with water-resistant finishes and a floor drain can prevent wind-driven water from reaching interior spaces.

When detailing window or curtain wall units, designers should only rely on sealants as the secondary line of defence against water infiltration. If a sealant joint is the first line of defence, a secondary defence should be designed to intercept and drain water that drives past the sealant joint.

Louvers and other openings necessary for ventilation must also be protected from windborne debris. Impact-resistant devices must anchor firmly to the wall and protect the louver blades. Armouring may affect airflow through the vents, so verify that the required aperture is sufficient with the addition of hardened screening.

ROOFS AND SOFFITS

Precast concrete roof decks may appear to have enough weight to resist uplift loads but the dead load is often smaller than the uplift. Detail connections to ensure continuity of load path and adequate shear strength to offset uplift forces.

Sprayed polyurethane foam and liquid-applied roof systems show reliable high-wind performance. If the substrate to which the foam or liquid-applied membrane is applied does not lift, it is unlikely that these systems will blow off. These systems are also more resistant to leakage after missile impact damage than many other systems.

Built-up roofs and modified bitumen systems also demonstrate good wind performance so long as the edge flashing/coping remains intact. Roof membrane blow-off almost always results from lifting or peeling at the edge flashing or coping, which clamps the membrane at the roof edge. Mechanical fasteners at edge flashing should be of non-corrosive materials and spacing to meet high wind criteria. Nailers to which the flashing is attached must also be securely anchored.

Deep overhangs, which are desirable for sun shading and reducing heat gain, can trap wind and exacerbate uplift forces. The standard overhang in a high wind region overhang is 14 inches or less to reduce aerodynamic lift. For larger overhangs in high wind regions, design brackets or cantilevers to resist uplift.

Gutters are seldom constructed from materials capable of resisting wind loads, nor are they fastened to the structure in ways that provide continuity of the load path. When a gutter lifts, it typically causes the edge flashing that laps into the gutter to detach, which can result in lifting and peeling of the roof membrane along the edge.

Soffits can be affected by both positive and negative pressure, depending on the wind direction. Some soffit materials, such as vinyl panels, may be inadequately fastened to rafters. The loss of a soffit in a high-wind event can result in wind-driven rain entering an attic or cavity, causing significant damage.

In hurricane zones, the Insurance Institute for Business and Home Safety (IBHS) recommends not installing gable end vents in new construction; suggesting wind-rated ridge or off-ridge vents to take advantage of the lower pressure in the centre of the roof. Existing structures with gable end vents should be properly braced, blocked, or have covers that can be installed when high winds approach. A vented soffit assembly can provide two-stage air pressure control using a narrow soffit strip vent coupled with an expansion chamber followed by a narrow structural baffle.

An unvented attic may also be an option. By eliminating vents, an unvented attic design keeps wind-driven rain out of the attic, which has shown to be a major water damage issue following hurricanes. An unvented attic also prevents embers from entering at the soffit or ridge. Insulating and air sealing along the roof line offers several advantages over insulating along the ceiling deck, including energy savings; an unvented attic is warmer in winter and cooler in summer, reducing the HVAC load.

Roof-mounted mechanical equipment, such as exhaust fans, HVAC units, relief air hoods, rooftop ductwork, lightning protection systems, antennas, and satellite dishes, is easily damaged during high winds. The equipment can detach and become wind-borne missiles, and water can enter the facility where equipment was displaced. The most common problems relate to inadequate equipment anchorage and corroded fasteners. If the demounted equipment is essential for the operation of the facility, damage from a high wind event can prevent re-occupation and continuity of use.

IMPACT

Social: Reducing the risk of envelope breach protects occupants and reduces property damage in high wind events. Designs with a reinforced envelope have a better chance of surviving a high-wind event and a quick return to operations.

Environmental: Wind damage can be resource-intensive and require a lengthy process to repair. While the structure is open to the elements, moisture intrusion and mould growth are likely, expanding the scope of repairs.

Economic: Depending on the magnitude of wind damage on a building, it can take months to years to repair damage or replace a facility. Interruptions to use of the facility can cause loss of services, lost production, and additional costs to rent temporary facilities. About 25% of businesses do not reopen after a disaster[5] and another 25% fail within one year.

Spatial Integration: When a structure is breached by the wind, its cladding, equipment, fixtures, roofing, and structural members can become wind-borne debris with the potential to damage neighbouring structures. Protecting buildings from envelope breach reduces the chance of severe damage that might require demolition.

NOTES

1 IBHS.org. Shut the Door: Closing interior doors can give your roof a fighting chance against high winds. https://fortifiedhome.org/article/shut-the-door/

2 FEMA. 2007. FEMA 543: Design Guide for Improving Critical Facility Safety from Flooding and High Winds, Risk Management Series. Washington DC. Accessed at: https://www.fema.gov/sites/default/files/2020-08/fema543_design_guide_complete.pdf

3 A complete list of wall sections that meet missile testing requirements can be found in FEMA P-361 (2021) Safe Rooms for Tornadoes and Hurricanes, Section B8.2.3. Accessed at: https://www.fema.gov/sites/default/files/documents/fema_safe-rooms-for-tornadoes-and-hurricanes_p-361.pdf

4 FEMA (2007).

5 FEMA. 2018. Stay in Business after a Disaster by Planning Ahead. Accessed at: https://www.fema.gov/press-release/20230502/stay-business-after-disaster-planning-ahead

RESOURCES

- FEMA. 2007. FEMA 543: Design Guide for Improving Critical Facility Safety from Flooding and High Winds, Risk Management Series. Washington DC. Accessed at: https://www.fema.gov/sites/default/files/2020-08/fema543_design_guide_complete.pdf
- The National Research Council of Canada, Institute for Research in Construction's Wind Design Guide for Mechanically Attached Flexible Membrane Roofs (B1049, 2005) provides recommendations related to mechanically attached single-ply and modified bituminous systems.

33 COLLATERAL DAMAGE

ADAPTATION **WIND** SCALE **BUILDING**

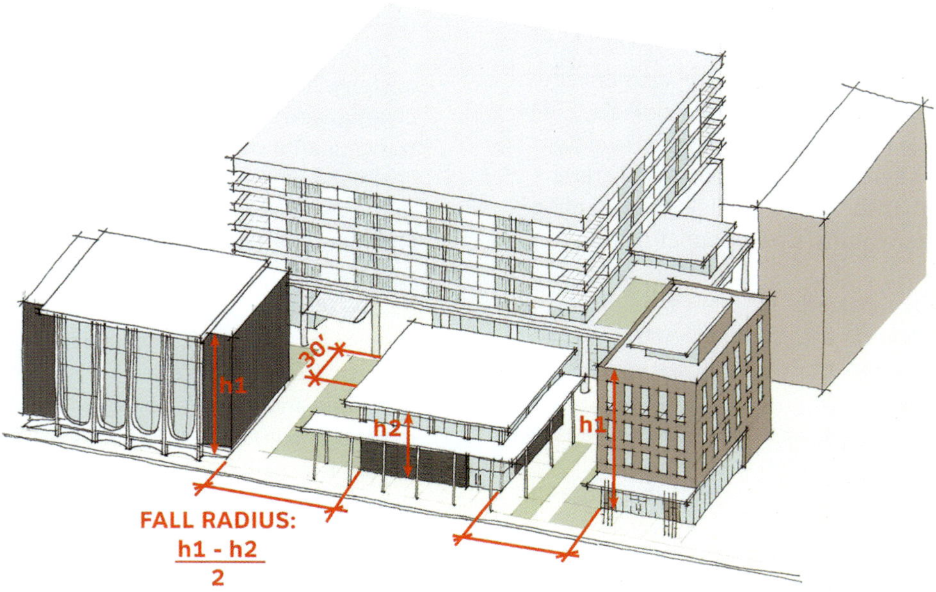

The roof plane of the building envelope is exposed to airborne debris, which can fall or strike the building from above. In a high wind, building cladding detaches, roofing is peeled off, equipment is dislodged from its mounting, walls disintegrate, and antennas blow over. These elements, detached from nearby structures, can become falling or windborne debris. Collateral damage comprises the impacts upon a building resulting from another object or structure collapsing onto that building.

Figure 33.1: Falling debris and lay down hazards cause roof damage. Solutions to prevent falling debris from adjacent structure failure include setbacks equal to the height of the adjacent building minus the height of the proposed building, divided by 2. The distance need not exceed 9 m (30 feet) as gravity narrows the debris field. Laydown hazards such as self-supporting towers or large trees should not be located where they could fall on the building.

DOI: 10.4324/9781032702964-37

BACKGROUND

The word 'collateral' derives from medieval Latin *col-* 'together with' + *later-* 'side'; its meaning describing the capacity of adjacent buildings to create a cascading hazard during a high wind event. The term *collateral damage* was widely used after Hurricane Katrina but is now reserved by the U.S. Department of Homeland Security for human conflicts; FEMA prefers the terms falling debris and laydown hazards. There are three types of collateral hazards that can impact buildings, according to the International Code Council (ICC)[1]:

- Lay down hazards: adjacent structures and other objects that could fall onto the roof including exterior walls, masts, towers, or large trees.
- Falling debris hazards: exterior components or cladding including masonry units, dislodged roofing materials, cladding, or equipment could fall onto the roof.
- Rollover hazards: vehicles or small buildings such as portable classrooms or storage buildings can roll or tumble onto a structure.

Not every roof must be armoured to protect against these hazards. Critical facilities - such as hospitals, fire stations, and large assembly halls - establish performance-based goals to reduce damage in a wind event. In conjunction with clients, architects can determine reasonable expectations for the building performance and design to meet that standard. If a building is expected to survive with only mild impacts, the surroundings must be analysed for potential hazards and the roof assembly must be robust. Other facilities may consult the ICC Performance Goals for Buildings and Facilities to determine the maximum damage level to be tolerated[2]:

- **Mild impact:** The building does not have structural damage and is safe to occupy. Nonstructural systems for normal building use are fully operational. Injuries to occupants from hazard-related loads are minor. Overall extent of damage is minimal in extent and cost.
- **Moderate impact:** There is moderate, repairable structural damage; some delay in re-occupancy is expected. Nonstructural systems are operational although some cleanup and repair may be needed. Injuries to occupants may be moderate with a low likelihood of life loss. Damage to building is generally moderate in extent and cost.
- **High impact:** There is significant damage to structural elements but no large falling debris; repair is possible. Significant delays in re-occupancy can be expected. Nonstructural systems are significantly damaged and inoperable; egress routes may be impaired by debris; and emergency systems remain operable. Injuries to occupants are moderate, with a moderate likelihood of single life loss. Damage to the building may be significant.
- **Severe impact:** There is substantial structural damage but all significant components continue to carry gravity loads. Repair may not be technically possible and the building is not safe for re-occupancy. Nonstructural systems may be completely nonfunctional. Injuries may be significant and there is a high likelihood of life loss. Damage to the building and contents may be total.

Mockups of roof assemblies undergo laboratory testing to evaluate performance against penetration or collapse from three types of debris: non-deformable debris, such as steel frames or hardened concrete barrels weighing up to 450 kg (1,000 lbs); semi-deformable barrels of sand weighing 370 kg (815 lbs); and deformable debris such as HVAC components and large objects weighing between 25 and 90 kg (50–200 lbs). The highest level of protection armours a roof against damage from a non-deformable 1,000-pound concrete barrel dropped from a height of 15 m (50 feet).[3]

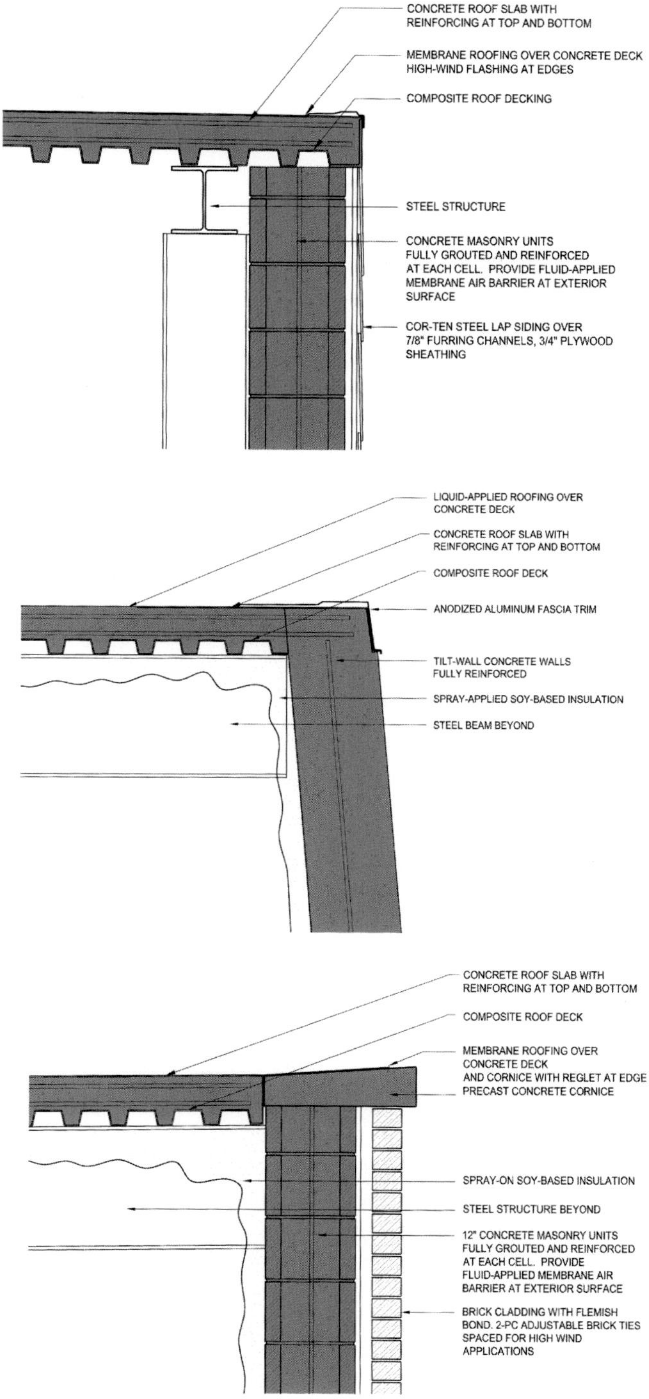

Figure 33.2: Sections of roof assemblies that meet falling debris tests using deformable, semi-deformable, and non-deformable debris released from heights up to 100 feet and allowed to free fall onto the roof assemblies. Roof designs that incorporate a uniform thickness (i.e., flat slab) provide a more uniform level of protection than other designs that incorporate a thin slab supported by secondary beams (e.g., ribbed slab).

KEY DESIGN CONSIDERATIONS

STANDARD PRACTICE

Discuss the clients' tolerance for risk and interruption, based on the four levels of impact damage outlined above. The client should understand the potential costs and benefits of protecting the building shell against high winds; the architect should document these expectations in the Owner's Project Requirements.

Perform a site assessment for a new or existing building to determine the level of risk from collateral damage. Identify potential hazards from the surroundings: unreinforced masonry structures that may fail during high winds; cladding on neighbouring buildings that is loosely fastened to the structural frame; or large objects such as light towers, antennas, satellite dishes, and roof-mounted equipment that might become fall or become airborne.

One design option is to maintain a consistent height for buildings along the street, which reduces the potential for equipment to fall from a high roof to a lower one. This strategy does not protect the roof from other sources of windborne debris.

Very large trees, overhanging branches, and hazard trees (lopsided, damaged, and trees nearing the end of life) should be assessed by a professional arborist and corrected or removed if advised.

Soil cover on the roof can protect against windborne debris because the soil absorbs the impact before it affects the roofing membrane and decking below. Impact resistance can be enhanced with as little as 30 cm (12 inches) of soil cover (see Chapter 35: Earth Shelter).

Temporary structures such as mobile homes, storage buildings, and portable trailers must be firmly secured to the ground. At critical facilities, the operations plan may require vehicles to be relocated in advance of a storm.

CRITICAL FACILITIES

Whenever possible, locate critical facilities away from collateral hazards. Set the building away from adjacent structures to prevent falling debris so that the distance is equal to the height of the adjacent building minus the height of the proposed building, divided by 2 (*h1 – h2/2*). The setback distance need not exceed 9 m (30 feet).

In critical facilities, design the roof to meet ICC 500 standards using a flat slab with a uniform thickness of cast in place or precast concrete. A 4″ thick reinforced concrete roof provides sufficient protection from a 15-lb wood 2 × 4 missile impacting at 67 mph (generated by a tornadic wind speed of 250 mph), which matches the free-falling missile impact speed in FEMA P-361, Safe Rooms for Tornadoes and Hurricanes.[4] Light cracking and minimal spalling are acceptable in the test protocols, provided that large fragments of concrete are retained at the roof by steel reinforcing or 22-gauge metal decking. If concrete is cast on metal roof decking, the steel beams and deck must have shear connector studs to contain the spalling concrete.

Roof penetrations on critical structures must be armoured to ensure mechanical, electrical, or plumbing penetrations do not become detached to create windborne debris and introduce moisture. Penetrations larger than 9 cm (3.5 square inches) for rectangular vents or 6.35 cm diameter (2.5 inches) must be protected by a steel sleeve cast into the concrete roof.

Roof equipment, ladders, access hatches, and skylights must be secured to roof decks. On membrane roofs, poorly anchored roof-mounted equipment can be detached by high winds or windborne debris impact. This often leads to tearing and peeling of the roof membrane as the equipment moves across the roof. Add a concrete curb or pedestal on which to mount rooftop equipment to provide a solid connection point without having to break through the surrounding roof membrane. Use tie-down cables and turnbuckles to secure equipment to curbs and prevent cowlings from blowing off. Use robust hatches with thick seals, steel hinges, and strong locking mechanisms. Use periodic flashing over lightning protection conductors so these do not become loose in a high wind event. In situations where roof-mounted equipment is difficult to anchor or the equipment is unlikely to withstand high winds, move the equipment inside the building or into a rooftop penthouse to protect the equipment and the roof from damage. Evaluate the strength of roof-mounted antennas to determine if additional guy wires, bracing or tower strengthening are required.[5]

IMPACT

Social: Armoured roofs provide life safety protection for occupants and maintain continuity of operations for critical facilities. Other structures may also take measures to protect against falling debris to protect inhabitants and quickly restore operations.

Environmental: The embodied carbon of an armoured concrete roof and enhanced structural frame is high, so buildings with these features should be designed for an extended service life to offset the carbon expended in its construction.

Economic: Facilities that can be occupied during an event or returned to service without delay minimise evacuation costs, loss of productivity, and relocation costs. They can also enhance the reputation of the facility (and by extension, its occupants, owner, and design team) as being prepared for challenges.

Spatial: Enhanced structural protection at the roof plane may support ancillary functions such as green roofs, activity terraces, or other uses with greater live loads.

NOTES

1 International Code Council. 2020. ICC 500/NSSA Standard for the Design and Construction of Storm Shelters. Washington, DC.
2 International Code Council. 2021. ICC Performance Code for Buildings and Facilities (ICCPC). Washington, DC.
3 FEMA P-361, Safe Rooms for Tornadoes and Hurricanes, Fourth Edition, B3–34.
4 FEMA P-361, Safe Rooms for Tornadoes and Hurricanes, Fourth Edition, B3–34, Table B3-3.
5 Telecommunications Industry Association. 2023. ANSI/TIA-222-1 Structural Standard for Antenna Supporting Structures and Antennas and Small Wind Turbine Support Structures. Accessed at: https://tiaonline.org/standardannouncement/tia-issues-new-structural-standard-for-antenna-supporting-structures-antennas-and-small-wind-turbine-support-structures-standard/

RESOURCES

- FEMA. 2022. P-2181, Hurricane and Flood Mitigation Handbook for Public Facilities. Fact Sheet 3.3.2: Roof Systems – Low-Slope Roofs. Accessed at: https://www.fema.gov/sites/default/files/documents/fema_p-2181-fact-sheet-3-3-2-roof-systems-low-slope-roofs.pdf
- International Code Council. 2020. ICC 500/NSSA Standard for the Design and Construction of Storm Shelters. Washington, DC.

SAFE ROOMS 34

ADAPTATION **WIND** SCALE **BUILDING**

A safe room is an armoured structure designed to provide life-safety protection in extreme-wind events, including tornadoes and hurricanes with winds up to 250 mph. Shelters fall into three categories: best available refuge area (BARA) in a building determined to be the least vulnerable to wind impacts; storm shelters that meet the requirements in the ICC 500 standard; and safe rooms that meet the requirements in the ICC 500 standard plus additional criteria. Shelters may be stand-alone structures or a space within a building that is capable of providing near-absolute protection for its occupants.

Figure 34.1: The curved concrete walls and roof at the Hancock County Community Shelters in Mississippi direct wind over and around the structure. A concrete roof, cast-in-place concrete walls with exterior buttresses, and earthen berms deflect the impacts of wind and debris. Openings are blast- and impact-resistant construction.

DOI: 10.4324/9781032702964-38

BACKGROUND

Hurricanes and tornadoes are among the most destructive weather events, causing injury and death to people who are unable to safely evacuate or find shelter from these events. Hurricanes and tornadoes vary in intensity and frequency, so it is critical to understand the hazard risks - probability, frequency, and intensity - as well as the potential consequence for casualties, property damage, and loss of life.

Hurricane-prone regions are coastal areas where the design wind speed for buildings with an average hazard to human life is greater than 115 mph.[1] The severity of hurricanes is categorised using the Saffir-Simpson Hurricane Wind Scale, which ranks hurricanes based on sustained wind speeds on a scale from 1 to 5. The Saffir-Simpson scale describes potential damage correlated with the highest sustained wind speed: Category 1 winds at 119–153 km/hr (74–95 mph) cause damage to roofs, trees, and power lines; to Category 5 winds at 252 km/hr (157 mph) or higher resulting in a high percentage of framed structures destroyed, power outages that last weeks or months, and uninhabitable areas.

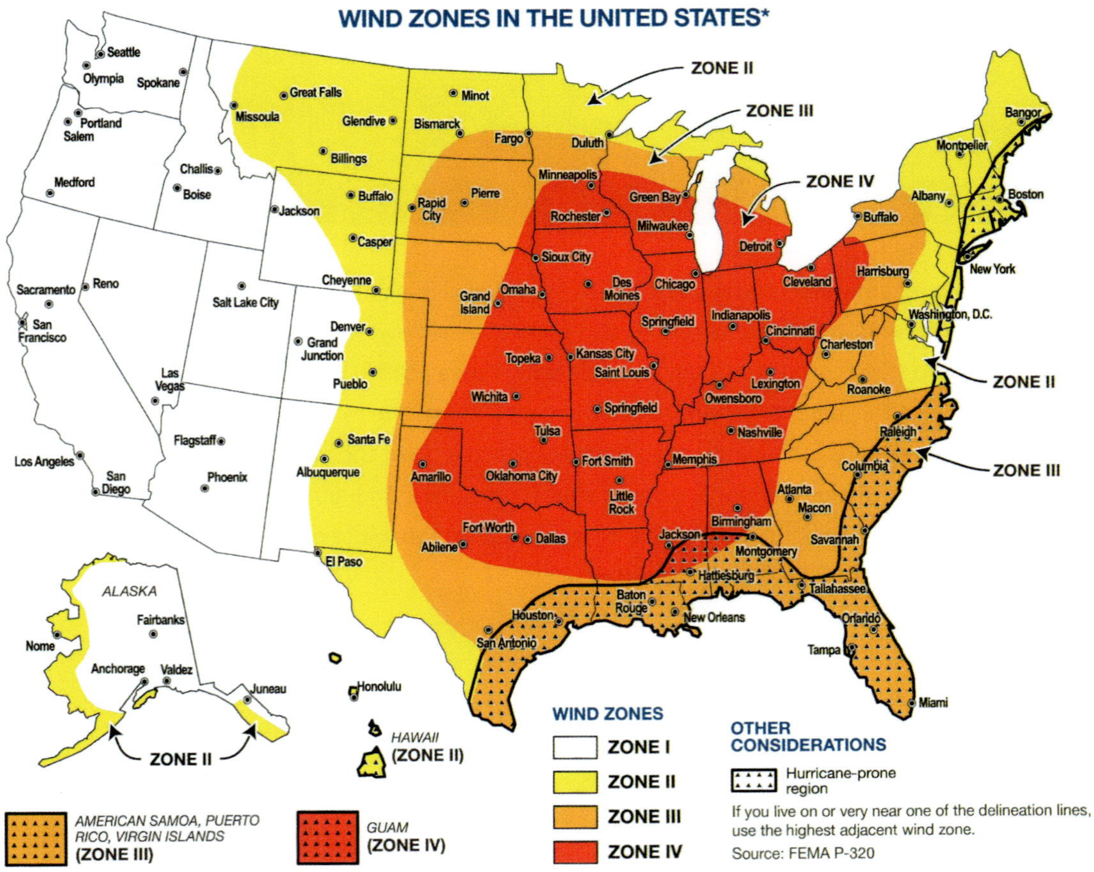

Figure 34.2: Wind map of the United States. Design wind speed contour lines are not drawn as precise geographic coordinates and therefore when the site is near a line of delineation, the prudent approach is to assume the site lies within the higher wind speed zone.

The United States leads the world in the number of tornadoes per year with about 1,250 per year, in comparison to Europe with 300–400 tornadoes per year. The Enhanced Fujita scale is a 'rating' based on estimated (not measured) wind speeds and related damage. When tornado-related damage is surveyed, it is compared to a list of damage indicators and degrees of damage, which help estimate the likely range of wind speeds produced. A rating (from EF0 to EF5) is assigned based on observations of the damage. A list of damage indicators for various building types is maintained by the U.S. National Weather Service at: https://www.weather.gov/oun/efscale. In one example, a three-story townhouse with 'significant' loss of roof covering indicates an expected wind speed of 124 mph (EF-2); for the same building type, the uplift or collapse of the roof structure indicates 138 mph winds (EF-3).

Communities can determine the need for a safe room by assessing the potential vulnerability of their building stock to wind damage based on structural integrity, age, condition, materials, and quality of construction. As part of the overall risk assessment for a safe room, consider the vulnerability of the population to extreme wind events. High-priority groups include children and youth, elderly, and people with medical conditions or mobility limitations, as these groups may be unable to seek shelter from the impending threat on their own. Other people may elect not to leave the area because they lack transportation, lack a place to go, or other economic reasons; emergency personnel need to remain in the area as first responders after an event. Assessing the population likely to stay behind or requiring assistance during an emergency can determine the location and optimal size to shelter these populations in an event.

Community safe rooms are designed and built to protect occupants from multiple hazards, an approach that ensures comprehensive risk assessment. They are typically sited outside of the 500-year flood plain within a large, cleared area to mitigate the potential of falling debris or wildfire. An evacuation shelter may be located either inside the anticipated disaster impact zone as a *risk shelter*, or outside the zone as a *host shelter*. A *recovery shelter* is intended for use after extreme-wind events, where those who have been displaced from their homes can go for shelter and other basic needs.

Individual or family safe rooms are rooms or stand-alone structures on private property that protect small groups from windstorms, typically tornadoes, which can occur with very little warning. Residents in tornado-prone areas may live in rural areas, far from access to community shelters. They may construct it because they feel unprotected without a safe refuge, or there may be insurance benefits associated with safe room construction.

Due to complexities of funding, some shelters are designated as single-use while others may be used for multiple purposes. Multi-use shelters can be used for many purposes, a benefit that allows people to become familiar with the spaces before an emergency and may encourage vulnerable people to gather there for shelter in an emergency. Single-use shelters are reserved for one purpose - to shelter people in the immediate period of a disaster - a period lasting from a few hours for a tornado up to 72 hours for a hurricane. Single-use shelters are not permitted to include showers or food preparation areas, and may have limited mechanical and electrical services. The most critical concern for single-use shelters is maintenance: when the building isn't needed for months or years, maintenance may be deferred and minor issues are compounded. When the structures are 'out of sight, out of mind', it may be difficult to gain community support for necessary maintenance.

CONSTRUCTION STANDARDS

The U.S. Federal Emergency Management Agency (FEMA) has developed and provided design and construction guidance for safe rooms since 1998. The International Code Council, in partnership with FEMA and the National Storm Shelter Association, developed a consensus standard for the design and construction of tornado and hurricane shelters, the ICC 500.[2] The standard defines the structural design and testing criteria, wind loads, debris hazards, siting, envelope design, and continuity of operations requirements. There are no reports of a cast-in-place concrete building experiencing a significant structural problem during wind events, including the strongest hurricanes and tornadoes.[3]

The envelope must be designed to withstand high wind speed, so storm shelters are typically constructed with cast-in-place concrete or precast concrete, assemblies that offer great reliability in impact tests. The envelope is concerned with:

- Design wind speed: 250 mph (tornadic)
- Windborne debris impact: Wall assemblies are tested with large missiles: 15-lb wood 2 × 4 that is typically 12′ long, launched at 100 mph toward vertical surfaces (horizontally travelling missiles). The test must reject two missile impacts without penetration; some cracking is allowed but pieces of concrete cannot be ejected to the interior.
- Windborne debris impact: and then subjected to a cyclical pressure test. The window may break but must remain intact and in the frame. The subsequent cyclical test determines if the glass meets the pressure requirements for storm-force winds. The test window is placed in a pressure simulator where positive and negative pressure flexes the glass for 4,500 cycles. Approved windows do not form cracks larger than 127 mm (5 inches) long and 1.6 mm (1/16″) wide through which air can pass.
- Windborne debris impact: Doors are tested using the same test protocols as walls. Approved doors must remain intact and hardware must operate to allow egress after the testing.
- A concrete roof deck is required to prevent large falling debris from penetrating the roof of a shelter. The test is conducted with non-deformable barrels filled with hardened concrete weighing between 200 and 1,000 lbs. The impacts are concentrated at the centre of the roof span and close to slab supports to observe bending, shear, and spallling (see Chapter 31: Collateral Damage).

Critical support systems must continue to support human occupancy during severe weather events, with essential systems (power, communications, water, and wastewater) remaining functional. Hurricane safe rooms must ensure a supply of potable water is available for drinking and sanitation for the entire period of disruption by the storm: 1 gallon per occupant per day for handwashing and 1.5 gallons for flushing. Safe rooms must also safely contain waste for the entire design occupant capacity through the storm. Water for potable uses and sanitation should be protected by an enclosure designed to the same criteria as the safe room. If the safe room water supply comes from a well, then the pump, pump house, piping, and associated equipment need to be protected and have an alternate power supply.

Standby power is also essential for the minimum period of occupancy (24 hours for a hurricane, 2 hours for a tornado) and longer for critical facilities such as first-responder shelters and hospitals. Emergency power includes generators and fuel, uninterruptible power sources, and battery backups for emergency lighting. Mechanical ventilation is required for safe rooms with occupancy over 50 people, with natural ventilation as a failsafe

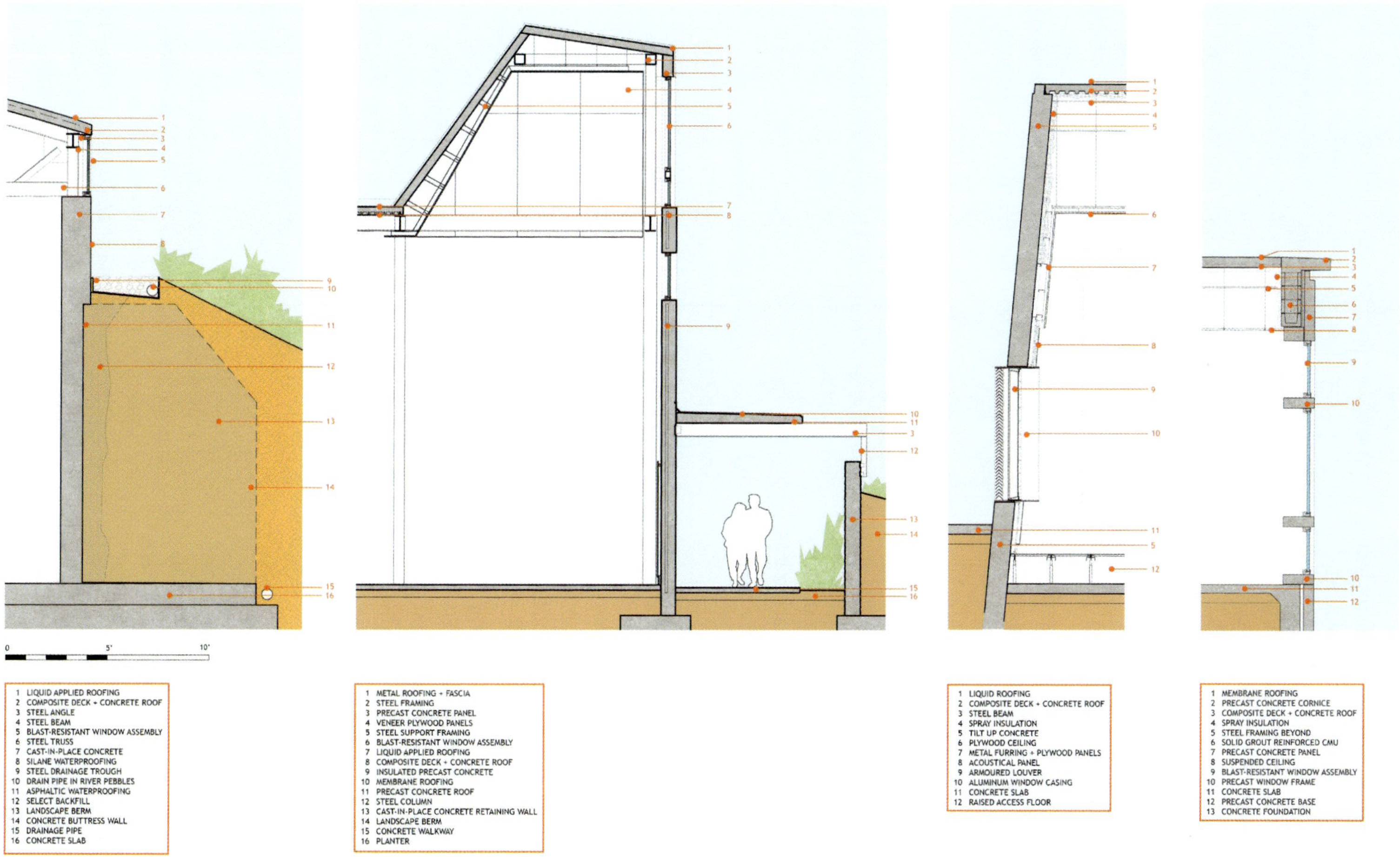

Figure 34.3: Four shelter designs with four different wall sections, from left: cast-in-place concrete, precast concrete, tilt-wall concrete, and reinforced concrete masonry units.

mode. In order to reduce the demand on generators and mechanical ventilation, efforts should be made to design a high-performance building envelope with adequate insulation, and to employ other measures such as ground-source heat exchange to minimise equipment size, fuel use, and energy demand.

KEY DESIGN CONSIDERATIONS

GENERAL DESIGN CONSIDERATIONS

Determine whether a safe room is necessary. Is the location likely to be threatened by an extreme-wind event? Do existing refuge areas leave occupants vulnerable to the impacts of wind and windborne debris? How many people are at risk and what are the potential casualties or losses associated with an extreme wind event? Evaluate the emergency warning system and estimate the travel time to a shelter to reduce the chances of exposing people to additional hazards when moving to the safe room.

In areas where the design wind speed for tornadoes is 250 mph, shelter is required at 911 call centres, emergency operations centres, fire, rescue, ambulance, and police stations. A safe room is required in educational occupancies where the number of occupants exceeds 50 people: schools, day care, and educational occupancies at places of religious worship.[4] Government offices, industrial plants, and other facilities may also require safe rooms. Where they are required, a safe room must accommodate 100% of the occupancy of the building.

Mitigating the potential for death or injury may be sufficient reason to build a safe room, even if not required. A business may want to protect employees and customers or improve recovery time after an event. If individuals or private concerns elect to build a safe room, it must conform to the same standards of construction as a public safe room.

Tornado shelters specify an occupant density of 5 square feet per person due to the limited time of use (less than 2 hours); for wheelchair users, it is 10 square feet per person, and persons on a bed or stretcher are allowed 30 square feet. Hurricane safe rooms specify a minimum of 20 square feet per person standing or in a wheelchair, and 40 square feet per person on a bed or stretcher.[5] In comparison, the floor area allowance for an assembly occupancy without fixed seats is 7 square feet per person, so a hurricane safe room will hold fewer occupants than if it is used for assembly purposes, while a tornado safe room can hold slightly more occupants.

If a facility has a shelter located in an accessory structure, the maximum distance of travel must be less than 1,000 feet from at least one door of the facility.

Annual evaluations of the storm shelter envelope and impact-protective systems ensure community safe rooms continue to meet protection standards. Storm shelters are often constructed with cast-in-place concrete, or prestressed, precast concrete, which may be prone to deterioration from chloride contamination, corrosion of embedded reinforcement, or freeze-thaw damage. Shelter owners should address leaks in walls and roofs as soon as they appear to prevent damage to the underlying structure. In addition to visual inspections, shelter owners may consider employing hammer-sounding and non-destructive evaluation methods to identify incipient structural defects.

A third-party peer review is required for community storm shelters with 50 or more occupants, shelters in schools with an occupant load greater than 16, and shelters in all Risk Category IV structures. Peer review is an important quality assurance measure.

WALLS, WINDOWS, AND DOORS

Wall sections that pass missile impact tests include a variety of framing materials: 6-inch-thick reinforced concrete, flat insulating concrete form with at least 4-inch-thick concrete encapsulated, and 6-inch-thick reinforced concrete masonry units. Even wood stud framing has passed the test, albeit with unusual construction methods: filling the space between studs with concrete and adding 14 ga. 1/2″ expanded metal sheathing or 14 ga. steel sheathing at the face of the wall.

Maximum wind pressures in a building occur at the building corners. Openings, even impact-resistant windows, should be set away from corners to ensure safety. Doors can be protected by an alcove or baffle system for greater safety against windborne debris.

Windows that pass missile-impact testing have multiple layers of glass laminated with polycarbonate interlayers. The layers are sandwiched together, typically without an insulating air space. Successful window test sections include: 2-ply 3/16-inch polycarbonate with 2-ply 1/8-inch heat-strengthened glass; and four- or five-layer laminated glass with 3/8-inch annealed glass and 0.090 PVB laminate. Missile-resistant windows typically have a deeper embedment in the frame to allow for deflection from windborne debris. The frame itself is also reinforced with steel splines, to prevent missile penetration. The thickness of the glazed assembly (over 3 inches), the weight (over 25 lbs per square foot), the potential for thermal bridging, and their high cost prohibit the use of large areas of glass in shelters.

Missile-resistant steel doors typically have 14 ga. skin and interior supports. The size of the door, frame, and hardware must be capable of resisting the highest wind pressure required at the site location. Double door systems with a central mullion must meet design pressures and the hardware must remain functional for exiting after an impact. All doors should be in an outswing configuration for both egress and wind resistance.

If there are operable impact-protection systems, such as hurricane shutters to cover windows, they must be capable of being operated by manual means from within the shelter.

Louvers and grilles for air intake or exhaust must also be protected from debris impacts with armoured screens. These screens typically reduce the amount of airflow through a louver, a consideration that may affect the size or number of louvers.

ROOFS

In addition to resisting wind pressures, ICC 500 requires roofs to be designed for extreme roof live loads: 100 psf for tornado shelters and 50 psf for hurricane shelters.

For precast concrete decks, the deck connections must be designed to resist uplift loads because the deck dead load itself is often less than the uplift force.

Debris hazards are present from taller adjacent buildings or other structures such as communication towers, taller sections of the host building, or large trees within the hazard's fall radius. Shelter designers multiply falling debris loads by a minimum safety factor of 2.0 to account for dynamic effects and apply falling debris loads simultaneously with the uniform roof live load (see Chapter 33: Collateral Damage).

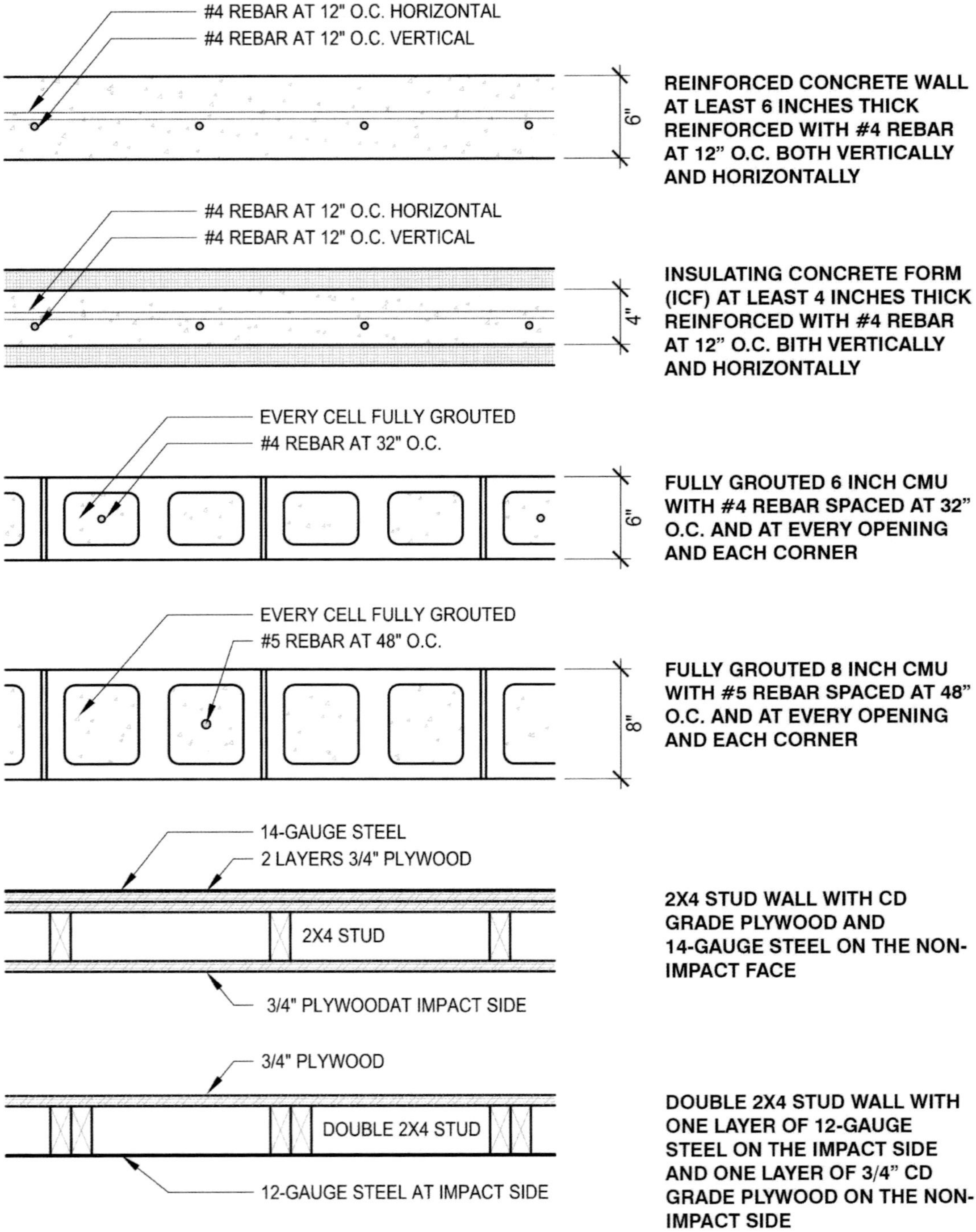

Figure 34.4: Wall assemblies that meet the requirements of FEMA P-361 missile impact testing.

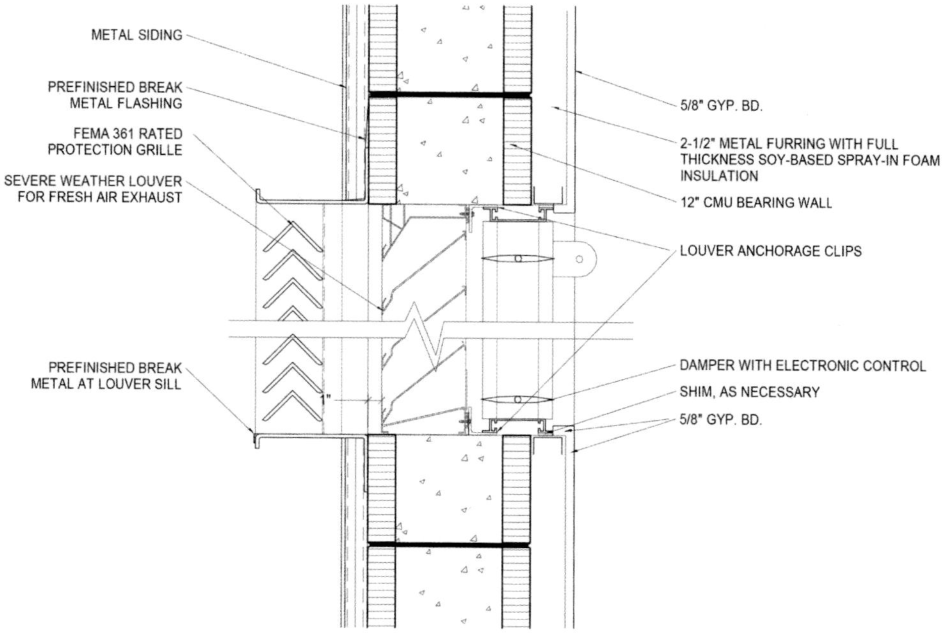

Figure 34.5: Cross-section of an armoured louver at the Bay Saint Louis Fire House No. 1.

Green roofs offer a promising alternative to conventional roof coverings, as the earthen material can absorb and deflect debris impact. Typically, the additional weight of a green roof system can be supported by the major wind-resisting structural elements already present in the safe room (see Chapter 35: Earth Shelter).

Renewable energy sources are difficult to integrate into safe rooms. The highest wind speed a solar mounting system can resist is about 140–160 mph; above 55 mph, wind turbinesautomatically shut off to prevent damage to the rotor.

IMPACT

Social: Hurricane and tornado safe rooms offer protection against extreme weather, reducing the risk of injury and loss of life during high-wind events. They enhance community resilience by ensuring communities can recover more quickly after a disaster and foster a sense of collective responsibility. Ensuring access to safe rooms for vulnerable populations promotes equity in disaster management.

Environmental: Although the embodied carbon in the armoured construction materials is high, these structures should be designed to last 200+ years.

Economic: While the initial cost of building safe rooms can be high, they may reduce the long-term economic burden on communities. Safe rooms can decrease emergency response costs by minimising injuries and avoiding the cost of evacuating large groups of people out of harm's way. After an event, shelter occupants can more easily return home to assess damage and begin the task of correcting any damage from the event.

Spatial Integration: The siting requirements for a shelter (outside of the floodplain and away from tall structures) mean that they are often built at the periphery of communities, often along major evacuation routes. This, and the potential for single-use designation, tends to isolate the buildings from daily use, which can have significant impacts on familiarity and the commitment to maintaining these structures.

NOTES

1 American Society of Civil Engineers (ASCE). 2017. Minimum Design Loads and Associated Criteria for Buildings and Other Structures (7–16).
2 ICC/NSSA. 2020. ICC500 Standard for the Design and Construction of Storm Shelters. Accessed at: https://codes.iccsafe.org/content/ICC5002020P1
3 https://www.fema.gov/sites/default/files/2020-08/fema543_design_guide_complete.pdf
4 ICC. 2024. International Building Code, Section 423 Storm Shelters.
5 ICC. 2020. Section 502.2.

RESOURCES

- FEMA. 2021. *Safe Rooms for Tornadoes and Hurricanes: Guidance for Community and Residential Safe Rooms, Third Edition (P-361).* Washington DC: U.S. Government Printing Office.
- ICC/NSSA. 2020. ICC500 Standard for the Design and Construction of Storm Shelters. Accessed at: https://codes.iccsafe.org/content/ICC5002020P1

EARTH SHELTER 35

ADAPTATION **WIND** SCALE **BUILDING**

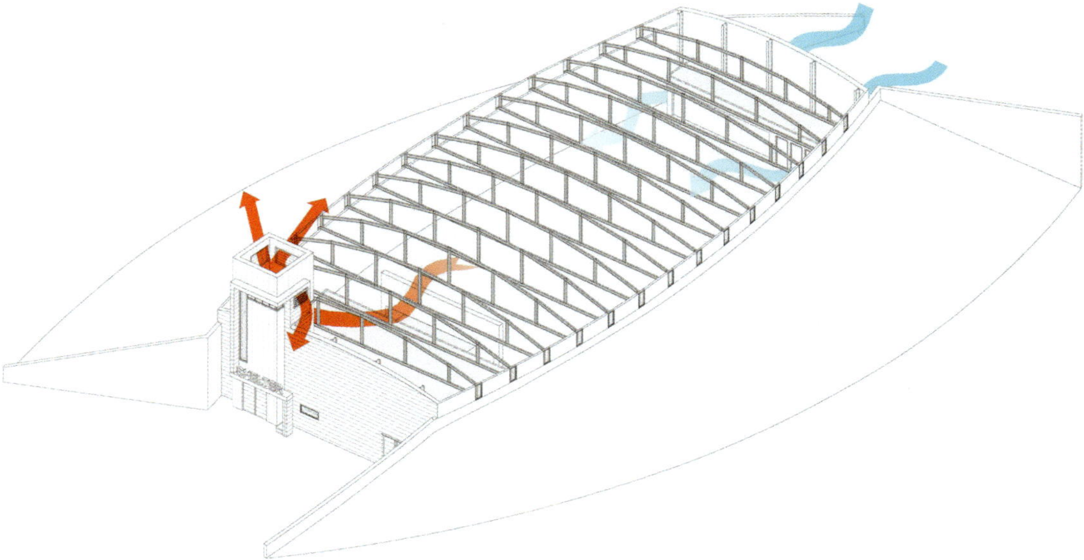

Earth sheltered structures use the natural properties of soil to resist climate extremes, employing the insulative value against heat and offering superior wind resistance against windborne debris impact, uplift, turbulent flow, and wake. Soil cover changes the surface morphology to alter wind interactions; both underground (completely below-grade) and bermed (all or partially above grade) structures streamline the flow of wind over the roof, especially at plane transitions and corners. Earth-covered buildings can use massing and orientation to reduce frontal areas that intercept wind while allowing the bulk of the structure to be covered with soil and plant materials that absorb the impact of wind-borne debris.

Figure 35.1: The Hancock County Shelters use earthen berms to deflect debris impact. The curved geometry of the walls and berms reduces peak pressure and turbulent flow. Natural ventilation uses the stack effect at the end walls to introduce airflow through louvers placed near the floor level at one end and high louvers to exhaust warm air on the opposite wall. The armoured louvers are on a dead-man switch to open automatically in the event of a power failure.

DOI: 10.4324/9781032702964-39

BACKGROUND

Roofs are the most vulnerable building components, often damaged by high winds acting on the geometric roof edges and corners. Various aerodynamic mitigation devices have been tested to reduce peak roof suction pressures. But what if the roof just ... disappeared?

Soil cover has been proven to protect from wind and debris impact[1] and the resulting low-profile structures deflect rather than confront wind-generated forces. The natural angle of repose of soil is about 35 degrees, depending on the grain size and shape; this slope gently directs wind over and around structures instead of creating sharp corners and spinning vortices. A bermed structure with partial exposure above the soil affects surface roughness and creates wind acceleration over the crest of the berm but reduces flow separation and lowers peak pressures.

The underground has long been a place of safety against threats. Both Hitler and Churchill built underground bunkers in WWII. Hitler's *Führerbunker* was constructed 8.5 m (28 feet) below the gardens of the Reich Chancellery with a 3 m (9′–10″) thick concrete barrier. The British Office of Works renovated the basement of the New Public Offices in 1939 to serve as the Cabinet War Rooms, but the essential offices were only 3 m (10 feet) below the surface, with an unreinforced concrete cover 1.5 m (5′–0″) thick added during the Blitz in 1940–1941. Although the underground bunker was structurally inadequate against a bomb, the staff believed in its protective ability and affectionately termed the addition, 'The Slab'. It was structurally inadequate against a direct hit, but psychologically, it reassured the staff who worked there around the clock.

America first detonated an atomic bomb in 1945, kickstarting the nuclear age and subsequent panic. The government offered two recommendations: (1) stockpile supplies and (2) build an underground bomb shelter to reduce exposure to radioactive fallout. Bomb shelter designs offered choices ranging from single-person blast refuges to family-sized structures in a range of designs with varying degrees of efficacy: corrugated steel (the corrugations promising to 'increase strength 1,000 times!'), oversized concrete pipes, and reinforced walls. Shelters could be supplied with ventilators, chemical toilets, bicycle-powered electricity, storage shelves, built-in furniture, swimming pools, Astroturf, fishponds, generators, batteries, and potable water tanks. Thousands of these structures were built as a contingency for a war that never happened.

Figure 35.2: There are three types of earth-sheltered structures: fully underground, partially-bermed, and a hybrid type for sloped sites that appear subsurface from one side and elevational on the other side.

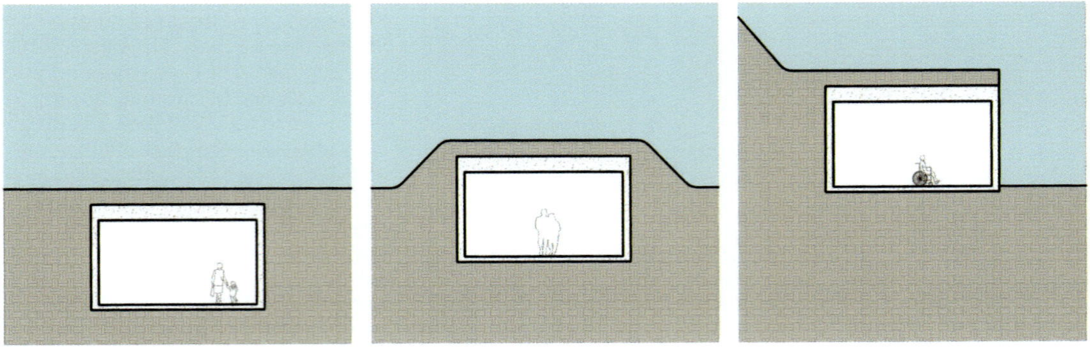

In an overheated world with increasing storms, earth-sheltered structures may have a role in saving lives along hurricane-battered coastlines and in tornado alleys ... at least for short periods of occupation. People cannot tolerate the physical and mental dysfunction that arises from confinement in a lightless environment, with human reactions varying from mild discomfort to severe claustrophobia. In Civil Defence tests of shelter occupation, families complained of mildew, low light, poor sanitation, and the psychological pressures of the extended stay. The study reported, 'At the end of the two weeks, the couple said they were able to cope with the pressures of the stay only by drinking whisky and giving tranquilizers to their children'.[2]

KEY DESIGN CONSIDERATIONS

Certain soil types are better suited to earth-sheltered construction. Expansive clays can promote cracking of the slab and walls. Excavation in areas with hard, rocky ground may be difficult and expensive. Unstable and coarse soils may be prone to landslides. Ideal sites have a slope where the structure can be partially-buried and permeable soils to allow water to percolate away from the structure. Test soils prior to the design phase.

Identify the groundwater level at the site and provide good drainage away from the building. Hydrostatic pressure has significant structural implications but also drives moisture transmission; a complete waterproofing and drainage systems at exterior walls reduces opportunities for leaks. Provide capillary breaks and vapour barriers beneath the slab and at exterior walls that will be covered with earth. A good primer on keeping water out of underground spaces comes from Building Science.com Corporation: https://buildingscience.com/documents/building-science-insights-newsletters/bsi-110-keeping-water-out-basements.

In an earth-sheltered structure, orientation is particularly critical. Follow cues from the site topography to determine whether the building can be built into a slope or bermed. Identify the prevailing winds that should be deflected by earthen berms. Design openings to allow light penetration and direct heat gain in regions with long winter seasons; in regions with long summers, shade openings with overhangs.

Earth-sheltered structures benefit from the insulative value of the earth surrounding the structure, significantly reducing the need for heating and cooling. Normal ground temperature seldom reaches the outdoor air temperatures in the heat of a normal hot day, conducting less heat into the structure due to the reduced temperature difference. If the air surface temperature ranges from −15°C to 35°C throughout the year at 3 m below the surface, the temperature of the earth will vary between 10°C and 15°C. The principles of annual heat storage describe how the earth collects solar heat all summer and cools passively while heating the earth around it; maintaining warmth in winter by retrieving stored heat from the soil. An earth-sheltered building is also protected from most direct solar radiation, eliminating the direct thermal load due to heat radiation through the building envelope. Heating energy consumption can be reduced 75% when compared to a baseline, moderately-insulated structure, using soil cover to equate to a super-insulated structure.[3]

Compacted fill around the safe room provides suitable protection from a tornado safe room test missile. At least 12 inches of vertical soil cover can protect horizontal surfaces and at least 36 inches of horizontal soil cover (sloped not greater than 2:12) protects vertical surfaces. The roof and wall assemblies beneath do not need to be tested for missile impact because the wall assembly is not exposed.[4]

A bermed earth-sheltered structure is less effective for wind protection than a fully earth-sheltered structure as one (or more) facades may be exposed. Ensure that exposed walls are braced to resist wind pressures and are protected from wind-borne debris.

Figure 35.3: Construction of the Hancock County Shelters with buttresses designed to resist hydrostatic pressure on the earthen berms.

Green roofs and earth-sheltered structures require a support structure sized to withstand the gravity and hydrostatic loads of a fully-saturated growth medium. Bermed exterior walls must be strong enough to withstand the overturning pressure, typically built with reinforced, cast-in place concrete or concrete masonry units. At the roof, full saturation of the soil harnesses the weight of water to resist uplift forces but increases gravity loads. Most high-wind events are accompanied by rainfall to ensure the soil is wetted and heavy: hurricanes arrive with rain bands and tornadoes form in the warm, moist air of severe thunderstorms.

Ensure adequate ventilation of earth-sheltered structures, which typically cannot depend on natural sources of cross-ventilation. Never

Figure 35.4: A green roof system was tested to Category IV hurricane winds and passed without damage or displacement of any of the components. The approved system was installed at the Lakeside Village student housing complex at the University of Miami in 2019, designed by Arquitectonica. Images courtesy of Henry, a Carlisle Company.

use appliances dependent upon fossil fuel combustion, such as log-burners or gas stovetops, which affect interior air quality. Avoid indoor pollutants from high-VOC materials that can build up in confined spaces. Use an energy recovery ventilation system to mix incoming fresh air and minimise heat loss. Higher ventilation rates (4–6 air changes per hour) reduce airborne infectious diseases.[5] This ventilation target can be difficult to reach in an underground or partially earth-sheltered structure.

A soil gas vent at the crushed stone layer beneath the floor slab provides pressure relief and prevents moisture upwelling. Earth-sheltered structures can potentially have higher radon levels; below-slab venting can reduce radon buildup. Radon levels inside houses below 4 picoCuries per litre of air (pCi/L) are considered acceptable.

Green roofs are not only a sustainability strategy but also a resilience option as a minimum soil cover of 12″ is sufficient to absorb most of the impact force from wind-borne debris. Concerns about the possibility of wind pressure dislodging components had discouraged the widespread use of green roofing in hurricane zones until the systems were tested and shown to withstand high velocity hurricane zone winds. A wind- and impact-resistant green roof systems includes: a waterproofing membrane fully adhered to the concrete deck; a capillary action drainage mat used in place of a standard moulded plastic drainboard to provide a balance of water retention and positive drainage beneath the growth media; extensive green roof systems with at least 10 inches of growth medium; anchoring components consisting of steel cables and a geotextile mesh to the concrete deck; and a double parapet enclosure around each roof to contain the green roof components separately from the building parapet.

A thriving plant colony helps to anchor the soil during windstorms. In sloped applications, a capillary action drainage mat is used in place of a standard moulded plastic drainboard to balance water retention and positive drainage beneath the soil. This layer manages hydrostatic pressure to retain adequate moisture at the higher end of the roof slope and avoid too much water at the base. Soil that is not uniformly moist offers less support for plant materials. A green roof is like a very large container planting, which can dry out when exposed to airflow and therefore should include a water supply at the roof level to maintain thriving plant colonies.

A green roof slope stabilisation system consists of steel cables and a geotextile mesh within the growing media anchored to the deck and bolted to parapets. This keeps the soil tightly confined and holds it in place. Plants grow through the mesh, undeterred by the slight barrier to photosynthesis it creates.

A biodegradable jute mat can be placed over the top of the growing media to provide erosion control during the plant establishment period. In testing, plants grew to cover the jute and entangled their roots in the mesh for further protection against wind uplift.

For green roof applications, a double parapet provides better wind resistance than a single parapet. The outer parapet wall intercepts high winds and reduces the turbulent wake along the edge of the roof, while the inner parapet wall reduces uplift pressure on vegetation and firmly contains the component layers. The space between parapets can be used for access and maintenance.

Figure 35.5: The Eco-Residence was completed in July 2005, five weeks before Hurricane Katrina. The grass roof remained intact during the storm, the weight of the fully-saturated grass roof and the strength of the wood support piers contributing to its survival, even as storm surge nearly reached the level of the deck. Photo by Charles Punzo.

GREEN ROOFS SAVE LIVES

When Hurricane Katrina came ashore on 29 August 2005, the people who elected to stay in place were long-time residents who had weathered many storms and believed that the benchmark storm - the worst-case scenario - was 1969s Hurricane Camille. They were mistaken. Coming ashore with Cat 3 winds and Cat 5 storm surge, Katrina broke Camille's record of destruction and killed more people than the previous storm.

My family had completed construction of a house in July 2005, five weeks before the storm. It was built on 'high ground' for coastal Mississippi, about 20 feet above sea level and (crucially for reducing insurance premiums) 1,000 feet from the coastal waterline. When we began excavating for the foundations, we found the remains of a house destroyed by Camille's winds, but there was no indication of the site being flooded in 300 years of recorded history.

Katrina's storm surge at our location was measured at 28 feet above sea level. Houses along the beach were washed out, foundations scoured, roofs ripped off, and walls overturned. Survivors swam out of windows, searching for something - anything - to hold onto. A brother and sister survived the slow disintegration of their house on the beach and were pushed inland by the waves. Trees were lashed by the winds, structures were breaking apart, and entire roof diaphragms floating through the landscape. They were looking for a place that wasn't moving and found shelter underneath our green roof. They said afterwards that they were hoping for a wave high enough to wash them onto the roof so they could get away from the surge.

The decision to include a green roof in the design was an effort to demonstrate

IMPACT

Social: Earth-sheltered structures can encourage a closer connection to nature and elevate considerations of sustainability and resilience. However, these structures may isolate occupants from interaction with neighbours, as the structures have fewer opportunities to integrate porches and windows.

Environmental: The insulative value of the earth and the stable internal temperature of the ground can lower energy consumption and reduce resource use. Although exterior walls and roof decks are typically constructed with concrete, a high-embodied carbon material, this building assembly can reduce the need for redundant layers such as cladding and insulation, reducing the overall environmental impact.

Economic: Earth-sheltered structures may cost less to insure because they offer enhanced protection against high winds, hailstorms, and some natural disasters. They can reduce the annual cost of heating and cooling in climates with large temperature swings and low humidity. However, the initial cost of construction can be up to 20% more than a conventional structure, and maintenance demands increased care to avoid moisture problems during construction and over the life of the structure.

Spatial Integration: Earth-sheltered structures create a visually distinct appearance, which can either allow them to blend into the natural landscape or to stand out from conventionally-built neighbours. Earth-sheltered structures may require more land to allow berming and are not a good solution for dense, urban areas. However, green roofs offer many of the same benefits for wind-resistance, insulation, and stormwater management.

to clients that this strategy could work in south Mississippi – that plants could survive alternating periods of drought and heavy rainfall, that the soil wouldn't be washed away, and that the system had good insulative value. We never imagined that the excess weight of the system and the oversized supports would become an anchor that held the structure in place. Nor could we have ever imagined that the structure would save the lives of our neighbours. Even more surprising – the green roof lost none of its soil in the storm.

After the storm, there were only a few structures left standing in the neighbourhood – including ours. The interior sheetrock had a waterline as high as one could reach, 7′–3″ above the floor. The downstairs was cleared out and we moved back in seven weeks after the storm. When inspectors from FEMA visited, they were confounded by the survival of the house, attributing it to three design decisions: the green roof, continuity of load path, and interior shear walls that run from the slab to the roof deck. Although green roofs in the region remain rare, we have a firsthand understanding of their resilience value and remain staunch advocates for green roofs.

NOTES

1 FEMA. 2021. Safe Rooms for Tornadoes and Hurricanes: Guidance for Community and Residential Safe Rooms, Third Edition (P-361). B3-31.
2 Roy, S. 2011. *Bomboozled: How the U.S. Government Mislead Itself and Its People into Believing They Could Survive a Nuclear Attack*. Pointed Leaf Press, p. 93.
3 Wendt, R.L. 1982. *Earth-Sheltered Housing: An Evaluation of Energy-Conservation Potential*. Department of Energy, Oak Ridge National Laboratory. https://www.osti.gov/servlets/purl/5203877.
4 FEMA (2021).
5 Kurnitski, J. et al. 2023. Post-COVID Ventilation Design: Infection Risk-Based Target Ventilation Rates and Point Source Ventilation Effectiveness. *Energy and Buildings* 296. https://doi.org/10.1016/j.enbuild.2023.113386.

RESOURCE

- Anselm, A.J. 2012. Earth Shelters: A Review of Energy Conservation Properties in Earth Sheltered Housing. From the volume Energy Conservation, ed: Ahmed, A.Z. Accessed at: https://www.intechopen.com/chapters/40549

EMERGENCY CACHE 36

ADAPTATION **WIND** SCALE **BUILDING**

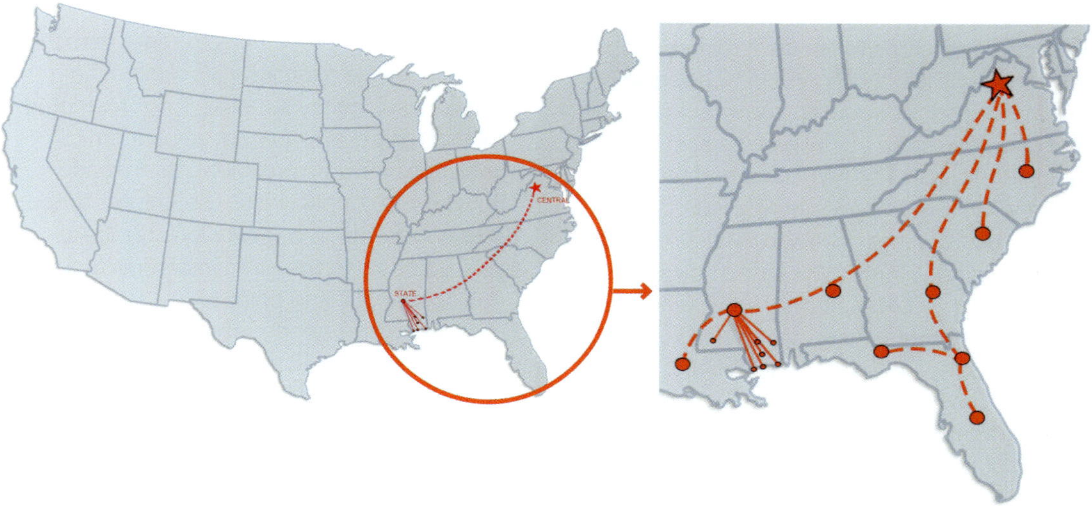

In the immediate aftermath of a disaster such as a tornado or hurricane, critical supply lines are blocked, power lines downed, other utilities interrupted by loss of power, and fuel supplies limited. Rapid distribution of essential supplies - water, food, and medicine - is the most critical emergency response activity. Supply chains rely on a sequence of interdependencies: the availability of vehicles and fuel, passable roadways, pre-positioned stocks of goods, local points of distribution (POD), and places for people to store individual supplies.

Figure 36.1: The emergency supply chain works in a hub and spoke organisation, with central warehouses moving supplies to state warehouses which then distribute supplies to points of distribution located in or near affected communities.

DOI: 10.4324/9781032702964-40

BACKGROUND

The primary goal of emergency management is to reduce the loss of life during and after an event. The director of the Federal Emergency Management Agency (U.S.) asserted in 2003 that the agency was taking steps to ensure that 'disaster teams will be able to respond anywhere in the country within 12 hours and disaster logistics packages, commodities, and equipment can be delivered anywhere within 24 hours'.[1] The first sustained test of the new system occurred during Hurricane Katrina in 2005, when the supply chain failed catastrophically. In this, the largest disaster in U.S. history, FEMA adopted a wait-and-see policy to determine if pre-positioned supplies were adequate rather than maintaining a constant flow to the disaster zone. The national agency had pre-positioned 4.6 million tonnes of ice, 3.7 million litres of water, and 1.86 million meals-ready-to-eat (MRE) at logistics centres just beyond the disaster zone but the ultimate scale of the disaster affected 2.5 million people and lasted for weeks and months, making initial supplies insufficient. States also failed to distribute the supplies in time. Louisiana used a central server that was quickly overwhelmed with requests for supplies while roads in hard-hit areas remained underwater for weeks. Federal shipments to Mississippi did not reach adequate levels until 10 days after landfall,[2] hampered by scant local resources and severe fuel shortages. The storm's death toll reached 1,833, with about half of these deaths directly from the hurricane and the other half resulting from inadequate emergency response.[3]

After a disaster, it may be impossible to procure sufficient resources to meet demands, establishing the need for a stockpile. The need for emergency supplies is not restricted to windstorms; events such as pandemics or conflicts have widespread effects that add stress to the supply chain. The uninterrupted delivery of supplies depends on storage at every point along the path: in central/regional hubs, local POD, and point of use storerooms. Designers can support community safety by understanding the flow of goods and planning adequate spatial resources.

After a disaster, delivering one case of drinking water, two bags of ice, and six MREs per day to affected households (the amount recommended by the Florida State Emergency Response Team), requires a sequence of steps from the central/regional stockpile to the local authority's POD to the household or point of use.

Figure 36.2: The space necessary to host a standard single-line Point of Distribution is extensive, with areas for unloading trailers, consumer vehicle stacking, staff/personnel areas, and storage for supplies.

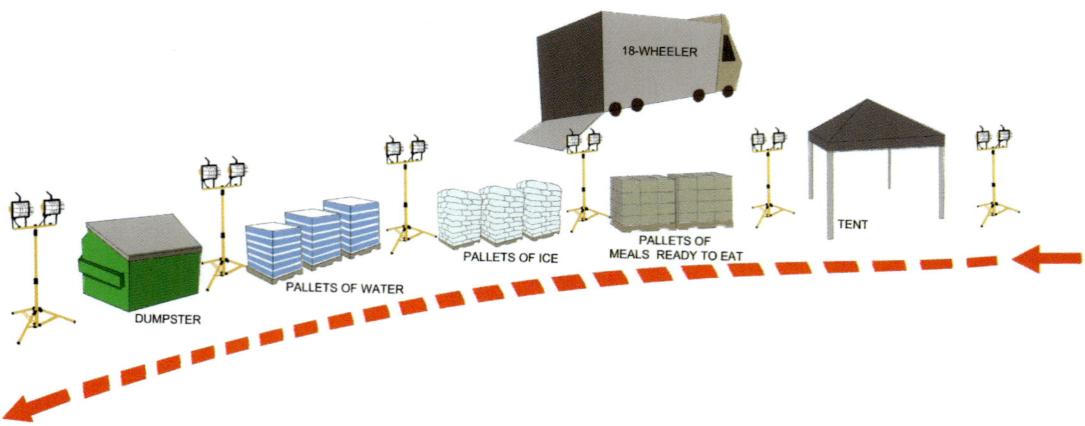

KEY DESIGN CONSIDERATIONS

CENTRAL/REGIONAL STOCKPILES

The Strategic National Stockpile, which includes medical supplies and equipment, is maintained in 12 secret locations around the United States. FEMA maintains an additional eight secure distribution centres for food, water, generators, and other disaster supplies around the country (Federal Operational Staging Areas), as well as 252 pre-positioned containers of disaster supplies in 14 states (Regional Staging Areas).[4]

Warehouses of long-life goods are staged in proximity to – but not within – the hazard area. Stockpiles may be located at military bases or government-owned facilities, but if adequate space is not available, storage options include the use of large warehouses, vacant shopping malls, and abandoned big-box stores.

Some supplies require special handling, such as medical supplies requiring security or refrigeration, and bags of ice requiring freezers. Planning for adequate cold-chain storage, uninterruptible power, and refrigerated trucks reduces potential loss and waste.

Security is critical to prevent facilities or distribution trucks from becoming targets for looters.

Proximity to the interstate system is desirable to deploy supplies quickly to local distribution points.

Large, national chains have logistics protocols for responding to disasters and also require their major vendors to establish disaster protocols to prevent interruptions. Wal-Mart has 100 distribution centres in the United States, eight of which have significant square footage reserved for disaster merchandise, including bottled water stockpiled for emergencies.

LOCAL POINTS OF DISTRIBUTION

PODs in the United States are ranked in size to serve between 5,000 and 20,000 people per day, and up to 560 vehicles per hour. POD sites are typically staged in large parking lots organised with one-way, drive-through traffic. Emergency operations managers conduct a hazard analysis to designate sites outside of floodplains, surge areas, and clear of potential falling hazards such as tall buildings or water towers. The sites must provide ample space for delivery trucks to unload, space to store pallets of supplies, and one (or more) car pickup lines. Traffic control, lights, equipment, and dumpsters must be accommodated on the site, as well as tents and toilet facilities for the POD staff.

Locations at high-traffic roadways have good accessibility, visibility, and familiarity. However, these large lots are often found on the periphery of urban areas and may be difficult to reach without a vehicle. In urban environments, PODs should be located so that people can walk or bike to get emergency supplies when fuel is unavailable or cars are no longer working.

Staffing is required – team leaders, forklift operators, labourers, law enforcement, and community relations personnel. In the United States., the National Guard often assists with distribution after major disasters.

The same locations may also provide information to connect people with necessary resources: financial, medical, family services, etc.

Charging points and Wi-Fi networks help people contact family members, register for assistance, and plan their next move.

If a private office or commercial establishment remains operational after a disaster, they may volunteer to become a distribution point for disaster relief supplies, charging station, meal preparation site, or hub for volunteers. Following Hurricane Sandy in the northeast U.S., thirty-five PODs were established in locations ranging from churches to daycare facilities, storefronts to surf shops.

Figure 36.3: A three-day supply of personal disaster supplies requires about 1.2 cubic metres (42 cubic feet) of space for storage.

POINT OF USE STORAGE

Households should designate space to maintain an essential cache of supplies. This should be located within the heated and cooled envelope to ensure supplies have a long shelf life.

The National Safety Council recommends a home emergency supply kit include the following items[5]:

- One gallon of water per person per day for at least three days
- Three days of nonperishable protein-packed foods that can be cooked without electricity, such as tuna, peanut butter, and granola bars
- Prescription medicines

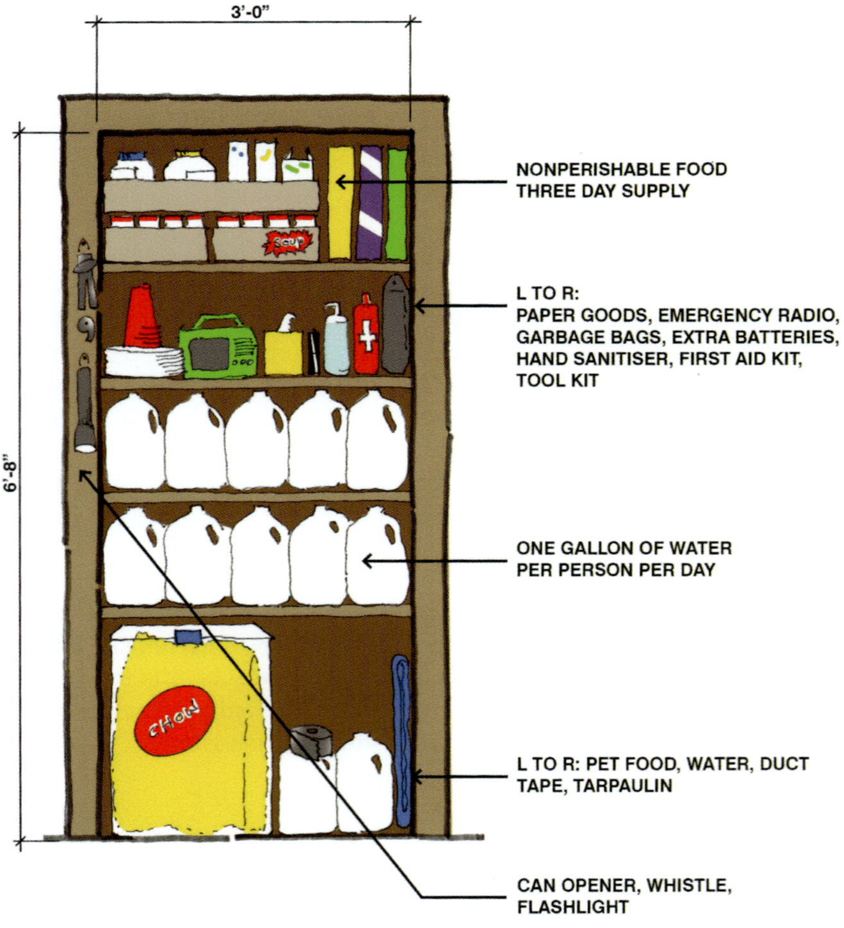

- Food for pets
- Can opener
- Hand-crank or battery-powered radio with extra batteries
- Flashlight with extra batteries
- First aid kit with gauze, tape, bandages, antibiotic ointment, aspirin, a blanket, nonlatex gloves, scissors, hydrocortisone, thermometer, tweezers, and instant cold compress
- Tool kit with basic tools to shut off utilities
- Hand sanitiser and garbage bags for sanitation
- Plastic sheeting/tarpaulin and duct tape in case of broken windows or a leaky roof
- Whistle to signal for help

Residents in isolated locations, such as the islands of Hawaii, are encouraged to maintain 14 days of disaster supplies due to the reliance on air or sea transportation and the islands' susceptibility to supply chain disruptions.

Households concerned about self-sufficiency can dramatically improve conditions after a disaster by storing additional nonperishable food, installing uninterruptible power and batteries to keep the household running in a power outage, installing rainwater harvesting and filtration systems and tanks to store potable water, providing solar hot water for hygiene, and planting gardens for food production. Note that these may be impacted by the disaster if not protected.

Offices and public facilities should also maintain resources to enable continuity of operations for the business; support staff and colleagues; temporarily secure the workplace; and restore technology and communications. Tenants and facility managers should assess the supplies needed. The AIA Architects' Guide to Business Continuity offers a workbook and checklists to prepare for disruptions including floods and windstorms.

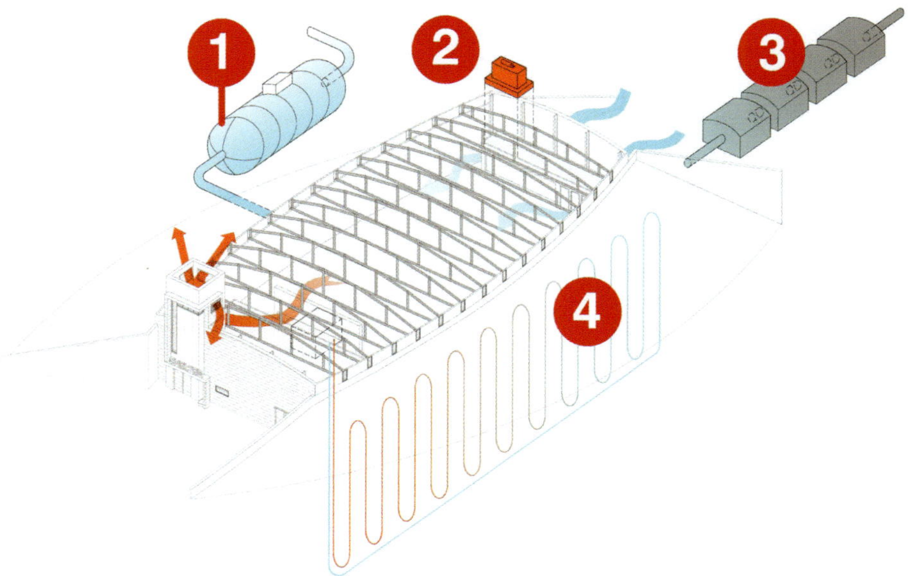

Figure 36.4: Critical facilities, such as community shelters and essential offices, require on-site Continuity-of-Operations (COOP) equipment. The Hancock County Shelters include: 1. A 10,000 gallon potable water storage tank to provide a three-day supply of water for occupants; 2. A diesel generator with a 3-day supply of fuel; 3. Wastewater chambers to detain sewage if municipal treatment systems are offline; and 4. Ground-source heat exchange system to transfer heat to and from the ground, which reduces cooling and heating loads.

IMPACT

Social: Pre-planning and emergency response ensures that people have essential provisions in a timely manner after a disaster, reducing human suffering and casualties.

Economic: The cost of emergency supplies may be inflated or have limited availability immediately prior to a threat due to a surge in demand. The cost of supplies in the aftermath of widespread damage may increase costs by 15–30% for three to six months or until re-supply can meet demands.

Environmental: The post-disaster period often takes large toll on environmental practices, requiring extra transportation, packaging, and fuel. With local sources impacted, transporting emergency supplies to the disaster area adds considerable vehicle miles to food consumed after a disaster. Residents may drive farther to access supplies or rely more heavily on personal vehicles if public transit is affected. Unsafe drinking water in the impacted area drives residents to consume bottled water and interruptions to recycling programmes are common after disasters.

Spatial: Reusing empty facilities for emergency stockpiles ensures these facilities are maintained and the embodied carbon still serves a purpose.

NOTES

1 Senate Report S. Rept. 109–322, p. 225. https://www.govinfo.gov/content/pkg/CRPT-109srpt322/pdf/CRPT-109srpt322.pdf

2 U.S. Congress. 2006. Hurricane Katrina: A Nation Still Unprepared, Special Report of the Committee on Homeland Security and Governmental Affairs. U.S. Government Printing Office, p. 9.

3 Sylvester, J. 2008. *The Media and Hurricanes Katrina and Rita: Lost and Found*. New York: Palgrave Macmillan.

4 Graff, G. 2017. *Raven Rock: The Story of the U.S. Government's Secret Plan to Save Itself—While the Rest of Us Die*. New York: Simon & Schuster.

5 National Safety Council, Emergency Supply Kit. Accessed at: https://www.nsc.org/community-safety/safety-topics/emergency-preparedness/emergency-supplies-for-the-home?

RESOURCES

- American Institute of Architects. 2023. Architects' Guide to Business Continuity. Accessed at: https://www.aia.org/resource-center/architects-guide-business-continuity
- USAID Global Health Supply Chain Program, Emergency Supply Chain Preparedness and Response. Accessed at: https://www.ghsupplychain.org/ESC-Preparedness-Response

PART IV

Scarcity

The climate crisis exerts a profound impact on resources. Droughts are turning arable land into deserts and affecting cities with thousand-year shortages in aquifers and reservoirs. For every 1°C of warming, global cereal crop yields decline by 10%. Increasing heat affects planting zones, which are moving towards the poles. Scarce resources affect building materials, too, through supply chain interruptions, low river levels interrupting shipping, and rising fuel prices. The myth of continuous economic growth tied to consumption is collapsing, as every degree of warming reduces economic growth by 1%.

The most significant effects of scarcity foster higher inequality as crises create wider gaps in income and access to health, food, water, and shelter. Food production declines, increasingly expensive disasters accumulate, transport grinds to a halt, and public health impacts spread, threatening human survival across the globe, driving up costs, and placing more people in vulnerable conditions.

Architects must incorporate creative solutions to fill gaps by creating buildings and communities that regenerate the productive systems upon which we rely.

At the Community scale, the built environment can support **Biodiversity** through rewilding buildings, sites, and cities. **Edible Cities** suggests ways for urban areas to localise food production and increase self-sufficiency. **Boundaries to Growth** limit the urban footprint to preserve green boundary zones and agricultural lands along the city's edge. Building community resilience is a process requiring sustained commitment, and **Community Participation after Disaster** places the responsibility for recovery in the hands of residents, giving them agency and influence over the process to address longstanding issues in their community.

At the Site scale, designs to enhance **Social Capital / Social Infrastructure** dissolves barriers between people to encourage acquaintanceship, friendship, and the ability to reach out to others for assistance. **Net-Zero Water** prepares each site to collect, treat, use, reuse, and return water to the original source, another effort towards self-sufficiency.

The Building scale introduces the **Circularity** of building material flows and a cycle of use, disassembly, and reuse that can mitigate the impacts of virgin resource extraction and harvest. **Adaptable + Adaptive** presents solutions for buildings that can be modified for new uses and with the capacity to change in response to climate and economic forces. **Antifragile** presents an argument for structures that benefit from shocks and stresses and continue to serve for extended periods of time.

In an era of continuing disruption and scarcity, people need to be able to rely on their immediate neighbourhood for essential goods and services. They may also have to depend on their neighbours to help in a crisis, a reliance that begins with small encounters at the park or coffee shop, participating in clubs and meetings, extending invitations to events and other opportunities to know one another, which can lead to leadership and advocacy for change. This is how social capital - and resilience - is built, one person and one place at a time.

BIODIVERSITY + ADAPTATION 37

ADAPTATION **SCARCITY** SCALE **COMMUNITY**

Biodiversity measures the variety of living organisms in an ecosystem, describing both the number of species in a particular habitat and the skein of interdependencies they rely on for survival. Biodiversity-friendly architecture prioritises the integration of natural elements and ecosystems in the built environment to improve quality of life for humans and the natural systems upon which we rely for food, water, material resources, income, and health.

Figure 37.1: Rewild My Street proposed adapting the terraces, gardens and streetscape of typical London residential streets, transforming them into havens for wildlife and adding wildflower meadows, patio ponds, bird feeders and insect hotels. The scale of the proposal – 3.8 million gardens covering 24% of land in the city – could have tremendous impact on biodiversity. Siân and Jon Moxon/ Rewild My Street (with altered photos courtesy of Charles J Sharp, Pau. artigas, Super.lukas, Didier Descouens, Ninjatacoshell, George Hodan, Piotr Siedlecki, Peter Mulligan, Potapov Alexander/Shutterstock).

DOI: 10.4324/9781032702964-42

BACKGROUND

The term 'adaptation' emerged from the biological sciences as the adjustment of organisms to their environment to improve their chance of survival. Adaptation relies on biological diversity for the natural selection of traits that enable survival and reproduction. Humans rely on biodiversity to supply essential services: food, medicine, and materials for clothing, shelter, and goods. For this reason, settlements have historically flourished in areas of concentrated biological productivity characterised by high levels of diversity in animals and plants. However, cities are dominated by one species – humans – whose actions are the leading cause of species extinction.

Architecture becomes a direct cause of biodiversity loss when a sterile structure replaces a site with an abundance of life. Architecture is also one of the leading indirect causes of global biodiversity loss due to forestry, mining, and other resource extraction for use in building materials. One quarter of tropical forests have been logged and a significant percentage of that timber has been used to construct buildings. Depletion of fossil fuels and mineral elements is currently proceeding unchecked, not hampered by dwindling reserves. Humans have artificially restricted biodiversity by planting concentrations of turf grass instead of wild meadows, farming fish rather than encouraging wild propagation, clearcutting mixed forests and replanting only monocultures. Monocultures, whether fields of crops, forests of timber, or turfgrass lawns, are associated with soil degradation, vulnerability to drought and disease, increased risk of wildfire, and the loss of wild pollinators. Decision-makers have committed human dependence upon a narrow selection of favoured species, a reliance that may prove deadly in this era of climate uncertainty.

The loss of biodiversity increases challenges to humans in both mental and physical health. A decline in biodiversity threatens food production by decreasing the number of species cultivated for food and attacking the habitats of pollinators, making global populations vulnerable to drought, famine, and price fluctuations. The loss of ecosystems and their services affects air and water quality, storm resilience, and bird and animal populations. Human encroachment on ecosystems leads to a greater risk of animal-to-human transmission of diseases, increasing the potential for pandemics. Every loss threatens the existence of historic crops and their genetic library, which could provide solutions for future innovations in medicines and food production. Through land use and the destruction of habitat, exploitation of resources, and contamination, humans have driven extinction rates 100–1,000 times higher than the baseline rate,[1] signalling massive losses to the planet's biodiversity.

Architects must recognise and value ecosystem services in order to design a built environment that prioritises biodiversity. Primary ecosystem services include:

- **Provisioning** (food, fuel, fibre, genetic resources, medicines, freshwater, and ornamental/aesthetic)
- **Regulating** (air quality, climate, water, solar, erosion, water treatment, noise mitigation, disease regulation, pests, pollination, natural hazard mitigation, and carbon sequestration)
- **Cultural** (mental and physical health, cultural diversity, knowledge, sense of place, aesthetic value, education, social relations, recreation, heritage, and inspiration)
- **Supporting services** (soil formation, habitat, photosynthesis, primary production, and nutrient cycling)

Biodiversity is measured by two aspects: *species richness,* or the number of species in a community; and *evenness,* which indicates how common or rare each species is within the community.[2] Sites with significant species richness or uncommon species exhibit high distinctiveness.

Slowing the rate of biodiversity loss requires understanding the economic value of the ecosystem services that natural habitats provide, and committing to actions that preserve and restore ecosystems. Architects can have a positive impact on biodiversity through responsible sourcing, low-impact construction practices, and planning for responsible end-of-life scenarios. Critical design decisions directly impact biodiversity at the site: green roofs v. impervious surfaces, bird-friendly glazing and living walls rather than blank exteriors, and the proportion of landscape and hardscape in sitework. Architects are culpable for these choices and share the responsibility for regenerating what has been lost, even in places far from the project site.

The U.K. government's 25-year Environmental Plan (2018) requires new development to provide an increase in biodiversity of at least 10% above the existing condition and maintain this net gain for at least 30 years.[3] The intent is to spur local nature recovery using a wide variety of solutions to enhance terrestrial habitats, hedgerows, and watercourses. Biological units are strengthened through nutrient mitigation, green infrastructure, river basin enhancement, vegetation and tree planting, restoring hedgerows, and other actions that provide habitat, food, and shelter for a variety of native species.

KEY DESIGN CONSIDERATIONS

COMMUNITY + SITE

Avoiding biodiversity loss is the most effective way of reducing potential impacts. Protect what is inherited at the site, especially the native habitats, rare species, and remnant patches of vegetation with very high distinctiveness.

Minimise building footprints to limit the extent of impacts to biodiversity. Where avoidance is not feasible, minimise negative impacts through the project design. One solution is cluster development, which calculates the maximum number of units that can be developed and then compresses units on the site to minimise the development footprint and leave critical habitats or high-hazard areas undeveloped.

Mitigate ecological damage by replacing resources that are lost through development, preferably on site or nearby. For each tree removed, aim to replace it with sufficient new trees to provide more than the equivalent

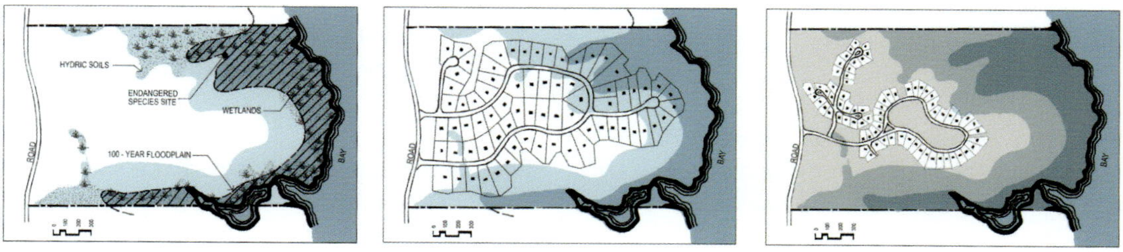

Figure 37.2: One tool for maintaining biodiversity is cluster development, which maximises open space conservation without reducing building density by clustering units on the site. leaving critical habitats and high-hazard areas undeveloped.

ecosystem services: flood control, air quality, windbreak, shade, fruit, and carbon sequestration.

The urban environment offers great opportunities for improving biodiversity within its heterogeneous structure. Although highly urbanised areas host only 10–50% of the species found in more species-rich habitats,[4] their ability to thrive under less-than-ideal conditions makes these brave colonisers sturdy and able to survive difficult circumstances. Restore areas of the street frontage to green space by reducing pavement widths and introducing parking space gardens and corner planting areas. Replace impervious hard paving with pavers or grasscrete and encourage vegetation to thrive in the interstitial spaces.

Restore and enhance habitats by protecting flora and fauna that thrive together. The overall size of a habitat area influences the number of species present in a single section, with large, remnant patches of vegetation hosting a higher number and variety of species. However, even small sites may have high distinctiveness, especially at bogs, woodlands, shorelines, and scrub. Provide a variety of habitat niches to serve different species.

Although many habitats have been fragmented by development, small landscapes in close proximity become part of a larger ecological network as islands that can later be connected into green corridors. Design connective greenway corridors to cross through cities to overcome barriers to species migration and human movement.

Rewild private yards and public gardens to make space for wildlife. Remove hardscape and turf grass to plant native trees, shrubs, groundcovers, and meadows. Create fence gaps and permeable hedges for small animals. Plant aerial highways between gardens for birds and squirrels.

Design landscapes to mimic the original condition in layer and structure. Increase the heterogeneity of species by designing the vegetation structure in layers: tree canopy, shrub layer, and ground cover. Provide adequate space to allow spontaneous vegetation to grow and natural succession to occur. Increase greenery and colour with a variety of seed-bearing, flowering, fruiting, and other food sources to support indigenous wildlife. Avoid introducing invasive species in landscape design, which compete unfairly with native plants.

Diversify to regenerate life. Re-introduce heritage plant species that support pollinators. Diversify the site with multiple ecosystems that will thrive in specific site conditions: wetlands, slopes, or hot, dry environments.

To insure against losses from pests and diseases, one rule of thumb is to select plants with no more than: 10% of any single tree species; no more than 20% of species in any tree genus, no more than 30% of species in any tree family.[5]

At small sites, minimise the space devoted to vehicle movement and storage; substitute rich, productive, and biodiverse habitats instead. Advocate for minimum parking standards and narrow lanes. Design to shade 50% of hardscape within five years (equal to one LEED credit for Sustainable Sites) or more. Improve accessibility for pedestrians and bicyclists.

Restore the native hydrology of the site. Daylight rivers, stormwater detention and conveyance, and reconnect hydrological

Quantity	Botanical Name	Common Name
Trees		
4	*Acer barbatum*	Florida Maple
2	*Acer rubrum*	Red Maple
23	*Cercis canadensis var. texensis*	Texas Redbud
17	*Fraxinus pennsylvanica*	Green Ash
13	*Lagerstroemia indica x fauriel 'Muskogee'*	Muskogee' crepe myrtle
7	*Liquidamber styraciflua 'Rotundiloba'*	Seedless Sweetgum
5	*Magnolia virginiana*	Sweetbay Magnolia
2	*Metasequoia glyptostroboides*	Dawn Redwood
6	*Pinus glabra*	Spruce Pine
4	*Pistacia chinensis*	Chinese Pistache
8	*Quercus virginiana*	Live Oak
48	*Sabal palmetto*	Cabbage Palm
55	*Taxodium ascendens*	Pond Cypress
2	*Taxodium distichum*	Bald Cypress
Shrubs/Groundcover		
200	*Agapanthus africanus*	Lily of the Nile
22	*Camellia sasanqua*	Sasanqua
10	*Cortaderia selloana*	Pampas Grass
100	*Gaura lindheimeri*	Gaura
68	*Ilex 'Mary Nell'*	Mary Nell Holly
800	*Hemerocallis Illoasphodelus*	Daylily
1200	*Muhlenbergia capillaris*	Muhly Grass
44	*Rosa 'Knockout'*	Yellow 'Knockout' Rose
18	*Rosa 'Knockout'*	Red 'Knockout' Rose
27	*Rosmarinus officinalis*	Rosemary
800	*Trachelospermum asiaticum*	Asiatic Jasmine
Wetland Plants		
55	*Canna flaccida*	Canna
89	*Crinum americanum*	Swamp Lily
148	*Iris virginica*	Blue Flag Iris
87	*Pontederia cordata*	Pickerelweed
61	*Sagittaria lancifolia*	Bulltongue

Figure 37.3: The native plant list for an urban streetscapes project used 30 types of native and adapted species, with only one species (Muhly grass, a low-maintenance ornamental grass) totalling over 18% of the overall plant material. unabridged Architecture + The Landscape Studio.

functions to nurture aquatic species and improve waterways. Increase perviousness at sites to reduce the heat island effect and allow water and oxygen to permeate soils and encourage vegetation growth.

Explore ways to find synergy in landscape solutions. Create or restore wetlands to treat stormwater runoff, which may also mitigate flood hazards and create wildlife habitat for birds, amphibians, and a variety of plant species.

Maintain healthy topsoil on site to promote soil health and beneficial organisms. Avoid topsoil stripping where possible. If soil must be temporarily removed, store it in shallow, linear berms to allow for air and moisture exchange. Add compost and organic material regularly to improve nutrient content.

Leave downed trees in wooded areas and minimise the manicured footprint on the site. Allow leaves to remain and break down, providing nutrients and habitat.

Shrink lawns. Replace monocultures of turf grass with a variety of native grasses or wildflower plant mixes. Choose plants that can survive without irrigation with potable water.

Replace monocultures of turf grass with a variety of native grasses or wildflower plant mixes. Choose plants that can survive without irrigation.

Design landscapes to avoid the use of pesticide and fertilisers, which have far-reaching impacts to biodiversity and the environment.

Habitat offsets or compensation for adverse impacts are the least preferable options for enhancing biodiversity. Purchased credits can include creation or enhancement of off-site habitats; however, many of these schemes have been discredited, poorly managed, or nonviable ways to replace lost biodiversity.

Look beyond the project site. Responsible material sourcing considers the social and environmental impact of the materials used in a project. There are several third-party reviewers who can verify that materials disclose red list chemicals, embodied carbon accounting, life expectancy, end of life options, and the chain of custody. Other standards ensure transparency in labour practices and validate social and ethical best practices.

BUILDINGS

Design bird-friendly buildings and sites. Birds strike at windows in an attempt to get to perches, food, or water seen through the glass or reflected. Guidelines to deter bird collisions include three categories of solutions: use minimal glass; place glass behind screening; and use glass with inherent properties that reduce collisions. The 2 × 4 rule reduces collisions from songbirds, the most numerous victims of bird deaths. A pattern with horizontal lines spaced 2 inches (5 cm) apart and vertical lines with a maximum spacing of 4 inches (10 cm) apart imitates a screen and deters most bird species. Bird-friendly retrofit options include installing netting, window films, screens, shutters, or replacement glass.

Elevate buildings to maintain site hydrologic connections. Allow for sheet flow to continue at the ground surface with minimal interruption from foundations and site hardscape.

Figure 37.4: A songbird-friendly glass grid has lines at 2″ on centre vertical spacing and 4″ o.c. horizontal spacing.

Limit site clearance around structures. Narrow the construction perimeter to 3 m (10 feet) or less. Do not allow clearcutting of sites. Plan driveways and hardscape to avoid mature trees.

Create opportunities for positive wildlife interaction at the interface between building and exterior. Integrate nesting boxes, hedges, ponds, trellises, bird feeders, birdbaths, hanging baskets, container pools, window boxes, and other mini-habitats to support wildlife. Note that the inclusion of an insect hotel or nesting box is no substitute for a healthy and thriving ecosystem.

Look for opportunities to introduce vegetative materials at the building envelope, including green roofs and living walls. Explore the range of plant materials that thrive at the specific site microclimate by considering the solar exposure, water, wind, and temperature.

Consider the effect of building materials on adjacent microclimates. For example, a reflective glazed or metal panel on a south façade can raise temperatures by 10 °F or more due to reflectivity.

IMPACT

Social: A human connection with nature confers mental health and wellbeing benefits. Biodiversity loss can have detrimental impacts to humans if ecosystem services are no longer adequate to meet social needs, affect livelihoods, income, mobility, and heighten tension and conflict.

Environmental: Healthy ecosystems support the animals, plants, and microorganisms that humans rely on for provisioning services: air, food, water, clothing, structures, medicine, and other needs. Furthermore, a healthy ecosystem can sustain disruptions from events due to redundancy and diversity in the composition, which supports regeneration.

Economic: The UN's System of Environmental Economic Accounting Framework organises biophysical information about ecosystem services and monetary value. There is a growing body of evidence to quantify the economic value of ecosystem services for pollination, stormwater management, heat mitigation, air quality, and many other regulating services, as well as direct provisioning, cultural, and supporting systems.[6]

Spatial: Ecosystems with high biodiversity improve the texture and variety of human experience, compelling attention with sensory cues from the surroundings. Biodiversity confers a sense of distinctness from everyday experience, whether immersed in a small but lushly textured space, or an extensive, open space; both contribute to individual and community satisfaction.

NOTES

1 Dasgupta, P. 2021. *The Economics of Biodiversity: The Dasgupta Review*. London: HM Treasury. Accessed at: https://assets.publishing.service.gov.uk/media/602e92b2e90e07660f807b47/The_Economics_of_Biodiversity_The_Dasgupta_Review_Full_Report.pdf

2 National Institute of Standards and Technology (U.S.) Statistical Engineering Division: https://www.itl.nist.gov/div898/software/dataplot/refman2/auxillar/shannon.htm

3 U.K. Department for Environment, Food, and Rural Affairs. 2018. A Green Future: Our 25 Year Plan to Improve the Environment. Accessed at: https://www.gov.uk/government/publications/25-year-environment-plan

4 Hansen, A.J., R.L. Knight, J.M. Marzluff, S. Powell, K. Brown, P.H. Gude, and K. Jones. 2005. Effects of Exurban Development on Biodiversity: Patterns, Mechanisms, and Research Needs. *Ecological Applications* 15, 1893–1905.

5 Santamour, F.S., Jr. 1990. Trees for Urban Planting: Diversity, Uniformity, and Common Sense. *Proceedings 7th Conference Metropolitan Tree Improvement Alliance (METRIA)* 7, 57–65.

6 Dasgupta (2021).

RESOURCES

- Dasgupta, P. 2021. *The Economics of Biodiversity: The Dasgupta Review*. London: HM Treasury. Accessed at: https://assets.publishing.service.gov.uk/media/602e92b2e90e07660f807b47/The_Economics_of_Biodiversity_The_Dasgupta_Review_Full_Report.pdf
- Rewild My Street website: https://www.rewildmystreet.org/
- Tan, P.Y., K.-H.Liao, Y.H. Hwang, V. Chua, A.O. Guizzo, and J. Chan. 2018. *Nature, Place & People: Forging Connections through Neighbourhood Landscape Design*. https://doi.org/10.1142/9789813236035_0005
- United Nations et al. 2021. System of Environmental-Economic Accounting— Ecosystem Accounting (SEEA EA). White cover publication, pre-edited text subject to official editing. Accessed at: https://seea.un.org/ecosystem-accounting.

EDIBLE CITIES 38

ADAPTATION **SCARCITY** SCALE **COMMUNITY**

Edible cities have sustainable and productive landscapes with local food production, distribution, and consumption. People are invited to connect more intimately with food, its origins and seasons, and the ubiquity of edible plants, which results in the increased consumption of fruits and vegetables necessary for healthy diets. Edible cities create opportunities for households, independent growers, and regions to boost food production and enhance self-sufficiency.

Figure 38.1: Street view of Amsterdam Avenue in Manhattan featuring a mix of traditional and advanced agricultural growing techniques to foster self-sufficiency in cities, creating its own food, energy, and other needs within its borders. New York (Steady) State, Terreform ONE, Mitchell Joachim.

DOI: 10.4324/9781032702964-43

BACKGROUND

In times of scarcity, citizens are encouraged to contribute to food production by growing victory gardens, keeping bees and chickens, and harvesting crops, efforts to maintain local food supplies. The climate crisis is demanding the same self-sufficiency, with global food production strained by drought, flooding, supply chain interruptions, migration, and conflict. The benefits of cultivating food locally go beyond the tangible - fresh, inexpensive, organic produce - to encompass better air quality, greener and more biodiverse cities, and increased exercise, improving public health.

Small towns and suburbs with large lots have long participated in small-scale food production in back yards and smallholdings less than 2 hectares. Urban areas and their concentrated demand for food are unable to grow sufficient food in the interstitial spaces between buildings. As a result, food is grown at a distance and transported to centres of population for consumption, with significant food miles for high-value perishable foods, especially produce grown out of season, which is shipped as air cargo rather than trucked or shipped in boats. In a single year, global food miles are responsible for 3 bn tonnes of CO_2 equivalent emissions.[1]

New models of urban food production envision streets and public spaces intensively planted with fruit and nut orchards, market gardens, and allotments. The fulfilment of this vision would create cities that are healthier, wilder, and more biodiverse. However, it would also mark a significant urban transition, change the stewardship and maintenance of public lands, and require the development of workforce training programmes and ongoing public investment. A great deal of the land in cities available for planting is privately owned with limited access, or held in the public trust with conflicting demands. Many of the

Figure 38.2: Andernach, Germany and the Edible City project. Gardens are planted near the walls of the castle at the centre of town featuring carrots, beans, fruits and berries, onions, tomatoes, wine grapes, herbs, and flowers.

food-producing plants to be introduced at the urban scale require specialist knowledge, equipment, and biological controls to curb pesticide and herbicide use. Despite these drawbacks, there are an increasing number of successful projects across the globe. The city of Andernach, Germany began an edible city project in 2010, planting 101 tomato varieties in public green spaces in the city centre to illustrate the diversity of heirloom plants. Residents and visitors embraced the project, expanding the scope to include more vegetables, berries, fruit trees, chickens, and sheep to enliven the townscape. The cost of the programme is covered by individual and business sponsorships, the Edible Cities Network - a EU-sponsored project - and the city. The workforce includes unemployed residents alongside a team of gardeners. Everyone is invited to pick the produce and experience food at the centre of life in the city. Instead of 'Keep Off the Grass', signs say 'Picking is encouraged - Help Yourself'.

Climate variability from droughts, deluges, and heat waves is driving the expansion of controlled environment agriculture (vertical farming). The process is becoming more viable with the rise of AI-powered systems to control temperature, water, and nutrients, and the use of robotic harvesting. Specialty items - berries, microgreens, lettuces - are grown in a modular system that can supply customers with year-round produce using significantly less water, fertiliser, and pesticides. Indoor grow facilities are located close to consumers and use up to 97% less land than conventional farming.

KEY DESIGN CONSIDERATIONS

Greenhouses with advanced vertical farming techniques can be installed in vacant office buildings, but introducing these systems into existing structures requires adding significant mechanical, electrical, plumbing, and potentially structural improvements to

Figure 38.3: Aquaponics integrates fish and hydroponic plant production in a recirculating water system. A small-scale aquaponic system consisting of a shipping container plus a greenhouse on a mobile chassis can supplement food deserts or be deployed to disaster areas..

create the growing environment. The added infrastructure and cost of energy is the biggest challenge for upscaling local food production, as energy demands for lighting, HVAC, and water systems may offset the energy previously expended on transportation from traditional farm sources.

Aquaponics couples two systems: farming aquatic organisms (aquaculture) and growing plants in a soilless medium (hydroponics). Nutrient-rich water from the fish is used as fertiliser for hydroponically grown plants, which in turn processes waste from the fish. Hydroponic systems reduce freshwater consumption and also reduce energy demand. A plant and fish farming box uses a mobile container to house fish tanks with a soilless greenhouse on top to form a closed-loop system.

Figure 38.4: Edible urban greenscreens can be planted with herbs, vegetables, vines, and flowers to beautify, cool, and nourish occupants or passersby.

Rooftops can be used for gardens, solar arrays, urban beekeeping, chicken coops – or all these functions at once. Assess the structural capacity of existing buildings before installing green roofs or solar panels, which may increase point or tributary loads. Green roofs may extend the service life of roof membranes by reducing exposure to UV weathering but do need regular maintenance and a water supply at the roof level.

Edible forests planted along streets, parks, playgrounds, and schools invite walkers to stop and pick fruits and nuts throughout the year. Edible trees provide shade, offer ornamental greening, and seasonal harvests. Existing stands of trees may be interplanted or extended with native fruit and nut varieties ranging from pecan, walnut, peach, medlar, pear, plum, persimmon, and apple to citrus, avocado, mango, and papaya, depending on the climate zone. Designers should select native and adapted trees that require little irrigation, pest control, or fertiliser after the initial establishment period.

Along urban facades, freestanding frames and exterior scaffolding can support stacked planters to create green facades and living screens of ornamental and edible plants. The varieties that grow well in this environment are hardy native or adapted species with a compact shape that are accustomed to growing in containers. Automatic watering systems can use rainwater collected from roofs, supplemented from municipal sources in prolonged dry spells.

Design habitats to include protein sources where possible. Cities might issue licenses in riverbeds for oyster farming or the growth of tilapia in freshwater tanks. Backyard chickens and flocks of sheep in parks improve the soil, graze lawns, and add visual interest at the same time they produce eggs, milk, and meat.

Address food deserts by installing tactical gardens to transform street verges, vacant lots, fence lines, and railroad easements. Cities are experimenting with cemeteries as urban food plots, such as Berlin's *Prinzessinnengarten* at the Neuen St. Jacobi cemetery.[2] The rationale for this controversial siting is that alternative burial choices occupy less space than traditional burials and the dwindling importance of religion means that some cemeteries are facing closure. Urban gardens fill deconsecrated spaces with new life, volunteers, and social interaction as well as providing sustenance for the living.

In larger cities, utilise peri-urban opportunities for food production in close proximity to high concentrations of people. The suburbs of Bangkok feature profitable fish, shrimp, rice, and fruit producers within 20 miles of 10.7 million people,[3] a distance that can be covered with cargo bicycles, small trucks, and boats so produce arrives fresh each morning.

Gardens at primary schools tie directly into the educational curriculum in science, art, mathematics, and literature. Young adults can utilise gardens for horticulture and culinary training, biology and genetics experiments, and a host of other uses. A recent study on the impact of school gardens on academic performance shows evidence that garden-based learning has a positive impact on students' grades, knowledge, attitudes, and behaviour.[4]

Hospitals and nursing homes often have underutilised space devoted to unproductive lawns and shrubs. Transform these into sensory-rich, edible gardens by planting herbs, pollinators, and vegetable gardens to inspire positive effects on residents and patients. Spending time in gardens and nature improves moods and quality of sleep in dementia patients, provides a welcome respite for ambulatory patients, and relieves symptoms of anxiety and depression in elderly residents.

Before planting a city garden, test the soil for environmental hazards. City streets may retain a legacy of lead contamination in the soil that remains from the time when gasoline and paint still contained lead. If the soil has elevated levels of lead, soils may be encapsulated, remediated, or removed. Phytoremediation, using plants such as sunflowers, river birch, and other plants to filter toxins may be a long-term option for remediation, although the resulting plant biomass should not be consumed, as heavy metals and other contaminants may be concentrated in the leaves, stem, and roots.[5]

Encourage urban foraging, the practice of identifying and collecting wild foods (tree nuts, plant roots, mushrooms, berries, and edible flowers) growing freely around the city. The foragers Manifesto (https://forage.link/the-manifesto/) includes a promise to protect sensitive areas and endangered species, and to freely share knowledge with others. Do not encourage foraging in areas prone to high pollution or near agricultural runoff.

Celebrate urban food production in restaurants that showcase vertical farming on site, community kitchens that serve and distribute fresh foods, outdoor markets, and events highlighting locally grown foods.

NEW YORK CITY'S FOOD/ FLOOD DILEMMA

New York City relies on six major distribution centres—the largest of which are located in flood hazard zones – to feed 8.5 million residents, supply over 20,000 restaurants, and stock grocery stores. Supermarkets typically maintain a stock of six to seven days of food, convenience stores four to five days, and bodegas and schools stock only three to five days of supplies. Hurricane Sandy in 2012 caused major disruptions to the food supply. The widespread loss of power meant that fuel could not be pumped, causing transportation delays because 99% of last-mile food transport in the city is made by trucks. Flooding caused interruptions to public transit, resulting in greater reliance on local food sources. When the power went out throughout the region, refrigeration and freezers stopped running and some foods became inedible in as little as four hours. Cell towers had no power and telecommunications services were down, with the result that orders could not be placed and payments could not be processed. Distribution centres and food stores were inundated, damaging produce, meat, dry goods, even compromising bottled and canned goods by the influx of salt water. The devastation was a stark reminder that a single extreme weather event has the potential to create widespread disruption across the food supply chain.[6]

The Rebuild by Design Hunts Point Lifelines project by Penn Design and Olin, a design studio of landscape architects, recommended a perimeter flood protection wall at +16′ around the city's Hunts Point Food Distribution Center, a cluster of wholesalers who serve 22 million residents

IMPACT

Social: Edible cities enhance social cohesion through an inclusive and participatory process of planning and growing food. Sources of food in the urban environment improve human health by providing lifelines with access to fresh foods, especially in food deserts where access to fresh fruits and vegetables is limited. Cities with more accessible food gardens encourage healthier lives and greater well-being.

Environmental: Cities hosting decentralised food production have more wildlife, trees and flowers to attract birds, small mammals, and insects. Transforming cities into decentralised food production hubs is a local, action-based strategy to enhance sustainability and climate adaptation. Local food production reduces food miles and associated carbon emissions.

Economic: When disasters strike and supply chains are interrupted, local food sources can help to temporarily fill the gaps until regular deliveries are restored. The additional cost of transforming the urban environment to a food-producing system may be offset by economic and ecosystem services: jobs, food security, and regulating services such as urban heat mitigation and stormwater management.

Spatial: Scaling up food production can fill gaps in the urban fabric. Disperse edible gardens and orchards widely to benefit more neighbourhoods. Reuse abandoned structures for food production centres.

and represent more than 20,000 direct jobs. The Center is located within the floodplain in a neighbourhood challenged by poor air quality and environmental degradation. The flood protection wall corresponds to FEMA 100-year Base Flood Elevation and the projected sea level rise of 31 inches by 2050. A series of edge conditions were proposed, including permanent terraces, adaptive walls, thin edges where space is constrained by roadways and structures, and thick edges where there is room to build earthen berms.

A tri-generation microgrid has been installed to provide back-up power to the Hunts Point Food Distribution Center, along with mobile generators for back-up power at other important citywide food distributors during emergencies. NYC was awarded a $14.68M grant for dry-floodproofing the Meat Market and 600 Food Center Drive, identified as two of the facilities most at risk from storm surge flooding. The full project proposal can be found here: https://rebuildbydesign.org/wp-content/uploads/2021/12/677.pdf.

Figure 38.5: A perimeter flood protection wall at +16′ around the city's Hunts Point Food Distribution Center integrates a marsh habitat, elevated walkway, infiltration zone, and the South Bronx Greenway. PennDesign/OLIN.

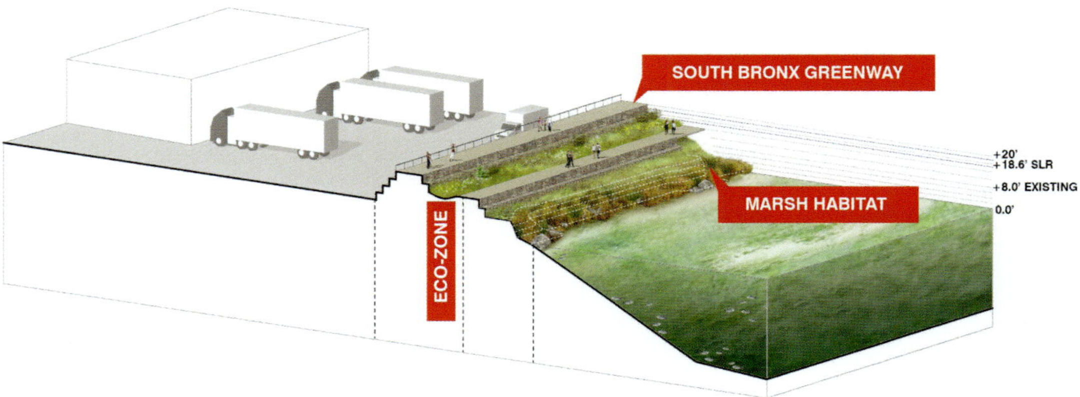

NOTES

1 Li, M. et al. 2022. Global Food-Miles Account for Nearly 20% of Total Food-Systems Emissions. *Nature Food* 3, 445–453.
2 Molina, S. 2021. An Urban Garden Brings New Life to Berlin Cemeteries. *The Urban Activist*. Accessed at: https://theurbanactivist.com/idea/an-urban-garden-brings-new-life-to-berlin-cemeteries/
3 Vagneron, I. 2007. Economic Appraisal of Profitability and Sustainability of Peri-Urban Agriculture in Bangkok. *Ecological Economics* 61, nos. 2–3, 516–529. https://doi.org/10.1016/j.ecolecon.2006.04.006.
4 Williams, D.R. and P. Scott Dixon. 2013. Impact of Garden-Based Learning on Academic Outcomes in Schools: Synthesis of Research Between 1990 and 2010. *Review of Educational Research* 83, no. 2.
5 Yan, A., Y. Wang, S.N. Tan, M.L.M. Yusof, S. Ghosh, and Z. Chen. 2020. Phytoremediation: A Promising Approach for Revegetation of Heavy Metal-Polluted Land. *Frontiers in Plant Science* 11. https://doi.org/10.3389/fpls.2020.00359
6 Hosfelt, B. 2019. What Climate Risks Mean for NYC's Food Supply. *City Limits*. Accessed at: https://citylimits.org/2019/12/30/what-climate-risks-mean-for-nycs-food-supply/

RESOURCE

- Edible Cities Network: https://www.edicitnet.com/what-is-edicitnet/

BOUNDARIES TO GROWTH 39

ADAPTATION **SCARCITY** SCALE **COMMUNITY**

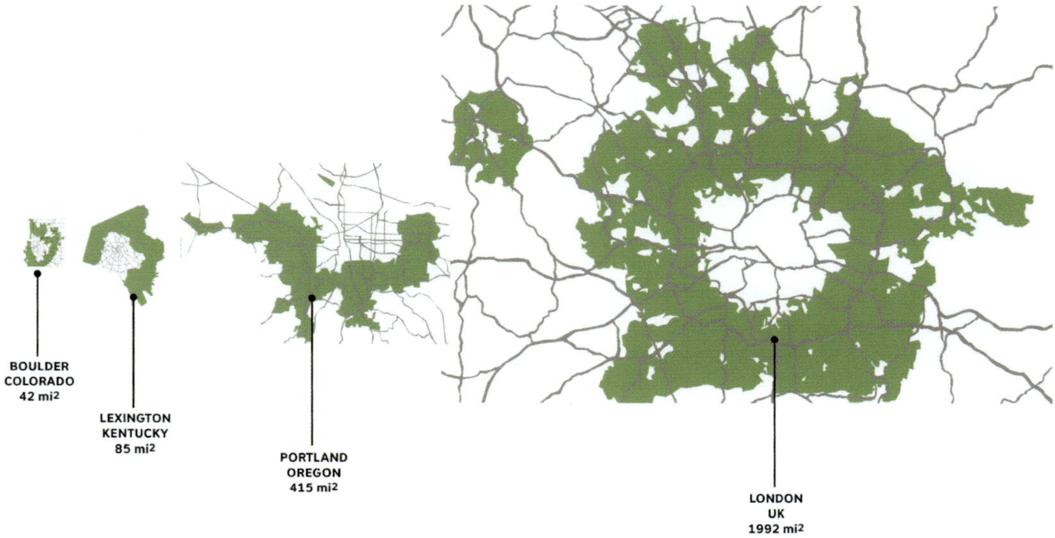

Increasing urbanisation is escalating development pressure on rural lands to provide more housing for people. Boundaries to urban growth preserve the natural and agricultural lands at the periphery and prevent encroachment from the edgeless city. Boundaries are established to define practical limits for urban service areas for firefighting, garbage collection, and other utilities, where dense settlement patterns and roadway traffic define the figurative limits of the city's identity. The boundary establishes a threshold, a green zone reserved for agriculture, forests, and natural features of the landscape. The value of the boundary as an adaptation measure is its capacity to regulate temperature, manage stormwater, improve air quality, and sequester carbon as well as to promote contact with nature.

Figure 39.1: Urban growth boundaries to scale. Left to right: Boulder CO, Lexington KY, Portland OR, and London, UK.

DOI: 10.4324/9781032702964-44

BACKGROUND

For thousands of years, the dimensions of a city were necessarily compact, to allow crossings on foot and expanding only to the limit where the city could protect and feed inhabitants. Few ancient cities housed large populations: Thebes in Egypt held 100,000 inhabitants circa 1000 BCE and Rome had a population of 1,000,000 circa 100 CE. It was the Industrial Revolution, along with motorised vehicles and refrigeration, that changed the method, speed, and distance at which people and goods could move, allowing cities to extend farther into the countryside. Cities continued to annex land as linkages extended out: motorways, rail, and shipping channels.

Mitigating the worst effects of climate change will demand cities control the widespread conversion of previously undeveloped land to low-density housing and commercial land uses.[1] Rings of low-density, spatially segregated land uses around major cities - suburbs - cannot support public transit, relying instead on personal vehicles, which consume fossil fuel resources and contribute to global heating. That auto dependence demands wider roadways and oversized parking lots, impervious surfaces that create heat islands and exacerbate stormwater management.

In place of the centralised, concentric alignment of greenbelts, there exists an alternative for drawing boundaries based on topographic eco-regions: the Hawaiian *ahupua'a*. Based on the limits of a watershed, each ahupua'a managed resources for the community living within its boundaries, from the source of freshwater in the high elevations to the sea. The *wao akua* or sacred forest lies at the top of the watershed in a sacred, protected area. The valleys below harbour forests for harvesting timber and recharging the aquifer. Slopes are terraced for cultivating crops: taro, banana, nut trees, and other produce, with scattered homesteads. In the plains near the coast, multigenerational housing, schools, and shared activities take advantage of the relatively open, flat ground plane for most of the community to live and work together. Close to the coastline, *loko i'a* are constructed and stocked with fish to ensure a ready supply for the table. Sacred spots - overlooks and other convergences - are dedicated as *heiau*, temples where culture is passed down in chants, songs, dances, and rituals. The ahupua'a provides every need for the community within a continuous gradient from the mountaintop to the sea, with the number of residents limited to the capacity of the land and waters to support life.

Sprawl has economic repercussions that stand in the way of more resilient communities. Extending roadways and utility services to support low-density housing places a tremendous strain on community coffers. Low-density residential patterns have life-cycle costs up to ten times higher to provide utility and roadway service than more dense patterns. The distance to service a low-density population affects the efficacy and affordability of other public services: police, fire, ambulance, solid waste collection, and libraries. Although the initial capital cost of constructing infrastructure is often seen as a barrier, most of the costs are incurred after it is built, with operations and maintenance comprising 60%–90% of the lifecycle cost.[2]

A growth boundary gives local governments a clear plan for making infrastructure investments. The high cost of disconnected development is a key economic argument to support denser, walkable, and mixed-use neighbourhoods. The ability to share the cost between a larger number of housing units can relieve financial pressure on municipalities and allow them to provide more services or reduce the tax burden for each family, building financial solvency and reducing long-term stressors.

SUBURBAN LOW DENSITY

LOT SIZE: 8100 SF/DWELLING
ROAD FRONTAGE: 98 FEET/DWELLING
16 PEOPLE/ACRE
TOTAL COST OF SERVICE PER DWELLING:
$3462

URBAN HIGH DENSITY

LOT SIZE: 760 SF/DWELLING
ROAD FRONTAGE: 5.2 FEET/DWELLING
92 PEOPLE/ACRE
TOTAL COST OF SERVICE PER DWELLING:
$1416

Figure 39.2: Neighbourhood pattern and density determine the cost of service for public infrastructure including roads, transit, water, wastewater, emergency services, and other public goods. Higher density settlements reduce the extent of new infrastructure, spreading the cost of providing these services among a larger population. Service cost analysis from Halifax Regional Authority, 2005.

Establishing boundaries to urban growth downsizes the spatial imprint of human enterprise and creates non-competing zones for natural systems to thrive. Preserving ecosystems and the skein of dependencies that support life may require protecting 50% of the planet's land area from development. Dedicating a zone strictly for nature does not mean that humans no longer derive services from that space; the ecosystem services prosper, continuing to deliver essential provisioning, regulating, cultural, and supporting services (see Chapter 39: Biodiversity). They preserve the rural character of surrounding communities and relieve development pressure. Building in green belt areas depletes resources that can be used in the future to mitigate climate change.

KEY DESIGN CONSIDERATIONS

Determine the purpose of the urban growth boundary: Will it support new development at urban densities within the ring? Preserve the character and identity of communities outside the boundary? Define the limit of municipal services? Preserve lands with environmental, scenic, or cultural value? Understanding the purpose of imposing a boundary will determine the regulations for management and protection of the lands.

Project the expected population growth and development, and the amount of land required to accommodate growth over the next 5–10 years. Create land use options using alternative densities including low-, medium-, and high-density patterns.

Delineate the urban growth boundary to accommodate reasonable economic growth and expansions that may already be documented in community plans. If a boundary severely constrains development, the lack of land for new development will inflate property costs and may push new

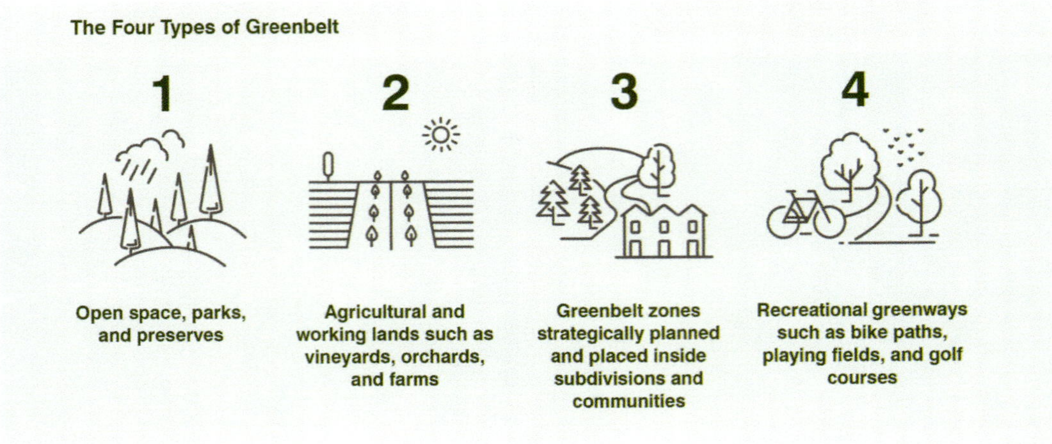

Figure 39.3: Four types of greenbelt: open space, parks and preserves; agricultural land and farms; greenbelt zones within communities and subdivisions; and recreational pathways and fields. Greenbelt Alliance.

development into nearby areas. This type of leapfrog development occurs when developers skip over the urban growth boundary to obtain available land, resulting in extended commuting distances and non-contiguous urbanisation.

Designate lands within the boundary as either rural or urban reserves. Rural Reserves limit urban development with long-term protection for agriculture, forestry, or landscapes; almost two-thirds of land in the UK Green Belts is used for crop production. Urban Reserves designate space for future town expansion.[3]

Identify the groups or stakeholders within the community who are most likely to be affected by adoption of an urban growth boundary. Include authorities that provide critical services: school boards, fire and police services, transportation, and other agencies. Include them in the process of developing the boundary to address concerns about affordability, displacement, access to transportation and jobs, and issues of equity.

Hard limits for growth create incentives for projects within the urban area. Create land use regulations to support the desired community patterns and define acceptable increases to density. Explore mechanisms for the transfer of development rights to preserve green space and jumpstart high-density nodes. Develop special taxation or financing districts to encourage infill development and strategic site investments.

Greenbelts around cities provide a critical separation between urban zones and wildlands. A managed greenbelt – recreational, agricultural, open space, or greenway trail – can provide a strategic location for wildfire defence against unmanaged forests and brushy areas. Increased stewardship within these greenbelts should include regular wildfire regimes to minimise fuel buildup.[4]

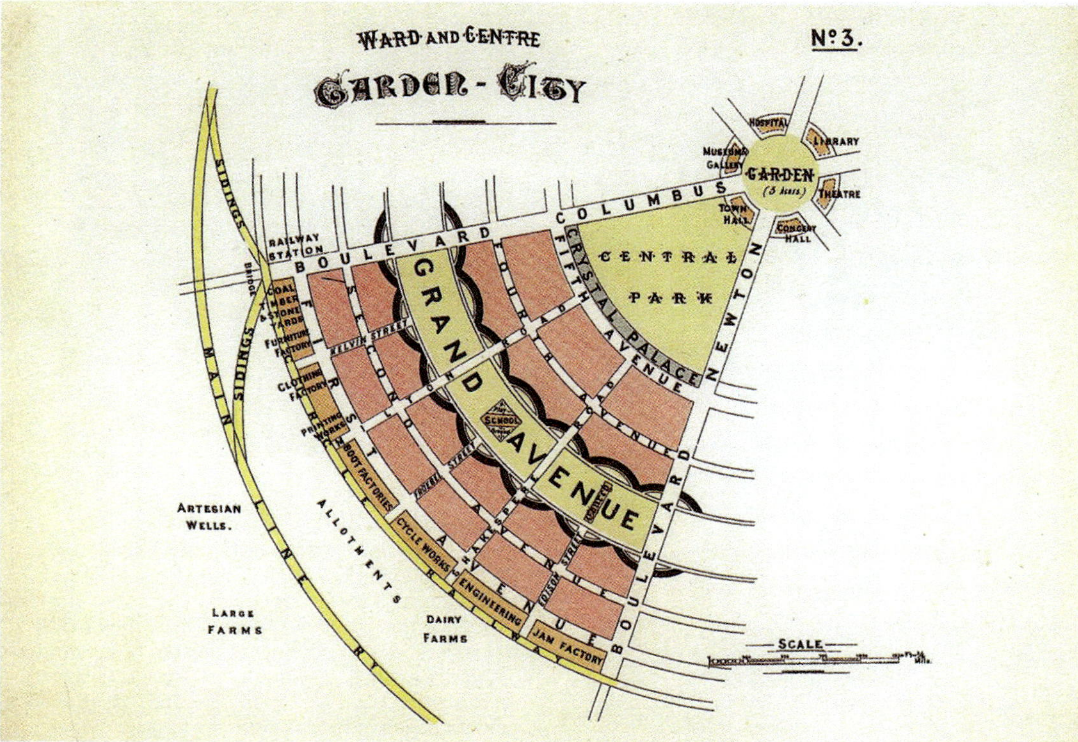

Figure 39.4: Ebenezer Howard began to reimagine utopian communities in 1898. 'Town' was characterised by Excessive Hours, Army of Unemployed, Fogs and Droughts, Costly Drainage, Foul Air, Murkey Sky, Slums, and Gin-Palaces. In contrast, 'Country' featured Lack of Amusement, No Public Spirit, Land Lying Idle, and Need for Reform. The Garden City was designed to join the best of both worlds in a city for 32,000 people within an encircling greenbelt. This was a hardworking landscape with reservoirs, waterfalls, stone quarries, brickfields, new forests, cemeteries, and convalescent homes.

Design equitable access to green spaces, enhancing social infrastructure with walkable paths, mixed uses nearby, bike- and pedestrian-friendly networks, public transit, and the fair distribution of public services. Strengthen existing service networks with transport links connecting the green belt to hospitals, libraries, and other public functions.

Position the green zone to preserve special features within the landscape. Inside greenbelts, provide a loop trail connecting to streets and nodes within each neighbourhood. Expand recreational functions, edible gardens and orchards, and biodiverse ecosystems. Design the urban growth boundary to manage current stormwater needs for adjacent communities, with additional capacity to cover future developments.

Exert flexible control over the boundary, re-evaluating the extent and regulations every 5–10 years as the population changes, nearby communities grow or shrink, shifts in market forces occur, and changes in affordability influence the community.

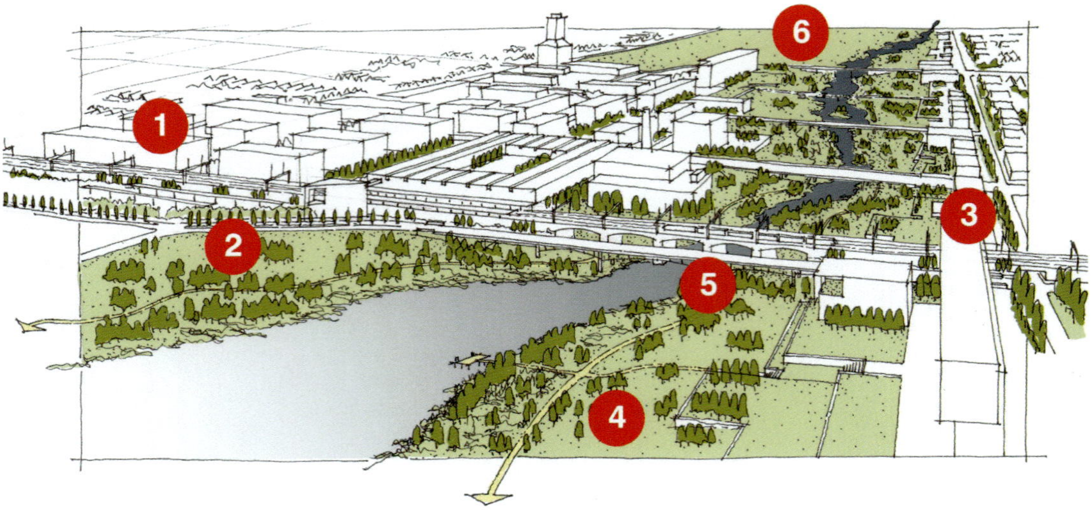

Figure 39.5: Rebuild by Design's Resilient Bridgeport team proposed a high-density Transit-Oriented Development at the edge of the Yellow Mill River which forms a green boundary and corridor at the city edge. (1) Allow higher density near major transit stations. (2) Connect transit to greenways for alternative mobility through the city and (3) link to essential facilities. (4) Expand recreational amenities and (5) preserve historic features to (6) provide equitable access to nature. WB/unabridged/GCCDS/Yale/Arcadis.

IMPACT

Social: Growth boundaries provide additional social infrastructure in urban areas and improve access to nature. Defining the civic edge promotes community identity and loyalty.

Environmental: Green space that girdles, crosses, or encircles communities helps to process waste, build oxygen, sequester carbon, and close nutrient loops, improving resilience to disaster events and long-term stresses. Urban growth boundaries result in higher density neighbourhoods that use less energy per capita and have lower per capita greenhouse gas emissions than suburban development.

Economic: Urban growth boundaries reduce the cost of capital investment in infrastructure by increasing the number of customers per mile, resulting in lower life-cycle costs for each household. Higher-density, walkable settlement patterns support public transit, lead to more diverse housing options, and increase real estate values.

Spatial: Green belts define the edge of the urban area, establish buffers between communities, and protect wildlands from encroachment, allowing them to retain ecological functions for future generations.

NOTES

1 Feng, Q. and Gauthier, P. 2021. 'Untangling Urban Sprawl and Climate Change: A Review of the Literature on Physical Planning and Transportation Drivers.' Atmosphere 2021, 12(5), 547. Doi: https://doi.org/10.3390/atmos12050547

2 Halifax, 2005. Accessed at: https://lede-admin.usa.streetsblog.org/wp-content/uploads/sites/46/2015/03/Halifax-data.pdf

3 74th Oregon Legislative Assembly. 2007. Enrolled Senate Bill 1011. Accessed at: https://library.oregonmetro.gov/files/senate_bill_1011.pdf

4 Greenbelt Alliance. 2021. *The Critical Role of Greenbelts in Wildfire Resilience*. Oakland, CA.

RESOURCES

- Howard, E. 2010. *To-Morrow: A Peaceful Path to Real Reform*. Cambridge: Cambridge University Press.
- The Charter of the New Urbanism. 1996. Accessed at: https://www.cnu.org/who-we-are/charter-new-urbanism

COMMUNITY PARTICIPATION AFTER DISASTER 40

ADAPTATION **SCARCITY** SCALE **COMMUNITY**

More frequent and stronger disasters place more communities and people at risk, often in places faced with substantial damage far from the traditional loci of impacts. Communities navigating disasters must commit to empowering residents in the recovery. An equitable process ensures the survivors' ability to participate, influence, and guide recovery. Bringing together residents to define the future of the built environment after a disaster improves recovery services, promotes equity, supports the legitimacy of the recovery plan within the community, and improves the chances of implementing the planning decisions.

Figure 40.1: Property owners review design options for rebuilding homes in six Houston neighbourhoods after Hurricane Ike. Project: City of Houston Disaster Recovery Program (DR2). Architects: buildingcommunityWORKSHOP, MSU Gulf Coast Community Design Studio, and unabridged Architecture.

DOI: 10.4324/9781032702964-45

BACKGROUND

Architects are are strategic partners in considering the needs of vulnerable and marginalised individuals after a disaster. Disasters can become tipping points for people with few resources - such as money, education, language, and social networks - pushing them into debt, insecurity, and homelessness. People with resources have the choice to evacuate, rent temporary housing, and rebuild in a more resilient manner, relying less on community and government resources but tending to have greater influence in community recovery. Designers have an opportunity to work at the grassroots level to help the community to define immediate and long-term needs, coordinate with state and local officials to bridge gaps between perspectives, envision alternative scenarios, and find consensus.

The period after a disaster is a good time to reconsider land use planning to find equitable solutions to guide people out of high hazard areas. People base the perceived risks on their own previous experience, but after a period with little to no threats they may become complacent. Complacency reduces the impetus to prepare for future disasters, as the apparent indifference of others to the threat becomes standard, constant exposure to threats without severe consequences leads to passivity, or people incorrectly diminish potential impacts and exaggerate their ability to withstand the disaster. Floods, fires, and other disasters increase concerns about the climate crisis and may lead residents of affected communities to adopt more pro-environmental behaviours.[1]

There are four phases in disaster recovery: assessment, design, implementation, and monitoring. In each phase, architects can play a critical role as an advisor and advocate for members of the community affected by disaster.

Assessment Phase: Each disaster is unique and standardised approaches are not always applicable. Architects are trained to gather and interpret data, report conditions, share forecasting of future hazards, and identify key stakeholders. Architects can partner with affected communities to uncover longstanding issues within the community that foster inequality or increase hazard risk: to collect information on the baseline conditions (what used to be there); prepare situation reports (what happened); identify outstanding risks and priority hazards; develop a list of critical community needs (what assistance is required); assess the community capacity to recover (what resources exist); and project gaps and critical shortfalls.[2]

Design Phase: Participatory design sets architects to work in collaboration with communities to formulate solutions to immediate concerns and barriers to long-term recovery. Architects can document historic patterns and the conditions immediately preceding the disaster. They can recommend precedents from other communities that may solve longstanding issues such as mobility and accessibility, the provision and distribution of public goods (public services, parks, and parking), or the redevelopment of economic corridors. Architects envision alternatives for the future and can illustrate a variety of possible options to share with residents during open discussions.

Implementation Phase: A disaster event often propels homeowners and small businesses to become small-scale developers at a time when making decisions about rebuilding is risky. Architects can assist survivors with finding sources of funding and other assistance, connecting people with reliable contractors, organising volunteers and repair teams, and sharing reputable sources for materials. Architects use their professional experience to observe and evaluate construction progress on projects in the community with an understanding of labour and resource flows, health, safety and welfare standards, and fluctuating costs.

Monitoring Phase: Architects can monitor community progress in rebuilding by assessing the social, environmental, and economic results, and evaluating which solutions worked for the community, information that will be instructive in guiding response in future disasters.

Figure 40.2: The Rebuild by Design: Resilient Bridgeport team brought together community members, state and local officials, nonprofits, and business groups in a four-day charrette held in a vacant storefront downtown. Public presentations were followed by work periods to document observations, test design strategies, and influence the design process. The resulting plan was expanded and improved by the collaborative process, eventually generating $75 million in funding for recovery and resiliency projects. WB/unabridged/GCCDS/Yale/Arcadis

KEY DESIGN CONSIDERATIONS

ASSESSMENT PHASE

Identify the key community assets that, if lost, will have a negative impact on community identity. Identify scenic places or cultural touchpoints that define the community and should not be lost to development.

Connect with key people to provide information and partner with community organisations with broad networks to connect with disaster survivors. Find the most reputable sources of information in the community and form connections with these people, linking them to initial recovery efforts and broadening the circle of advisers as trust grows in the community.

Ensure communities remain aware of the challenges they face and efforts made on their behalf. Informed communities can take advantage of recovery opportunities, access available services, voice concerns, exercise civil rights, and negotiate for improvements. Disaster recovery often seems like it proceeds at a glacial pace, so use this time to cement networks, plan strategies, envision best-case scenarios, and organise legal standing. Dismantle the persistent barriers to equitable housing recovery. Every person should be able to rebuild or access quality, affordable, accessible homes in safe neighbourhoods of their choice.

Work with community-based organisations, faith-based organisations, local governments, and non-governmental organisations that have worked in the community for a long time or have strong approval within the community. Recognise cultural or social norms that may enhance or impede participatory design. Where possible, integrate members of the community within the architecture team to serve as cultural observers, guiding teams on how to proceed with caution and respect for affected sites.

Work with community participants to determine their appetite for retreat. This is a difficult conversation for many, but others may be predisposed to rebuilding elsewhere so as not to endure another disaster. Assess the regulatory environment and plan strategies to support retreat. Delineate high-hazard areas, which may have expanded due to the last disaster. Identify locations to redevelop with higher density, a richer variety of housing types, and allow Accessory Dwelling Units. Propose appropriate new sites for urban expansion away from risks.

Assess the historic context and neighbourhood patterns to identify consistent materials, features, and design choices that might be used in recovery planning to re-establish familiarity and comfort.

Identify structures with the capacity to be recovered. Assess the scope of repairs or reconstruction and assist property owners in finding sources of funding which may be available after a disaster.

Figure 40.3: The Disaster Recovery 2 Plan Catalogue offered house designs specifically calibrated to match each of six Houston neighbourhoods affected by Hurricane Ike. Residents walked with the architects at the outset of the project to point out familiar features and later voted on which designs best assimilated with the existing urban fabric. The plans calibrated differences in lot width, style of surrounding homes, materials, and special features such as columns, brackets, screens, or carports. Architects: buildingcommunityWORKSHOP, MSU Gulf Coast Community Design Studio, and unabridged Architecture.

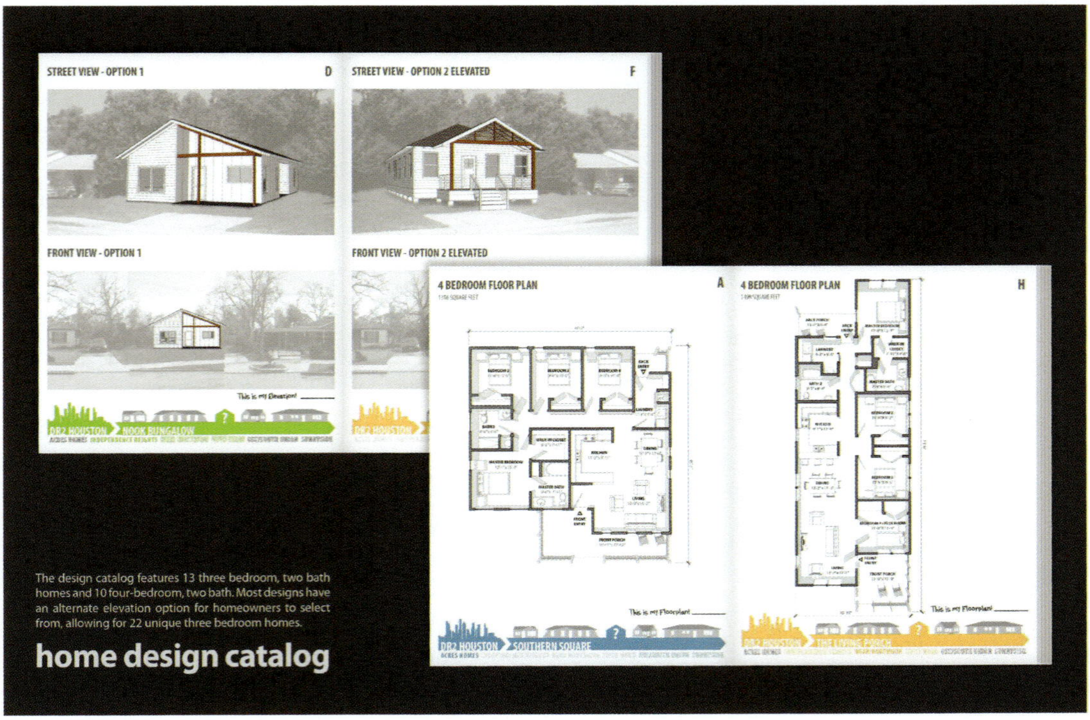

Identify and inventory local material stocks available for rebuilding. Materials are often difficult to source after a disaster, with lengthy delays, irregular quality issues, and higher costs. Keep tabs on local sources and find reclaimed sources if possible.

DESIGN PHASE

Design a strong community participation process. Identify under-represented groups and explore options to reach out and include their perspectives. Ensure the participation of young people to promote their influence on the future. Plan meetings to take place inside the community boundaries to understand issues firsthand and directly address concerns and questions. Establish a neutral ground, a space where conflicting opinions can be expressed and resolved together.

Facilitate dialogue and exchange. State clear objectives for community meetings, outlining the main topics for each event. Share information freely and provide background information in advance of the meeting, if possible. Have multiple members of the design team participate to collect more ideas and concerns. As far as possible, remove obstacles to community participation. Offer options at different times to avoid conflicts with work and childcare schedules. Provide language interpreters, if necessary, to give everyone an opportunity to comment. Feed people. Compensate people for their time, if possible.

Build a consensus reflecting the diversity of views obtained throughout the process. Initial results can be both/and solutions highlighting the diversity of thought. Document the meeting in drawings, photographs, and notes, and gain stakeholder approval before moving forward.

Acknowledge the existence of property lines. Many former homeowners are continuing to pay mortgages for structures that no longer exist to avoid foreclosure. Do not develop options that aggregate lots for re-development, as this is a fear of property owners after a disaster.

Provide information on costs, benefits, and questions needing further review to help survivors make decisions that prioritise resilience to future climate conditions.

Plan for long-term economic development, not just disaster relief. Plan more equitable, healthier, and more prosperous communities. The adaptive capacity of any household is inextricably linked to underlying social systems, health disparities, and historic social inequities. Utilise recovery grants to create essential and transformative changes to make communities safer and more resilient. Put structures in place that will confer lasting benefits for economic development: streetscapes, zoning ordinances, utilities, and projects that catalyse private development.

Prioritise the rehabilitation of historic fabric wherever possible. Historic structures are links to the community's identity and memory, and their rehabilitation stands as a testament to resilience.

Establish a plan bank of pre-permitted designs for residents to choose between, with a variety of sizes, configurations, and designs to fit into established neighbourhoods.

Design for expansion, using resources available for immediate housing that can be expanded later for permanent housing.

Rebuild communities free from environmental hazards. Address lead in soils, poor air quality, and low levels of green space. Identify contaminated sites in the disaster area and prioritise hazardous waste removal and abatement. If communities have been affected by chemical or other releases, ensure that cleanup measures are complete and certified prior to rebuilding and reoccupation. Improve protective infrastructure around potentially hazardous sources to contain waste in future events.

If neighbourhoods are deemed to be at higher risk after a disaster, work with officials to clearly illustrate the impacts of rebuilding decisions. In the aftermath of Hurricane Katrina, many residents rushed to rebuild before the flood maps changed; this shortsighted decision caused insurance rates to skyrocket as these nonconforming homes no longer meet the standards, with insurance penalties that affect the entire community.

IMPLEMENTATION PHASE

Ensure new or rebuilt public infrastructure is safe, accessible, and resilient to future climate conditions over an extended service life of 100 – 150 years.

Work with permitting authorities to streamline the permitting process for those wishing to rebuild at appropriate sites: a catalogue of pre-permitted plans, zoning restrictions lifted for rebuilding within the same footprint, or relief from application fees.

Use disasters as a catalyst for skilled job training in sustainable construction methods: improved structural strength, high-quality thermal envelope, high-efficiency fixtures and equipment, and renewable energy.

Create opportunities to develop skills through workforce training and mentorship.

Maintain a list of reputable sources of labour and materials. Prioritise the skills and participation of local tradespeople to rebuild the local economy.

Set up salvage and exchange sites to recover and reuse materials. Skilled volunteers can plane and recut lumber to nominal sizes, repair ornamental metal, and repoint masonry. Unskilled volunteers can remove nails, chip mortar off salvaged bricks, sort metals, and clean furnishings. Identify sites for collecting, sorting, and refinishing. Incorporate digital skills to set up online exchange sites with photos, description, source, location, and cost of reclaimed materials.

Work with local officials to adopt beyond-code standards for rebuilding in the affected area. This may include adding freeboard above the Base Flood Elevation in flood risk zones, requiring impact-resistant openings and fortified roof decks in high wind areas, or requiring fire-resistant materials in the wildland–urban interface.

MONITORING PHASE

Maintain a presence within the local community to provide continuity throughout the rebuilding process. Depending on the scope of the recovery, establish a timeline for regular check-ins: 1 year for small-scale events; 1-, 2- and 5-year reviews for larger-scale events; and 1-, 2-, 5-, 10-, and 15-year reviews for highly-destructive events.

Keep records of recovery progress: infrastructure (dates that utilities are restored and transportation networks reestablished); reconstruction progress (building permit applications, certificates of occupancy issued, temporary housing units, permanent housing units restored); economic milestones (% of population restored, gross sales, assistance disbursed); and ecological progress (debris removal, number of trees planted, marine environment cleanup). Establish a set of pre-event and post-rebuilding metrics to evaluate community strength, ecological health, and economic productivity.

Document changes in land use after the event. Were properties aggregated by developers to form large-scale developments? Did shifts in zoning occur as a result of the planning efforts? Were these changes welcomed by the community?

Document changing economic conditions after the event. Were rebuilding costs inflated by demand? What percentage of properties changed hands? Were property values inflated or reduced in the aftermath? Did insurance costs go up significantly? Did employment rise or fall significantly?

Evaluate the success of design recommendations and include property owners, building users, the design and construction team, and community members. Identify what went well in the recovery process and what could have been improved. This process might include interviews, surveys, or facilitated group discussions.

Keep track of hazard mitigation activities that strengthen the community against future challenges. Evaluate how these perform in future events.

IMPACT

Social: Disasters cause chronic, community-wide trauma but participation in the recovery phase gives those affected by the disaster agency, influence, an opportunity to expose longstanding issues in the community, and a forum to express their vision for the future. A strong community engagement process enlarges the networks of social interaction and strengthens social capital when it is needed.

Environmental: Community participation prioritises the structures to be preserved and the sites to be conserved, decisions with long-term environmental impacts. If retreat strategies become part of the community's future planning, the restoration of high-hazard areas to become absorptive and protective sites will enhance resilience for the entire community.

Economic: In the post-disaster milieu, economic forces have tremendous impact on decision-making. Responsible decisions in land use planning should be based on observed and foreseeable climate challenges. Strengthen programmes that retain longtime residents in the community.

Spatial: Recovery is an opportunity to rebuild in ways that avoid or mitigate hazards by reducing exposure and instituting higher standards for building performance. Community participation may guide investments to new sites, intensify underutilised neighbourhoods, and plan areas for retreat.

NOTES

1 Gallego, R.I.F. and L.M.S. Tejero. 2023. The Passivity-Responsiveness Continuum in the Disaster Preparedness and Mitigation Process: A Synthesized Theory. *International Journal of Disaster Risk Reduction* 88, 103616. https://doi.org/10.1016/j.ijdrr.2023.103616

2 T. Skavdal. 2003. *Introduction to Disaster Assessment and Assessment Methodologies*. UNOCHA, Kobe, Japan. Accessed at: https://www.adrc.asia/publications/TDRM2003June/16.pdf

RESOURCE

- Guidelines for Community Participation in Disaster Recovery, United Nations Development Programme (UNDP) 2020. Accessed at: https://www.gfdrr.org/sites/default/files/Guidelines%20for%20Community%20Participation%20in%20Disaster%20Recovery.pdf

SOCIAL CAPITAL + SOCIAL INFRASTRUCTURE

41

ADAPTATION **SCARCITY** SCALE **SITE**

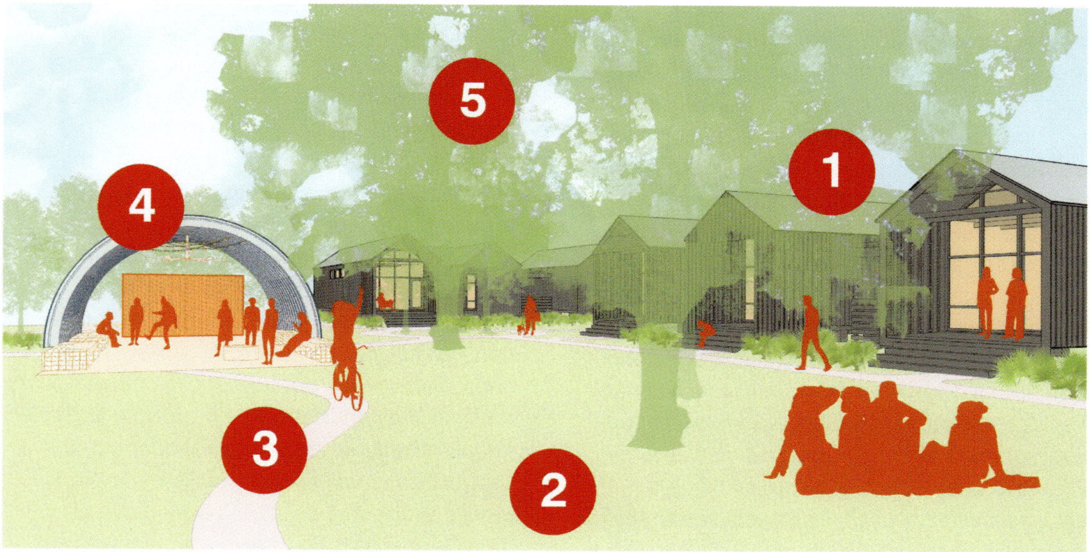

In an era of increasing isolation and loneliness, improving social interaction is critical to happiness, economic advancement, and resilience. Social capital encompasses the network of close friends and family, as well as acquaintances with weaker ties, that facilitate cooperation for mutual benefit. Social capital is the most critical resource in disaster recovery.[1] Social infrastructure corresponds to the elements and spaces that bring people together, including places where people assemble in public spaces, playgrounds, outdoor markets, and libraries, and in private spaces such as churches, restaurants, or clubs. It is distinct from the standard infrastructure of utilities, transportation, and public services, but has no less importance in its contributions to physical and psychological needs.[2]

Figure 41.1: A cottage court with common space strengthens the natural tendency of a small group of neighbours to watch out for one another. (1) Provide porches overlooking common spaces and (2) activity areas. Provide (3) walking and bicycling paths, (4) a sheltered outdoor area, and (5) trees for habitat and shade.

DOI: 10.4324/9781032702964-46

BACKGROUND

Places with good social infrastructure inspire people to forge connections. The spatial patterns that support social capital can be measured on a dozen indices: clean and tidy, accessible, attractive, comfortable, inclusive, vital, functional, distinctive, safe and secure, robust, green and unpolluted, and fulfilling.[3] Danish architect Jan Gehl compared outdoor areas with poor quality where only strictly necessary activities occur to places that are meaningful and attractive, where people engage in a wider range of social and spontaneous activities.[4] A ball-player orchestrates a team of children; a taxi driver monitors the crowded sidewalks around the pub; and a dog-walker speaks to a fisherman, each casual contact a ripple widening to touch everyone in the community. Interactions weave a pattern that, in times of trouble, creates a safety net that protects vulnerable members of the community.

Disasters are a critical time for social capital because of the many decisions that must be made before and after an event. When and where shall we evacuate? When should we return? Are our friends returning? When will services be fully restored? How will we get supplies? Are schools open? Can we travel safely to work? How will we rebuild? These decisions are often made in conjunction with others or influenced by key social networks: family members, school friends, churches, and organisations.

People in peril depend on others for assistance, and in the advent of an emergency each person becomes a conduit to others. Most people hear disaster warnings several times before they take action: they must listen, understand, believe, personalise, and decide how to act.[5] Alarm has a highly social component requiring people to know the warning is credible, and confirmed by others they trust. Even if individuals believe the message, if they do not believe that the message is intended for them or applies to those they care about, they are less likely to take precautions. Trusted people amplify critical messages to others in their social circle.

After a disaster, reconstituting disrupted social networks is one of the fastest ways to rebuild community spirit. The aftermath creates opportunities to bond over shared adversity causing social networks to broaden after a disaster when people check on their neighbours, borrow equipment, or share food and supplies. Each person acts as a bridge among different clusters of friends, introducing a colleague from work to a neighbour with a truck or a family member that can help gut a house. As survivors fulfil immediate needs outside of their normal, daily routine, they encounter new groups, and new people; these expanded social connections support emotional coping skills by solving urgent problems, enlarging their circle of friends, and gaining a sense of purpose from helping others. An expanded social circle helps alleviate trauma from the event and fear of the community's future; people with friends from diverse backgrounds and with strong social connections generally feel less anxious about the future.[6]

Storms and other disasters disrupt social capital. When the built environment is damaged and people displaced, normal social interaction is one casualty. Katrina displaced over one million people in 2005; ten years later, 20% of residents hadn't returned to their previous community. The evacuees' social capital became tied to new people and new communities, finding family, job opportunities, and sanctuary away from the storm-damaged landscape.

Communities with good social infrastructure find it easier to respond to, withstand, and recover from crises. 'Third places' such as libraries, coffee shops, community halls, pubs, and public parks bring together a diverse cohort of users on neutral ground, without imposed hierarchy or barriers. Spaces where

people can drop in, speak up, relax, and have a conversation are essential to building cohesion across the community, minimising gaps between generations, ethnic groups, economic classes, and religious beliefs.[7] This type of social infrastructure jumpstarts access to services after a disaster by providing physical places for social interaction: to learn, get warm (or cool), recharge a battery, access the internet, pray, have a meal, obtain childcare, or gain access to resources. Access to social capital is a necessary component of individual and community resilience.

Figure 41.2: Social capital is the most critical resource in disaster recovery. Social infrastructure corresponds to the elements and spaces that bring people together. This proposal for a Rapid Economic Development Initiative (REDI) was designed for New Orleans after Hurricane Katrina. The community resiliency hub is built of prefabricated sections to house a coffee shop, catalogue shop, labour exchange, and community information board. An open activity area for gathering is enhanced with sheltered porches, recreational amenities, sidewalks, and trees for shade. unabridged Architecture + Rockwell Group.

KEY DESIGN CONSIDERATIONS

Social infrastructure establishes a framework for serendipity in the urban environment. Will there be other people present? Will they be doing something interesting? Will the weather be favourable? Is there a chance to see new blooms, changing leaves, or interesting pets? Include a variety of activity spaces ranging from small and intimate to large gathering areas. Plan walkways to intersect with the community's street grid, commercial centres, cultural sites, and natural areas to create links between established activity nodes.

Design social infrastructure to incorporate green spaces: beaches, ballfields, amphitheatres, dog parks, community gardens, walking tracks, play streets, public schools, skate parks, pools, waterfronts, fountains, and playgrounds. Design streetscapes to include seating, shade, drinking fountains, public art, transit stops, lighting for nighttime, and services such as concessions, parking, and transit connections. Provide good visibility to ensure the safety of the elderly, youth, and other vulnerable residents.

Develop guidelines for public street frontage to include social features: porches, stoops, low fences, front-facing windows, and balconies. Reduce setbacks to improve connections to the sidewalk. Do not allow parking courts to consume the entire front yard.

Provide seamless connections to (and through) public spaces. Link neighbourhoods with a network of public transit, linear greenways, bikeways, riverine paths, and shaded boulevards.

Ensure that social infrastructure is equitably distributed across the community. In many places, spatial accessibility to green spaces and other social infrastructure is not evenly distributed, with studies showing reduced open and green spaces in communities of colour and socially disadvantaged areas.[8] Plan new investments to serve communities with fewer places of social infrastructure, establishing event halls, health clinics, public markets, museums, childcare, colleges, and libraries.

Variety in programming at public spaces draws different segments of the population, providing opportunities to meet people outside of normal circles of acquaintance. Programming should include active recreation (family bike rides, morning yoga sessions, and kayak lessons) and cultural events (concerts, movie nights, art festivals, poetry slams, and trivia games). Attractive programming entices people to visit new places and can foster new connections among people with a passion for the same activities.

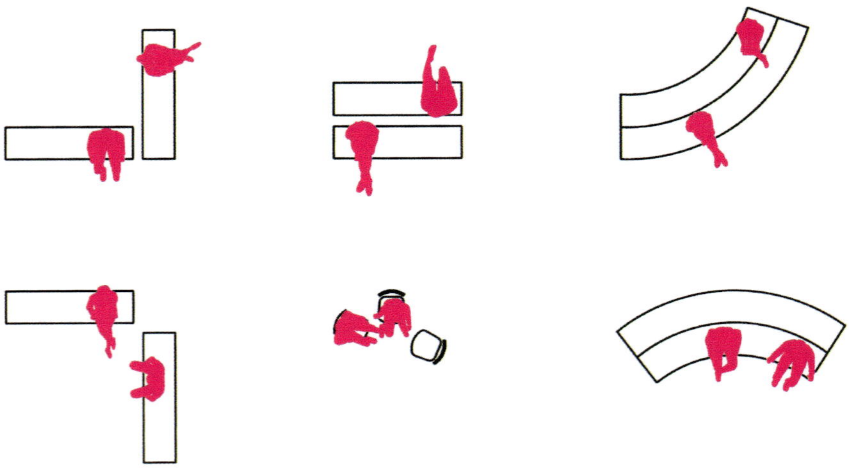

Figure 41.3: Seat configurations encourage or discourage social interaction. Sociofugal seating (top row) is designed to minimise interaction between people. Sociopetal seating (bottom row) is designed to encourage contact between people.

Erik Klinenberg describes how commercial areas also serve as social attractions in *Palaces for the People*. 'Grocery stores, diners, cafes, bookstores, and barber shops draw people out of their homes and into the streets and sidewalks, where they create cultural vitality and contribute to the passive surveillance of shared public space'.[9]

Cluster multi-family housing around common areas, courtyards, play areas, and entries to promote the natural tendency of a small group to watch out for one another. The landmark 1973 publication *Defensible Space* by Oscar Newman advocated for buildings and spatial configurations that create areas of shared concern which residents adopt and monitor closely.[10]

Provide social interaction spaces within buildings, too. The Salk Institute by Louis Kahn (1965) is famed for orchestrating informal connections between researchers in disparate fields of science. Collaboration spaces and open labs create a dynamic place that fosters social interaction. Thomas Albright, a neurobiologist who worked at the Salk for three decades, told *The Los Angeles Times*, 'My lab flows into the lab next to me and that's the valuable thing. The sparks fly at the boundaries of different areas of scientific research. People are always running into other people'.[11]

Seating configuration also has an impact on social interaction. Inward-focused seating (sociopetal) enables conversation while outward-focused or side-by-side seating (sociofugal) discourages interaction. Proximity, as well as direction, has an impact on conviviality. Movable seating offers the greatest opportunity to adjust to fit different size groups, personal preferences, cultural norms, and desires for sun or shade, quiet or noisy, intimacy or gregariousness, in exposed or sheltered locations.

IMPACT

Social: Communities with high social capital are less affected by disaster, can be quickly restored, and provide an essential resource for accomplishing critical tasks. Communities with high social capital also tend to be happier with post-disaster development planning as they typically have greater influence in the process.

Environmental: Incorporating social infrastructure into environmental functions (benches beneath shade trees, paths through stormwater management ponds) has win-win results, encouraging usage by a broad group of people to meet their daily needs, get exercise, and enjoy chance encounters.

Economic: Good social infrastructure promotes the use of commercial spaces, inviting people to linger and establish informal connections that lead to broader networks and more economic activity. Proximity to a popular commercial corridor affects the long-term recovery of a community.

Spatial: Social infrastructure has profound implications for spatial quality, with its reliance on walkable streets, street-scale commercial districts, enhanced vitality day and night, slower road speeds, and increased independence for the elderly, children, and vulnerable citizens.

OCCUPY SANDY

When Hurricane Sandy made landfall on 29 October 2012, the Occupy movement had been in existence for a year, marshalling support for social and economic justice through opposition to the global financial system through Occupy Wall Street. The hurricane provided an opportunity for members to organise disaster response and relief efforts, providing mutual aid in the hard-hit neighbourhoods of the Lower East Side of Manhattan, Brooklyn, the Rockaways, Staten Island, and New Jersey.

Members canvassed neighbours to identify people who were trapped in apartment buildings with electrical outages which shut down elevator service, refrigeration, and heating. They set up a motor pool to mobilise volunteers to deliver water, food, flashlights, blankets, and clothing. Volunteers established 24-hour hubs in churches, community centres, and storefronts, stocking them with information, food, basic needs, and heat. Registries for relief items and tools directed materials to local businesses and neighbourhood groups. In the immediate aftermath, the rapid-response team handled donations, distribution, volunteer services, field site operation, and organisational skills such as information-sharing, ordering, and mapping. Where public services failed – FEMA, National Guard, city police, Red Cross – the Occupy volunteers, summoned by a text or tweet, delivered aid to the most vulnerable people in the community via door-to-door visits.

The Occupy Sandy volunteers used existing social networks to enhance social capital at a critical time. The self-organised community communicated more clearly, convened to deter problems, and inspired people to act collectively in the rebuilding process. It is an example of social capital inspiring faster recovery times by helping survivors coordinate efforts.[12]

NOTES

1 Dynes, R.2006. 'Social Capital: Dealing with Community Emergencies'. Homeland Security Affairs 2(2).
2 Klinenberg, E. 2018. *Palaces for the People: How Social Infrastructure can Help Fight Inequality, Polarization, and the Decline of Civic Life*. New York: Penguin Random House.
3 deMagalhaes, C. and Carmona, M. 2009. 'Dimensions and models of contemporary public space management in England'. Journal of Environmental Planning and Management vol. 52, Issue 1, p 111-129. https://doi.org/10.1080/09640560802504704
4 Gehl, J. 2011. *Life Between Buildings*. Washington, DC: Island Press.
5 Fitzpatrick, C. and Mileti, D. 1994. 'Motivating Public Evacuation'. International Journal of Mass Emergencies & Disasters, vol. 9, Issue 2. https://doi.org/10.1177/028072709100900202
6 Aldrich, D. 2012. *Building Resilience: Social Capital in Post-Disaster Recovery*.
7 Oldenburg, R. 1999. *The Great Good Place: Cafes, Coffee Shops, Bookstores, Bars, Hair Salons, and Other Hangouts at the Heart of a Community*. Cambridge, MA: Da Capo Press.
8 Dai, D. 2011. Racial/Ethnic and Socioeconomic Disparities in Urban Green Space Accessibility: Where to Intervene? *Landscape and Urban Planning* 102, no. 4, 234–244.
9 Klinenberg, E. 2018. pp. 75–76. Op.cit.
10 Newman, O. 1973. *Defensible Space: Crime Prevention Through Urban Design*. New York: Macmillan Publishing.
11 Miranda, C.A. 2016. Louis Kahn's Salk Institute, the Building that Guesses Tomorrow, Is Aging – Very, Very Gracefully. *Los Angeles Times*, November 22, 2016. Accessed at: https://www.latimes.com/entertainment/arts/miranda/la-et-cam-salk-institute-louis-kahn-20161107-htmlstory.html?utm_medium=website&utm_source=archdaily.com
12 Aldrich, D.P. 2012. *Building Resilience: Social Capital in Post-Disaster Recovery*. Chicago, IL: University of Chicago Press.

RESOURCES

- Klinenberg, E. 2018. *Palaces for the People: How Social Infrastructure Can Help Fight Inequality, Polarization, and the Decline of Civic Life*. New York: Penguin Random House.
- Spacey, J. 2023. 60 Examples of Social Infrastructure. *Simplicable*. Accessed at: https://simplicable.com/society/social-infrastructure
- Urban Land Institute. 2023. *Social Spaces, Resilient Communities: Social Infrastructure as a Climate Strategy for Real Estate*. Washington, DC. Accessed at: https://knowledge.uli.org/-/media/files/research-reports/2022/social-spaces-resilient-communities-1.pdf?rev=8d6ee91d053d41e0a469618a69583cf8&hash=659AC190AC8440A9634CFACF80965A

NET-ZERO WATER

42

ADAPTATION **SCARCITY** SCALE **SITE**

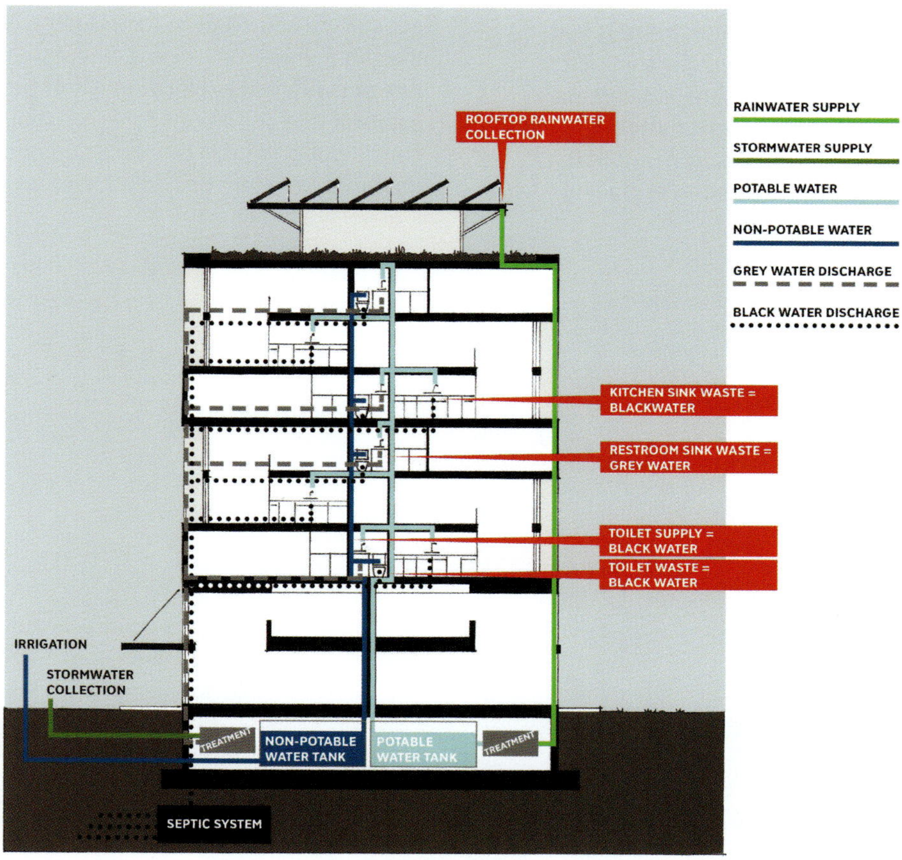

Climate change is increasing drought with every degree of warming. Projects that meet net-zero water targets preserve the quantity and quality of natural water resources by not depleting, compromising, or re-directing the flow within the watershed. A net-zero water project minimises total water consumption, utilises alternative water sources such as rainwater, minimises wastewater discharge, and returns the water to the original water source, balancing the overall water intake and release over the course of a year. Net-zero water is a strategy for adaptation, in the near term through passive survivability in the case of municipal utility interruptions, and in the long-term by adapting to a decreasing supply of freshwater.

Figure 42.1: The ideal net-zero water building.

DOI: 10.4324/9781032702964-47

BACKGROUND

Only 0.05% of water on Earth is accessible freshwater for human consumption. Climate change is dangerously affecting the freshwater supply in many parts of the world and the availability of drinking water could decline by two-thirds by the 2050s. This is a manmade problem, exacerbated by irresponsible settlement patterns, unsustainable drawdown from aquifers, contamination of water sources, failing infrastructure, and disregard for the most fundamental human need.

Although the built environment is not the primary consumer of water - 70–80% of freshwater is used for food production and agriculture and 10–20% for industry - it is the most immediate nexus where people interact with water. Net-zero water projects establish the conditions for more thoughtful consideration of this resource and ensure that annual water consumption balances

Figure 42.2: An Annual Water Balance Diagram shows water input and output throughout the year. Watershed Row, Place Collaborative.

the water harvested from the site and the water returned to the site. Net-zero water buildings demonstrate how new development can operate within the constraints of the site's specific place and climate. Where freshwater sources are constrained, the net-zero approach limits development on a site to its carrying capacity, which represents the number of people and type of functions the site can support without environmental degradation.

Annual water consumption measures the amount of water consumed within a building from all sources, both potable and non-potable, over the course of a year. Traditional freshwater supplies include wells, lakes, rivers, and aquifers. There are also a variety of alternative water sources that do not come from typical freshwater sources. Harvested rainwater from roofs requires the least treatment before use; stormwater collected at the ground level or water from sump pumps at the building foundation may require additional filtration to remove contaminants.

Greywater discharge from lavatory sinks, showers, bathtubs, and washing machines can be treated for non-potable reuse. Condensate from HVAC systems is a good source along with water denied by water purification systems. Dishwashers are not a good source for greywater because the detergents typically have a high salt content and kitchen sinks often have food particle contamination. Greywater is collected in a non-potable water tank and used for toilet flushing, irrigation, and car washing. Blackwater from kitchen sinks, dishwashers, and toilets is processed through septic systems or living machines before release.

To verify that a net-zero building is operating as designed, architects collect annual water use data for each type of water flow:

NET ZERO WATER USE

POTABLE WATER USE	______
NON-POTABLE WATER USE	+ ______
ALTERNATIVE WATER USE	+ ______
TOTAL WATER USE	______
WASTEWATER TREATED ONSITE	______
WATER INFILTRATED ONSITE	+ ______
TOTAL WATER RETURNED	______
TOTAL WATER USE	______
TOTAL WATER RETURNED	- ______
NET ZERO SUMMARY	______

(if sum is equal to or less than zero, the building is considered to have net zero water use)

Figure 42.3: This chart explains how to calculate total water use and total water returned, subtracting the difference to determine if a building meets the standards for net-zero water use.

- Potable water use
- Non-potable water use from freshwater sources
- Alternative water use
- Wastewater treated on-site and returned to original water source
- Stormwater infiltrated to the original water source through green infrastructure.[1]

Freshwater and alternative water use to calculate the building's total annual water use. Wastewater and stormwater must be returned to the original source after on-site treatment.

In a net-zero water building, the total annual water intake must equal to (or less than) the amount of water returned to the original source. Potable and greywater can be returned to the site by treating it without the use of chemicals or by allowing stormwater to infiltrate through green infrastructure to rejoin the aquifer or stream. Blackwater can be treated in mechanical filtration chambers or onsite living machines, which work like natural wetlands using a series of cells to treat effluent. Although treatment systems vary, the first step typically takes place in an enclosed tank where microbes and enzymes break down waste, remove odours, and transform effluent into nutrients. The liquid passes through filters that polish and scrub nutrients from the water using plant materials, UV light, and sand. At the end of the treatment train, the remaining liquid is nearly potable quality and safe to release.

KEY DESIGN CONSIDERATIONS

GENERAL

Determine the origin of the water supply at the site. Does it come from wells tapped into groundwater aquifers, rivers and streams, or lakes? In the United States, the EPA has an interactive map to locate drinking water providers, sources, treatment plants, and violations at: https://www.epa.gov/sourcewaterprotection/drinking-water-mapping-application-protect-source-waters-dwmaps. Understanding the source of a project's drinking water and projected changes to water quantity and quality can drive adaptation with net-zero water solutions.

Estimate annual water use and develop a water balance strategy incorporating alternative water sources, green infrastructure and recharge, water storage, and onsite treatment options.

Determine the pre-development hydrology flows across the site. If the site has already been developed, infer the original conditions as far as possible. Restore the site's hydrologic function to serve the larger watershed through water conveyance and natural infiltration, which contribute to regenerating both aquatic and terrestrial ecosystems.

Calculate the carbon impact of water use in carbon per gallon of water supplied to the site. Install meters to measure potable water use and track data.

Advocate for better supervision of water resources by governments. Municipally-treated freshwater loss is estimated to total about one-third of treated drinking water, and about 90% of those leaks are underground. Innovative AI analysis of pipe acoustic profiles offers a new tool for locating and measuring leaks, the first step towards addressing the problem. However, the deferred maintenance of water infrastructure systems worldwide far exceeds the financial capacity to correct the problems.

Developing a net-zero water building shifts some of the costs for water storage and treatment from the municipality to the property owner. If a sufficient number of utility customers implement these measures, it may delay the need to increase capacity (and investment) at the community scale.

WATER SUPPLY

Collecting rainwater from the roof is preferable to harvesting stormwater from the ground due to the possibility of additional contaminants that may be present, including pesticides, fertilisers, soils, or petrochemicals. Design the roof materials, preferably using polymer-coated steel, galvanised, steel, zinc, concrete tile, or cool roofs. Rainwater harvested from galvanised steel roofs had lower concentrations of faecal coliform than other materials.[2] Low-slope acrylic polymer membrane cool roofs and concrete tile roofs also require minimal treatment. Asphaltic shingles can produce high levels of dissolved organic carbon when the roof is new, which can lead to high concentrations of disinfection byproducts after chlorination. Water quality generally improves with an effective first-flush diverter but contaminants above EPA safe drinking standards make additional treatment necessary prior to potable use.

Conveyance systems must also be constructed with low toxicity materials. Steel- or glass-lined cisterns are preferable for storing potable water.

Provide an uninterruptible source of potable water on-site for use in emergencies or grid interruptions to serve all regular building occupants for a period of three days to one week.

OPERATIONS

Design a water efficient building. Minimise the use of potable water for non-potable functions such as toilet flushing, irrigation, or other purposes. Reduce demand by employing innovative technologies that consume less water: efficient fixtures, automated controls, leak detection, and moisture sensors.

Consider non-water-using fixtures such as composting toilets and non-water urinals. If these options are selected, communicate proper operation and maintenance practices to all building users.

Incorporate water efficiency with native landscape materials that require no supplemental irrigation after an initial establishment period.

Set up a leak detection system. In the United States, 10% of homes have leaks that waste 90 gallons or more each day from worn toilet flappers, dripping faucets, or outdoor valve leaks. In larger buildings, the problem is compounded. Install a leak detector to monitor plumbing and alert building owners to microleaks and larger issues.

Heating and cooling equipment requires water for its processes and also generates condensate, which can be used as an alternative source of water. Rainwater collection can provide makeup water for evaporative cooling towers during the peak heat seasons when systems require a tremendous amount of water.

RECYCLING WATER

Water flows through a continuous recycling process that includes precipitation, condensation, evaporation, ice melt, storage in aquifers and surface water, and emerging as springs. Treatments to make water potable intervene in the cycle to separate solids, filter organic and inorganic contaminants, and add chemicals to make the water clear, colourless, and fit for consumption. All water is recycled, but the timeline between use and reuse is growing shorter due to changing precipitation patterns, population growth, and pollution.

Industrial facilities often reuse process or cooling water that is generated onsite from boilers, chillers, and industrial production in a closed-loop cycle. Because this water has limited opportunities for contamination, it can be less costly and less energy intensive to treat and reuse for offsite purposes, such as human consumption or agricultural reuse.

A mostly untapped source of reclaimed water is municipal wastewater. In urban areas with

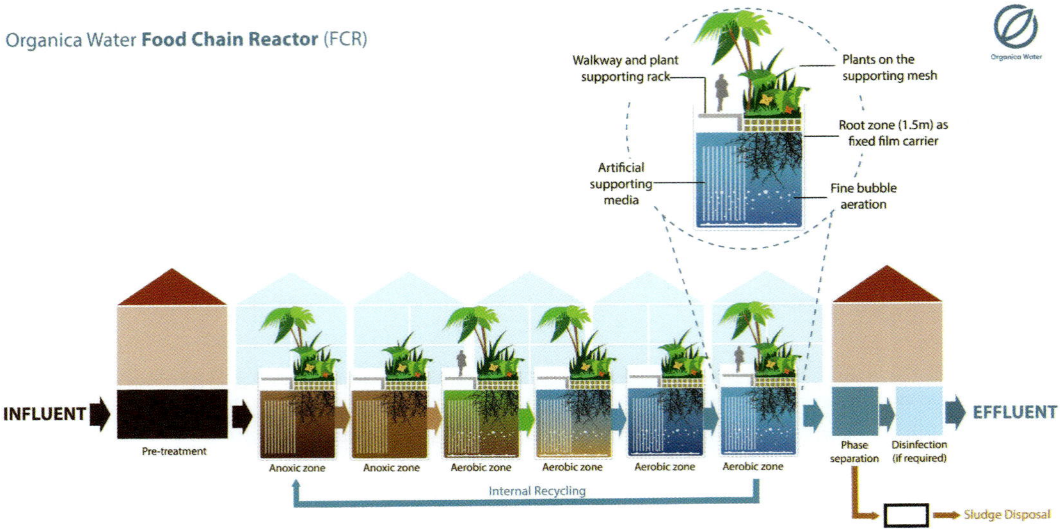

Figure 42.4: Diagram of nature-based water treatment technology with a series of biological reactors to consume contaminants from the wastewater and produce reusable water. The reactors, populated with microbes, aquatic flora, and fauna are arranged in a cascade fashion with pretreatment steps in the beginning and final polishing at the end. Organica Ecotechnologies.

high population density, pressure on local water resources is growing as local aquifers are overdrafted, making it inadvisable to use water once and dispose of it. However, most people will refuse to drink reclaimed water, preferring to pump it to distant locations for treatment and release. The psychological considerations associated with drinking reclaimed wastewater - the yuck factor - are a powerful drawback to reuse. Traditional water treatment plants are large, unattractive, and smelly, which relegates them to the outskirts of a community, increasing the distance to pump effluent and the reclaimed, treated water and reducing the competitive advantage of reclamation. Successful solutions will manage the unappealing aspects of recycled water by re-associating water reclamation with nature through the incorporation of plants: spray irrigation systems, biofiltration through vegetated tanks, injection wells, groundwater recharge basins, and other methods.

Water Resource Gardens incorporate nature, technology, and architecture in a confined treatment process that directs untreated water through a sequence of treatment cells using common techniques: sedimentation to separate solids and suspended particles; membrane filtration or sand filters; aeration panels to enhance mixing; and bio-reactors with natural biomass and engineered root systems featuring microorganisms and aquatic flora and fauna that remove pathogens.

Architecture plays a key role in changing attitudes towards recycled water in urban systems. A more cost-effective and spatially efficient solution reclaims wastewater directly within an urban setting, in a way that is aesthetically pleasing, eliminates noxious odours, and uses advanced technology to clean and polish water for potable reuse. A large capacity water reclamation plant can be designed as a large greenhouse or botanical garden, with diverse plants growing on top of the biological reactors, often with a cascade of multi-story treatment cells creating tiered gardens.

RELEASE

Septic systems are often used for on-site treatment in rural areas using anaerobic digestion and settling within a tank before filtration through a leach field. The systems provide moderate treatment efficiency; however, there is growing consensus that septic systems have a sizeable negative impact on the environment due to age, deferred maintenance, incompatible soils, methane emissions, and high embodied carbon. Septic systems that combine aerobic aeration systems and biofilters improve treatment efficacy. Living machines offer both a carbon and cost incentive when compared to traditional septic system designs and may improve treatment, reduce greenhouse gas emissions, and reduce desludging frequency.[3]

A living machine or on-site wastewater treatment technology utilises a series of tanks supporting vegetation, microbes, and snails to treat effluent to high ecological standards. The tanks incorporate sedimentation, filtration, clarification, adsorption, and other processes used in conventional biological systems, but the on-site treatment can cost less to operate than conventional systems and don't require harmful chemicals to achieve tertiary treatment.

Design green infrastructure features to return water to its original water source using bioswales, wetlands, and detention ponds that filter, cool, and aerate stormwater. These may include horizontal or vertical reed beds to process greywater before reuse or release.

IMPACT

Social: Net-zero water strategies improve public health by treating wastewater prior to discharge. A building with net-zero water reduces dependency on infrastructure that may be compromised in a disaster event or severe water stress, improving self-sufficiency and passive survivability.

Environmental: Netzero water projects conserve water and pretreat outflow before release, resulting in better water quality. Enhancing green infrastructure at bioswales and wetlands can lower microclimate temperatures and add texture and biodiversity to the landscape.

Economic: Although the initial cost of a net-zero water system, including piping, storage tanks, and site improvements is not zero, the payback from lower monthly costs and fewer interruptions may take only a few years. Community-wide water quality improvements may have positive economic impacts for the entire area by expanding tourism, recreation, aquaculture, and the blue economy.

Spatial: Net-zero water communities or campuses encourage block-scale solutions but may have to limit density based on the site's capacity to process wastewater. On-site green infrastructure for water treatment and recharge can provide benefits including space for recreation, gardens, and buffers between properties.

More frequent and extreme storm events increase the inflow into municipal sanitary systems and combined sewers, causing untreated material to be released into nearby bodies of water. Net-zero water projects offer the potential to reduce those impacts by adding capacity, storage, and treatment in peak wet weather, and relieving pressure on municipal systems.

NOTES

1 U.S. Federal Energy Management Program, Net-Zero Water Building Strategies. Website accessed at: https://www.energy.gov/femp/net-zero-water-building-strategies
2 Mendez, C. et al. 2011. The Effect of Roofing Material on the Quality of Harvested Rainwater. *Water Research* 45, no. 5, 2049–2059. https://doi.org/10.1016/j.watres.2010.12.015
3 Brown, G.C., J. MacAdam, G. Dotro, and B. Jefferson. 2023. A Wholelife Cost and Carbon Perspective of Alternatives to Septic Tanks Using Nature-Based Solutions. *H2Open Journal* 6, no. 3, 361–372. https://doi.org/10.2166/h2oj.2023.002

RESOURCE

- Design Elements of a Net-Zero Water Building. Federal Energy Management Program. Accessed at: https://www.energy.gov/femp/design-elements-net-zero-water-building

CIRCULARITY 43

ADAPTATION **SCARCITY** SCALE **BUILDING**

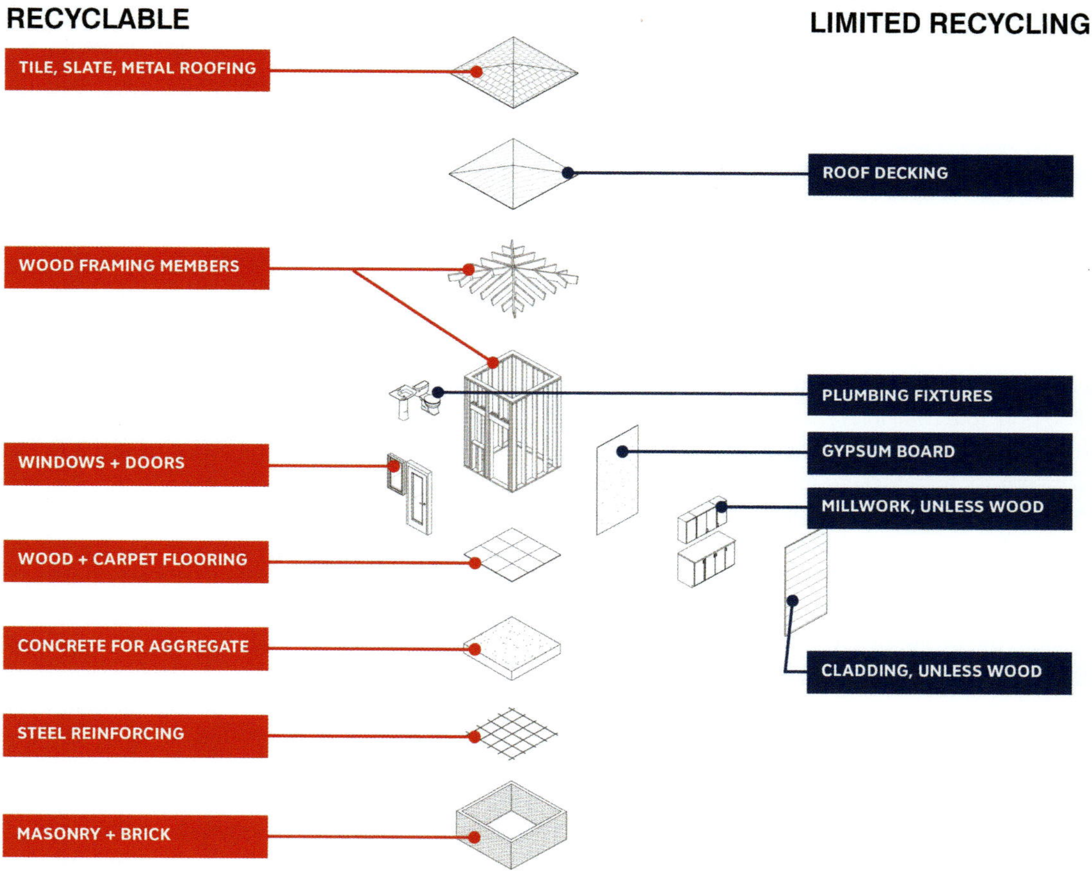

Circularity is the systematic recovery and reuse of material so that resources may be endlessly transformed into something new. Circularity encourages the imaginative reuse of 'waste' materials near their initial deployment, rather than the default practice of extracting or harvesting new materials, processing and manufacturing building products, transporting products to sales yards and stores before moving them to the project site, and assembling materials for a single use. Deconstruction, disassembly, reclamation, reuse, refurbishment, remanufacturing, recycling, and redistribution preserves finite materials and reduces the amount of fuel and material necessary for new production, leaving essential resources for future generations.

Figure 43.1: Diagram of deconstruction/reuse potential of common residential materials.

DOI: 10.4324/9781032702964-48

BACKGROUND

The global population growth demands more and more construction materials for housing, workspace, and public facilities. At the same time, the increased frequency and severity of disaster events creates mountains of waste material - but not all of it is unrecoverable or without value. Construction and demolition (C&D) waste resulting from the construction sector accounts for about 30% of the total waste produced globally, about 1.68 kg/capita/day.[1]

The groundbreaking book by William McDonough and Michael Braungart, *Cradle to Cradle* (2002) laid a foundation for circularity in architecture and construction. The principle that 'everything is a resource for something else' remains a revolutionary concept for architecture in an era marked by overconsumption, obsolescence, and architectural frivolity. If architects were to design buildings as material banks to serve future generations as storehouses of essential goods, the profession would make significant progress toward waste reduction, extracting fewer virgin resources and protecting ecosystems.

There are two ways a material can be reused. Upcycling transforms waste materials or unwanted items into new products with higher quality, artistic value, or environmental utility (for example, taking old jeans and turning them into building insulation). Downcycling converts materials into lower value products, such as recycling hard plastics into softer plastic fibres that are weaker than the virgin plastic source material.

Buildings have always been repositories of valuable materials: wood from ancient forests, metals and minerals from deep sources within the earth, and composites that required groundbreaking chemical innovation. Instead of seeing material use in buildings as linear, the walls, frames, and finishes can be designed to be taken apart, recovered, and reused in the construction of other buildings, thus reducing the need to extract primary resources. Extracting smaller quantities of abiotic resources (fuel, minerals, sand, and stone) and biotic resources (wood, fibre, and peat) contributes fewer greenhouse gas emissions to the atmosphere and prevents further damage to habitats.

There is another, economic rationale for considering the condition of a building as temporary. Buildings are a primary investment for property owners; their value is in the utility of their spaces to produce revenue or meet essential needs. But what if buildings themselves were valued as a stockpile of resources in which products and components are temporarily 'deposited'?[2] Whenever conditions change or sites are threatened, the materials and components may be retrieved for another building or investment. If buildings are to become material stores for the future, then durable materials that can be repurposed in the future are preferable to the take/make/waste model that is conventional practice.

A 'cradle to grave' perspective examines how resources are extracted from the natural environment, processed into useful materials, assembled, used, and disposed at the end of their useful life. For building materials, there are both economic and environmental costs to demolish and dispose of a structure and its contents. One cost-benefit analysis compared recycling C&D waste versus conventional disposal, finding recycling C&D waste to result in a net profit of 2.5%.[3] The study quantified the direct economic benefits: cost savings from reusing and recycling materials in place of new materials, savings on waste collection and transport, savings from landfill charges, and money recouped by selling scrap metal. Indirect benefits included: reducing the required landfill space, reduced liability for environmental problems, reduced chance of soil and groundwater contamination, and an improved public image for the company's environmental concern.

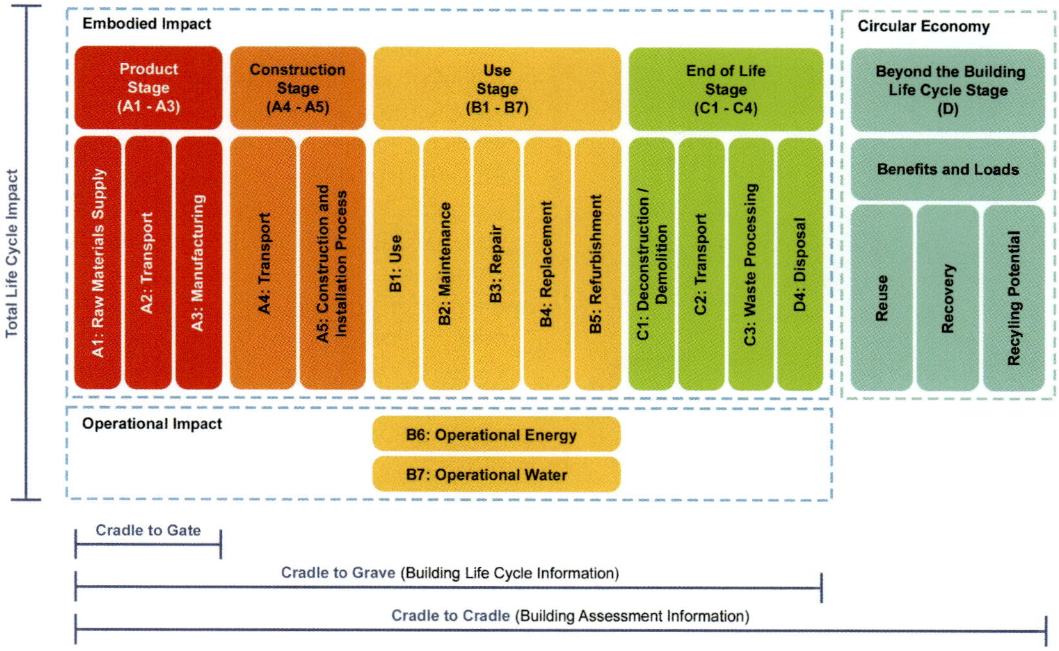

Figure 43.2: Cradle to Gate measures a project's embodied carbon to the point where it leaves the factory gate. Cradle to Grave includes the full life cycle of the material, including waste disposal at the end of life. Cradle to Cradle models the stage beyond the building's lifespan and considers how the materials are repurposed or recycled to keep them circulating through the economy. The total life cycle impact of the products and assemblies includes the carbon associated with operational energy and water. Daniel Overbey.

Material choices and detailing can either streamline or hinder the ability of future generations to disassemble, reuse, or recycle components. When construction materials can be reclaimed or re-processed into valuable commodities, embodied carbon and other environmental penalties are lower. The ISO 15686 (2014) standard describes alternative end-of-life scenarios. These include disassembly or demolition, treating hazardous material to render it safe, transportation to waste processing, disposal, reuse, recovery, and recycling potential. Architects using recycled metals, concrete, and glass in new construction, plus prioritising recycling in disposal, can achieve an overall environmental impact up to 65% less than conventional construction methods.[4]

Circularity in building materials relies on reducing waste through design, selecting sustainable and durable materials, designing for disassembly, and developing plans for future material recovery. Working with manufacturers and contractors, architects must explore the processes and materials that contribute to circularity in building construction.

KEY DESIGN CONSIDERATIONS

PROCESSES

Reduce waste through conscious design. Maximise clarity and simplicity in design and minimise complexity to reduce the

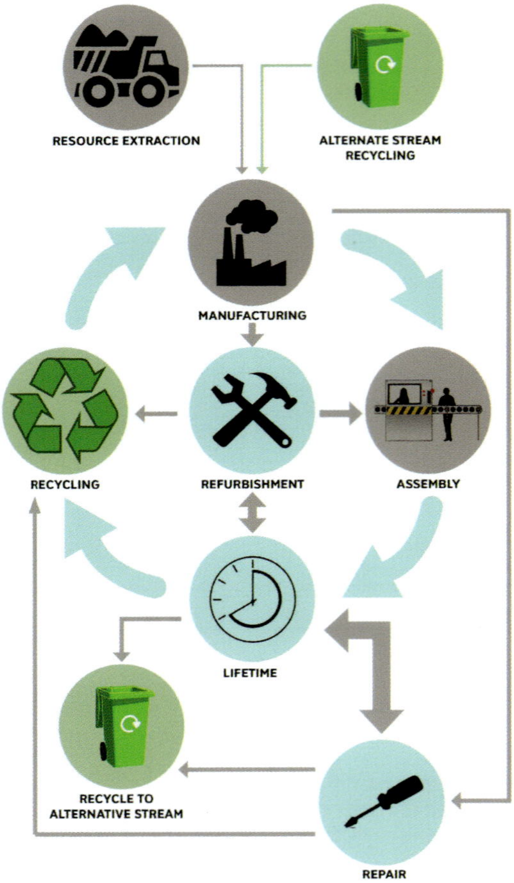

Figure 43.3: Diagram representing material flows in a circular economy. The arrow sizes represent a weighting for the amount of material in the flow as well as the preferred direction of the material flow. unabridged Architecture, after Anastasiades et al. (2020).

number and type of materials in a building. This includes foregoing redundant finishes and finding more efficient ways to employ materials. Look for opportunities to optimise resources, using a little rather than a lot.

Develop a Deconstruction Plan to outline the re-usable elements and best practices to ensure they are handled in a way that preserves maximum reusability. List building elements in an inventory of all components used in the project with full specifications, manufacturer information, and warranties. Identify the intended service life and options for reuse, reclamation, recycling and disposal. Provide instructions on how to deconstruct elements, including the equipment needed and implications for health and safety; if components require a special tool to be dismantled it should be provided with the initial construction, kept nearby, and labelled. Place copies of the Deconstruction Plan alongside the legal deeds of the building, safety records, warranties, and maintenance files.[5]

Deconstruction of an existing building should begin with an inventory of reusable and recyclable components. Select a protected location to store salvaged items. Dismantle and remove elements from the building, with workers sorting materials as they proceed. Only after all eligible items are removed can demolition begin.

Design for future disassembly may require more space surrounding the building components but the improved access for repairing or replacing components can extend the longevity of a building. Strategic routing of building services to reduce interpenetration between other systems enables greater access for modifications. Temporary or quickly evolving services may be surface mounted; alternately, a service plenum or chase provides access at critical junctions.

Components with the shortest lifespan should not be blocked by permanent elements. This becomes difficult when installing liquid-applied weatherproofing layer (50 years) under a fibre cement rainscreen (100 years); wood foundations (5–40 years) under a building with a heavy timber frame (100 years); or flooring underlayment (25 years) under a wood floor (100 years). (See Chapter 44: Antifragile.)

Specifications can facilitate the use of reclaimed products by allowing non-standard sizes or offering product options. Provide clear guidance about who (architects, contractor, or owner) has the responsibility for sourcing, approving, refurbishing, storing, and installing reused materials.

Contract documents can specify performance characteristics and other measures to allow recycled product substitutions when a specific product is not available.

Identify reclaimed material sources early in the design process. Allot additional time for material sourcing, testing, and preparation of the materials for construction. Create a network of salvaged material contacts, pre-test structural materials, and reserve or purchase items to ensure that there is a quantity sufficient for the intended design use, as finding matching materials later may be difficult.

The use of reclaimed materials may have more upfront costs, including potential doubling handling costs to deconstruct, store, transport, and install materials. However, these costs may be offset by lower material costs, making the decision to use reclaimed materials cost-neutral.

Expand the range of materials and components available for salvage beyond specialty items such as railings, fireplaces, floorboards and trim pieces. Look for ways to reuse standard building materials: doors, windows, masonry, and entire panels such as gable ends, roofing squares, or sections of decking.

Note that existing structures may contain hazardous materials (asbestos, lead paint, and mercury) or contain chemicals that are on the ILFI Red List (solvents, polymers, formaldehyde, and other harmful chemicals). Identify chemicals of concern and separate these materials for safe disposal.[6] Selective demolition for hazardous materials should occur first to remove items such as fluorescent tubes, asbestos insulation or tiles, and others. Handle and dispose of these materials carefully to prevent cross-contamination of salvageable materials.

Design reversible connections between materials, such as bolted rather than welded connections. Minimise the number of fasteners, using fewer, stronger fasteners. Use mechanical fasteners in lieu of sealants and adhesives.

Design to use standard dimensions of locally available materials for easy replacement of materials that may become damaged.

In the demolition and construction process, provide space to collect materials for sorting, repair, replacement, and reuse. Provide a site area for composting, where organic matter can break down and become nutrient rich soil. Choose deconstruction before demolition and reuse before recycling.

MATERIALS

Select materials worth recovering or retaining in 50 or 100 years.

Wood: Framing lumber, decks, flooring, subfloor, and panels in good condition can be reused. Painted wood trim (mouldings and baseboards), plywood, and OSB often end up in landfills. Kitchen cabinets and shelves may be reused or donated. Solid wood doors are often reused but hollow-core doors are less durable and have lower value for reuse. Salvaged wood requires very little additional energy to process, so new emissions are

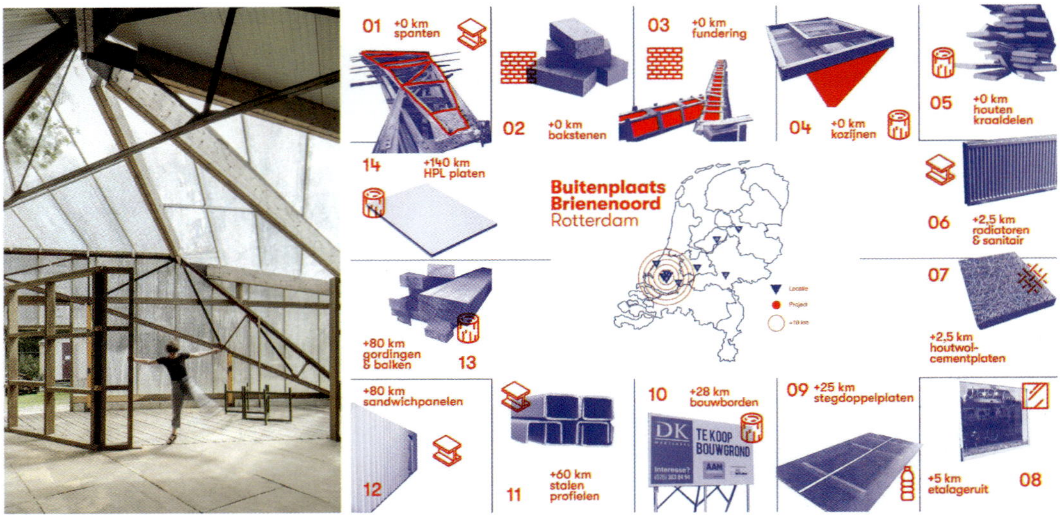

Figure 43.4: Jan Jongert employs the extensive reuse of building materials, including a gathering space and learning centre at Buitenplaats Brienenoord in Rotterdam, Netherlands. Riccardo De Vecchi + Superuse Studios.

limited primarily to transportation. The key to retaining wood's value through cycles of reuse is to maintain it for the highest and best use. The value of wood products vary based on the size, cut, and character of the wood; in general, larger pieces retain more of their value as they offer the most flexibility for reuse and are easier to salvage than small pieces. Notching or drilling framing lumber creates defects in the wood that reduce its value and potential for reuse. Reuse preserves about 72% of the resource, with 28% loss for small or damaged pieces.[7]

Steel: Structural beams and columns, siding, and roof panels may be reused but are more often recycled. The steel in white goods (appliances) can be extracted and recycled. Steel from rebar can be separated from concrete as it is pulverised and recycled. Structural steel contains at least 93% recycled content and recycling preserves about 90% of the resource (with small losses for welds, fittings, and imperfect sorting).

Aluminium: Window, door, and curtainwall frames can be separated from glass for recycling. Single-pane windows are rarely reused. Gutters and downspouts can be recycled. Recycling preserves about 93% of the resource.

Concrete slabs and foundations: Concrete can be crushed into 5–10 cm (2–4 inch) chunks of aggregate for use as a sub-base for new paving or foundations, as aggregate for new concrete, or as rubble for soil stabilisation. Recycling equipment that pulverises concrete equipment has a powerful magnet to separate steel reinforcing for recycling. Recycling preserves about 96% of the resource.

Masonry: CMU and bricks must be stripped of mortar before reusing. Veneer bricks are thinner and more brittle, posing greater difficulty in salvaging for reuse. Lime mortar between bricks can be broken down to fine aggregate or powder and reconstituted with a small amount of additional lime.

Asphalt shingles: Shingles can be downcycled to become roadway asphalt. Shingles are ground into 0.6–5 cm (0.25–2 inch) pieces. Larger particles can be used as a base stabilisation course for roadways, and smaller particles in the surface course. Hot mix asphalt can be composed of up to 5% recycled shingles with the remaining bulk made up of soft asphaltic material.

Glass: Sheet glass, mirrors, and laminated glass can be recycled. To recycle window assemblies, the glass must be separated from the frame and scraped clean of putty or sealants. Glass is purified, separated by colour, crushed into cullet, melted, and re-formed. Glass is infinitely recyclable, and every metric tonne (1,000 kg) of waste glass recycled saves 315 kg (694 lb) of carbon dioxide from being released into the atmosphere as compared to the manufacture of new glass.

Gypsum board: New scrap material generated at construction sites can be recycled by removing paper face and downcycling the core gypsum as an additive in concrete, plaster, and stucco. Previously-installed gypsum board is

IMPACT

Social: Buildings and materials that are reused continue to support community history and culture through narratives of their former uses, present condition, and future possibilities. The process of deconstruction preserves community assets (albeit not in place) and expands the local construction workforce.

Environmental: Circularity reduces embodied carbon emissions by re-purposing materials that have already been harvested, transported, and processed. Circularity also reduces the need to expand landfills but may increase the toxicity of landfill sites due to the concentration of non-recyclable materials.

Economic: Building disassembly promotes a continuous loop of materials in use and reuse, creating new markets for recycled materials and products. Reusing materials from existing buildings supports regional self-sufficiency and reduces transport costs and emissions.

Spatial: Geology, hydrology, photosynthesis, and nutrient processing yield astonishing diversity in creating resources adapted to their locales. Material reuse preserves these natural resources in situ – forests, mines, and fields – for future generations.

generally not recycled as it contains materials that are difficult to separate, such as tape, paint, and joint compound.

PVC: There are two main methods of recycling PVC: mechanical and chemical. Mechanical recycling shreds PVC into particles, which are cleaned, re-melted, and reused with or without new material. Granulate from mechanical recycling cannot be used for food packaging due to the potential for hazardous substances; the recycled material is typically black-grey in colour. Mechanical recycling preserves the molecular structure of the material, while chemical recycling converts PVC into crude oil, naphtha, or fuels through chemical processes such as pyrolysis or hydrolysis. The resulting sodium chloride, calcium chloride and hydrocarbon products, are used to make new PVC, raw materials or fuels. Chemical recycling requires more energy than mechanical recycling, and if the fuels are later burned, the greenhouse gas emitted is higher than if the plastic had been converted in a waste incineration plant.

Laminate flooring requires specialty removal of the chemical-imbued top layer prior to recycling the wood layers beneath. In practical application, the adhesives used to laminate the thin layers make reuse unlikely.

Four billion pounds of carpet ends up in landfills in the United States every year. Carpet recycling separates the outer fibres from the backing and processes each type of fibre separately. Tack strips are not recyclable, so some manufacturers limit recovery to products installed with a releasable installation system, such as tape.

NOTES

1 Chandrappa, R. and D.B. Das. 2024. *Construction and Demolition Waste, in Solid Waste Management*. New York: Springer, pp. 609–638.

2 Baker-Brown, D. 2019. *The Re-Use Atlas*. London: RIBA Publishing.

3 Begum R.A., C. Siwar, J.J. Pereira, and A.H. Jaafar. 2006. A Benefit-Cost Analysis on the Economic Feasibility of Construction Waste Minimisation: The Case of Malaysia. *Resources, Conservation and Recycling* 48,86–98. https://doi.org/10.1016/j.resconrec.2006.01.004.

4 Papadaki, D., D.A. Nikolaou, and M.N. Assimakopoulos. 2022. Circular Environmental Impact of Recycled Building Materials and Residential Renewable Energy. *Sustainability 14*, no. 7, 4039. https://doi.org/10.3390/su14074039

5 Morgan, C. and F. Stevenson. 2005. *Design for Deconstruction: SEDA Design Guides for Scotland: No. 1*. Edinburgh, Scotland. Accessed at: https://static1.squarespace.com/static/5978a800bf629a80c569eef0/t/5aa999f7652deaa430532afd/1530223259684/Design+%26+Detailing+for+Deconstruction.pdf

6 International Living Future Institute. 2019. *Living Building Challenge 4.0: Materials Imperative 13, Red List*. Seattle, WA.

7 Quéheille, E., A. Ventura, N. Saiyouri, and F. Taillandier. 2022. A Life Cycle Assessment Model of End-of-Life Scenarios for Building Deconstruction and Waste Management. *Journal of Cleaner Production* 339, 130694. https://doi.org/10.1016/j.jclepro.2022.130694.

RESOURCES

- Morgan, C. and F. Stevenson. 2005. *Design for Deconstruction: SEDA Design Guides for Scotland: No. 1*. Edinburgh, Scotland.
- Paula Melton and American Institute of Architects. 2020. *Buildings That Last: Design for Adaptability, Deconstruction, and Reuse*. Washington DC. Accessed at: https://content.aia.org/sites/default/files/2020-03/ADR-Guide-final_0.pdf
- Quéheille, E., A. Ventura, N. Saiyouri, and F. Taillandier. 2022. A Life Cycle Assessment Model of End-of-Life Scenarios for Building Deconstruction and Waste Management. *Journal of Cleaner Production* 339, 130694. https://doi.org/10.1016/j.jclepro.2022.130694

ADAPTABLE + ADAPTIVE

44

ADAPTATION **SCARCITY** SCALE **BUILDING**

Reducing resource use can mitigate climate change, spurring architects to design structures that are both adaptable to future uses and adapt to the future impacts of climate change. The distinction between Adaptable (able to be modified for a new use or purpose, indicating plasticity in the programming of a building) and Adaptive (the ability to change in response to conditions beyond the building) is subtle. Both tactics are useful for architects in planning for climate adaptation by rightsizing building footprints and pre-planning modifications to keep pace with temperature, flooding, and precipitation changes.

Figure 44.1: An adaptable room changes functions easily, as in this example of a school gymnasium that can also serve as an assembly hall or dining room with alternative furnishings.

DOI: 10.4324/9781032702964-49

BACKGROUND

Adaptable spaces offer flexibility for multiple functions and reconfigurations. Interchangeability, the ability to reprogramme a space designed for one planned function to different uses, creates spaces that can be used in multiple ways over their service life. A standardised set of rooms may be used for a variety of different functions, a concept known as 'Long-Life, Loose Fit'. The term was first used by the architect John Weeks who developed the Duffle Coat Theory of space planning as a guide to interchangeability:

Figure 44.2: The tenets of loose fit include two main principles: (1) adaptability increases when there is greater interchangeability between activities and spaces and (2) designs with a smaller number of distinct room sizes offer greater interchangeability and reduce complexity in construction and maintenance. Activities can take place in a space that is slightly too big for its purpose, but often, activities can tolerate spaces that are slightly too small, making this approach useful in building types with repetitive spaces such as offices, classrooms, and healthcare. Multiple healthcare functions can utilise a 14 m^2 (150 SF) room: nursing station, patient examination room, doctor's office, etc.

> *In order to get maximum flexibility within a (hospital) department it is necessary to provide rooms which fit around the activities which are to be carried out in them like a duffle coat. The duffle coat, provided by the Navy for its officers, was not a tailor-made garment. A few sizes were made and these were related to the known sizes of sailors so that it was usually possible to find one that would fit reasonably, and keep the sailor quite snug.*[1]

Researchers discovered that between 50 and 65% of the rooms in hospitals were less than 19 m^2 (200 SF) in area, and most between 9 and 14 m^2 (100–150 SF). These rooms were regularly reprogrammed, causing extended demolition and reconstruction to fit the spaces to their purpose. Weeks contended that flexibility in hospitals improves when there is greater interchangeability between activities and spaces, and that a small number of distinct room sizes improves interchangeability.[2] A room of 14 m^2 (150 SF room) allows patient examination, storage, doctor's office, waiting area, and a host of other functions depending on the space's proximity to other equipment or functions. Only minor renovations are necessary to

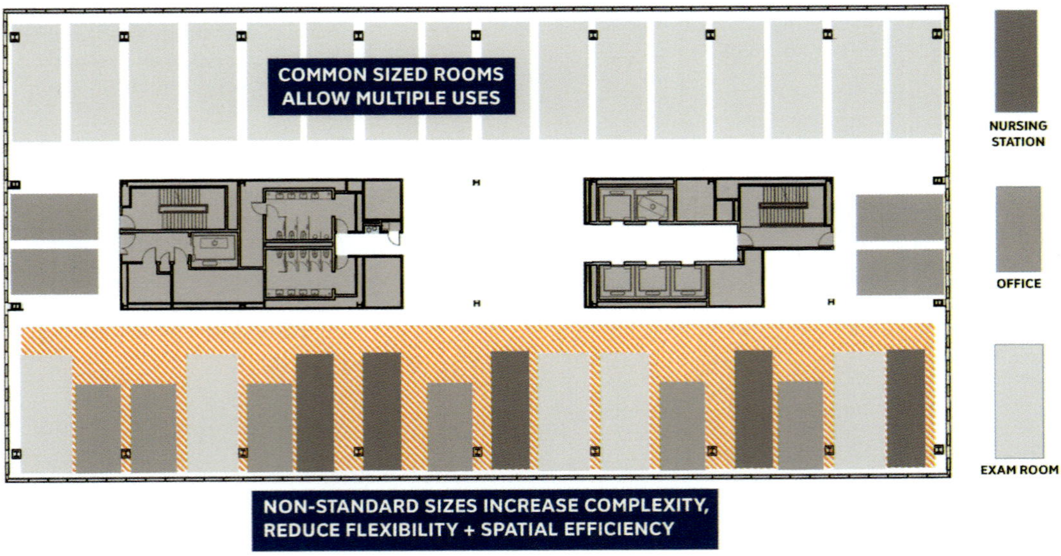

Figure 44.3: Waveland Business Centre changed functions from a business incubator and restaurant to an art gallery and glassblowing studio. The restaurant hood was fitted with a slightly larger exhaust fan to manage the higher temperatures of the glass furnace. Eugenia Uhl + Allison Anderson.

accommodate various uses over the life of the structure, reducing cost and downtime.[3]

Adaptive buildings are designed to adapt to conditions beyond the building and changes in the environment. They can respond to changing weather patterns, changes in access and security, or an influx of building users automatically through the use of sensors.[4] Building control systems are adaptive, adjusting thermal comfort and lighting systems over the course of the day to meet user demands; modifying the space to improve daylighting or solar shading; adjusting privacy, transparency, and security to match user preferences; responding to air quality issues inside or outside the building; prioritising cleaning or maintenance in high-traffic areas; rotating solar collectors to track optimal sun angles throughout the day and season; and communicating emergency messages. These adaptive actions use sensors and controls to improve comfort for occupants and promote conservation.

Climate-adaptive buildings are developing high-performance tools in response to low-cost sensors and high user demand. Sites with perimeter fire suppression will automatically soak the ground when fire weather conditions are detected. Hurricane shutters are automatically deployed when high winds are forecast. Buildings may soon be able to raise their finish floor level to avoid floods. Perimeter floodgates can rise in concert with water levels. These and many more advancements in data analysis and automation are on the way.

KEY DESIGN CONSIDERATIONS

ADAPTABLE

Identify common sizes of rooms in the building programme and standardise sizes where possible for interchangeability.

In building typologies with rapidly changing programmes, leave 5% of space undefined, for use as collaboration space, open work areas, or expansion. This gives building users the freedom to manipulate the space to meet daily demands or a seasonal schedule.

Design 'soft spaces' for administration, lounges, and storage adjacent to areas that anticipate growth. Consider where to accommodate these functions if they must be relocated.

Plan future expansion areas so they do not displace other functions. Design structural bracing and frames at end walls to allow for horizontal expansions. In dense urban environments, consider the potential for vertical expansion and plan foundations and structural frame to support future growth.

Consider the impact of the structural grid on potential tenant layouts. Don't overcommit to a rigid plan organisation. Design fixed programme elements (core, elevator, stair, and columns) to allow future changes in working styles and preferences.

Specify demountable partitions at interiors so spaces can be reconfigured without waste. Use modular casework that can be repositioned or reused in place of built-in pieces.

Plan for evolving technical innovations, especially in mechanical, plumbing, and electrical utilities. Provide regularly spaced power and communications points to ensure coverage.

Consider alternative future uses early in design. For example, if there is the potential for a future conversion from office space to residential use, adequate interstitial space to run additional power, piping, and ductwork is critical. Leaving space for vertical chases and horizontal plenums may have immediate and long-term payback.

Recognise that too much redundancy in the pursuit of flexibility can strain budgets and demand excess resources. A space or a structure cannot meet every possible programmatic use without other trade-offs in budget or design.

Design quality matters. Spaces with unappealing architectural features, low-quality construction, poor daylighting, and inadequate building envelopes will be abandoned for better or more modern structures.

Design accessory structures that are also adaptable for future uses. Parking garages with higher floor-to-floor heights and flat floors are more likely to be repurposed rather than demolished as transportation patterns change.

ADAPTIVE

Design the building to react in real time to climate challenges. Automate building systems to perform necessary adaptation tasks without human intervention, reducing the chance of human error.

Analyse future climate conditions and explore whether there are new or near-term technologies that might be incorporated to manage threats from floods, wind, heat, wildfire, or earthquake. The technological advances being incorporated in buildings today were unimaginable 20 years ago and the pace of change is accelerating.

Design the building envelope to adapt to higher temperatures. Install insulation thicknesses to meet 2060 temperatures or prepare a plan to add insulation in the future. Design shading to dispel heat now or provide the structural capacity to fasten additional shade devices in the future. Plan roof loading capacity and equipment space for renewable energy systems or green roofs to offset higher demands in the future. Reinforce building bases now so they can meet dry floodproofing requirements in the future. Other features can be integrated now for win–win results that streamline building adaptation as conditions change.

Design the building to signal distress. Communications may include lighting or messages that are shared with building users and the surrounding community about excessive heat warnings, fire danger, flooding, or other conditions likely to result in power interruptions.

IMPACT

Social: Adaptable and adaptive spaces maintain occupant comfort and add options for personal choice: dark/light, quiet/noisy, cool/warm spaces. Unprogrammed space improves social interaction, collaboration, and flexible uses.

Environmental: Adaptive buildings extend the service life of a structure by preparing for future modifications to the structure over time; this avoids the embodied carbon penalty from demolition and reconstruction. Preparing now for increased heat may reduce operating energy over the life of the structure.

Economic: Interchangeable rooms reduce initial capital costs due to standardisation and save renovation costs as purposes change. Adaptive buildings protect against hazard impacts to avoid damage and reduce interruptions to operations.

Spatial: Planning future modifications may have spatial implications on siting (setbacks for floodwalls, terraces, or infiltration), structural framing (enhanced capacity to support vertical expansion, larger spans for greater interior space flexibility), and the building envelope (more space to accommodate future shading, insulation, photovoltaic panels, and screening).

NOTES

1 Weeks, J. 1960. Planning for Growth and Change. *Architects' Journal*, 7 July, p. 20.

2 Fawcett, W. 2012. *The Sustainable Schedule of Hospital Spaces: Investigating the 'Duffle Coat' Theory of Flexibility*. Chapter 12, Sustainable Environmental Design in Architecture (pp. 193–209). https://doi.org/10.1007/978-1-4419-0745-5_12

3 'Our predecessors', said Alex Gordon, RIBA, 'left us with a stock of buildings, which generally have been pretty adaptable and served for a long time. One suspects that many of our buildings are only going to be really suitable for the functions for which they are designed for a comparatively short time'. John Weeks. 1965. Indeterminate Architecture, p. 20.

4 Schnädelbach, H. 2010. Adaptive Architecture – A Conceptual Framework. Accessed at: https://www.researchgate.net/profile/Holger-Schnaedelbach/publication/235218510_Adaptive_Architecture_-_A_Conceptual_Framework/links/5b83ee9192851c1e123501d1/Adaptive-Architecture-A-Conceptual-Framework.pdf

RESOURCES

- Schmidt III, R. and S. Austin. 2016. *Adaptable Architecture: Theory and Practice*. Routledge.
- Schnädelbach, H. 2010. *Adaptive Architecture – A Conceptual Framework*. University of Nottingham. Accessed at: https://www.researchgate.net/profile/Holger-Schnaedelbach/publication/235218510_Adaptive_Architecture_-_A_Conceptual_Framework/links/5b83ee9192851c1e123501d1/Adaptive-Architecture-A-Conceptual-Framework.pdf

ANTIFRAGILE 45

ADAPTATION **SCARCITY** SCALE **BUILDING**

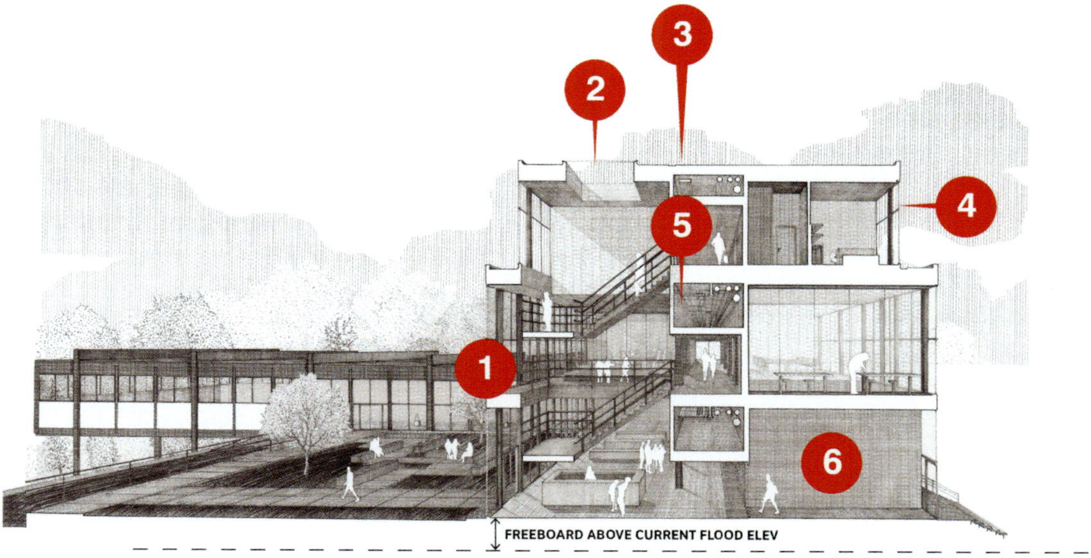

The built environment in this era of uncertainty is not striving to reach a fixed condition of resilience but to become antifragile, benefitting from shocks and improving during periods of disorder and stress. The most likely antifragile buildings are the ones that have been in existence the longest, for their very continuance is evidence of being antifragile.[1] The antifragile building is one that can be used indefinitely; adapts to new functions and intensifying climate conditions without extensive overhaul; harvests sunlight and rainwater to supply occupants with essential services; and is beloved by the community in which it stands.

Figure 45.1: A building designed to adapt to future climate challenges and program changes: (1) the structural frame has capacity to add load, (2) the atrium allows future infill at multiple levels, (3) roof framing is sized to add a green roof, (4) cladding can be replaced for a different style. (5) A plenum allows access to systems for easy modifications, and (6) the grade level will allow decommissioning for future floodproofing. Yevgen Gozhenko.

DOI: 10.4324/9781032702964-50

BACKGROUND

Nassim Nicholas Taleb wrote in *Antifragile: Things that Gain from Disorder* (2012) that some things benefit from shocks, thriving when exposed to volatility and disorder.[2] Buildings aren't typically considered as objects that improve under difficult circumstances, having inherent weaknesses to impact, movement, infiltration, and arson. However, the buildings that survive for centuries have proven capable of absorbing shocks and stresses and are likely to continue to thrive against future perturbations. Having proven their firmness, commodity, and delight, they have also demonstrated their safety, reliability, and capacity to serve generations. Adaptive reuse is a climate-centred practise that celebrates longevity in the built environment, longevity that is enhanced by the visible markers of time: weathering, cracking, accreting, encrusting, and the myriad of transformations wrought by the way people have occupied the spaces within.

The continued renewal of buildings is a critical tool for climate mitigation. Every built work has consumed resources: materials harvested from the earth, processed to refine the materials used in the structure, transported to the site, supplied with energy and water to keep it running, and provisioned with new materials to clean, replace, and maintain the structure. The use of such resources has contributed greenhouse gas emissions. Even though an existing building's original emissions may have occurred 25 or 200 years ago, their legacy of emissions still contribute to the climate crisis, as greenhouse gases stay in the atmosphere for tens to hundreds of years after being released. To demolish and replace these buildings – if they could reasonably be reused – adds unnecessarily to levels of atmospheric carbon.

Cities need to retain old buildings, the ordinary structures that make up the city fabric, according to Jane Jacobs,[3] transforming them to manage new climate challenges. In adapting to climate change, humans naturally look to historical disasters and use this to estimate future risks. However, disaster events often exceed the magnitude of the previous disaster. For this reason, people of the Mississippi Gulf Coast say, 'Camille killed as many people in 2005 than it did in 1969', because many residents felt safe if their home survived Hurricane Camille, once considered the benchmark storm. Many chose to ride out Hurricane Katrina with grave consequences. Camille's death toll was 259 people, with peak hurricane winds of 175 mph and 7.32 m (24 feet) of storm surge; Katrina's death toll in Mississippi was 238 people, with winds of 175 mph and a storm surge of 8.5 m (28 feet). Storms are intensifying and large storms are becoming more frequent, so Katrina won't remain the new benchmark storm for long.

Each component of a building has a different lifecycle, and buildings can be modified more easily when layers remain independent, allowing elements with shorter lifecycles (such as building services) to remain independent from layers with longer lifecycles (such as structure). This concept of layers was described by Stewart Brand in *How Buildings Learn: What Happens After They're Built* (1994). The six layers include: site, structure, skin, services, space plan, and stuff, each with an estimated service life. These six categories also describe potential building modifications to accommodate future climate conditions, as outlined below.

Not all existing buildings can – or should – be saved. Structures on high-hazard sites, or without the structural integrity to remain stable under threats, should be deconstructed and removed. Structures that cannot be insulated against increasing heat or elevated against higher floodwaters will ultimately be lost and their demise

Figure 45.2: To use a building indefinitely, a building must be easily modified and repaired. Stewart Brand noted that this was easier when the layers remained independent: site, structure, skin, services, space plan, and stuff. Each layer has its own estimated service life, ranging from the lifetime of the site to a lifespan of 5 to 15 years for furnishings.

should be a planned and orderly process of salvage and removal, rather than a slow deterioration.

KEY DESIGN CONSIDERATIONS

SITE (PERMANENT)

The permanence of the site layer may be reconsidered in this era of rapid change. Fixed boundaries are in flux, reshaped by rivers and coastlines, by economic pressures to subdivide and densify, by the reconfigurations caused by wildfire and earthquake. Climate change may alter site conditions so profoundly that they are likely to be lost to encroaching threats. Consider site viability in 100 years, 200 years, and beyond. If a disaster is foreseeable, plan for the careful, systematic, and productive salvage of building components, or disassembly and reassembly on another site.

Buildings capable of adapting to site changes are good candidates for reuse. However, when conditions indicate higher or more persistent risks such as flooding or wildfire exposure, existing buildings may need to consider decommissioning a portion of the structure. Alternatives include constructing barriers such as floodwalls or exterior fire sprinklers, or significant modifications such as elevation, re-cladding, or wet floodproofing. A cost-benefit analysis will determine whether the embodied carbon of these interventions is offset by saving the existing structure.

A building may outlive its economic purpose on a site, no longer contributing to the community or economic development. If an acceptable reuse scenario cannot be conceived, the building can be deconstructed and its materials salvaged for reuse. Repetitive damage to buildings from the same type of hazard should guide future uses, modify performance standards, or indicate abandonment of the site. An antifragile approach does not replace the same structure on a site after a loss, and hope for a different outcome in the future.

STRUCTURE (30–300 YEARS)

The structural foundations and frame account for a high proportion of a building's overall embodied carbon. In an average commercial building, structure comprises 82% of the total shell, including floor slabs (47%), structural foundations (17%), structural framing (12%), and structural columns (6%).[4] Maintain the structural frame wherever possible to retain the value of the embodied carbon.

Monitor the structural health of a building to prolong its lifecycle. Pests, rot, corrosion, undermining, deflection, unplanned loads, and mechanical impacts on a building frame can have harmful or catastrophic consequences.

Consider low-carbon options for new or replacement structural members: wood, reclaimed materials, smaller cross sections of material, and more efficient frames.

Structural geometry has an impact on efficiency, adaptability, strength, and longevity. Consider design options that permit longer spans, as long span structures accommodate a wider variety of potential uses. Higher floor-to-floor dimensions allow a variety of different functions and permit the construction of mezzanines. However, these design choices may increase the initial cost; a cost-benefit analysis can advise if these enhancements will pay back within the building's service life.

Design overhangs to protect openings from increasing rainfall variability, and ensure they are braced to manage increased uplift from high winds and storms. Consider adding anchor points at overhangs to allow for future enclosure of exterior space or the later addition of shading devices.

Use 'screws not glues', at structural frames for ease of disassembly. Bolted connections are preferable to welded frames. Fastening systems that can be reversed aid in deconstruction and reuse.

SKIN (20+ YEARS)

The building skin responds closely to style, transparency, privacy, texture, and material. Climate adaptation may dictate new façade components to block solar heat gain, allow natural ventilation for passive survivability, enhance biophilia with living walls and bird-friendly sites, create a dry floodproof base, brace overhangs, or respond in a myriad of other ways to manage heat, water, wind, and scarcity.

Design the building skin to manage higher exterior temperatures with appropriate shading, insulation, and openings.

Roofing is the critical fifth façade of the building skin. Monitor and replace roofs regularly – likely every 20 years for membrane roofs, 20–30 years for asphalt shingles, 40–80 years for metal roofs, 60–150 years for slate, and 100 or more years for clay tile.[5]

Green roofs have a life expectancy of 40+ years, extending the life expectancy of the membrane roof below, according to the U.S. General Services Administration, which maintains about 2 million square feet of green roofs.[6] Assess existing buildings and determine if their existing structural capacity can accommodate the additional weight of a green roof.

Ensure any new additions – vertical or horizontal – do not exceed the load capacity of the walls or frame. Maintain and strengthen continuous load paths.

SERVICES (7–20 YEARS)

Services to the building - electrical, mechanical, plumbing, and communications - are highly dependent on rapidly-evolving technology. Provide plenum space, vertical chases, and raised access floors for easy reconfiguration as technology changes.

Plumbing is especially difficult to add later due to requirements for supply, waste, and venting, one reason for the high cost of transforming offices to residential units with more dispersed plumbing needs. Certain construction types - wood framing or elevated structures - make it easy to add or move fixtures. Designing vertical duct chases and horizontal plenum spaces can make future conversions easier.

Antifragile buildings are fossil-fuel-free buildings. As buildings are renovated, remove outdated natural or propane gas equipment and plumbing, and replace them with electric services prepared for grid integration.

SPACE (3 YEARS)

Interior layout, organisation, and the distribution of people within the building shell changes often in commercial spaces. Antifragile spaces adapt to multiple functions and users. Architects can use demountable interior walls, and modular pieces with built-in electrical and communications conduits that can be moved or reconfigured easily.

Open office space has multiple benefits and drawbacks but one benefit for antifragility is reducing the amount of construction within the building shell. Where possible, reduce interior walls to allow flexibility of uses and maintain line of sight to windows for views and daylighting.

Figure 45.3: LMN Architects illustrates the embodied carbon impact of a 2013–2015 office renovation to highlight the surprising - and high - embodied carbon of tenant improvements.

Tenant improvements in commercial spaces may have high embodied carbon.[7] Plan new interventions using low-carbon or reclaimed materials for millwork and finishes. Eliminate ceilings and carpets if a suitable substrate is provided. Select non-PVC materials wherever possible due to the high embodied carbon and toxicity of PVC.

Design millwork so that it can be moved, converted, reused, or disassembled and reassembled in a different configuration.

STUFF (>3 YEARS)

Furnishings and finishes are susceptible to the vagaries of trends and styles. To be considered antifragile, 'stuff' must be durable, fit for purpose, and easily restored in the event of minor damage.

Specify solid wood in place of fibreboard, scrubbable surfaces instead of upholstered, and reclaimed pieces where possible.

Specify recyclable carpet tiles instead of broadloom. This allows stained or worn sections to be replaced easily. Discarded materials can separate the backing from the fibres for recycling into new tiles.

Balance the embodied carbon in new furnishings against the potential improvement to comfort and productivity when selecting office chairs and desks.

IMPACT

Social: Adapting beloved existing buildings for new purposes supports community landmarks, preserves history, and prepares buildings to resist increasing disruptions. Antifragile buildings and sites reassure residents that survival and recovery is possible.

Environmental: Building reuse avoids 50–75% of the embodied carbon emissions that an identical new building would generate. Adaptation can improve the building's environmental performance in water efficiency, energy use, and health.

Economic: Keeping antifragile structures in service has a profound impact on city settlement patterns. Revitalisation spurs economic development, engages the workforce, and affects liveability, wellbeing, and connection.

Spatial: Adaptive reuse prevents damage and loss to those specific assets; but at high-hazard sites, reinvestment can lead to doubling down on sites that should transition to other uses.

NOTES

1 Blečić, I. and A. Cecchini. 2017. On the Antifragility of Cities and of Their Buildings. *City, Territory and Architecture* 4, no. 3. https://doi.org/10.1186/s40410-016-0059-4
2 Taleb, N. 2012. *Antifragile: Things That Gain from Disorder*. New York: Random House.
3 Jacobs, J. 1961. *The Death and Life of Great American Cities*. New York: Random House, p. 187.
4 Pearson, C. 2019, December 20. Structural Engineers Study Embodied Carbon of 600 Buildings. Accessed at: https://www.buildinggreen.com/newsbrief/structural-engineers-study-embodied-carbon-600-buildings
5 International Association of Certified Home Inspectors. Standard Estimated Life Expectancy Chart for Homes. Accessed at: https://www.nachi.org/life-expectancy.htm
6 U.S. General Services Administration, Green Roof Tracker. Accessed at: https://www.gsa.gov/governmentwide-initiatives/federal-highperformance-green-buildings/resource-library/integrative-strategies/green-roofs/green-roof-tracker
7 LMN Architects. 2022. Tenant Improvements Embodied Carbon Study, Version 2. Accessed at: https://lmnarchitects.com/lmn-research/tenant-improvements-embodied-carbon-study

RESOURCES

- International Association of Certified Home Inspectors. Standard Estimated Life Expectancy Chart for Homes. Accessed at: https://www.nachi.org/life-expectancy.htm
- LMN Architects. 2022. Tenant Improvements Embodied Carbon Study, Version 2. Accessed at: https://lmnarchitects.com/lmn-research/tenant-improvements-embodied-carbon-study

Acknowledgements

No architect, and certainly no writer, works alone. The lessons of so many colleagues, friends, and critical thinkers have shaped my work, whether on paper or constructed.

Thanks to that boy on a camping trip who told me architecture was 'too hard for you,' a red flag that challenged me to apply. To my first architecture studio teacher, who asked if I really wanted to be an architect and then recommended that I work in the studio rather than at home. And to the well-meaning university colleague who warned me that research in a host of random directions would never result in tenure. I didn't take your advice – the world of architecture is endlessly interesting and design ideas are found in unexpected places.

Thanks to my teachers who shared their passions for making better buildings, engaging people, and telling stories with greater impact. Special thanks to Charles Moore for demonstrating through his teaching, practice, writing, and approach to life how architecture could become more personal, meaningful, and joyful.

Thanks to the Gulf Coast for challenging us to build more resilient communities after Hurricane Katrina and to our clients for giving us the opportunity to apply lessons from the catastrophe and prepare for the coming storms.

Thank you to the American Institute of Architects who convened the Resilience and Adaptation Advisory Group and invited me to join leaders from across the country who strive to implement climate adaptation in the practice of architecture.

To my students. Your enthusiasm for this profession is a source of hope in a world of uncertainty.

To my colleagues in the studio who uncomplainingly draw, redraw, and refine every line, note, and detail: David Tanner, Mike Grote, Michelle Fredericks, Ann Panopio, Susan Daigre, Cory May, Nichole Chauvin, Islay Burgess, Steven Miller, Shawna Henry, Lora Teagarden, David Grapusa, Joseph Colón, Cassidy Maschler, Dylan Roth, Sami Spoon, Chloe Barton, Amelia Haasl, Mandi Newton, Jonathan Hall, Isabel Coelho, Hannah Anderson, Terri Lamperez, and Tamera Labat Whavers.

Thanks to everyone who read, commented, guided, contributed, and encouraged the early versions of this book. Your advice made a tremendous difference but any remaining mistakes are mine.

Special thanks to Lydia Kessell, who reached out on LinkedIn and entertained a book proposal for a very different book, which she helped shape into the one in your hands.

To my parents who told me I could do anything and supported me through everything. Both were excellent storytellers, cheerleaders, and counsellors. Our whirlwind life in cities shaped my love of architecture and your devotion to books formed my love of reading.

To my sister, who remains the smartest, the most beautiful, the youngest, and the one they write songs about.

To my children, the greatest joys in my life.

And to my partner in life and work, John Anderson. Your creativity, talent, and dedication to the craft of architecture - and to our life together - are a constant inspiration.

Index